Martial Musings

A Portrayal of Martial Arts
in the 20th Century

Martial Musings

A Portrayal of Martial Arts
in the 20th Century

Robert W. Smith

Via Media Publishing Company
Erie, Pennsylvania

Library of Congress
Cataloging-in-Publication Data

Smith, Robert W., 1926–
  Martial Musings:
  A Portrayal of the Martial Arts
  in the 20th Century/Robert W. Smith
  Includes glossary and index.
  ISBN 1-893765-00-8 (alk. paper)

1. Martial arts–History. 2. Martial arts–
Social and cultural aspects.
I. Title. II. Smith, Robert W.

Library of Congress
Catalog Card Number: 99-66170

Disclaimer
Please note that the author and publisher
of this book are not responsible in any
manner whatsoever for any injury that
may result from practicing the techniques
and/or following the instructions given
within, since the physical activities
described herein may be too strenuous
in nature for some readers to engage
in safely, it is essential that a physician
be consulted prior to training.

First published in 1999 by
Via Media Publishing Company
821 W. 24th Street • Erie, PA 16502 USA
Tel: 1-800-455-9517 • Fax: 1-877-526-5262
E-mail: info@goviamedia.com
Website: www.goviamedia.com

Book and cover design by
Via Media Publishing Company.
Cover painting by Michael Lane.

Printed in the United States of America.

The paper in this book meets the
guidelines for permanence and durability
of the Committee on Production
Guidelines for Book Longevity of
the Council on Library Resources.

10 9 8 7 6 5 4 3 2 1
05 04 03 02 01 00 99

Dedication
To Agnes in the hope that one day
God's glorious gift of sight may be restored to her,
and to the indefatigable publisher, Michael DeMarco,
without who's iron-urging this book would never have been written.

Acknowledgments
Here is a list of those who helped in large and small ways.
There were so many and I'm sure I've missed some good souls.
If so, they should blame it on a waning brain rather than cussedness.

Howard Alexander	James Grady	Paul Lynch
Sam Ahtye	Jay Groen	Diane Macchiavelli
Bob Arief	Roseann Guterman	Larry Mann (deceased)
Hunter Armstrong	John Harding	Russ Mason
Chris Bates	Pat Harrington	Pat McGowan
Mike Belzer	Richard Hayes	John Mocella
Will Bibby	Ray Hayward	Gerald Moose
Jon Bluming	Christine Herrod	Mike Mushinsky
Doug Bone	Jeff Herrod	Graham Noble
Richard Bowen	Terry Hill	Paul Nurse
Kim Bozark	Ted Hillson	Hank Ogawa
Janet Bradley	Al Holtmann	Theresa Perkins
Jim Bregman	Kent Howard	Doug Perry
George Bristol	Betty Huxley	Henri Plée
Dave Brown	Frank Iaccobo	Allen Pittman
Frank Buiting	Bart Ingram	Oscar Ratti
Y.W. Chang	Martin Inn	A.J. Reid
William C.C. Chen	Dainis Jirgensons	Kevin Roberts
Juliana Cheng	Dan Johnston	Don Sayenga
Katie Cheng	Harry Johnston	Mike Schnapp
Partick Cheng	Ken Johnston	Meik Skoss
Frank Congee	Kim Kanzelberger	Alan Shapiro
Warren Conner	Pat Kenny	Joel Sucher
Paul Cote	James Klebau	Sidney Tai
Victor Crawford (deceased)	Robert Kostka	Kirk Talbott
Joe Cunniff	Saul Krotki	P.S. Tao
Barbara Davis	Michael Lane	Aaron Thompson
Terry Dunn	John Lang	Ken Van Sickle
Danny Emerick	Neil Laughlin	Mike Ward
Jay Falleson	Rose Li	David Waterhouse
Billy Fox	T.T. Liang	Stan Wiggins
Joe Gantner	Pat Lineberger	Geoff Wilcher
Martin Gardner	Liu Xiheng	Lenzie Williams
Tim Geoghegan (deceased)	Ben Lo	George Wilson
Dick Goheen	Joe Lowe	Wang Yennian
Steve Goodson	Wolfe Lowenthal	John Wolfe
Bob Goodwin		Frang Wong

NOTE: In this book, individuals' names are usually presented with surnames following the given name, including those of Japanese heritage. However, Chinese names are presented in the traditional Asian order, with family name first.

Table of Contents

Introduction

Somewhere between nostalgia and neuralgia
everything old becomes new again.
– Robert Lipsyte

I came down to the Smoky Mountains in 1989 to recreate myself. I'd spent fifty or more years learning and teaching the martial arts, not to mention the infinitely more important achievement of staying with the same marvelous wife (Alice) and helping rear a family of three girls (Susan, Annette, and Christine), a boy (David), and assorted dogs (Missy, Cobber, Muffin, Trampas, and Charlie). Along the way I had put head, hands, and no little heart into carving out a career in intelligence, and managed never to be indicted.

Dorothy Parker, the New York wit, had it right: old age ain't for sissies. But still, as the Thirties tune put it, "I'm in good shape for the shape I'm in." Which is sort of stiff and a little crumbly. A good day for me is one when nothing hurts very much. I've licked the age problem by adjusting humorist James Thurber's methodology. He simply used fifteen instead of twelve months to a year. With his deflator, I've been able to reduce my age from 72 to 56.

All of us, if we are lucky, have happiness of a sort. Too often it is a cheap or shallow thing attached to some everyday occurrence. Or, if more than that, so ephemeral that we hardly notice it. So much so that in the 1960's, we had the Law of the Happy Moment, "This is wonderful, wasn't it?" To round it into something fuller, we must – as taiji teaches us – become more aware when the bluebird comes by. *It is wonderful to know when you are happy.* Memorize that line, for it is key. But that's only the first step. After you recognize and savor happiness, how are you going to keep it?

All things considered, these are the happiest days of my life – the present always has been. I've been poorer and more ignorant, but that never mattered. Infused with all this joy and juice, I've always thought that now was best. Sometimes I didn't have or get things to delight in, so I became delighted with delight. Often I couldn't do or go where I wanted – particularly in the martial arts realm – so I tried to make the lure of the thing as good as the doing or going itself. W.B. Yeats, unarguably the greatest poet of this century, once wrote that he was one of

The author relaxing in Bethesda, Maryland, 1988.

"the last romantics." Not so. There are still romantics around, people whom the ancient Greeks wouldn't address with such nonsense as, "Nothing matters very much and very little matters at all." I am one. So was H.L. Mencken. Indeed, a romantic can be defined as someone who knows Mencken was funning when he said, "We are here and it is now; all the rest is moonshine." He meant it as a needed put-down of intellectualism and science, but knew well the endless possibilities of Beauty and the wild probabilities of Truth.

Critics have called me outspoken and controversial. But someone has to be, otherwise who would tell the emperor that he is naked? I protest against things I think are wrong: evil, hatred, hunger, and war. I'm for goodness, love, full bellies, and peace.

Apropos here is the old story of a rabbi who stood in the market place each week and rebuked the rabble for their sins. No one listened. A small boy watched and grew bigger. Finally, when the boy had become a man, he felt sympathy for the now antique rabbi still harassing the crowds to care and love more. So he said to the rabbi, "Father, it is a holy thing you're doing, but these people don't care. They wouldn't live if they couldn't sin. They're worse than when you started preaching to them twenty years ago. Can't you see that they're not listening?" The rabbi looked at him and said softly, "But young man, you're mistaken. I'm not doing it for them: I'm doing it for me!"

Generally, I incline toward the Daoist view of life, believing that if we all followed nature we'd find that less is better and that small is, indeed, beautiful. Key here is the notion of nothing in excess. We exercise or fail to exercise too much. We eat too much, compete too much, have sex too much, win too much. We sleep too much, think too much, do too much, and talk too much. (Confucius warned that we mustn't talk while eating or in bed.) Perhaps we even write too much. Mad William Blake's words catch us well: "Too much/enough." If there is anything to the theory that there is only a certain amount of pleasure allotted to each of us, then perhaps we should spread it thinner so it will last longer. This would let us burn always with Walter Pater's hard, gemlike flame rather than bouncing along from conflagration to ashes and back again.

Unfortunately, Daoism doesn't appear overly interested in love. That's not good, because the one thing none of us does too much is love. Professor Zheng Manqing, the most remarkable man I met in my life, in his book on Laozi commended Confucius for embodying an ethical dimension – loving and doing good – and lambasted Laozi for lacking one. For me then, I like Laozi for his nature and the Buddha, Christ, and Confucius for their love.

Looking back, my love for the martial arts always took second place (properly) to my love for family and friends. Early on, we had little and my family and school left little time for concerted vigorous practice. Later, I had more money, but work took all my time. The martial arts, nevertheless, were never far from my mind. I can remember doing countless repetitions of throws (*uchikomi* or *butsukari*) against walls, with Western boxers, and even (Lord forgive me!) a willing pregnant wife (but only once, for twenty minutes). I sometimes wished I could go full-bore on practice and contests, confident that I could gain skill fairly quickly, but responsibilities prevented it. But mustn't complain, as the old British gardener said, "We've had our innings." So I don't dwell on it, especially when I see that better competitors often were not as happy as I: their skills improved but their lives sometimes didn't.

When I came south for the bluebirds and the mountains, I had no desire to write further on the martial arts. But old friends carped at me, urging that I do so. Canadian judoka Paul Nurse among them, learning that I had a title (if no book), wrote: "I hope *Martial Musings* will cover some background on your own life-path. If Homer is right and we all become like Odysseus, the sum of all we come into contact with, then I believe your particular progress could be of interest and instructive to readers. Not in any egocentric manner, but as a record of an uncommon life."

My recent series of articles for the *Journal of Asian Martial Arts* (JAMA) was done as much to protect the name and teaching of Professor Zheng Manqing against detractors among his students and others as to explicate and inform. Knowledgeable students used this motivation, urging me to protect my own poor ideas in the future by publishing a clearer statement of my position.

And so, when James Grady, long-time student and crackerjack novelist (*Six Days of the Condor*, 1974), asked to interview me for JAMA, I relented. In the past, I would have said no, but now as the candle gutters, I decided to let him try. Not for ego, God knows, but for the opportunity to get my view on the martial arts out in public so that someday when I'm strewing arbutus in Heavenly glades, someone doesn't misrepresent my ideas.

In readying myself for that interview, I began dredging my brain and writing notes. The almost feverish recall quickly became a book. Jim will be along with the interview shortly.

As a result of the discipline of the fighting arts, my garbage detector has improved over time. "The cheaper the crook, the gaudier the patter," warned writer Dashiell Hammett. The garbage detector identifies the sleaze through the patter. The detector goes to tilt more often now than in the past.

Still, memory is no mean thing. It warms and stimulates so much that sometimes I feel more alive with the memories of the past than I do with the perception of the present. I am not alone in this. In his autobiography, the esteemed author V. Nabokov sees memory as a "robust reality" that makes a ghost of the present. "To know how to change the past into a few saddened smiles," Maurice Maeterlinck said, "is this not to master the future?" So recollection has its reward. But one has to beware lest he recalls pigeons as swans. The writer has to exercise the same rigor and restraint examining the past as he does in viewing the present. I've tried to do it so that I could say (with Mark Twain), "Not that it matters, but most of what follows is true."

Writing about the martial arts can't compete with watching blue-birds. But it has its virtues. A retrospective view lets me amend, correct, and update previous work. It also permits me to go in new directions and develop ideas I've not expressed before. Its main virtue, however, is that it lets me revisit some of the many exponents of these arts whom I've met down the years.

I would be happier if I'd used fewer "I's" (I thought of using the third person, but that seemed artificial and a little precious). There was simply no way around it. I asked myself why should anyone want to know about me? As politicians never say, I'm modest and have every right to be. I wrote to inform readers of these arts and those who grace them, not to celebrate myself. Also, I ask readers forbearance for my opinions on society and politics that they may not share.

I hope that readers enjoy and learn a bit from this scribbling. My thanks go to the many good people who helped me. High praise goes to Joe Svinth, Seattle area karate teacher, one of the first to encourage me in the enterprise. He eased the writing by insightful suggestions, and typed the manuscript. I salute also Mike DeMarco, publisher of by far the best martial arts journal in the world, for asking me to do it. Additionally, Warren Conner and Russ Mason did heroic editing through several drafts of the manuscript. Some who helped me are mentioned in the body of the text and others are listed in the acknowledgement. It goes without saying that any defects in the book are my responsibility, not theirs. Invoking poet Hilaire Belloc, I say to all the good people who figure in this saga as actors or helpers:

From quiet homes and first beginning,
Out to the undiscovered ends,
There's nothing worth the wear of winning,
But laughter and the love of friends.

Early Days

Born on December 27, 1926, on a small Iowa farm to a family that foundered in the Depression, I was deposited at three into an orphanage in the railroad town of Galesburg, Illinois. I remember the orphanage mostly as a refuge for fifty thin children from those economic hard times. We had firm discipline and swift copious punishment for rules infractions.

In 1987, I revisited the Home and noticed a decal on the door leading out into the backyard that read, "People are not for hitting and children are people too." This wonderful declaration wasn't present during my ten years there (1930 to 1940). Despite the Spartan life, I look back fondly on those early formative years.

"We all loved the same old bitch in those days and her name was nostalgia," Scott Fitzgerald wrote. And my warm recall largely reflects the one glorious thing in that rambling, big building – a large library that cascaded color on an otherwise dark ambiance. I devoured almost every book in it two or three times before I left. The most educative aspect of my life, reading became a habit there and then, a solace and life-long friend that led to a life of writing. The books made for easy schooling in Galesburg. (Ronald Reagan, the amiable dunce of a B-actor, attended first grade in the Galesburg school system but I guess we must have read different books.)

Among the books were whole sets of Tom Swift and *The Boy Allies*, lots of Dickens, Rider Haggard ("Run for your lives!" he shouted in Arabic), Frank Baum's Oz books, Sherlock Holmes ("I observe that you have recently been in Afghanistan"), and of course Emerson,

The author (front, center) at age four, doing what no fighter should: standing with his hands in his pockets. To his left is his best friend, Leroy Maxwell, killed in World War II.

Thoreau, and Burt Standish's *Frank Merriwell* books. Frank was athletic and purportedly clean living. It was thirty years before I was to learn that on Frank's first day at Yale he kicked a dog and helped Rattleton cheat on his entrance exams. There were a hundred volumes of poetry (the biggest defect in modern America is the absence of good poetry) and many nature titles. At this remove, I can almost feel the texture and heft of some of them and how they smelled on cold winter afternoons. And yes, I can remember my loins being stirred by a passage in Walter Edmonds' *Drums Along the Mohawk* (1936).

Mrs. Irma Gale, granddaughter of Galesburg's founder and a favorite history teacher at the high school across the street, stayed with us for three years during the Thirties. After putting us to bed at night, she would regale us with wonderful stories from history, George Mallory's ill-fated attempt to conquer Mount Everest in 1924, for instance, or from literature. I still resonate to her marvelous voice telling Nathaniel Hawthorne's story, "The Great Stone Face." This tale concerns young Ernest, reared at the base of a mountain that bears the likeness of a good and wise man, who legend says will come someday to minister to the people. As Ernest grows under its influence, great men of industry, education, and war periodically come to compare their own faces with it, and the poor and credulous townsfolk all too quickly shout, "It's him! It's him!" But Ernest's hopes are shattered each time when he sees their defects and knows they are not the Face. In the twilight of his years, Ernest, now a poet, is sitting with an old friend when the setting sun illuminates the Face in such a way that his friend cries, "Ernest, you are the Man!" But Ernest only smiles sadly and turns away, still hoping for the one who is to come.

Years later, as a seventeen-year-old Marine, I gave up carousing in Oceanside, California, one evening to sit in the small city library rereading that story. My addiction to reading and learning was stronger than my raging hormones. Hawthorne's story always stayed with me, being descriptive of life in general and the martial arts in particular. I've yearned for the great and good men and women in these pursuits and though I've been extremely lucky in finding some, I'm always looking for more. Lately, I must tell you, it's been hard going.

One of my first literary brushes with self-defense was when the arch-villain Professor Moriarty got his godownance (opposite of come-uppance, see?) from Sherlock Holmes. It came not from some great throw, punch, or kick, but from a secret Japanese system of unbalancing known as *Baritsu* (sic). Here are Holmes and Moriarty struggling at the Reichenbach Falls:

> He drew no weapon, but he rushed at me and threw his long arms around me. He knew that his own game was up, and was only anxious to revenge himself upon me. We tottered together on the brink of the fall. I have some knowledge however, of baritsu, or the Japanese system of wrestling, which has more than once been very useful to me. I slipped through his grip, and he with a horrible scream kicked madly for a few seconds, and clawed the air with both his hands. But for all his efforts he could not get his balance, and over he went.

I later learned that Holmes' trick was based on a turn-of-the-century art called *Bartitsu*, which combined English boxing and wrestling with jujutsu. The name was derived from its founder, a man named E. W. Barton-Wright.

And, like every American kid, I liked the comic strips, and the forces for good in them. I leaned toward subtlety and understatement rather than muscles and strength. Instead of Punjab, the towering protector of Orphan Annie, I preferred the quiet suited chap with the oriental features known as "the Asp." His style was picked up in movies by novelist John Marquand's "Mr. Moto." Done up brown by Peter Lorre, Moto-san would touch your wrist and up you'd go, making today's nerve touch masters appear amateurs. Charlie Chan I never cared for, finding him too inert and lugubrious, though I still recall this line as oddly marvelous: "Relinquish the firearms, Mr. Jennison, or am I forced to make fatal insertion into vital organ belonging to you?" Oh, the old movies – I watched them for ten years and saw not one explosion.

On Saturday afternoons, we trooped off three blocks to the Colonial Theater to see a cowboy show, an adventure serial, and a newsreel. More than forty children

Orphan Annie comic, 1935. Even monkeys sometimes fall out of trees. In the "Little Orphan Annie" comics, the Oriental Asp invariably won. But sometimes he got banged up a bit. Here he is in the '30's with a bandaged Daddy Warbucks, Annie, and Sandy.

strolling hand in hand down the street must have been quite a sight. My older sister, Margaret, told me laughingly once that as we passed them, two fellows eyed us and one shook his head admiringly and said, "What a man!" – a remark I wasn't to understand for some years.

As charity kids, we were seated too close to the screen but didn't mind, though I'd often go home with a headache. We watched such stars as Tom Mix, Buck Jones, and my favorite, Ken Maynard, who it was said, was the only cowboy able to go around the belly of a horse and back into the saddle while it was in full stride. If I remember right, Ken's horse was named "Tarzan," and Tom Mix's "Tony." These horse operas established for me at an early age an awareness of good and evil, white hat and black. And also the fact that seeing such frenetic action was not cathartic, but instead a raging stimulus on young children. We went back home and galloped on imaginary horses and shot imaginary guns for two hours afterwards. Jack Valenti and his vile Hollywood apologists don't know the truth of this yet, whereas I knew it at nine.

During that same period, I have a vague recall of seeing in a newsreel two white-jacketed persons throwing each other around on a large white mat laid out on a lawn. The recall is a bit better than vague because the image is of T. Shozo Kuwashima Sensei and partner in New York or New Jersey. They were on for a short time and off again and back we went to Tim McCoy and George O'Brien. McCoy didn't need a gun – he stared the crooks to death. From this we started having staring contests, the longest lasting a full day.

We boys were generally a rough but well-behaved bunch. At the elementary school we went to across the street the boys were also rough, but cussed and were rowdy in the rawest sense. The villain of the school was Kenny Craig, a likable lout who in the fifth-grade could whip all the sixth-graders. One day at recess, we got cross-wise and in an instant he pushed me to the ground. For some time I had kept clear of him. I not only was in awe of him, I was scared to death. I didn't realize this until he put me down. Then, all ambiguity fled and I realized in a panic what real terror was.

Luckily for me, when he followed me to the ground, he tripped and ended up on his back. Like a drowning man finding a floating spar, I managed to roll on top and clutch him to me with fear-crazed arms. Though we wrestled often at the Home, I was no champion. (From the comics we all knew the full-nelson Tarzan used to kill his first lion, though, lacking his power and skill, we were never able to do it.) But my memory of Kenny annihilating with his fists another guy who I had thought was tough fueled that fear. I did not want to face those fists. So I tightened and squeezed. He reared like a bucking bronco, but he had no chance against fear. Soon the bell rang and the janitor came out and picked us up by our ears and took us in to the principal. Strangely, after that we became close friends. Kenny survived World War II but then came to a bad end – going into politics and becoming a Republican state senator.

You hear a lot nowadays in all our pro sports of the need for passion. Nuts. There was passion at the Alamo and no one survived (though had there been a back door, we never would have heard of it)! No, as a better lubricant for effective fighting skills, I'll take fear over passion any time.

Fist fights were fairly common and our women overseers were in no hurry to break them up, probably seeing them as a cathartic venting of repressed dreams and loneliness and ennui. I remember Robert Schmidt and John Shaner going at it an hour or so in late afternoon, then stopping for supper and sleep, and continuing another hour the next morning. My memory is of hot swirling dust and two bodies, with Shaner down more than up but unwilling to quit until he'd established his sincerity. The women finally stopped it.

Later, I began a small boxing stable there, two of the boys boxing for me later in Quincy. It was a modest thing – we had no gloves even – so head punching was necessarily banned.

In The Marines

In 1940, I emerged from the Home to attend a Catholic school in Peoria, Illinois. I quit high school after the second year, worked in a variety of jobs, and finally hitchhiked to California at sixteen. There, I worked at Mare Island shipyard until I turned seventeen, when I joined the Marine Corps. After almost three years in the Marine Corps, half of it overseas (Hawaii, Peleliu, Guam, and with the first units to occupy southern Japan after the surrender), I was unbloody, unbowed, and considerably better educated.

Ah, the memories of the Corps. The first day at boot camp, a small corporal disgustfully appraising sixty of America's finest. "You meatheads," the two-striped runt says, growing in quantum jumps with each word, "America has hit the skids. I think I'll defect to the Japs. But before I do, I see some cocky big fellows amongst you. Here and now I challenge any and all of you to come forth and take your beating like men, you miserable midgets!" (His language, of course, was not that elegant.) Not a man, from the 6'-6" Los Angeles police lieutenant to skinny and shivering me, not one stepped forward. It was a psych job impure and simple. Ten weeks later, the corporal had turned into Dale Carnegie and loved everyone. Still, it made for memories.

In the Marines, we did a lot of bayonet drill and our instructor was the pro footballer Wee Willie Wilkin. I recall reading years later that his pro career tragically was cut short by cancer. Wee Willie was instructing with a sheathed bayonet one day out on the boondocks when an unprepossessing bird from Arkansas answered his challenge. You know the kind of man, the sort one meets but not often in every martial arts dojo; the kind who, *sans* training, naturally have a sense of balance, root, and rhythm deriving from bodies that have weathered hell. Many martial art instructors, in fact, want to see the last of these because they don't fit the overly structured milieu of typical classes, but a judo teacher will welcome them with glee.

Anyhow, this guy bracing Wee Willie that day was one such and a nice guy to boot, unlike the stereotype Marine of today, the one who all too often lives just this side of hysteria. Wee Willie also was a nice guy, so they started easy – Willie, huge and muscular; the farm-boy, middle-sized and wiry. Wee Willie tried some structured stuff but Arkansas whacked his rifle with a stroke that would've broken a bar with the bartender. Then a full-scale scrap ensued. No one died, no one even got bloodied, but Wee Willie never had such an interesting five minutes: for him, the NFL after the war must have seemed like the Teddy Bears' Picnic with Big Jon and Sparkey in comparison. Someone once called Stan Ketchell "an Indian uprising." So it was that day with Arkansas belaboring Wee Willie. Some of our bigger members, when the thing looked to go to extra innings, finally threw a seventeen-year-old stripling (thankfully, not me) into the melee. Before his thin and ravaged body was tossed back out of the milling, it had reduced the momentum of the savage pair to where our big guys could break it up.

Marine Corps judo bore no resemblance to the sportive jacketed wrestling I encountered in Chicago after being discharged in 1946. Marine judo was a melange of punches, chops, elbows, and low kicks – most of them aimed at the groin. No throws or locks, just strikes by the number. We were told that every Japanese private was a samurai who would eat two of us with his one bowl of rice and then hike fifty miles with a seventy-five-pound pack. So we had to out-terrorize them. We believed it.

It was a rough patch, but the discipline was consistent – consistently harsh. In the first few hectic days of boot camp there was no time even for suicide. We heard that a guy from an earlier platoon had gone out of his head and broke ranks, got up on the roof of the barracks and tried that exit (never mind that the barracks was only two-stories). He made a bad job of it, only breaking his ankle. The Marines were death on suicide and bad tries – the man was put back in ranks and made to continue marching.

A couple guys, who for whatever reason didn't like to wash (modesty? an aversion to soap?), were ganged and sand-washed by most of the platoon. I preferred dirt to fascism and angrily said so to a few of the "sanitary" thugs. On this occasion, I noted the absence of the drill instructor. I haven't altogether liked humans en masse since.

A war zone was a hellish place to do schooling, but I wanted to make up those two lost years and get a diploma. So I enrolled in the Marine Corps Institute's correspondence course. In Peleliu, the temperature reached $110°$ with no electric fans, the perspiration wetting the paper and smearing the ink. But avid reading and a heady love of learning softened the rigor and made it almost fun.

Boxing

In 1946, just out of the Marines as a corporal, I started firing on the Chicago, Burlington, and Quincy railroad (CB&Q – now the Burlington Northern). I was in Galesburg and going good. I had a high school diploma (by correspondence) and a good-paying job: if I could hold it against the laconic severe engineers on the right side of the cab. The elite in that town of 30,000, I came to believe the engineers were tougher even than the Marines. Not so, they only seemed tougher because their existence was a gray one in which cheerfulness never broke in. In the Corps, a twenty-six-mile hike would become a lark with the same tough corporal who had challenged us to personal combat the first day of boot camp now kidding about extending the hike to thirty miles, and a seventeen-year-old saying OK, but only if we could do the extra four miles backward. And sweaty smiles all round.

At the Galesburg YMCA, I began learning boxing from Andy Duncan, a gifted ex-pro who could showboat or take you out with either hand. All too quickly in 1947, I was transferred to the river town of Quincy, Illinois, to cope with Mississippi River flooding. At the YMCA there I took over a good group of Golden Glovers. I trained them hard, and while practicing judo and firing on the railroad, I also put on amateur cards across a three-state area. For kicks, I would now and then go boxer versus judoka with them and, despite occasional bells ringing in my head when they connected, I found that once vertical became horizontal the boxer was done.

Andy Duncan (right) of Galesburg, Illinois, who taught the author the rudiments of boxing after World War II. Below, Duncan later teaching that old black magic to other lads.

Once I took the team to a bigger city for a card. While he was pay-ing me our fee, the promoter, a big guy named Salto, asked me for a favor. Salto, the spitting image of tough guy Sheldon Leonard on early TV, said he had a little black kid fighting featherweight who'd been boxing only two years. Salto was a former boxer of note: he had once held a young Joe Louis to a ten-round decision loss. And he still looked tough with big black eyes boring holes through me. Worse, he owned the mayor and most of the rackets. "You'll take care of us won't you, Smitty?" he urged. This was one man I wanted to please. I told him sure, we'd carry his boy – he didn't have to worry. I then told my feath-er, Dick, a top contender in area Golden Gloves competition, what had happened. I warned him not to get suckered, but to feel the kid out carefully and if indeed he was a novice, to dance him the three rounds. He agreed to go easy.

Dick's bout came and I warned him again to take it easy. He nod-ded. The first bell rang as I was coming down the ring steps. A roar went up from the crowd as I settled into my seat. The black boxer, a good looking little guy, hadn't made it out of his corner. Dick had him against the ropes shooting the works. The kid could do nothing but receive and wilt. This terrorism took a couple minutes during which I looked over at Salto. He wasn't even watching the fight, he only had eyes for me: obsidian ones staring into and through me. I was so scared I almost threw the towel in for his fighter. Happily, the referee stopped it soon enough.

It was a long night with several bouts to follow. But Salto didn't seem interested. His eyes never left me. When his crack middleweight won a KO upset over ours, I kissed up to him by almost cheering. But Salto didn't seem to notice: he just kept staring at me. Before the last fight, I called our team together and told them that afterwards we were leaving quick and whoever wasn't in the two cars a minute after the bout would be left behind.

As the last bout ended we ran for the exits. And made it home. Salto had disappeared. On the way to Galesburg, I asked Dick why he hadn't followed orders. He said lamely that he'd never fought a black before and was so scared he couldn't stop himself. Before I went to bed that night, I looked under my bed. Salto wasn't there.

There were always adventures. My lightweight three-state champi-on Bill Platt was having a *zombie* (one to a customer, at $2 a glass – serious money then) with me one night and went outside. Though never much of a drinker, I continued sipping mine, gradually achieving the condition the Spanish call "joyous." A chap ran in, shouting, "Platt is fighting a big guy!" I mused and continued drinking. In the chap ran again. "Now he's banging Bill's head against the building!" This changed the equation: Platt was to headline a big boxing show two days later in Keokuk, Iowa, and I wanted him halfway healthy. Out I waltzed to find the report true. A 200-pounder had Platt's head in hand and was pounding it against the wall. Platt, meanwhile, was laughing uproariously. (He loved to fight and laugh.)

I touched the guy and asked him to desist, as we wanted Platt fairly intact for the upcoming bout. He leered at me, said, "Screw your jujitsu," and for emphasis banged Platt's noggin against brick once more. In manhandling Platt, he turned his back to me. I again touched his shoulder and this time he released Platt, wheeled, and threw a huge right haymaker. If it had hit me, I'd still be dead. But it didn't. Everything seemed to slow as I avoided his blow, turned in and took

Some of the Quincy Golden Glove team the author managed:
Bill Platt is at the left in second row; author is at center of first row.

him up with a shoulder throw (*seoi-nage*). Things seemed so slow that as I got him up I leisurely deliberated on whether to whip him over to the ground. I decided on the other option. Jigoro Kano, the founder of judo, found that on most throws the receiver's head faces down and the ethic of judo was for the thrower to continue his pull, ending by pulling up on the receiver's jacket so that his head didn't hit, and he was able to breakfall with his arm – this, to show that sportive judo had functional use. But in that alley, I eschewed the sportive and released Platt's attacker at the zenith of his arc. He was then on his own, but managed it poorly. I rolled him over and applied a choke, but the heavy leather of his Air Force-style jacket made for tough going, till a friend of the man begged me to quit choking – he was out. And so he was, his face open and bleeding. *Katsu* (resuscitation) brought him around.

I was a hero in the burg for a while, but was sobered the next day by the news that the brute I'd braced was one of the prime street fighters there. He had even once hit the main supporting member of a small house and brought the whole structure down around him. Not too bright a guy, but strong. So thereafter when I'd see him around town, I'd straighten up and "muscle out" for his questioning eyes ("How'd he do that?") and hope like hell he wouldn't have another try. Though this certainly proved the efficacy of judo for me – especially since the thrower was operating with a *zombie* and only two years of judo in him at the time – I was aware then and now that Lady Luck was providing her favors that night.

Not all the excitement was in Quincy. Once we went to a town with a reputation for bringing in top amateurs from Detroit. We got our heads handed to us, losing four to two. ("Managers, trainers, and seconds all say 'we' when speaking of a fight, if they wish to be polite to the fighter," says A.J. Liebling, our finest boxing writer. "Otherwise they say 'I.'") Platt was shellacked by Candy Anderson, who later turned into a leading welterweight in the pro ranks. The promoter was a feisty little guy who had boxed successfully in the late 1920's. Evidently, he was also hell in the street. According to my wife's uncle, who knew him well, the promoter once had whipped a big lad from a local factory. The defeated big one thereupon went into six months of drastic training and then tried again. He got beat worse that time. However, I only learned how tough the promoter was later. Had I known that night, I probably would have been more prudent. As it was, as he paid me off, he griped that Platt was an over-rated patsy. I answered in kind that he knew Platt's record, and that Candy was just too much for him. The conflict escalated with me doing most of the talking. We even squared away, but wiser heads and bigger guys prevailed.

Bill Platt came into the "Y" one evening to announce that Ernie Brix was coming that night to box him. Ernie was the town hooligan with time done in prison who fancied himself a boxer. "Is it okay?" Bill asked. "Sure," I told him, "if it's all right with you. Why do you ask?"

In answer, he said that he had heard that Brix was a tough bastard who in the thick of it might forget that boxing was a sport and, well, was it worth the risk? I told him to suit himself but, if Brix went bad, he'd have to beat both of us. That did the trick – bring on the brute!

And on he came a half-hour later with a big pair of shoulders and a smile belying the something in his eyes you get only in the joint. I laced his gloves on for him. I had seen him around town where we'd nod, but he was warmer now. "Smitty, how goes it?" he asked, and I said fine, adding, "Ernie, you got fifty pounds on Bill, so have at him, but try to stay with the rules, okay?" He smiled again, nudged my shoulder, and said, "Sure, that's why I wanted the workout, to see if I could box like a boxer, legit, you know."

With that preamble over, I squared Platt and Brix away and told them we'd go two three-minute rounds with a couple minutes rest in between. Without headgear – we were not affluent – I called time at a team member who was to keep time. I refereed.

I tell this now because it was educational. Brix had had gloves on before, held up a good high guard, and he circled Platt well. This, I recall thinking, is going to be interesting. But it wasn't. Platt, measuring for distance, tried a tentative jab and when he felt Brix's nose hit it, he dropped, shifted his weight, and crossed with his right. Because of the weight factor, Platt could never have knocked Brix out. But that first right cross almost did it. It jolted Brix against the ropes and took him out of his game plan. Half angry but laughing, he started pitching baseballs, throwing high hooks whose wind velocity alone should have floored Platt. But didn't. Nor did his savagery scare Platt, who was more of a boxer than a slugger and was now in his element.

He went to town on Brix, countering every hook with short stiff lefts and rights to body and head. Undeterred, Brix kept throwing but Platt kept sliding inside to counter. The thing came apart when Platt got in his pet right uppercut. Brix stopped throwing and his legs walked funny. Just then time ran out for the first round. And last. Brix sprawled on a chair, sweating profusely, and shoved both gloves up at me, gasping: "Take 'em off, Smitty – I'm too tired." And he was, taking ten minutes before he could tell us how he evidently wasn't meant to be a boxer.

True, he didn't have the temperament for boxing. His reputation had been built on street fighting. A month later, another boxer and I stopped at a bar and got a couple beers. We were at the end of a crowded bar drinking when some kind of altercation broke out at the middle. No punches were thrown but people were moving rapidly away from something. We moseyed closer and there was my buddy Ernie Brix and Bill, one of his younger roughneck brothers. As I got in earshot, I could hear a short muscular guy, built like a fireplug and dressed to kill, say to Ernie, "I'm here to beat the hell out of Jim Brix. Are you him?" Ernie smiled, "No, I'm his brother. Will I do?"

Out in the alley behind the tavern we all went, even a pale special police officer. We had us a ring in the half-light and these two had a fight. But not before the swarthy dresser announced his name as Sal Gianetti and said, "I'm undefeated in New York City," to which Ernie allowed as how he was who he was and that he'd never been whipped in Chicago. So it was to be an inter-city go.

But it wasn't much of a fight. Shakespeare was right, "The advertisement detracted from the performance." The short guy bobbed and weaved and hooked and missed. Ernie threw his right and didn't. Down went New York City and Ernie kicked him accurately and sharply in the head. He was groggy and Ernie wanted to put the other boot to him. He was near me and I pulled him away forcefully, saying, "It's all over, Ernie, you got him." He looked at me unsmiling now, his blood up. I got ready. But then he recognized me and smiled. "Hell, Smitty, I didn't see you. Yep, I guess it's over."

The moral of the story is that boxing and street-fighting are two different qualities. Don't conclude, however, that one is invariably superior to the other. John Gilbey cited Ralph Ellison's story in *Invisible Man* (1952) of the prize fighter who completely overwhelmed a big awkward yokel from the country. The boxer turned him inside and out, knocking his ears off. Then one of the stupefied yokel's haymakers got through, "knocking science, speed, and footwork as cold as a well-digger's posterior. . . . The yokel had simply stepped inside of his opponent's sense of time."

Nor was this a fluke. One night, as a young high school kid, I went along with Tosco Frederick, at 230 pounds the biggest guy in school and our ace fullback, to a carnival in Galesburg. A good looking blond boxer with gloves on was standing in front of a tent while a barker extolled his lethality and dared any of the men present to try conclusions with him. The guy was "Snooks" Wilson, a local middleweight with a good reputation. Anyone lasting three minutes with Snooks, the barker said, would get a sawbuck. Tosco thought he'd gone to Heaven. The Frederick clan – Gilbey later called them the Fanchers – was the town's toughest. Tosco had two big brothers at home who could whip him and an ailing but mean old man who could whip all of them simultaneously. He presented himself to the carnies and I thought I glimpsed a worried look in Snook's eyes. We had trouble getting Tosco's huge hands into those little gloves, and then they began.

Snooks was pretty and a cute boxer. Clever would have been better. He shot out a lightning-fast stiff left jab to Tosco's mouth, cutting his lip. Tosco didn't notice. He walked through it and tossed a short right hook that bounced Snooks to the floor.

Snooks then made another mistake: he got up. Tosco met him with a left hook and down he went. For a cute guy – he probably had to beat the ladies off – Snooks had grit and managed to almost make it to the vertical before meeting Tosco's barn-burning right. Snooks snoozed, Tosco got his sawbuck, and we had cheeseburgers and shakes.

Toward the end of his life, Jack Johnson, then in his sixties, and the greatest heavyweight boxer of all time, worked for peanuts in carnivals. With only three or four others, I saw Jack along with Jess Willard in a Los Angeles sideshow in 1944. Jack was "Lil' Artha," big, powerful, and smiling; Jess looked like a retired feed merchant. For a quarter you could ask the pair questions. I don't remember mine, but I can't forget how, when I held the rope up for Jack to climb into the ring, he affectionately slapped my shoulder with his huge right mitt, gave that gorgeous grin showing more teeth than even Louis Armstrong could, and said, "Thanks, son." (So, in a real sense, you are reading the scribbling of a man who survived Jack's punishing right hand.) Two years after I saw him, Jack was dead in a car crash near Raleigh, North Carolina.

If you won't take my word on Jack Johnson's prowess, listen to Jack Dempsey, who said that the farther back you go, the tougher they were – and that Johnson was toughest of all. "He was all elbows and arms," said Dempsey, "the greatest catcher of punches who ever lived. He could uppercut moving backward and could cut to the body off a jaw feint and hook off a jab better than any heavyweight who ever lived." That's definitive enough, I think.

Curiously, there is something of Johnson's marvelous defensive wizardry today in Chris Byrd, a 225-pound ranking heavyweight. As of July, 1999, he had twenty-seven wins and one loss. Byrd plays pitty-pat with heavy punchers like Bert Cooper. He is so unorthodox no top boxer will meet him. And he doesn't run – he'll put his back to the ropes and still slip and slide, duck and dodge, and turn opponents into knots. Unlike Johnson, he has utterly no power in either hand, his twelve knockouts being the result of frustration fusing with exhaustion on the part of his victims. He beats them with great condition, greater reflexes, and the greatest boy-next-door smile. He's having fun as he raindrops on the roofs of his opponents.

The best boxer I ever watched was Joe Louis, "the Brown Bomber," who held the heavyweight title for twelve years and defended it twenty-five times. I saw Joe train three hours in Chicago in 1947, preparing for his first Joe Walcott fight. He worked several rounds with Bob Satterfield, no tin can, and seeped with style. Bulkier and slower than he was during his pre-war "Bum of the Month" days, Joe's crisp, powerful left jab was still the best I ever saw. And the exquisite short right cross that followed the jab rocked Satterfield even with sixteen-ounce gloves and headgear. Joe shuffled, economized, and was so expressionless that no one ever knew if he was hurt. He was a dignified fighter, unlike loud-mouth Ali, who would have been just another bum of the month for Joe. As for Mike Tyson, he couldn't have gotten past Rocky Marciano, who took eight rounds to knock out an aging Joe, who had

Jack Johnson (left), probably the best heavyweight boxer of all time.

Joe Louis (right), the Brown Bomber, the best boxer the author ever saw at work.

returned from retirement in 1951. Mike, however, would have gone down a lot sooner than Ali, because he would have tried to push Louis, a mistake against the best counter-puncher since Jack Johnson.

In John Gilbey's *Western Boxing and World Wrestling* (1986), I dilated on boxing at some length, and here I want only to show part of the role it played in my life. But while I'm on Gilbey, let me correct him (page 36). He wrote that, because Louis never learned how to defend against Schmeling's right in the two years between their first and second fights, fear drove him to knock out Schmeling in the first round lest Max get that dreaded right in. This tale circulated in the Louis camp probably to sandbag Schmeling. It is nonsense. Louis destroyed Max in one round out of anger, not fear. All Louis had to do to correct the defect (dropping his left after a jab, thus letting Max use his right over it) was to keep his left fist up when retracting it, which he did for the rest of his career. Max Baer had the most powerful right of all heavy weights then, but Louis had no trouble knocking him out. No defensive marvel himself, Baer wasn't bothered by Schmeling, and kayoed him in ten.

Although I grew up liking professional boxing – and Lord forgive me, I even promoted amateur boxing – I have long since believed that all boxing should be banned. Boxing is too brutal for civilized societies. Boxing is the only sport that has injury as its aim. To survive, a boxer has to have a good chin, in A.J. Liebling's words, "an unlimited absorptive capacity for percussion." A pro footballer faces the risk of pain and sometimes serious injury; a boxer the certainty of it. This sterile intentionality is what stamps this remnant of primitive savagery as unfit for human beings. Available data demonstrate that on a per-participant basis, boxing is the most dangerous sport. Over five hundred men and a couple of women have been killed in the ring since 1918. But, you say, why shouldn't two people who relish trauma mix it if they wish? Because boxing is a business, a bestial business, exploiting and staining all it touches.

Plato probably was right in asserting that any recourse to physical force is an indication of meager intelligence, but it's even worse if men fight without anger simply for money, promoters, and the ephemeral plaudits of the crowd. Many have suggested various palliatives to correct boxing (heavier gloves, headgear, etc.), but these amount to replacing the whorehouse's water glasses with Dixie cups as a sanitary measure, and in any case would not be countenanced by the crowd.

To show how vulgar these times have become, women – yeah, my mom and your sister – are now getting into boxing. A bad thing, boxing, has now gotten worse. Men shouldn't box because of brain damage. Ditto for women. And neither should box because it's uncivilized. (Critic Christopher Lehmann-Haupt doesn't mince words: "Boxing is a nasty, brutish activity whose point is to attack the very source of human civilization, the human brain.") But women have a problem men don't have, except actor Victor Mature, of whom it was said that when he played Samson, he had bigger mammaries than Delilah in the classic film of the pair. (I can never be critical, though, of a guy who said once that the toughest job in film acting was keeping his stomach sucked in.) The problem is that women have exposed breasts that were never meant to be punched. In 1976, a woman lost on a second round KO when she dropped her guard to adjust a slipping bra. After the loss, her trainer said her bra would have to be redesigned. But the gal did him one better: she redesigned her body by having her breasts removed surgically. I have heard of a woman golf pro who had one breast removed to ease her golf swing, but giving two breasts to any sport is beyond comprehension.

A friend has asked me why I changed my view on boxing. Simple, I got smarter and a bit more civilized as I grew older. I started to research the subject of boxing injuries and became acquainted with good-hearted Mannie Velasquez of Greenville, Illinois, and Tucson, Arizona, who had been collecting data for decades and passed it on to me.

Later, the martial arts brought Andy Guterman, a judo black belt from Florida, into my ken. Andy was an extraordinary person, very erudite, who had earned both a doctorate in medicine and a Ph.D. in pharmacology. His obituary read that he'd had post-doctoral residencies in neurology and psychiatry, plus numerous fellowships. His lecturing and writing were praised widely. A humble man, he told me little of these honors and his sometimes bawdy jokes and ways masked much of his accomplishment.

Andy Guterman, M.D., a judo black belt who helped the author research boxing injuries.

He considered himself my student in the martial arts, though we never did judo and only a little Chinese boxing. He knew me mainly from my books, but as a student he was exceptional. He held doors open, listened to what I said, and believed and acted on it. He was quiet when it was called for and noisily boisterous other times. Genuinely polite, he showed no trace of sycophancy. He would not let me buy a meal in his presence, "The teacher does not pay," he said. Of course I thwarted this but commended the spirit. I hadn't met these traits much and queried him. He told me it wasn't just me, it was an institution. This is how, he said, a student of the martial arts should act. Only a few of my long-time students approached this kind of studentship.

We planned a book on boxing injuries and collected material for it. Although his untimely death in 1991 at age thirty-nine put the quietus on that, we did manage to co-author an article, "Neurological Sequalae of Boxing," for a New Zealand medical journal (*Sports Medicine* 4:194-210 (1987). At the height of his rocketing career, he developed brain cancer and all too soon he and his enormous promise were gone. At the end, on the phone with a weary laugh, he told me that the episode held one happy result. Whereas before he had lectured from theory on epilepsy and brain malfunction, now that he carried the cancer, he was lecturing from intimate experience and lecturing much better. A grace note in passing – little wonder his widow Roseann and two children treasured him so.

We wanted boxing banned and Andy helped me document its dangers. In *Western Boxing and World Wrestling* (1986), Gilbey stated that boxing should be banned. He mentioned that his friend, Al Holtmann, 6th-dan at the San Diego Judo Club, hoped that judo could replace it. It was a good thought, except that judo – sensibly limited (regulated) and thus creative – never found an audience in America. With limited contact and emphasis put on skillful attack and defense, karate would be a useful surrogate. But in the end, commercial demands are such that violence must out. The crowd still wants Barabbas – they require blood and knockouts. Go to a fight and watch the faces in the audience, not the fighters, and you'll see what I mean.

At the end of V. Blasco-Ibanez's *Blood and Sand* (1908), the gored matador is doing his last *faena* on a cot while another "fight" is in progress. The crowd roars. The book ends: "Outside roared the beast, the real beast, the only beast!"

One rainy day in 1948, I and a few boxers wanted to run some miles on the YMCA indoor track. Once there, we found high school students putting up balloons and crepe paper streamers. I asked a winsome lass if we could use the track. She said no, that the high school had it. Turned out that they were preparing the gym for a big dance. I protested that we needed it. In a nose-to-nose confrontation, she persisted and won. And still does: I married her three years later.

The author and his gal Alice, 1949.

Judo

I wrestled in high school and at YMCAs and learned rough-and-tumble "judo" in the Marine Corps. But the "judo" I learned there bore little resemblance to the sportive jacketed wrestling I began learning after my discharge in 1946.

In Galesburg, I fired for the CB&Q Railroad. This was before the switch from steam to diesels and your job was only as good as your shovel. Despite the curmudgeonly engineers, I loved the two years I fired on the railroad – rolling along at midnight, hearing the melancholy whistle at crossings, an awed nineteen-year-old alone in a peaceful world. Or the time I had a *satori* at dawn looking out from the engine on misty coal fields at Lewistown, Illinois. Many were the memorable moments. Rail versus air travel? There is no comparison. One is civilized (or at least was during the 1940's) – the other is a sardine can. Edna Millay says it all for me: "There isn't a train I wouldn't take, no matter where it's going." Alas, as Lucius Beebe wrote, "The iron ponies are now stabled forever amid fields of asphodel and beyond the margin of Acheron."

Other benefits of the system included a rail pass to Chicago. So one day early in 1947, I decided to look in on the Chicago Judo Club on South Michigan Avenue. Like "Country Cousin," a writer for the London Budokwai, I took up judo on medical advice. My doctor made no bones about it. "Give up boxing," he said, "or you'll get killed."

On entering the basement dojo, I saw a fairly small Japanese fellow in street clothes sweeping the mat. He didn't look much of a suchness and, disappointed, I asked him his grade. "Third," he said matter-of-factly. "Third Brown?" I queried, knowing a bit about the belt system. "No," he laughed, "Black." This was a letdown for me and he sensed it. "Had I done any judo?" I looked at his size and deftly lied, "Yes." Did I want a free practice? You bet. He gave me a uniform, put his on, and we grabbed hold and squared off. Against such a small guy, my past experience seemed great. I was as confident as a Christian with four aces.

We went for less than ten minutes, most of it air time. Mine. I've since gone with better judoka but none more devastating than Hik Nagao (who became a good friend). Hik's forte was *hane-makikomi.* My hand trembles as I write the name of the damned technique: the spring

Jigoro Kano, founder of judo.
He is where it started.

hip throw. Of course, I didn't know then what was happening and the trauma was amplified by the fact that I didn't know how to fall properly. ("Country Cousin" wrote that "the famed Yukio Tani spent five minutes showing me how to breakfall and the rest of the time showing me how necessary it was to learn to do it properly.") So I stumbled around in a daze pulling him, and every time I pulled, he rode it in, pulled me to him and pumped his right hip and leg against the inner surface of my right leg popping me up into the air. But that wasn't all.

Jigoro Kano, the founder of judo, once decreed that one should be able to *ukemi* (breakfall) for every throw. This means that every throw should afford you a chance to slap your arm on the mat, thus easing the force of the fall. Hik did his hane-makikomi a bit differently. Once he had me in the air, he wrapped me tight and then threw (sacrificed) his body into the air doubling the force. Down we came. Circles being what they are, I lit first and instanter Hik landed on me. A double whammy, if you will. I went home three hundred miles on a slow train, rueful and wondering what had happened. My back was so sorely stressed that I was stooped for two weeks and, when I shoveled coal into the firebox of the engine, I couldn't straighten up, much to the merriment of the engineer and brakeman.

With time, I could stand and walk fairly steadily. The episode, however, must have damaged my brain: a month later I walked into the club and signed up with the club's star, Minoru "Johnny" Osako, 3rd-dan. He gave me my first lesson: "Before you can throw, you must learn to fall properly." I was a poor loser. "You mean there's a proper way to fall?"

Though I stayed with judo for more than thirty years thereafter in different places and times, I never met a nicer bunch than at that first dojo. Old Hilaire Belloc captures my feeling pretty well:

> For no one in our long decline,
> So dusty, spiteful, and divided,
> Had quite such pleasant friends as mine,
> Or loved them half as much as I did.

What a bonny bunch! Mits Shoji (2nd-dan), who'd give $5 (a considerable sum then) to anyone who could throw him with *tomoe-ange* (circle throw); Al Valanis (2nd-dan), a detective who specialized in picking up guns from felons and drawing likenesses of suspects from descriptions; and Art Broadbent (5th-dan, deceased), my best friend who followed me all over America boosting a dream and, as best man at my wedding in 1951, showed up the first day of my honeymoon, and was welcome even then. And so many others: Lloyd Tuma, a 6' 6" giant, so tall you had to throw him in sections; and Richard Doi, a 1st-dan so tiny he could throw you with a shoulder throw and never have to bend his knees. (Richard taught at St. Charles Reform School and would regale us with stories of bonelocking inmates.) Quiet Harvey Dea, a 200-pound Chinese who once loaned me a box of jazz records of Louis and the boys, rare records now worth more than my house. Ruth Gardner, a legal stenographer and a 1st-dan, gave most of us trouble in *randori* (free practice). I fell sometimes for Ruth and invariably for Johnny. And there were Ron Heyse, Bill Gray, Fred Beem, and more I can't bring to mind.

I have a bit of treasure I just pulled from my bookcase, a 3"x4" piece of plaster, shrapnel from the wall of the club, one side inscribed "Property of Chicago Judo Club," and signed in 1949 by Johnny Osako, Art Broadbent, Shag Okada, Fred Beem, Paul Nessel, and Howard Dea. And on the back, in Art Broadbent's hand, the inscription, "Good Luck Always." The mats abutted the wall and occasionally someone would break the plaster. But not often. We cared for each other and avoided throwing into the wall.

It was so wonderful, it resembled music then and even now, remembering the times we had.

Chicago had several judo hot spots at the time. Hank Okamura had a hardy crew at the Lawson YMCA, and Oak Park always fielded a tough team. I recall a classic match once between Hank and Hik Nagao. Hank was all over Hik the whole way until the last seconds of the match when here came little Hik with that great big spring hip, and up and over highly-favored Hank went.

Sketch showing Hik Nagao pinning Hank Okamura with *kesa-gatame* (scarf hold).

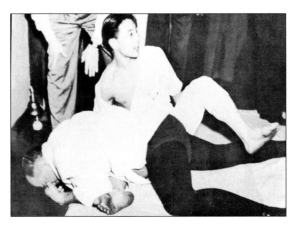

Mas Tamura
chokes out
champion
wrestler Karl
Pojello in
Chicago, 1943.

Meanwhile, at the Jiu Jitsu Institute in the Loop, the esteemed Masato "Mas" Tamura had his younger brother, Vince, and Bill Berndt and other stalwarts. Tamura, who was originally from Fife, Washington, had been a powerhouse on the west coast during the Thirties. His real claim to fame, though, was his 1943 match with the great Lithuanian grappler, Karl Pojello. The amateur Greco-Roman champion of Russia, Pojello taught doughty Britisher E.J. Harrison in Petrograd during World War I. Old, past his prime, and out of shape, Pojello was prevailed on by a Chicago newspaper to fight Tamura to establish whether Japanese judo could win over western wrestling. The bout was held in Chicago before a select audience of U.S. military observers and Avery Brundage, former head of the AAU. (My source is The Minidoka Irrigator, a relocation camp newspaper, dated March 13, 1943.)

Tamura and Pojello made an odd couple. Tamura was a 3rd-dan at the top of his game, but weighed only 143 pounds. Pojello weighed 205 pounds, but they weren't as muscled as when he'd taken on all comers in Petrograd. But the match they put on was a classic. They fought in jackets. No sooner started than Pojello slammed Tamura to the mat, and followed into groundwork only to be countered by Tamura from underneath and choked unconscious. The time elapsed was one minute, twenty seconds. After the referee sent Tamura to his corner, Pojello awoke and jumped up. Resuming the battle, he grabbed Tamura and threw him several times, but when he tried to pin the small judoka he was "kicked into the air" (that is, probably thrown with tomoe-nage, circle or stomach throw). After twenty-five slam-bang minutes the referee stepped between them and yelled, "This has gone far enough. Nobody is getting any dough out of this. Let's call it quits. It's a draw."

On that mercantile note, the match ended. Curiously, the *Chicago Sun-Times*, which promoted the bout, ended its account with Pojello unconscious. It must have been a beaut. Both men embodied the true warrior spirit. The 51-year-old Pojello deserves credit for fighting in the unfamiliar jacket when he should have been smoking a cigar on the front porch swing (his last fall was to cancer in 1954), rather than recovering from unconsciousness to carry the fight to Tamura, who was twenty years younger and far fitter. Tamura, too, has to be applauded for holding off one of Europe's top shoot (legitimate) wrestlers, despite giving up sixty pounds in weight and having only a forefinger and a thumb on his left hand. As a youth, he lost the last three fingers in an explosion. But, in the true judo spirit, he made this liability an asset, and developed a devastating right seoi-nage, most of the pulling being done by only that left thumb and index finger.

Anyway, while in Chicago, I learned to fall and a good thing. Though I won first place at the 1947 Chicagoland Judo Tournament, I was pretty much a second eleven sort of guy in great need of falling skills.

As I said, our club's big gun was Johnny Osako. He and Ruth Gardner had bought the place from T. Shozo Kuwashima, who had relocated to California. Back in 1917, Kuwashima had been selected by

Yoshiaki Yamashita Shihan (Jigoro Kano's right hand man) to go to the U.S. to teach judo. He arrived as a 5th-dan and spent World War I teaching combatives to U.S. military units on the west coast. He started the Chicago Judo School in 1919, changed the name to "Club" in 1940, and sold it to Johnny and Ruth in 1947.

Johnny (3rd-dan then, later 7th-dan, deceased) was then king of the U.S. mats. There was Ken Kuniyuki in Los Angeles and Mits Kimura in San Francisco; some fellows in Seattle I would meet later; and George Yoshida in New York ("I'm 3rd-dan in judo and

Johnny Osako at his club, 1949.

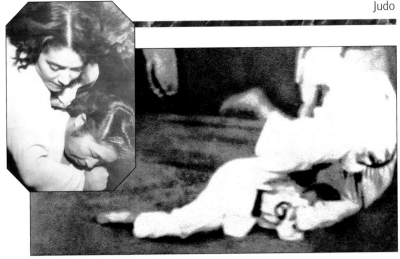

Ruth Gardner, the co-owner of the Chicago Judo Club, in Tokyo, 1949.
Above, she is throwing Takahashi Sensei with a circle throw at the Kodokan and,
at top left, Noritomi throws her with a shoulder throw.

6th-dan in beer drinking") whom, worst luck, I never did meet. But at that time, Johnny was supreme. Although born in Stockton, California, he had been Kagoshima Prefecture champion in 1940, but he returned to the United States before the war. He taught judo in the relocation camps during the war and won the 180-lb. championship in 1955, the heavyweight and grand championships in 1958, and the grand championships in the Pan-American Games held in Cuba in 1952 and 1954. During the 1960's, he taught appreciative students in Cincinnati, Cleveland, and Detroit.

Johnny was the only man I ever saw who never walked – he slid his feet along (few of even the big boys in Japan ever got him with a footsweep). He had a devastating inner thigh throw (*uchimata*) and footsweep (*okuri-ashi*), and an endless repertoire of chokes and pins. Some, perhaps many, quit judo early because of the necessity of enduring his powerful and high throws separating them rather quickly from the ground we live on. I never met any judoka anywhere who possessed such deliciously devastating sweeps (*ashi-waza*) as Johnny did. Sure, his swooping inner thigh (uchimata) did the trick quick, but the sweeps were even more rapid. They moved the earth for a lot of us. One moment you were vertical thinking devious thoughts and the next there was this lightning transition and you were skyward and horizontal and down again to the earth, your breakfall the thunderclap. Physically, it was so fast it never had time to become uncomfortable.

Group of top Japanese and American judoka at Chicago Judo Club.
From left: Sumiyuki Kotani (10th-dan), T. Otaki (obscured), Mas Tamura,
Johnny Osako, Hik Nagao, Hank Okamura, and Tak Otsu. Date unknown.

The uncertainty of moving around with Johnny, never knowing when one of his feet would react to a raised eyebrow and lash out sending one skyward, may have taken a psychological toll on others. But I got this terror early and it taught me to move economically and prudently. I seldom fell to sweeps after those early experiences with a master.

And there was always Art Broadbent. Until his untimely early death working as a carpenter on a construction site in Chicago, we were as close as brothers. With this imported Britisher, judo was fun and work, and even the work was fun. He visited me often. Once the promoter of a boxing show in Iowa asked if I would put on a judo exhibition at the show, "They ain't never seen jujipsu (sic)." Art said he'd help and so I agreed. At an interval in the fights held in a crowded Iowa pasture, most fans standing, in we came wearing our white pajamas. Merriment was general, titters were heard, and we had to fight our way through the grudging farmers to the ring. We gave them ten minutes of high-flying judo complete with *kiai* (spirit shouts) and throws to warm the coldest heart. The falls alone were worth the admission price, done as they were on two-inch felt on a wooden base that cracked with sound on every throw. We were heavily applauded throughout and when we left the ring to walk back to our quarters, the crowd parted like the Red Sea for Moses to let us pass.

On one of those visits, we got to see how judo would fare against freestyle wrestling. A friend, J.H. "Tyke" Miller, owned a firm in Quincy that made plaster dolls and such for U.S. carnivals. He was also my boxing team's corporate sponsor. Tyke told me once that he had won the 1946 and 1947 AAU national wrestling championships at

Left: The author throwing charitable U.S.
Champ Osako with shallow shoulder throw.
Right: The author in reverse side body hold that often worked against high-grade brown
belts and low-grade blacks. It didn't faze Osako, however, who appears to be asleep.

around 150 pounds. Years later, I checked Mike Chapman's *Encyclo-pedia of American Wrestling,* and, unlike most folks who tell me of their sporting prowess, sure enough there he was, listed as the winner at 147.5 pounds both years.

In 1949, Johnny Osako and Art Broadbent came three hundred miles from Chicago for a visit. Tyke invited all of us out to his place for the day. With ulterior motives, he had spread a big mat across the lawn of his splendid estate and bade us go ahead with our judo, as he had never seen it before. Art and I had no sooner started when our host cockily walked onto the mat and asked to borrow my jacket. He told Art he was a wrestler, and was curious to know how wrestling would do against judo. A business bigwig, one of the town elite, sitting there shouted that he would give three to one odds on the wrestler, but there were no takers. The two-time AAU champion had never been defeated around Quincy.

Johnny Osako and one of
his devastating footsweeps.

The author
(2nd-kyu),
Johnny Osako
(4th-dan), and
Art Broadbent
(1st-dan)
that day
at Tyke's.

Art and Tyke began. Tyke tried for a leg. Art slid to the side. Tyke kept trying and Art kept him at bay by moving laterally. After Art figured he had been polite long enough, he shot in with *harai-goshi* (sweeping loin). Tyke took a pretty dive and fell hard. He bounced up, eyes blinking in astonishment, but game to the core. To make a short story shorter, after falling for two more harai-goshi, an uchimata, and a *yoko-sutemi* (side sacrifice), Tyke was glad to rest. A couple times during the match, both men had slipped to the mat. There, Tyke tried to press his advantage. But Art, wary of Tyke's prowess in groundwork, gingerly escaped.

Johnny Osako and I worked out next. By this time the other guests were quite enthusiastic. Except for the boisterous chap who had wanted to bet the wrestler – he was singularly silent. As usual, Smith versus Osako was all Osako.

After a few minutes of this, Tyke asked if he could go with Johnny who was at his peak right about then. No one could resist his devastat-

Johnny Osako applies
combined armlock
and foot-to-head strangle
on the author, 1948.

ing throws. No sooner had he and Tyke taken hold than Johnny put Tyke into orbit with uchimata. Then he took Tyke to the mat and gained the conclusion using chokes and locks. The first time this happened was dramatic. Art had been wary of Tyke on the ground. Not Johnny. He went to the mat and stayed, the spider inviting the fly. Thinking this was his big chance, Tyke dived in and in less than five seconds was helpless in Johnny's *katajuji* (half-cross choke). A few more applications by Johnny, and an out-of-breath, out-of-gas Tyke discontinued.

A few days later, I met Tyke downtown. I asked him how he liked judo. He replied, with a wry grin, "Smitty, I think I better stick to wrestling!"

The boy who twisted the mule's tail, it is said, isn't as pretty as he once was, but he knows more. Tyke was a highly seasoned and skilled grappler. And game as they came. Judo is a lot different from freestyle wrestling, something that some famous Japanese judoka discovered to their chagrin when they entered the freestyle events at the 1932 Olympics. Tyke made the mistake of trying to mix the two, and, as a result, got an awful lot of education in a very short time.

Above:
Art Broadbent
doing randori with
Hank Okamura.

Left:
Art about to
be trapped from
underneath by
Hank Okamura.

After leaving the railroad in 1948, I worked at various sales positions and later lived as the caretaker at the Chicago Judo Club while working for Dashiell Hammett's old bunch, the Pinkerton National Detective Agency. Even after enrolling at the University of Illinois at Urbana in 1950, I continued to help Donn Draeger and others establish judo throughout the United States. Donn's efforts were largely responsible for a fairly solid national organization by 1953.

The first U.S. Judo Championships were held that year at San Jose, California. This was notable because of initial Japanese resistance to American unification. I gave an ephemeral speech there about retaining Jigoro Kano's ethics while improving our judo. My best friend, Art Broadbent, did better: he placed second in the 180-lb. class despite turning his Nisei opponent every way but loose, a decision that even some Japanese in the audience booed. Later, Art tossed his medal into a mountain gorge while motorcycling home and never told his dad of the medal. Although Art hadn't enjoyed the judging that day, he liked my speech and told Alice as much. Forty years later she told me.

Officials at First U.S. Judo Championships at San Jose, California, 1953.
L to R: Dr. Harry Kurisaki, Charles Yerkow, Sam Luke, author,
Bernice Jay, Donn Draeger, Esther Takamoto, Mr. Doiguchi,
Henry Stone, Yosh Uchida, Mits Kimura, Richard Yennie.

Evidently she didn't want me to get too cocky.

Before returning home, Art visited Alice and me in Seattle for a few days. We had been living there after I graduated from the University of Illinois in 1952 and began a graduate program at the University of Washington. We had our first baby, Sue, and a tiny two-room wooden hut in veterans' housing next to the city garbage dump. (How right Raymond Chandler's comment, "Life is not very fragrant.") To continue eating, I worked the swing shift at Boeing, thus could only practice judo on Saturday afternoons. Two or three *yudansha*, but mainly Ben Ishii (2nd-dan), would work with me two or three hours, go to a Japanese-style communal hot-water bath, and then restore sagging spirits with buckwheat noodles (*udon*) in a tiny restaurant.

Above: Jigoro Kano eating an ice cream cone at the Inazo
Nitobe Memorial in Vancouver, British Columbia, in April 1938.
With him is Shigetaka Sasaki, 6th-dan. Sasaki introduced Kodokan
judo into Canada in 1924, and is considered the father of Canadian judo.

Kano aboard the Hikawa Maru at Vancouver, British Columbia, in April 1938. Directly behind him (only half in frame) is Yasuyuki Kumagai (6th-dan), then head of Seattle Dojo, who returned to Japan in 1940. The bespectacled man is the Japanese consul, and the other men are civic leaders from Vancouver.

Seattle had a lustrous judo history. Yamashita Shihan gave a private demonstration of judo to a group of local business leaders and their friends in October, 1903. Two years later, some other Japanese gave public demonstrations of judo at the University of Washington. And by March, 1907, the Seattle Dojo was flourishing. The Seattle Judo Black Belt Association, which dates to 1935, was one of the first in the country.

The Seattle Dojo's current building opened June 10, 1934. When I was there, its floor was tatami spread on boards, themselves laid on top of eighty big springs. I enjoyed myself there, though the indigenous Japanese were generally an unsmiling lot. As one of the first Caucasians to join the club after World War II, I expected to get the samurai treatment for the United States' idiotic relocation of over 120,000 Japanese-Americans into remote camps. This wasn't the case: while I was thrown resoundingly by Isamu "Sam" Furuta (5th-dan), Susuma Nitta (4th-dan) and others, they never threw me off the mat area. But, being localistic, they did tell me that they didn't want to hear about Johnny Osako and Japanese (!) judoka in other areas.

Seattle Dojo at time of Nagaoka Shihan's visit in October 1934.
A suited Nagaoka is seated in center, second row; standing on his left, also suited, is F. Yasutaro Miyazawa who headed the dojo when I came along eighteen years later.
First row, L. to R: Minoru Araki, Minoru Togasaki, William Yoruzu, Hiroshi Watanabe, Shinji Kozu. Second row, L. to R.: Haruo Fujino, Yeichi Kozu, Michio Shinoda, Shuichi (Hideichi) Nagaoka, F. Yasutaro Miyazawa, Toru Araki.

NOTICE

Headquarters
Western Defense Command
and Fourth Army

Presido of San Francisco, California
May 15, 1942

Civilian Exclusion Order No. 80

1. Pursuant of the provisions of Public Proclamations Nos. 1 and 2, this Headquarters, dated March 2, 1942, and March 16, 1942, respectively, it is hereby ordered that from and after 12 o'clock noon, P.W.T., of Wednesday, May 20, 1942, all personal of Japanese ancestry, both alien and non-alien, be excluded from that portion of Military Area No. 1 described as follows:

All of that portion of the County of King, State of Washington, within the boundary beginning at the point at which the Snohomish-King County line meets Puget Sound; thence easterly and following said county line to the western limits of Snoqualmie National Forest; thence southerly and following the Middle Fork of the Snoqualmie River, and the Snoqualmie River to its intersection of W. S. Highway No. 10 at Fall City; thence westerly along said Highway No. 10 crossing Lake Washington Floating River Bridge to the west line of Lake Washington; thence northerly along the west line of Lake Washington to East 85th Street extended; thence westerly along East 85th Street extended and 85th Street to Puget Sound; thence northerly and following the shoreline of Puget Sound to the point of beginning.

2. A responsible member of each family, and each individual living alone, in the above described area will report between the hours of 8:00 A. M. and 5:00 P. M. Saturday, May 16, 1942, or during the same hours on Sunday, May 17, 1942, to the Civil Control Station located at:

122 Kirkland Avenue,
Kirkland, Washington.

3. Any person subject to this order who fails to comply with any of its provisions or with the provisions of published instructions pertaining hereto or who is found in the above area after 12 o'clock noon, P. W. T., of Wednesday, May 20, 1942, will be liable to the criminal penalties provided by Public Law No. 503, 77th Congress, approved March 21, 1942, entitled "An Act to Provide a Penalty for Violation of Restrictions or Orders with Respect to Persons Entering, Remaining in, Leaving or Committing Any Act in Military Areas or Zones," and alien Japanese will be subject to immediate apprehension and internment.

4. All persons within the bounds of an established Assembly Center pursuant of instruction from this Headquarters are excepted from the provisions of this order while those persons are in such Assembly Center.

J.I. DeWITT
Lieutenant General, U. S. Army
Commanding

The nefarious Relocation Notice.

This was interesting about the Japanese: few ever smiled. Other than Mits Shoji and Tak Otsu in Chicago, and some of the younger fellows in Seattle, men like Chris Kato, Ben Ishii, Kelly Nishitani (older, but young in spirit), and Kenji Yamada, I never knew many Japanese judoka who smiled much – and I only knew about Tak through Art Broadbent, who said that he was a real cut-up. He'd toss you into the air with a kiai that sounded suspiciously like "Timber-r-r."

A dapper Hank Ogawa celebrates a Northwest all-star judo team's victory over a Southern California all-star team in late February or early March, 1939.

Powerhouse Matsuo Sakagami is flanked by Yasuyuki Kumagai (l.) and Chuji Sakata (r.), cir. 1939.

I don't know whether the taciturn judoka of Japanese ancestry I met in America then were characteristic of the Japanese now. I suspect they've lightened up a bit. The Japanese I met in Tokyo in the 1950's and 1960's, however, were pretty much of the same serious mien as those in America in the 1940's.

When I got to studying the Chinese martial arts in 1959, I quickly sensed a contrast. The Chinese have been called the Frenchmen of Asia with good reason. Not only is their food better, but I found the people generally much more extroverted and jovial than the Japanese. It may have been cultural or genetic, and it has been noted and analyzed by various writers. If true, it doesn't mean that one is less loving or moral than the other, only that their cultures are different.

Reverting to Seattle and Sam Furuta, his *kuzushi* (unbalancing pull) for right shoulder throw was so powerful it would've ripped you out of your socks if you'd been wearing any. A chief petty officer in the Japanese Navy during the war, Sam told of returning to Hiroshima after the A-bomb fell to find his house a pile of sticks and dirt, and his beloved family utterly gone.

Other yudansha in this tough club headed by grandfatherly F. Yasutaro Miyazawa (6th-dan) included Kenji Yamada (2nd-dan), Shuzo "Chris" Kato (1st-dan), George Wilson (1st-dan), Fred Sato (1st-dan), and Charlie Woo (2nd-dan, deceased), to name a few. All were good and willing fighters. Once when Mas Tamura (6th-dan, deceased) visited from Chicago (his parents lived near Tacoma), he and Sam Furuta did some "give" randori in which both sparkled. I captained the winning team in the contest that night and with uchimata beat little Charlie Woo, who got second in the lightweight class at the 1954 Nationals.

One peerless Seattle judoka whom I met, though I didn't know it at the time, was Hank Ogawa, now 7th-dan, of Ontario, Oregon. Still active in judo today at the age of eighty-one, Ogawa started doing judo in 1937 because some high school buddies needed more people in their judo club if they wanted to retain a team trophy. Three months later, he went to his first tournament where he threw three brown belts and three black belts, six players in all, and won first place. That victory wasn't a fluke, either, as in 1939 he was a member of a northwest all-star team headed by Mas Tamura and Matsuo Sakagami; and in 1940 he took first place in a tournament so rough that Tamura was eliminated in the second round and Sakagami in the third! After the war, Ogawa moved to Ontario, a farm town on the Idaho border with a large Japanese-American population, where he soon became head of the local judo club. I met him in April, 1953, when he brought the Ontario club to Seattle to participate in our spring *shiai* (competition). At the time, I said that the Ontario juniors were good, but that its intermediates relied too much on strength and not enough on technique. I wish now I'd paid less attention to the Ontario club's techniques and more attention to its teacher.

The Seattle team champions at the Second U.S. Nationals in 1954. From L to R: G. Wilson, F. Sato, S. Kato, T. Kojima, and K. Yamada. Standing is coach I. Furuta.

CIA

Merely three months after that 1953 shiai, I graduated from the University of Washington with a master's degree in Far Eastern studies. When I applied to do intelligence research for the CIA, a freeze on government hiring just then led me to look around for other work. A friend told me that the American Red Cross was hiring people as Assistant Field Directors and, after a year, a person could get posted to Japan. That sounded copacetic. I applied and was accepted for a position in San Francisco. A promotion to Field Director, however, washed out the Japan prospect. So when the CIA later opened up and beckoned, our family relocated to Bethesda, Maryland, and I went to work for the Agency.

Jim Takemori (3rd-dan), who had been impressive at the San Jose Nationals in 1953, headed up the Washington Judo Club. Jim was a spirited performer who was tough in randori but tougher still in contest. I affiliated with him and his crew and soon had a branch dojo established at the Bethesda-Chevy Chase YMCA. The Washington, D.C. area bristled with judo talent. Besides Takemori, the top area black belts then were Ken Uyeno (3rd-dan), Ken Hisaoka (3rd-dan), and from nearby Baltimore, Lanny Miyamoto and John Anderson. Youngsters of great promise included Jim Bregman and Warren Minami.

At the CIA, I worked for the Intelligence rather than the Operations ("spook") side. As part of a highly professional team, I analyzed the political, economic, and military capabilities and intentions of foreign powers. In those days, that meant chiefly the USSR and the People's Republic of China. It was invigorating to work with such brain power, but sad to see bureaucratic inertia increasing over time: friends and colleagues there brought "agonies and exhaltations." My work was essentially desk work and, compared to the operations people, fairly humdrum. I have since heard all kinds of nonsense said or written about my OSS and CIA activities (I was far too young to be in OSS).

Once I did make an official suggestion that the outfit hire T. Ishikawa, twice all-Japan judo champion (1949, 1950), to head combatives instruction in the Operations Directorate. But it was rejected for "budgetary reasons." Another time, when Donn Draeger told me that the Library of Congress had a copy of the rare Akira Kurosawa film

masterpiece *Sanshiro Sugata* (1943), portraying the early days of Jigoro Kano at the Kodokan, I was able to get a search made. Unfortunately, it yielded only a mass of congealed celluloid stacked on top of a radiator. Happily, the film is now available from Japanese originals. It was remade in 1965 with Toshiro Mifune playing the role of Yano (Kano). But I never parachuted into Beijing with Bruce Lee and Count Dante, to hold their coats while they beat the daylights out of Sun Lutang and Yang Luchan. Nor, despite Internet gossip-mongers, did I do anything for or against Chiang Kaishek.

Out to Asia

While assigned to the station in Taiwan (1959-1962), I took a few weeks off in 1961 and went to Tokyo to test for 3rd-dan. While there, I lived with Donn Draeger and his bonny crew for six weeks. To prepare for the test – I had been doing Chinese martial arts almost exclusively for the past two years – I worked out at both the Kodokan and Morihei Ueshiba's hombu dojo. My first day at the Kodokan, I had a morning audience with Risei Kano, son of judo founder Jigoro Kano, and his successor as President. We had a pleasant talk about judo. Not a judo man himself, Risei Kano was an able administrator with a cool, dignified bearing.

In the early afternoon, I also met Jon Bluming for the first time. We hit it off from the beginning – he had the spontaneity and humor of a youngster – but he tested me as he did everyone he met. In the corridor outside the foreign dojo we got to chatting about Chinese boxing. He "innocently" asked me what the Chinese would do against a frontal kick, and there that big right foot came, happily controlled. I said I'd attempt to deflect it with my left arm, secure it, and then cut his left leg out from under him (*o-uchi*, big inner cut. Okay, so it's a judo technique – but any old port in that storm)!

Risei Kano,
President of
the Kodokan.

This took him down, but en route, he said that he could get an armlock, and did. This put me athwart his lower regions. While entangled there, I pointed out that, if I was fast enough, his privates were accessible. I grabbed his gi pants in simulation.

That was the tableau: two silly kids sprawled in a hallway, one with an armlock, the other, a groin gouge. So who should come down the hallway just then but Risei Kano and an entourage of ten or so foreign guests led by interpreter Donn Draeger. By then, I'm sure Kano knew Bluming and his errant ways. Bluming, the Dutchman, was always in Dutch with the Kodokan. (An official memo was posted on the bulletin board once saying that Bluming must stop touching women on the elevator or he'd lose his privileges. Bluming, seeing this, posted his own memo agreeing to comply

Jon Bluming,
judo powerhouse.

if the Japanese sensei stopped doing the same thing to women.) Fearing that he'd recognize me, too, I turned my head away. As I did, I glimpsed Kano's face. No recognition, just Vermont granite. Donn's face I also glimpsed in that moment. It was a battlefield where disgusted dignity and laughter fought it out to a draw.

Aikido Interlude

To help get my body ready for the *sandan* examination I put in over forty hours at Morihei Ueshiba's hombu dojo falling and rolling around in aikido. The dojo had an excellent way of imparting the art. You paid a nominal monthly fee and could then practice from 6 a.m. to 12 midnight every day. No one did, of course, but the art was certainly available. You grabbed a partner – my main one was a big farm boy, a 2nd-dan, from Kyushu – and away you went. My partner had huge wrists and I was no match for him in doing push-ups on bent wrists. (I realized how he got the wrists he had.) Those wrists meant that it was rough trying to lock them. But hellish good exercise.

Morihei Ueshiba Shihan (1883-1969) dropped by two or three times while I was practicing. He was quite impressive, tiny and trim, with a face that radiated good health. His cheeks had such a blush to them that I wondered idly whether he'd rouged them a bit. The mischievous little boy smile never left him. He did little but it was good having him around.

On the second visit he did something so spectacular I still think of it sometimes. In lecturing us on resilience and rooting, he had two stout students (one was my frequent partner from Kyushu) each grab a wrist so that one grabbed Ueshiba's left wrist with his right hand while the other grabbed Ueshiba's right wrist with his left hand. Thus, all three men were on a line looking at us. Then the master asked them to really bite in with their grips, which they did, bending their knees a bit at the same time. Then quicker than a flash, Ueshiba bent his knees and sent his ki to his wrists. The wrists didn't move much but his students simultaneously snapped skyward in unison. The thing was done so perfectly that a skeptic would say it had to have been choreographed and rehearsed. I was not of that mind. Instead, I was simply perplexed how Ueshiba was able with only slight knee flexion to create the rapid torque necessary to throw two big bodies into the air simultaneously.

When we resumed practice, I went with Kyushu to Ueshiba's son, Kisshomaru, and, with Kyushu interpreting, pleaded my case. I identified myself as a judoka friend of Donn Draeger. He nodded that he knew Donn. I then told him that I was a researcher and had always applauded his father's spiritual ideas and his attainment in aikido, but that the last feat seemed to defy physics. Would his father demonstrate the technique again, this time with me at one of the wrists? I knew that the result would be the same, but as a researcher, it would be far better if I actually participated.

Ueshiba's son smiled and said, "Mr. Smith, the ukemi (fall) for that *te* (technique) is brutal and you might be injured." I politely responded that in judo I fell so often that I'd become quite expert in that phase of the art. So there was no chance for injury. He smiled again, "We'll let you know" – the Japanese (and American) way of never having to say "No."

M. Ueshiba: ki with a stick.

Morihei Ueshiba,
founder of
aikido, resisting
superior force.
(Was it real?)

And it's a crying shame. I wrote about my aikido practice in Tokyo in the September, 1961, issue of the Budokwai quarterly *Judo:* "The teaching is based on the deductive principle: watch and do! It was arduous but fun. . . . My earlier evaluation that there is still a lot of unfunctional material in aikido still holds. There are too many wide circles, multiple moves, and derring-do dance steps. Ueshiba himself, though old, looked vigorous and effective. Here again, I was unable to speak with him because of a tight schedule. I regret this."

Thirty-nine years later, I still regret it. In that report, like a good soldier, I blamed my tight schedule for my not meeting Ueshiba Shihan. Actually, I couldn't get past his son. To me, the feat seemed authentic and marvelous. Alas, I've never been able to give Ueshiba the credit he probably deserves because I lacked hands-on proof.

Later, in Southeast Asia, a Chinese master was performing feats similar to this but he too wouldn't let me participate. This one I knew was hippodroming, but I was never sure of this regarding Ueshiba Shihan. His performance may have been legitimate. Zheng Manqing left no such ambiguities, when he said, "Do as you wish with me," he meant it. However that may be, I still have the same misgivings about aikido as a system as I did then.

Recently, I asked Al Holtmann (6th-dan judo) of San Diego, one of the premier judo/aikido figures in America since 1949, for his view. He wrote (December 4, 1996):

> The standing techniques that are a take-off of jujutsu and aikijutsu are very effective indeed. There are more than twenty movements that are more effective than jujutsu – due to their spiral nature.

Al Holtmann (judo 6th-dan) opened his school in San Diego in 1949. He's now teaching the grandchildren of previous students.

Anyone who considers aikido a realistic self-defense, however, is misinformed. It has no groundwork, a serious fault since most fights – the Gracie family is correct on this – end up there. Like karate students, aikido students simply aren't trained to fight there.

Most aikido techniques are not realistic. Students are filled with illusions on this. Techniques are applied against various wrist and body grabs, and Japanese-type strikes that will not occur. Most aikido students, however, are not interested in self-defense so much as in a philosophy built on ki which benefits students physically, mentally, and possibly spiritually. Though it is estimable from these standpoints, it is limited combatively.

Despite my analytical problems with aikido, I have to assume that Ueshiba was a singular figure. The evidence for this is his top student Koichi Tohei. I first heard of Tohei at the First U.S. Judo Tournament in San Jose, California, in 1953. Some of us were chatting about the judo and one veered off with the information that an expert in something called aikido was present from Hawaii and would demonstrate his art. Rumor had it that this Tohei had defeated the top fighters of Hawaii before securing a teaching niche there.

Later, in a lull in the program, here came Tohei, a little man with a smile bigger than he was. He took the stage and submitted to varieties of insult to his person. Three big judoka simultaneously put locks on his neck and both arms. He tossed them airward with abandon. Next he demonstrated rare proficiency in stick work (*bojutsu*). All this was interesting and pleasant to watch. The main course, next up, left us flabbergasted. Tohei stood and invited five black belt judokas to have at him simultaneously. Fifteen lined up and five fanned out and jumped him. This was no multiple attack choreographed so that the defender had enough time and space to deal with each attacker singly – the meretricious stuff that bores and stultifies. Not a bit. The surrounding circle hit Tohei almost in unison. He moved amongst them throwing them in all directions, even into each other. Up they got, tried again, and down they went. Three were greedy and tried thrice only to hit the mat again. After that, enthusiasm waned and the group desisted.

Though Tohei was said to have a high judo rank, his throws didn't resemble judo techniques. He seemed to do things like *te-waza tomoe-nage* and wrist twists with such élan that murmurs of "ki" spread through the awed audience. Everything dissolved in front of his gentle rapid applications. Big Jim Nisby, a giant judoka and former California All-State footballer, one of the five attackers, attempted a driving tackle from fifteen feet. Tohei put out a light hand and stopped Jim dead in his tracks, then, in almost the same movement, pushed him into the pile of bodies. It was all marvelous.

I never knew Tohei well but followed his career in America and elsewhere. Later, he broke with Ueshiba Sensei and traveled widely. Once Donn Draeger and I lunched with him between flights at National Airport in Washington. I don't recall much of the talk – the cafeteria clamor being so loud I couldn't hear what he said – but it may have been there that I asked him what happens to a master who flies on a plane that crashes. He said, smiling and waving his hand dismissively, "True masters don't fly on such planes!"

Another time, two of his 3rd-dans visited me in Bethesda. Inevitably, these likable ones wanted to know of taiji. "It's soft," I said. "But," one responded, "our aikido is also soft." He thrust his arm at me for a test. His arm was not stiff. But neither was it soft and I was able to use "pull down" (*cai*) of taiji successfully several times. His colleague jumped into it, and though his arm was more supple than his friend's, it still "was against" my arm, permitting me to pull him around easily. They took it in good part and proceeded to show me aikido's "unbendable arm."

Which reminds me of a story I heard years ago from two of my students who previously had studied with Tohei and American aikido teachers. They had met a Canadian judo 4th-dan whom I had known earlier as a clean-cut, humble 2nd-dan. With rank, evidently he became rank. My students met him at the Kodokan where he told them he was off to test Tohei – did they want to tag along? Tohei was a deity to my boys and to see someone trash him – of course they'd go.

Arriving at Tohei's dojo, the three were made welcome by Himself who knew my students well. The Canadian he'd never met, but did now. Oblivious of the aikido students practicing, Canada braced Tohei. Could he see the "unbendable arm"? Tohei nodded and put the arm out. Canada tried the bend with medium strength but, that unavailing, he swerved full bore taking it in an arc downward leaning Tohei over in a precarious position. Then he released the hold and announced, "So much for the unbendable arm," and strutted like a peacock out of the dojo. Tohei went back to his students, doubtless miffed, but not showing it. Embarrassed, his two visitors left shortly after.

Koichi Tohei

After telling me the story, they asked why Tohei had suffered such a fool. Did Tohei sense that Canada was his superior and let it go at that? Or had he been so surprised by the bad manners that he let the lad have his way?

I told them to pick up their long faces. Neither of their suggestions was close. I knew Canada and even with several more grades he would never be or beat Tohei. I told them that they had seen a wonderful thing: a master who, when tricked by a pipsqueak, chose not to react rather than to punish or even to counter the miscreant. Tohei took the risk of losing face with his students as to avoid any relationship with such a discourteous thing. Only a very secure man could have done that. Finally, I told them – they were brightening a bit – that Tohei has publicly announced that he will not accept challenges and what they had seen that evening was of a piece with his announcement. He had proved himself, probably dozens of times, and doubtless would again. If Canada really wanted to try conclusions with him, he should do it in the context of class. That would be the venue for unstructured violence, in which I was sure Tohei would oblige his basest request.

There's an old Chinese saying: "You must earn the right to ask a question." Canada hadn't earned the right to be demolished. The operative etiquette says that you don't get beat up till you join up.

At the Kodokan

As for the judo promotion test itself, it took place at the Kodokan. The panel was headed by Sumiyuki Kotani, the last of the 10th-dans. Years later, I participated in a seminar under Kotani, who was visiting in Washington, D.C. As he made us do falls for hours, I was re-educated and finally learned what the late Richard Fukua, a California judoka, meant when he said that the essence of judo "is in the bows and the falls." During my test, I was asked to do the standard "Forms of Throwing" (*nage-no-kata*). I was a bit rusty but having as receiver (*uke*) Jim Bregman (the 3rd-place winner in the 1964 Olympics in Tokyo) made it a piece of cake. Jim had been fighting beautifully since his early teens, but he was equally elegant at kata. So much so that as I came off the mat Donn Draeger told me that I'd done a right for a left throw, but not to worry; Bregman, like a monkey, had conformed and fell properly for a left throw. At this remove, I don't quite know how Jim accomplished it, but if anyone could have done it, he was the boy.

After that, the panel asked me some questions regarding certain groundwork. Then I had a ten-minute match with a 3rd-dan. Because I had fought on fair terms during preceding weeks with several 4th-dans and 5th-dans in their thirties and forties (and been tossed all over by others), I expected an opponent in my age category. Instead, I got a guy who looked to be about twenty-five or so and who had a similar build to mine. There was no advance intelligence; you took him as he came. And he came fast. When he took a two-handed bite of my jacket, his arms were like iron. But since he was pushing I pivoted into *tai-otoshi* (body drop). He didn't even notice it. I had no time to think thereafter because he hit me with a classic uchimata (inner-thigh throw) that nearly succeeded. If I had cut the toenail of my right foot any more, I would have gone – that toenail adhering to the mat saved me.

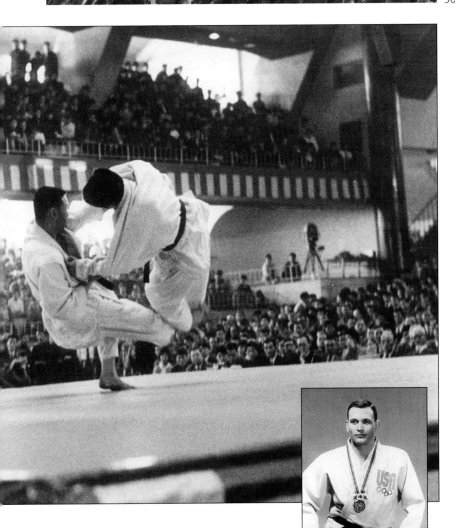

Above: Jim Bregman sweeps in Tokyo's Kodokan, 1961.
Right: Bregman, bronze winner at the Tokyo Olympics
in 1964 – pound-for-pound, one of America's best ever.

Although uchimata was (and probably still is) the top-scoring technique in judo, being thrown so often with it by Johnny Osako of
Chicago and Kenji Yamada of Seattle in the old days perhaps had inured
me to the throw done by lesser lights. And this 3rd-dan was a cut below
those masters of the throw. But he wasn't bad: he kept attacking with
it, mixed in now and then with *o-soto-gari* (large outer reap).

T. Ishikawa uses the same cross armlock on
Donn Draeger that the author used during grading in Tokyo.

About half-way through the match, I wobbled in stepping. (Humorist James Thurber wrote that when he was young he was always falling down from walking into himself.) My opponent took it as a reaction to his latest uchimata and again attacked with it quickly. I bellied out but this time he was tardy withdrawing and left his right arm too far in. I chopped his leg out from under him, hugged his arm and sat down into a cross armlock (*ude hishigi juji-gatame*). I was in tight, and had his arm imprisoned and stretched. I slowly lifted with my pelvis and waited for his submission tap. Nothing. I raised a bit more. Nothing. And more – and everything gave in a massive elbow dislocation. Talk about a samurai: this one was too proud to tap. The referee hit me on the shoulder, called *ippon* (full-point), and made us get up and go to the middle of the mat.

I thought the match was done because of my opponent's seriously sprained arm, but he wanted to go the limit. I asked him in Japanese if he were OK, and he said, "It's all right!" And picked up his right arm with his left hand and put it to where his right hand could take hold of my jacket. But there was nothing there and he tried nothing else. For my part, I felt like hell about his arm and aggressively danced the rest of the way. Hemingway once said something to the effect that one must not confuse movement with technique, and that was me, unwilling to take advantage, so doing my jig.

I hasten to add that I was lucky; he was not. He was so strong that none of my stuff dented his armor. My only shot was to counter him. He gave me that chance and I took it. More than enough said.

Cathedral Caper

Speaking of lucky, one Sunday I went to Mass at Sacred Heart Cathedral in Tokyo. (This was before I broke with the Catholic Church over its insane support for the Vietnam War.) The cathedral was big as a football field and crowded. I sat next to a big, good-looking Filipino chap in the last pew. About halfway through the Mass the damnedest thing happened. We were kneeling there, eyes closed in prayer, when some cries and commotion brought our eyes to the altar. There, an unkempt Japanese was savaging the elderly Caucasian priest celebrating the Mass. The next thing I knew, I was at the altar, just in time to confront the middle-sized man who was throwing sacred objects onto the floor. He had a feral look to him, and he swung his fist eagerly at me. I don't know what happened to his fist, but I do know I trussed him up with Han Qingtang's "Tyrant Invites Guest." The lock worked perfectly, and it was nice to know that these things one spends untold hours learning do work when put to the test.

As I walked up that football field of an aisle, however, I began feeling sorry for this poor mental case. And the longer I walked looking into a sea of vacant Japanese faces – I'd have paid good money for a smile or a wink – the sorrier I felt for the guy. My body must have followed my mind, sympathizing, and I eased up on the lock. He half extricated his arm and then tried to elbow me. I quickly re-applied the lock hard and he tiptoed the rest of the way. I held him inside the front door while behind me Japanese ushers tended the shaken but apparently unhurt priest who then continued the Mass. In five minutes, four burly Japanese police came and, unsmiling, took him off my hands. As I resumed my kneeling posture in the last pew beside the Filipino fellow, he leaned over to me and whispered in English, "You were pretty damned good in there!" To which I panted, "If I was so good, why is it that I can't breathe?" It was true, the repressed excitement and my emotions had caught up with me, so that even with the five-minute wait for the police, I still hadn't "caught my puff."

My Karate Kick

Long before karate became popular, I critiqued it none too favorably. Here is what I wrote after a 1960 trip to various Asian dojos.

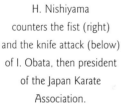

H. Nishiyama
counters the fist (right)
and the knife attack (below)
of I. Obata, then president
of the Japan Karate
Association.

I first spent several days at S. Nagamine's dojo in Okinawa, where I practiced with and watched the best karate brown belts I've ever seen. The only black belts I saw were visiting 6th-dans from Japan, both excellent, who must have been awed too, but they weren't talking much. Nagamine's stuff was balanced and authoritative. I noted the technical similarities of his system to some of the southern Shaolin methods in Taiwan. The big difference is that Nagamine exerted more discipline and rigor than most Chinese teachers. His students really worked. Some of my enthusiasm for him was punctured, however, when after saying my farewells, I had to return for my notebook the next day before catching my plane. Walking in, I was astonished to find yesterday's brown belts now sported black. This Potemkin maneuver doubtless was done to impress the high-ranking Japanese visitors.

In Japan, I saw workouts at the Japan Karate Association, Mas Oyama's Kyoku-shin Kai dojo, and some demonstrations by other masters. The Association is kind. It is trying to unify all karate in Japan, but of course it will never achieve it. Hidetaka Nishiyama is their star and he dazzles you as he shines. He is quite effective. My criticism of their method is (1) their over-use of foot techniques, (2) the barrenness of their katas, and (3) their feeling that they are above criticism, comments offered being treated with condescension. For instance, I mentioned Wang Shujin to a Chinese 6th-dan. He out-smirked the Japanese karateka, saying that Wang Shujin couldn't take their punches and they weren't interested in him. (By then, Wang had beaten every fighter coming to scratch against him.)

Though Mas Oyama's karate seemed to me functionally better than the Association's – it blended grappling with striking techniques – he too chilled Donn and me on our second visit when we suggested that he consult with Wang.

Mas Oyama
busting up
the place.

In sum, karate can stand some sobriety. It is one system – not the ultimate. It needs new forms, creativity, and humility. Its players are generally small and I would say that they over-estimate their destructive power. This would be natural in an art in which contact is eschewed. But in China and Taiwan contact is permitted, and I can say that punches that break bricks often don't bother a man. The beauty and precision of kata is also lost in the milling. If you attempt a kick, you're swarmed. Weight tells and grappling is as important as striking.

I would go further. I would make the same criticism of karate that I make of its father, Shaolin. The basic stances are too deep to permit speedy countering. You build a good defense by "holing in" but you must climb up and out before you can attack. And this takes time. The principle referred to here, over-defending, is present in other aspects of karate as well. For example, in *ude-uke* (forearm block), whether inside or outside, it is snapped and focused strongly on the point of impact – which is the opponent's arm. But is this much defense necessary? It reduces reaction time certainly. Karateka will argue that it is offensive as well as defensive – you can break the opponent's arm with a block. If you argue thus, then you do not know fighting. The arm is not a vital point. You will never, unless you are very lucky, injure his arm. What you should seek is to block, a la western boxing, with a minimum of effort, using the slight deflection to move immediately into the counter – which is aimed at a vital point.

Rereading this, I'm struck by my presumption. But I wrote this in a far country a long time ago. I hope my karate friends will forgive me the excesses of youth. In extenuation, a top British karateka told me two

Gichin Funakoshi.

decades later that when he'd read those comments by the upstart Smith, he cursed my words. Then he told me that over the years he'd come to agree with me on most points. That made me feel a bit better. And I still feel kindly about karate's original teachers. Gichin Funakoshi, who introduced karate to Kyoto in 1917 and Tokyo in 1922, was a doughty, interesting man in his own right. I have misgivings on a couple points culled from his autobiography, *Karate-do: My Way of Life* (1975), namely the fact that he (1) took an hour to brush and comb his hair every morning and (2) left his wife for thirty years to teach karate in Japan. These aside, I applaud his credo, *karate ni sente nashi*, "Karate has no offense."

Art Broadbent

Me & Art.
We were the best of friends.

The fine Irish poet, James Stephens, once wrote that the test of the value of a man is how many male friends he has. I've had many. But in the cosmic sense that Stephens meant, I have had two good friends. Leroy Maxwell, a little friend at the orphanage who was all too soon gone from there, and later, in World War II, gone from the earth. Art Broadbent, the transplanted British dairy-cart driver, was the second friend proving my life to have had some utility.

It wasn't long after I joined the Chicago Judo Club in 1947 that I heard about a lanky newcomer from England. I liked him right off – it was impossible not to. A boyish smile forever decked his face and he fit in well with a club that for sheer friendliness has never been topped. The club was always in financial distress but not overly bothered by it. I was firing on the CB&Q railroad in those years and used to travel three hundred miles each way once a month to get to the action. Though we began at the same level in judo, Art pulled away from me rapidly and I never caught him. But though the distance in our skills widened, we always stayed close.

He loved to travel. The big Harley with the bulging saddlebags. Gi always there. No, not always. Once...in the heyday of first judo love, when the mat was sheer heaven and gi's were royal purple (it was dignity to put one on no matter the sweat and smell), and a young 3rd-dan named Osako with an arcing uchimata, a swooping okuri-ashi, and a whirling harai-goshi, was its God...Art went to visit a dojo on the west coast. He was 2nd-dan then, anxious to try the technique of the Kimuras and Kuniyukis. He went to the largest dojo in L.A. "Could he practice?" The big one asked if he had a gi. No, he hadn't brought it.

"Then you can't practice." A judoka offered to loan him one and the chief relented. But the great one wasn't quite done. After Art had dusted off the first three black belts to face him, he noticed bulkier birds coming in the door. The riot call had gone out. By the time they were through with him, he had to crawl from the mat. (N. Kazantzakis, the fine Greek writer, says we have to stoop low to get into Heaven – the gate is very low.) He recalled that their eyes were very wide when he staggered in the next night.

Next stop, San Francisco. Same story: no gi, no practice. Thankfully no one offered a loaner, and he left unbruised except by the discourtesy which, of course, hurt him more than physical affronts. Here a point needs making. Courtesy is the keystone of Kano's judo; without it, talent and prowess avail little. Ironically, the higher the grade, the more frequent the sin on this score. Novelist John Masters, in speaking of the Pathan Mountain warriors of India mused, "In that large and easy-going country – there are so many sins that there is no sin, except inhospitality."

Ever mobile, Art took himself off to Paris where he stopped at Henri Plée's dojo. His first practice was with a 2nd-dan (this needs underscoring: in free practice (randori), Art would fall for any technique correctly applied whether the attacker was a white belt or a 4th-dan). The Frenchman bowed, took hold, reaped, piled on, and choked.

Art practicing a
waist technique in 1953.

Art gave a smart capitulation tap. They rose. Again, another leg reap technique ending with a strangle hold. Up again with Art thinking to balance things a bit – but the other one bowed out! And again some years later in Washington, D.C., Art practiced with a much inferior 4th-dan. Another throw with Art up then down. Art up – ditto. End of randori. Art, amused, to me, "He really has to win, huh?"

Before a general disgust stopped my writing about judo many years ago, I had wanted to note some of these things. Art said no, decidedly. What would embarrass him while living I hope honors him now that he is gone.

Art made the sport fun. Here he throws nearly 400 pounds (two people).
That's the author on top – he still feels the landing.

He loved nature. He hurt nothing and was himself oblivious to hurt. A stretch of midwestern road between sprawling cornfields would grab his eyes, a mountain would positively entrance him. He would hold a wasp in his hands to carry it out of a house. The insect, he said, stung only if frightened or if it sensed fright. And man, whom Robinson Jeffers placed below nature, Art put above. He exemplified Kano's greatest concept, "Mutual Welfare," which translates *love*. He never asked a cent for teaching thousands of hours of judo. It was enough for him that a student worked hard, sweated, and listened. If cheerfulness crept in, if a student laughed frequently, that was bonus. Gaiety always pleasured him.

Art was humble in the truest sense. His father never knew until his funeral that he had won second place in the 180-lb. class at the First U.S. Nationals in San Jose. There is even word around that he won the French Nationals one year. I haven't checked this out because I'm afraid it will turn out to be fact and humans can stand only so much humility. We do know that at a U.S. Nationals in the late '50's Art was in the semi-finals and expected to go all the way. He threw his antagonist hard and injured him. It was thought the man's back was broken.

Art immediately withdrew from the proceedings. The 4th-dan who told me this lost a match once when as a judge I prevailed on the referee and the other judge that his o-soto-gari (large outer reap) fifteen feet off the mat into the chairs was a mite much. He mused that Art would have been a great one but for his lack of a killer instinct!

A couple years at the Kodokan might have filled such a lack. In Seattle in 1954, I prepped Art to go to Japan for study. But, lacking the bucks, he missed the boat. Had he gone, I think he would have surpassed Ben Campbell and Gene LeBell, the American aces of that period.

Art put no store on worldly things. He was a third generation carpenter but this and the other

Art and dad Pete:
God did a helluva job on both.

jobs he tried in his too-short life were simply to keep him fed and lodged. Many have stated that Art could have done much better vocationally than he did – he was perceptive and articulate to boot. I remember I rode him for years about this very thing until I learned that Art was being himself and that, after all, being a carpenter shouldn't cast a stigma after that experience 2,000 years ago. But the nature of society – which is spelled *money* – probably meant he got a lot of such advice. And this may have created problems.

His dad lamented to me, "He never really knew what he was searching for." I argued against this. Art always knew what he wanted: in its simplest form it was Belloc's "laughter and the love of friends." His problem was that he didn't find it in the quantities desired. (Who can?) "My heart has followed all my days something I cannot name," the poet says. Perhaps Art couldn't have articulated that something but his life did it for him. It was simply to be a decent and gentle person, thus exemplifying the philosophy Jigoro Kano set forth for all of us.

G. Koizumi,
Father of the Budokwai,
does a body drop throw
on Trevor Leggett.

The Good Old Budokwai

From 1949 on, I wrote judo articles for that grand bastion of the art in the English-speaking world, the Budokwai in London. It had been started in 1918 by Gunji (G.K.) Koizumi (8th-dan) and Yukio Tani (4th-dan). Among its members were E.J. Harrison, H.A. Tricker, Marcus Kaye, George Grundy, Charley Grant, Trevor Leggett, Ted Mossom, John Barnes, and Dicky Bowen. Their quarterly bulletin, *Judo*, born in 1945 and decked out in literate and stylish garb by Dame Enid Russell-Smith (2nd-dan), caught my eye early. I wanted to write for it. And, would you believe it, they let me. I can't say how much this kindness impressed me. It let me know that somewhere judo was being approached without friction or factionalism, and that I was welcome to help them in their endeavor. So for a decade or so I wrote for them. Slight, tentative little newsletters on American judo doings with an occasionally bigger piece written jointly with E.J. Harrison thrown in. No one ever told me what I could write.

Dame Enid Russell-Smith (3rd-dan) played good judo and was a consummate editor of the Budokwai *Judo* quarterly.

The success of the Budokwai's quarterly bulletin *Judo* must be attributed in great part to its estimable editor. In July, 1953, E.J. wrote me of this woman who, adventurous to the hilt, climbed Mont Blanc at an advanced age:

By the way, I have been hymning your praises in raucous tones to our Dame Enid Russell-Smith. Doubtless you know that she is a high-ranking Civil Service officer at the Ministry of Health at a salary of well over £2,000 a year [perhaps $8,000-$10,000 in 1953, and probably $80,000-$100,000 today]. In the Coronation Honours she was made a Dame – a dreadful word, isn't it? Anyhow, she really does know a good deal about judo and is 2nd-dan, the highest woman *yudansha* [black belt] to date outside Japan.

In 1948, the Budokwai quarterly *Judo* celebrated the thirtieth anniversary of the Budokwai by publishing its most interesting issue. The top contributors were E.J. Harrison and Shaw Desmond.

The Man from Hiroshima by E.J. Harrison

One evening after a series of quite strenuous bouts I prepared to have a hot and cold douche and pack up for home when the principal of the dojo, himself a decidedly dangerous opponent in "groundwork," intervened and ceremoniously informed me that a yudansha from Hiroshima would shortly arrive and was most anxious to enjoy the privilege of a bout with Harrison San before he returned to his home town. Tired though I was, noblesse oblige, and so I waited. Soon a strange Japanese of more than average Japanese height appeared on the scene, changed into *keikogi* and requested the honour of a bout. To my natural satisfaction I got the better of him, and at the close of our friendly tussle I again made a move in the direction of the bathroom, again to be checked by the principal who apologetically explained that my late opponent was not the eagerly awaited Hiroshima yudansha! Then shortly afterwards a second strange Japanese on the large side made his appearance and invited me to try conclusions on the mat. Wearier than before I was still able to finish the practice bout on level terms. So for the third time I got ready to go, when once more the principal stopped me and almost simultaneously introduced me to the genuine Hiroshima yudansha, a splendidly built and distinctly handsome young Japanese who bore all the distinctive hallmarks of the trained judoka. At this juncture I was not ashamed in my best Nihongo to point out to the newcomer that I had already put in a very long evening and was therefore in no fit condition as a wretched *mudansha* to do myself justice against a sensei of his acknowledged reputation. But of course the Hiroshima man would take no denial, effusively assuring me that he would gladly make every allowance for my weariness of the flesh. On the other hand, should he return to Hiroshima without the honour of the longed-for bout with the celebrated (sic) Harrison San, whose fame had already reached his home confines, he would never forgive himself!

As was to be expected, in the ensuing encounter I came off second best, but nevertheless scored more than once and generally speaking fairly sustained my reputation. In the end we parted with many expressions of mutual esteem and friendship.

A year or so later, when I had already won my black belt at the Kodokan, the young Hiroshima man turned up there on a visit, recognized me immediately and with a humorous grin apologized for the rise he had taken out of me on the occasion of our first meeting. The appropriate

Yukio Tani, who with "G.K." started the Budokwai in 1918: a tiger on the mats and a terror in the music halls.

phrase was *"Konaida wa, jitsu ni shitsurei itashimashita!"* ("I was really rude to you the other day!") On my part I was rather tempted to retort, *"C'est magnifique, mais ce n'est pas la guerre!"* *Verb sap.* [It is magnificent, but it is not war. A word to the wise is sufficient.]

Old Budokwai Nights by Shaw Desmond

"Those dear dead days beyond recall," writes the poet. The nights when our friends Koizumi and Yukio Tani were in their prime and the latter was finishing a twenty-five-year unbroken success on the music-halls by taking on anything that could crawl!

The night when Ishiguro, the painter on silk, "painted out" one of the wrestling champions of the time and then proceeded to jump around the dojo on his knees! And how he spun 'em with that shoulder-turn!

Then there was the stream of judo-ka from the Kodokan, Tokio. The five-footers, Otani and Kotani. The giant "champion of the world" Nagaoka, with his grave dignity, teak-like head, bronzed and noble, and his matchless movement. "The man who never moved more than six inches." I shall never forget the night I had to face him and the terrible neck-wrench, exquisitely administered, when I thought my spinal column had gone – but also his perfectly kindly courtesy, out of all of which I got my "brown belt." The black belt took me exactly ten and a half years to attain – but, although I kept it to myself, I had reached the half century ere I took up ju-jutsu. It's never too late to mend – or to be broken!

I am back once again under the top-lights in the upper dojo, with "Tiger-Koizumi," the gentlest of carnivora! And with his catlike exquisite movement "working" over me. I am also once again being held in a terrible carotid strangle, lying plexus to plexus in the groundwork of the katame-waza. Either Tani "saw black" or I forgot to tap, but I remember thinking that this was my last moment on earth – and what a beautiful transition stage to heaven!

There was the night when the Moslem challenger for the Graeco-Roman world-title turned up and to whom I gave his first judo lesson in the lower dojo. As I was showing him stance and synchronisation of gait, I felt myself lifted skyward – and then the roof fell in. The "roof" was my Moslem friend who had 18-1/2 inch biceps, a chest somewhere in the late fifties, and an eye with blood in it! He had gripped me in the Graeco-Roman hold, had lifted me, dashed me to the mats and then fallen on me. After which I took my Muhammadan friend upstairs to the tender mercies of Yukio Tani, then in his sixties, who had been wrestling powerful young men for perhaps a couple of hours, who permitted my Moslem man-mountain to waste his sweetness on the desert air of the dojo, what time he rushed like a baited bull from side to side, as the gamest champion of them all evaded him. What Yukio Tani did that night, will never be forgotten, for he proved beyond cavil that even Graeco-Roman champions were but dust in the hands of the trained judo-ka. (Strictly between you and me, neither Koizumi nor Tani ever permitted us to see them go all-out, except on one occasion, which nearly affrighted me forever!)

Shuichi Nagaoka (10th-dan),
who never moved
more than six inches.

The elegant and effective
Gunji ("G.K.") Koizumi.

I remember a 6th-dan Kodokan little man, perhaps five feet high, throwing me into the air with a *sutemi*, and then, ere my body reached the ground, technically "kill" me three or four times, I feeling the finger-impact. "There were giants in those days," as it was writ in Holy Writ, from which the oldest of us all, a dear old gentleman from the Island of Man, was always quoting. He could still put them down at seventy-odd.

To my splendid friend Gunji Koizumi, as to gallant little Yukio Tani, I, like hundreds of others, owe not only physical health and power, but infinitely more vital, the mental clarity which comes from the steady practice of "the gentlest art in the world." To these gentlemen and comrades, I pay my acknowledgments and make my bow. Banzai!

For a hilarious read, Dicky Bowen has just now advised me to find Desmond's *Windjammer: The Book of the Horn* (London: Hutchinson and Co., 1932). I can't wait. I have read Desmond's autobiography *Pilgrim to Paradise* (London, Rider, 1951) and in the patois of Hollywood – it's a wow. Come to think of it, Desmond is the only one I can think of who out-Hollywood's Hollywood. In fine, a master of manure.

In its January, 1950 issue, *Judo* asked the same two gentlemen to tell "Why, How, and Where I Started Judo." And they sure did. Note the editor's caveat on Desmond.

Why, How, & Where I Started Judo

[So that a younger generation may know something of the spirit which animated the early European pioneers in the art of judo, the Editor asked some of the best known of the older judoka to answer the question at the head of this article. We print below the answers given by Mr. E.J. Harrison (3rd-dan) and Mr. Shaw Desmond (1st-dan), both well-known writers on judo and kindred subjects, to whom we owe a lot for all they have done to stimulate interest in the art. Mr. Shaw Desmond's views do not on all points represent those of the Budokwai. – Ed.]

E.J. Harrison (4th-dan)
a bonny fighter whose
playing and writing
illuminated early judo.

E.J. Harrison:

The "why" in my case is not far to seek. A native of Manchester, many a time and oft in those distant days facetiously described by irreverent contemporaries of mine in British Columbia as "near England", I took to a somewhat crude form of wrestling while still a mere boy as naturally as a duck takes to water. Being a pretty sturdy youngster, while still at school I taught myself to swim and skate, and generally participated vigorously in the games of childhood, with emphasis on tree climbing and even some elementary use of the foils and single-stick. Then a few years before emigrating to British Columbia at the age of nineteen, I joined the Manchester YMCA gymnasium, where I developed into quite a fair gymnast. I entered journalism at Vancouver, BC, and worked for some time as a reporter on the *Vancouver News Advertiser*, and although I never had an opportunity during my stay there to indulge in wrestling I enjoyed plenty of other healthy outdoor sports, more particularly swimming in English Bay and rowing, both alone and as a member of racing crews, in the placid mirror-like waters of Burrard Inlet, on which Vancouver stands, under the shadow of the noble range of mountains on the opposite shore.

Later I left Vancouver to accept a post as news editor on the Free Press at Nanaimo, then a small coalmining town on Vancouver Island. And it was during my sojourn there that I was able for the first time to study catch-as-catch-can systematically and seriously as a member of the local miners' sporting club and gymnasium. My instructor was little Jack Stewart, favourite pupil of the famous Dan McLeod, known far and wide in those days as the "Californian Wonder", although actually a native of Nova Scotia. Jack Stewart himself was a really talented and brilliant lightweight, to whom I owe a lasting debt of gratitude for the pains he took to transform me into a reasonably efficient mat-man. Two other stalwarts of the club, who also helped me greatly, were the brothers Swanson, the older a colossus of fifteen stone or so and the younger, "Sinc", then only seventeen, a super

heavy lightweight of splendid muscular development. Years afterwards in Japan I read that "Sinc" had met and defeated a Japanese reputed judoka somewhere in California. Be that as it may, I do not doubt that had "Sinc" been able to study the art of judo in Japan he would assuredly have become a top notcher.

Dan McLeod, "The California Wonder," who taught E.J. Harrison's wrestling mentor Jack Stewart.

With such antecedents it seems but natural that soon after my arrival in Yokohama from California, where for a year or so I engaged in journalism, I should have heard about jujutsu, to use the older term, and joined a dojo of the Tenshin Shinyo-ryu at Yokohama under Hagiwara Ryoshinsai, a wonderful little man whose praises I have sung to sympathetic hearers on several previous occasions. The time was then 1897. I gained the grade of *shodan* [1st-degree] at this school, but subsequently moved to Tokyo and became a *montei* or disciple of the famous Kodokan. Here, too, I soon found that I was a mere tyro in the art and had to unlearn a good many bad habits engendered by the practice of relying too much upon mere brute strength in preference to skill. But I have already exhausted my allotted space allowance and must therefore leave to my readers' imagination the task of filling up the inevitable residuary lacunae in this veracious recital.

Shaw Desmond:

I was just turned my fiftieth year when I had my first lesson in jujutsu. I was three months older when I "signed on" before the mast for my six months' voyage round the Horn in a Finnish four-masted barque and then walked across Africa, the result being my now world-known log "Windjammer" and "African Log".

All this I owe largely to yoga breathing, plus mental force and judo. Anyone who starts his incarnation with a carefully chosen body like mine can do the same – perhaps!

Almost from youth in Ireland I had been enamoured of the idea of jujutsu. When I was at twenty three secretary of half-a-dozen companies in "The City" and later a director of an international company (the youngest director in the city), I was still more concerned with theoretical jujutsu and how to strangle my friends than with stocks and shares, only there was no school of judo. When I walked out of the City to get on with my real work of novelist, dramatist and poet and musician I was still hankering after "locks" and "throws", strangulation, and above all, what I have created, i.e., "psychic jujutsu", or, to give it its scientific name, "psycho-kinetics", or "stopping at a distance" without contact. But it took me half a lifetime to reach that point in my now well-known experiment in John's College, Cambridge University, when on Sunday, 24th October, 1943, I knocked out a powerful athlete at a distance of four yards without contact and made six others "sick". Had I wished after that I could have made an excellent living as a teacher of murder! I had many applications.

This "psychic jujutsu" I had got from my studies amongst the Mississippi negroes and the Zulus, who adopted me as a sort of "Chief", my name in Zulu being *Inkosi* ("king-magician").

The irrepressible Shaw Desmond
who romanced judo to new heights.

But this has nothing to do with how I not came, but tried to come, into jujutsu. For, God help me, I could not find a school of jujutsu anywhere upon which I could rely, although there were dozens who claimed "to teach you jujutsu in twelve lessons".

Eureka. I had heard through *Health and Strength,* for which I sometimes wrote, of Gunji Koizumi and the Budokwai.

I got into my tunic and drawers that first night with two exactly opposite feelings. One was that as an Irishman with an Anglo-French Huguenot mother, a La Fontaine, I was unconquerable and that I would possibly quickly teach Mr. Yukio Tani a thing or two about rough-house work! (It was seeing Mr. Tani in the music halls which had first fanned the flame of jujutsu desire!) The other was the feeling that within a few minutes I should be carried out lifeless (I had looked up the nearest hospital to find it was St. George's, in case), or at the very least with a broken arm, leg, or pelvis. (I was particular about the "pelvis".)

Then somebody walked me about on the dojo mat. Delightful! It was like ballroom dancing, only nicer. Then, upon my special request for "the real thing", the dojo canvas came up and hit me under the ear. On the rest of the proceedings I will draw a veil.

So, belt by belt (only I never wore any belt till I reached "brown", as I felt anything lower was infra dig), I climbed my hard and horny way up to the "brown" after Nagaoka had tried me out. Of course, I wasn't quite so mad as not to realise that any of the little five-foot Japanese could have murdered me in a minute, much more the giant Nagaoka, who was exquisite in his touch and affection – for it was what a trout feels when he is played on the line of a dry-fly fisherman! For this I got the "brown", for it is not I who "wrestled" that night but my familiar spirit, who is as real as you who read these words. Incidentally, we all have guardian angels! In judo you need 'em.

But the night I got the "black", all the stars of the morning sang together. I went home and, carelessly flinging it into her lap, said lightly to my young daughter, "You might work my name into that – it's my Black Belt.' To which Deidre said nothing – literally nothing, little guessing that before her stood someone greater than Achilles or Ulysses – or even Cuhullin, my Irish progenitor!

God forgive her, for I can't!

Sample of British humor from the Budokwai's *Judo* quarterly.

I guess Shaw Desmond must have arrived.

The Budokwai was also blessed with Trevor Leggett (7th-dan), as splendid a writer as he was a judoka. Among the following selections, "Learning the Flute" is his. It also nurtured the splendid cartoonist JAK (Raymond Jackson) who died in July, 1997, aged seventy. For forty-five years JAK's seldom cruel artistry adorned the *Evening Standard* and made life more livable for London's homebound commuters. A black belt, JAK liked to live well and did. He was lauded by Prime Minister Tony Blair and other VIPs at his death. The Budokwai had other fine cartoonists and humorists, but the pieces weren't always identified. The author of the Ebor Judo Club article was probably Phil Edwards, but the author of "Gentle Art" is unknown.

Learning the Flute by Trevor Leggett

[The following traditional story (which has several slightly varying versions) is given to students of kendo and judo as an example of the right method.]

To a province in Southern Japan came on holiday a famous teacher of music from the capital. The local musicians begged him to address them, and he showed them a new type of flute then coming into favor at the capital. Sitting motionless in their midst, he so entranced them with its melody that at the end they cried out: "Like a god!"

They persuaded him to accept one of their number as a pupil, to study under him and return with the certificate of mastership, to teach the others. They chose a young flute-player to be the pupil, and subscribed the money for the journey.

The young man was naturally overjoyed, and at the capital worked night and day to master the difficult technique of the new flute. To his disappointment, the master would only let him try one melody, a classical air. Again and again he was made to play it, but never to the master's satisfaction. The time went by, and he came to the conclusion that he had failed, and the master did not intend to give him the certificate.

He left the master's house; ashamed to return, he stayed in cheap lodgings in the capital. Now he tried out other melodies on the new flute, but realized that in them too his performance was unsatisfactory. He thought of giving up the flute altogether, but became intolerably restless and was forced to take it up again. Now he was playing to himself merely to calm his spirit every day and evening, sometimes on the new flute and sometimes on his old one, and in this way his shame and distress of mind gradually became less. In the end he drifted back home, but did not play in public or show his face to the society of musicians.

One day the musicians organized a great concert and sent a messenger begging him to attend with his flute, for the sake of their former friendship. They would not, they said, hold the concert without him. Touched by their kindness he went with the messenger, but on arrival found he had unconsciously picked up and brought the new flute, of which he was not an accredited master. It was too late to change it for his old one, but in any case he had no reputation now, so careless of what the others might think he sat down and played for himself the old melody, repeated so many times for the master. He became lost in the melody, and did not know whether he played well or badly. Afterwards there was dead silence, and then the musicians cried out, "Like a god!"

He ran home in tears and wrote a long letter to the old master, praying his forgiveness and blaming his own lack of understanding of the training. The master immediately sent the certificate of mastership, with a letter saying: "You need not blame yourself too much. Your personal desire for fame gave you the energy to work hard at the technique. But mastership is much more than technique. You had to practice till your practice became no-practice, till it was a natural activity. When you had forgotten your selfish aim, forgotten yourself, forgotten any effort in playing, forgotten even the flute – when nothing remained but the melody itself, you achieved mastership.

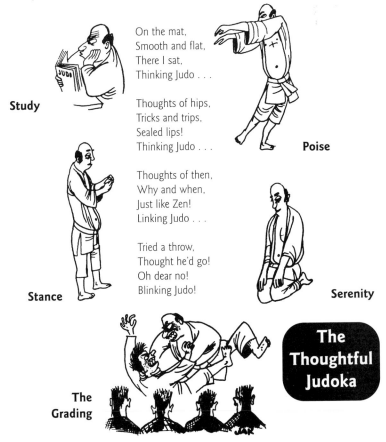

Study

On the mat,
Smooth and flat,
There I sat,
Thinking Judo . . .

Thoughts of hips,
Tricks and trips,
Sealed lips!
Thinking Judo . . .

Poise

Thoughts of then,
Why and when,
Just like Zen!
Linking Judo . . .

Tried a throw,
Thought he'd go!
Oh dear no!
Blinking Judo!

Stance

Serenity

The Grading

The Thoughtful Judoka

Sample of British humor from the Budokwai's *Judo* quarterly.

The Tribe of the Eborites

A True History of the Ebor Judo Club (1934-1949)

Now it came to pass in the year 1934 A.D., that Phil, son of Edwards, in the City of Eboracum, gathered round him the faithful, saying unto them – Let us practise the ancient rites of our cult, even all the katas of judo.

And straight-away in the school called Bright Street were heard the loud sounds of Haiuchi and Chugairi, yea, even the Kiai, and the Eborites laughed, and waxed exceeding glad.

But the people of Bright Street rose up in anger, saying – Verily our babes are mewling and puking, and our husbands, who are weary from work, cannot sleep for this fiendish noise. Get ye hence, O Eborites.

And behold, the Eborites sought an ancient building with an upper room, and the faithful came to practise, so the loud sounds were heard again, even Kiai.

Now, on a certain eve, John, son of Cappleman – he being a Constable of the City of Eboracum – was thrown with great force, and lo and behold, did disappear into the room below leaving a great hole in the floor – yea, with a great breaking of chattels. And the sounds were no longer heard in the upper room of the ancient building.

So, like the forgotten of God, the Eborites travelled, even to the gate called Marygate to an Inn, wherein there was an upper room.

But it came to pass that much damage was done to the Inn, and the landlord tore his hair saying: – "Oh Eborites, I love ye like mine own sons, but this I cannot stand. Get ye hence before the brewer finds ye."

Then two of the Eborites, being Constables of the City of Eboracum – did search, and did find for the faithful a cellar under a tabernacle called Centenary, in the Gate called St. Saviourgate.

And there was great rejoicing, and loud cries of happiness, for the Eborites again rolled upon the mats, and performed the rites of Judo – and lo, loud noise is heard, the Hai-uchi, the Chugairi, yea, even the Kiai.

Gentle Art

In the field, cows were mooing; it was milking time. In the street, a crowd was queuing; it was a meal time. A bus came along but could take only a small number. The conductress stretched her arm across and called out, "That is all, no more." A man suddenly jumped off as if he had forgotten to lock his office safely. A man at the head of the queue jumped on to the platform. The mistress of the bus would not have it and said: "Sorry, the bus is full." The man tried to reason with her: "But a man just got off. Surely I can take his place." The conductress would not have her authority questioned. She insisted he should get off, and told him the bus would not move with him on it. The man was obstinate. Long waiting did not improve tempers. The people began to show some agitation. The conductress, as if she was going to lecture a naughty boy, pointing her finger, said, "Do you know what I will do to you if you do not get off?" The man pulled himself up to his full six foot and stretching his bullying chest retorted, "What will you do?" Softening her voice she said, "I will tell your mum about you." The whole bus smiled. The man took his defeat like a sportsman and the bus moved on in a better mood.

South African Family Robinson

And, sometimes, there were even problems. In a 1953 letter to me, E.J. Harrison referred to the Robinson clan of South Africa, who periodically caused the Budokwai some distress. The family patriarch, "Professor" Jack Robinson, a bellicose fellow, loudly lauded the superior judo ability of himself, his three sons – Joe, Norman, and Dougie – and his daughter Sheila. He didn't like the Kodokan, which he claimed wouldn't let his boys enter its tournaments. So he sent son Joe to the Budokwai to show them up and throw them down. From all accounts Joe did pretty well. E.J. filled me in:

You ask me about young Joe Robinson whom I met some time ago with his father at the South London Judo Society. Physically he is a magnificent specimen of manhood. He stands something like six feet three or four in his socks and scales quite sixteen stone or as you would say about 224 lbs. Stripped. He has Atlantean shoulders. Moreover a handsome bloke of the Greek god type, with regular features and a marvellous head of auburn hair. He subsequently spent some time practicing at the Budokwai where, thanks to his prodigious strength, he was very rarely thrown and, on the contrary, used to toss most of his opponents. It was generally a simple matter for him to pick up his adversary bodily and lift him clean above his head before depositing him on the mat. But it was precisely in this erroneous reliance upon *wanryoku* [forceful strength] that his danger lay because sooner or later he was bound to come up against an antagonist whose combined physical strength and skill could prove superior to his simple strength, and then he would meet his Waterloo. Apart from judo, Robinson is an acknowledged Catch (freestyle) champion. He has since been expelled from the Budokwai for professionalism, so that's that.

Any of you chaps care for a spin?

Left to right: E.J. Harrison, Eric Dominy, "Daddy" Jack Robinson, Joe Robinson, and Hylton Green. Photo taken outside the London Judo Society, circa 1951.

All the same I must admit that personally he seemed a quiet, unassuming, likable enough fellow, and even had a course of dramatic training at the Royal Academy of Dramatic Art here in London. His father is another story: a really tough looking specimen with bloodshot optics and replete with hot air. Yes, I think Daigo would prove more than a match for Joe Robinson; but if the latter could have been trained in Japan he might conceivably have turned out a serious force to be reckoned with.

Six years later (1959), the Robinson controversy still raged. In the British monthly *Judo Magazine* (Judo Ltd. of Croydon) for February, letter writer W. Sipple, calling himself a "Very Yellow Belt," wrote that Professor Jack Robinson (10th-dan and world judo champion 1928-1938) had issued a challenge from his Judokwai Club to Dr. Sebastian Hawkins (5th-dan) of the rival South African Kodokan club for a contest. Robinson was 62 and Hawkins 58, but the challenge was not picked up, so the Professor's son Norman, 6th-dan, made do with taking on ten stalwarts in an hour. Norman disposed of the crew in just over six minutes and then did some self-defense with his sis, Sheila (5th-dan). Then Norman and Mr. South Africa, Doug Baggott (3rd-dan), did an unrecognizable *nage-no-kata* (forms of throwing).

The finale had Professor Robinson displaying pressure points and a throw "of which I am the only exponent in the world." As one man pinioned his feet from the rear, and a second man attacked him from the front, the Professor scissored the second man's neck, tossing both men airward in the process. Professor Robinson was then head of the South African Judo Board of Control.

A month later, "Very Yellow Belt" Sipple was crucified. G. Billson from South Africa didn't like his "blatant lies," and proudly proclaimed that Norman Robinson could beat anyone in the world today, "with the possible exception of his brother Joe, who is at present in London. This includes Sone, Yamashiki, Geesink, and any other of the top graded men." (With friends like Billson, Norman needs no enemies.) A second letter in that issue was from Professor Robinson himself. He called Yellow Belt a liar and quibbled on data. (Hawkins was a 2nd-dan, not a 5th-dan, trained by Kenshiro Abe, and Sheila was 3rd-dan, not 5th-dan.) The Professor went on that there was only a "split second" between Norman and his brother Joe, and even if the Budokwai in London wouldn't admit it, Joe could "beat any white man living." Surely old Jack isn't implying that some hated black somewhere could beat son Joe, so instead he must be saying that Joe can beat (barely) brother Norman.

Daddy Jack goes on to say that Joe went through the whole Budokwai crowd (in 1955), and when T. Leggett, G. Koizumi, and T. Kawamura (a legitimate 6th-dan visiting instructor from the Kodokan) failed to take up the cudgels, Kenshiro Abe (7th-dan, also from the Kodokan) bravely braced Joe. Abe, he wrote, lost by a point, but the Budokwai, to save face, later changed the result to a draw. Finally, the Professor said that if the Budokwai wanted to see what Norman could do, they had only to invite him to London, line up Messrs. Bloss, Young, Gleeson, and Palmer opposite him, and "...you will soon see whether he is 6th-dan or not."

Recently (summer, 1997, letters) Dicky Bowen wrote cogently on the Robinsons.

Joe Robinson is a decent guy, which is more than can be said for the others. The old man would sit bending a six inch nail while he talked – I am sure the nail had been softened. Joe could have been an excellent judoman had he had proper teachers. Yes, he joined the Budokwai. In randori he tended to crouch, both arms out straight and rigid. The only throw he initiated was a rather vicious ankle sweep, otherwise he relied on counters. Several people threw him in various throws – not easily but they did. I would say that honours were about even. He would never go near the ground – he had no *ne-waza*.

April 1997 photo of
Dicky Bowen (4th-dan),
current Budokwai Vice President
and still one of its bright lights.

Two to three randoris was his limit – he told me that after that his arms gave out! In the three months or so he was at the Budokwai he was quite popular. As I said, he is a decent person. He had to leave the club because he was doing judo professionally, on the stage as an entertainer, and this was not allowed by the Budokwai rules (based on Jigoro Kano's ideas). Joe was not the first to be asked to resign, over the years it happened numerous times. But any comment by the old man that "Joe recently went through the whole Budokwai crowd" is a lie.

One thing is certain, in spite of all the noise coming from old man Robinson, he never took his sons to the Kodokan. There is no doubt that none of them would have had much chance. Geesink would have murdered him.

As for the Kenshiro Abe versus Joe match ... Well, I saw it! This took place at the London Judo Society in the top dojo, where the mat extends right up to the wall on two sides. Kenshiro was, of course, a fool to get tangled up in such a match.

Abe was then in his forties and in his youth would have had little trouble with Joe. As an exciting spectacle it was dead boring. To increase interest at the time, some said that Abe threw Joe with a hane-makikomi and that later Joe knocked Abe down – both romantic inventions.

So that's a good hunk of a bad story. I should mention that the British judoka criticized by grandpa Jack for not doing battle with young Joe were all much older and no longer in the contest mode. Trevor Leggett, for instance, who had been the top British contest man in the 1930's, had had to remove himself from that scene for health reasons. Given that, I don't understand why the Budokwai didn't do as one of the correspondents suggested: line up Britain's best and let Joe and Norman go at them. At that time, the last vestiges of amateurism were being clung to, and the Budokwai may have abstained on that seemly score.

Joe Robinson, right, tries to hold Abe off during their match in London in 1955.

Dicky Bowen's letters nicely resolve this issue. None of the Robinson boys ever entered the world championships. I doubt that the Kodokan would reject any applications, irrespective of whether anyone was a professional. It's too bad: I would have paid mightily to see young Joe brace Dutchmen Bluming, Geesink, or Ruska, not to mention the Japanese biggies. I know Joe would have whupped Inoki, Rocca, and other so-called champions. But, could the Robinsons have beaten the Gracie family from Brazil? I wouldn't bet either way, but I'd pick boisterous grandpa Jack against any of the Gracie elders – this estimate simply on the score of his scarifying rhetoric. In all this unresolved mess we're left with another couple loose strands. Whatever happened to young Dougie, and is it true that, to enhance the martial gene pool, Sheila married a textile manufacturer yclept Gilbey?

The comedian Benny Hill learned judo for a couple years in London from Dicky Bowen. Above, Benny grins for Dicky's left shoulder technique. Then, Dicky throws Benny with a right body drop and Benny groans: "What'd you do that for?"

George "Scottie" Kerr (2nd-dan) from Scotland.
He was successful at the Kodokan in the late 1950's.

Some time after 1955, I stopped writing for the quarterly *Judo*. E.J. wrote me in 1959 that it had been renamed *Budokwai Bulletin*. I continued to write for the monthly *Judo* journal of Judo Limited in Croydon, however. The *Budokwai Bulletin* ceased publication in 1968.

In 1966, I finally got to visit the Budokwai. After being told by the doorman that Trevor Leggett was "under the weather" and wouldn't be in that night, I sat down near the mat and watched a resident black belt demolish an eager but out-manned American black belt. The Britisher was Syd Hoare, whom I had last seen in 1961 at the Kodokan. His judo was not the firewagon style of Brian Jacks or George "Scotty" Kerr, two other British stars of the period. At least it hadn't been in Tokyo where he had plied his trade erect, easy, and efficient with no flamboyance. But here at home, Hoare seemed to have new fire as he tossed the American about. We didn't speak or acknowledge each other – he may not have noticed or recognized me. But he did throw his man so near me once that his body whacked some wood framing, causing me to raise an endangered leg. I had the feeling he was saying, "Here Smith, this is for you." Perhaps I was putting too fine an edge on it, for we had always been good friends. I had another appointment in London that night and left soon after.

E. J. Harrison

E.J. Harrison was another fine man whose friendship played an important role in my life. I corresponded with him for a decade (1950-1960), but was never lucky enough to meet him in the flesh. We had much in common – we both liked to wrestle and to write.

Harrison was the first foreigner to knock at the Japanese judo door. Born in Manchester, England, in 1873, he emigrated to British Columbia at nineteen and worked in Vancouver and Nanaimo as a journalist. At Nanaimo, he was fortunate to begin freestyle wrestling (called "catch" then) under little Jack Stewart, a favorite pupil of famed Dan McLeod. Stewart and his crew made Harrison into "a reasonably efficient mat-man," readying him for Japan where he went in 1897. There in Yokohama, he joined a Tenshin Shinyo-ryu jujutsu dojo under Hagiwara Ryoshinsai, taking a *shodan* from this "wonderful little man" before moving to the Kodokan in Tokyo.

At the Kodokan, Harrison met such men as the great S. Yokoyama and K. Mifune, plus foreign stalwarts like Dr. A.J. Ross of Australia. In fact, E.J. had married Jack Ross' sister Cicely in Japan. Although he subsequently divorced her, he kept in touch with her through letters. Ross went to Japan with his parents in 1901 when he was eight-years-old. As a teenager, Ross was coached by E.J. in Japan and received 1st-dan before returning to England to study medicine. After getting his degree he migrated to Australia and established his practice in Brisbane. In his prime Ross stood six feet in his socks and weighed fifteen stone (210 pounds).

E.J. Harrison as a journalist in Japan in the early 1900's.

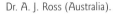
S. Yokoyama.
Many believe he
was the top judo
fighter of all time.

Dr. A. J. Ross (Australia).

Ross introduced Kodokan judo to Brisbane, Australia, in 1928. During the depression, he wrestled all comers in fairs; and, during World War II, he taught close-combat to the Australian Army. According to E.J., Ross maintained the colossal strength of his youth into his sixties. That power plus great skill enabled him to preserve his almost unique record of unbroken triumphs against all comers. Although sick and physically failing in 1957, Ross "set off for Dai Nippon with the truly fantastic intention of participating in the 1958 May World Judo Championships at the Kodokan! However, one might say 'providentially' he arrived at the scene too late to implement his plan. On his return to Australia he had a relapse." I never met Ross, who had a flourishing medical practice when he wasn't dispensing bruises – except through his *Text Book of Judo (Jiu-Jitsu)* published in Brisbane in 1950.

After gaining 2nd-dan in Japan, Harrison, during World War I (1914-1918), practiced Greco-Roman wrestling in Petrograd under Karl Pojello, the Lithuanian exponent of the "all-in" style and amateur middleweight champion of Russia in Greco-Roman. (For information about Pojello's match with Mas Tamura in Chicago in 1942, see page 29.) Harrison married a beautiful Lithuanian woman and, as British Vice-Consul, spent years comfortably in Lithuania before being ousted by the "Soviet sub-humans," as he called them, forcing his return to England.

E.J. joined the London Budokwai in 1919. He had many judo friends there. Dicky Bowen, who knew him but not very well, says of him: "He was hard as nails, even in old age." But before he got old (and presumably before he returned from Lithuania), E.J. continued to play a role in Budokwai activities. Here is his lovely true story on the virtue of *mochi* (rice cakes) from the mimeographed monthly *The Budokwail*, a house organ that ran just eleven months (April 1929-March 1930).

The Mutts & the Mochi Cakes

[It wouldn't be *bushido* or playing the game to keep a good thing to myself, and so I have decided to tell to readers of the 'Budokwail' the joyous story of the mutts and the *mochi* cakes, whereof I was one of the sparkling protagonists. It isn't a story of judo prowess, but it is a story of an experience in Dai Nippon, and should on that account, I think, pass the rigid censorship of our editorial board. (O.K. – Ed.)]

This was in the long ago, when we were very young and just a trifle verdant, although, in our own opinion, we knew it all with a bit over. Anyway, my bosom pal Johnson and I had not been more than a year in Japan, and our enthusiasm for the land of our temporary adoption was in inverse ratio to the length of our sojourn. As our first New Year festival drew near, we began to hear references to the *mochi* cakes of which every self-respecting Japanese partakes at that season, and it seemed absolutely essential to our further initiation into the ways of the country that we too should sample the succulence of the reputed dainty. No matter what the toll upon our gastric juices.

"*Mochi*," murmured Johnson, dreamily, as he looked at his dictionary. "Rice cake, to wit. What say you, young fellow, if we sally forth into the native quarter and buy some of it for a test this very night? The hour is but six p.m., and we can easily get back in time for dinner."

I agreed, and off we went. As the sinologue, or better, the japanologue of our mess, I accosted a wayfarer and in my best high-stepping Nihongo asked him where we could buy *mochi*. The Japanese politely pointed to a shop almost immediately opposite, and disappeared into the night. On drawing closer to the shop we saw that it was a drug-store.

"Passing strange!" remarked Johnson.

"Oh," said I, "I don't know so much about that. Japan is a weird place, one can never tell what the people will do in a given case, and so I suppose *mochi* here are sold in drug-stores instead of confectioners as they would be with us."

In we went, and again I tried my skill in the vernacular. To my delight the shop assistant understood me instantly, and picking up a short slender stick he dipped into a receptacle under one of the mats and drew it forth again with a dark decidedly unappetising substance adhering to the end. Both the stick and the substance he handed to Johnson with a courtly bow. I expect he chose Johnson for distinction because Johnson was a far bigger and more imposing individual than myself.

Johnson gazed dubiously at the exhibit and addressing me said: "Ask the Johnny how we cook the stuff."

To the best of my ability I put the question in Japanese. The assistant looked a trifle puzzled, but made reply: "It isn't necessary to cook it; you need only heat it a little before using."

Perforce content with this explanation, we paid our score and returned to our quarters with our prize. There was a good fire in our common sitting-room, and Johnson, a man of action, lost no time in squatting down in front of it, and then began to toast the *mochi*, as instructed. The substance speedily spread over the stick, but its appearance wasn't at all improved by the process.

Nothing daunted, Johnson tried to eat some of it. To our common horror the stuff stuck to his teeth so effectively that it was only with the utmost difficulty that he could liberate his jaws and in tones suited to the occasion express his candid view alike of this particular sample of *mochi* and the moral of a nation that could tolerate such dark practices. Even his ruby lips were somewhat burnt by contact with the infernal compound.

Finally, convinced by this unexpected development that there must be a flaw in our reasoning somewhere, we decided to descend into the kitchen and consult our cook and her husband for an elucidation of the mystery.

Well, it was some little time before the true inwardness of the situation dawned upon the Japanese couple, but when it did the effect was astounding. They broke out into screams of mirth, they laughed till the tears flowed and they were both reduced to a condition of helpless collapse. Meanwhile, Johnson and I stood looking on somewhat sheepishly, waiting to be let into the merry jest. There was a catch somewhere, we fully realized, but knew not exactly where.

Then the cook's husband, who was first to recover sufficiently to be coherent, essayed the obviously congenial task of "putting us wise" to the truth, and our own momentary status as the world's prize mutts. The sticky, glutinous substance which we had all-unwittingly bought under the impression that it was rice-cake was actually bird-lime! [A substance made from holly bark, and used to ensnare small birds.]

The explanation, afterwards vouchsafed to us by a noted Japanese scholar, proved to be simple. You see, in colloquial Japanese the word for bird-lime – *tori-mochi* in full – is usually contracted to '*mochi*'; there is a slight somewhat elusive difference in the accentuation of the last syllable, as compared with the word '*mochi*' meaning rice-cake, and, of course, the ideographs used for the two words are entirely different. Evidently, when I asked the Japanese wayfarer where we could buy '*mochi*', my clumsy Western lips had failed to give proper stress to the two syllables, and so the Japanese had understood me as wanting to buy bird-lime!

The saying that truth is often stranger than fiction received one more application a few days later, when I told the story in the paper in which I was working. Another English friend, who was also a zealous student of the language, despatched me a 'chit' on the very day the story appeared in print, reading laconically: 'Harrison, you're a d—— liar! The incident never took place! You simply invented it!

And such is the reward of virtue and veracity! I ask you.

Judoka everywhere owe a great debt to "E.J.", as I came to call him in years of correspondence during the 1950's when I was studying about and working on the Soviet problem. No one else matched those early books and articles in *Judo* (the London Budokwai's quarterly bulletin) in which E.J. told the West of this Asian form of jacketed wrestling in rational but compelling phrases. Donn Draeger once remarked apropos his writing style: "E.J. can make a privy sound like a palace."

Yes, he propagated judo as none of us could. To start with, he was admirably equipped for the job. He was: (1) a brilliant journalist and editor with years in foreign service, mainly in Asia; (2) 3rd-dan in judo at a time when that grade equated to a present 5th or 6th; (3) a linguist with facility in six or seven languages; and (4) a humanist and a gentleman.

I still think that E.J.'s first small paperback published under the auspices of Yukio Tani and with that terror's photo on the cover is the tersest and most inspiring of judo texts. Although not heavily detailed or illustrated, it gave the sport a firm basis in the West. And who can forget *The Fighting Spirit of Japan*, that early 1913 dive into the esoteric depths of the Japanese martial arts that has yet to be superseded?

The man was colorful. After two decades of journalism, E.J. successively became an officer in a Chinese labor battalion, a member of the British propaganda bureau at Archangel, and British consul at Kaunas, Lithuania. There he met and married a much younger Lithuanian woman. When the Russians occupied the Baltic States, he and his wife were forced to return to England. After losing considerable wealth in Lithuania, he found himself in marginal circumstances in London running a guest house. Like W.H. Hudson, the great naturalist and writer, he had support from a loving wife in translating and writing judo books and articles. Malcolm "Kid" Gregory, one of the Budokwai's top yudansha and live-in student of T. Ishikawa in Tokyo, told me that on the wrong side of seventy five, E.J. once defied him to strangle him. Gregory tried to escape, but E.J. insisting, the strapping youngster put the choke on. "I really choked – E.J. would've been insulted if I'd faked it – and his face reddened, but he withstood my efforts until his wife hurried in to see what was going on."

E.J. never left off exercise. Past eighty years, he stood 5'6" and weighed 175 pounds. In May, 1959, he wrote that, "I still adhere to my spartan matutinal regime of a good half-hour's PT after my shave and bath, and the curriculum always includes a good ten minutes of deep abdominal breathing according to the Fukushiki-Kokyu formula."

He was helpful to the end, too. In answering a letter from me in Taiwan in 1960, he wrote:

I was interested to read your mention of a shoving exercise at which your 120-lb. opponent proved more than a match for your 180-lb. avoirdupois. At the risk of telling you something you already know, I'll briefly describe a shoving technique taught me – was it by Kunishige? [The famed *kiaijutsu* expert; see *The Fighting Spirit of Japan*, New York, 1982:108-116.] Anyhow, the kernel of this *waza* is for the exponent to crouch lower than his opponent and from that stance to push upwards against him. So that it often happens that the shorter man does enjoy an advantage over a taller adversary.

Waxing egotistical: I recall an amusing experience of my own while "batching" with a huge Cossack friend named Silinski in Yokohama. We used to speak only Russian and then only English on alternate days. Silinski, a political exile from eastern Siberia, one day remarked to me: "Now Ernest Ivanovitch, you may fancy yourself with this judo of yours but I'm quite sure I could shove you all over the place." As you know I'm always quite careful not to prophesy the issue of a physical encounter unless I'm pretty sure of all the factors involved. Therefore, I modestly proposed that we should have a go. And we did, indeed more than one go, the result being that I repeatedly pushed the six-foot odd Russian until he banged his back against the wall! He hadn't an earthly. Believe me he was fairly baffled. Since he couldn't make himself believe that I was stronger than he what else could he do than admit there must be something after all in the art of judo? And since those palmy days of my comparative youth and even during my active membership in the Budokwai here I have often demonstrated the same trick to fellow members and have always been successful.

An Exchange of Letters

Several times we joined hands across the sea to collaborate on articles on specific aspects of judo. Below is an example of our exchange (1952).

NOTE: The question of weight categories has brought on the warmest controversy in judo circles in years. Bulletin readers may be given some added insight into the problem from the extracts printed below. These have been drawn from an exchange of letters between R.W. Smith, 26-year old 1st-dan of America, who posits the question and gives his views, and Mr. E.J. Harrison, 80-year young 3rd-dan, who answers it.

• SMITH: The problem is this vexing one of weight categories. Do we need them? Is it contrary to the very essence of Dr. Kano's teaching? I have been reading French journals of late where the pros and cons are bitterly sounded out. As the most authoritative pilgrim of the West into the judo realm what say you? Are weight categories apposite or opposite what Dr. Kano taught?

Briefly, my thought is this. Judo is dynamic and Dr. Kano surely recognized this. The kata and techniques have undergone some little change since he first outlined them. They were to serve as foundation-stones for the future to build on. So we may expect judo to evolve – but never depart from the basic concepts. And it was the idea of the little man by dint of skill in technique and mentality besting the big man which freshened Dr. Kano's whole philosophy. I submit that the universal application of weight categories will smother its essence.

Daigo and Yoshimatsu, the last two title-holders were, it is true, big men but they were also very speedy (I've seen them both in action) and adroitly able players. Ishikawa, the 1950 champion, weighed about 175, I believe, and was able to throw much bigger judoka handily. Osawa, 148 pounds, was the 'hit' of the 1952 tournament in Tokyo. It took Yoshimatsu to defeat him, and this only after the small man had just missed his throw. All things being equal the big man will win, but when is such a state seen in this life? Just as different throws are applicable to various physical types, so there are advantages accruing to the small man vis-a-vis his larger opponent. He will most certainly have speed on his side and this in itself is often more than a set-off to bulk. So far as I have been able to learn, Dr. Kano as an active member of the International Olympic Committee never mentioned the problem or its consideration.

For shiai purposes the time-honored belt classifications should be continued. Perhaps for inchoate purposes (say, the Olympics where there are rigid weight categories), we might have to permit the use of weight gradations, but for the sport per se a vehement no! Your views will be appreciated. Mine have been jotted down without too much thought of logical continuity etcetera but perhaps you can grasp them.

• HARRISON: Like you, I'm much interested in the problem of weight categories. And in this context I am wholly of your opinion that the general adoption of such an innovation would be, as you rightly say, contrary to the very essence of Dr. Kano's teaching. It would invalidate the *raison d'être* and basic concept of the art as originally elaborated by its founder. Unfortunately, the heresy underlying this movement has already taken root in several countries, Germany and Austria among others. Thus the seeds of future confusion in the judo world have been sown. Of course we are agreed that, other things being equal, a good big man will always beat a good little man, but as you add, when or how often is such a coincidence seen in real life? It does so happen that Daigo and Yoshimatsu are not only big but speedy. I was able to convince myself of this truth as regards Daigo because I saw him in action at the Albert Hall and in our Dojo on the occasion of Risei Kano's visit. You cite the case of the light-weight Osawa. To that I can add at least two other striking instances. The first is that of [Ted] Mossom, 3rd-dan, a light-weight shorter than I am (my height is about 5' 6'), and several stone lighter than my twelve stone stripped. Yet some years ago when the international contests were resumed, he threw the huge French champion de Herdt, 6' 3" or thereabouts and I don't know how many stone, twice in rapid succession without the smallest apparent difficulty. I don't quite recall what throws he used but I think they were the *ashi-guruma* and perhaps the harai-goshi. The second case concerns our 3rd-dan Charley Grant, not more than 5' tall and perhaps ten stone in weight. On more than one occasion I've seen him tossing six-footers, and black belts at that, with his seoi-nage. And similar instances could be multiplied.

Meet the
maestro:
Kyuzo
Mifune.

My old time instructor and personal friend, Kyuzo Mifune, 10th-dan, to whom I have dedicated my *Manual* [*of Judo*] and who has given me for inclusion in it his photograph and a special message reproduced in facsimile, is a smaller man than I am and very much slighter in build. But he, too, in the old days made short work of far bigger men and rarely threw fewer than six men in contest. It is, as you point out, the great merit of judo and almost its chief title to predominance among athletic sports that its eclectic repertoire comprises something for everybody, e.g., the six-footer would not be well advised to try to throw a five-footer with the seoi-nage any more than a five-footer would be well advised to try to throw a six-footer with the uchimata! In my *Manual* I have been at pains to emphasize that although other things being equal superior weight and strength will carry the day against less weight and strength, yet as often as not superior skill and speed in the smaller, lighter and weaker man will suffice to bring him victory over his heavier and stronger opponent. I am therefore wholeheartedly with you in your insistence that although we may have to permit weight gradations for the Olympic Games, for the sport per se, emphatically no!

In his last letters, E.J. viewed the approaching end bravely. With a whimsical sadness, he quoted the well-known haiku:

Hito ni koso	It is only man
Toshi wa yori nure	Who becomes aged
Haru no kusa.	Oh, thou grass of spring!

He also quoted Touchstone's immortal words, "And so from hour to hour we ripe and ripe and then from hour to hour we rot and rot and thereby hangs a tale."

When I visited the Kodokan in 1961, I learned of E.J.'s death that year at age eighty-eight. The first fellow I ran into there was a fine British yudansha, Syd Hoare. He greeted me with "Hi, Brother Bob," and a laugh, letting me know that he had seen an article I had written for a British journal in which I said that I had been working so hard with half a dozen Chinese boxing teachers that my wife now called me "Brother Bob." Then he sobered and asked, "Did you know that E.J. died?" My face fell and something in my belly knotted and I died a little. I hadn't, I told him, and he gave me some necessary time and space.

It was very sad, but E.J. Harrison lived life with dash and relish, and he would want to be remembered on a happier note. So, in his last letter to me, dated March 21, 1960, inked in a good hand, E.J. said that he'd be eighty-seven in August, adding, "I rate you as one of my best friends albeit, alas, we are not fated to meet in the flesh." This was not a last-minute thought. In another letter, he had put me in the company of cherished friends such as Malcolm Gregory and the Austrian savant Dr. Baudisch, the only man E.J. had ever seen who was able to do the *kekka-fuza* posture of Zen – and he had learned this impossibility when past fifty! Not wanting to burst his bubble, I never told E.J. that I similarly had accomplished the almost miraculous fifth posture of the *Kama Sutra*, but I did it so precariously that I always kept my fingers crossed.

E.J. Harrison, who was always a buoyant and cheerful bloke, wouldn't mind my ending this on a humorous note. Laugh we may, but sad it is to see him go. I hope judoka everywhere never forget the man and his work.

Donn Draeger

Looks like
a kid going on an
adventure.

Donn Draeger I have long regarded as one of the great samurai of
the last half of the twentieth century. He was:

- The first and only non-Japanese to hold the rank of *budo kyoshi,*
  or full professor of the classical martial arts and ways.
- The first non-Japanese judo instructor at the Kodokan in Tokyo.
- The first non-Japanese to compete in the "All-Japan High
  Rank Holders" judo tournament at the Kodokan.
- The creator of the recognized academic discipline of hoplology
  (the study of weapons and fighting systems). He also established
  the International Hoplological Research Center and published
  its newsletter.
- The creator of the U.S. Jodo Federation. (The jo is a Japanese short
  staff used as a weapon.)
- Almost solely responsible for uniting the various American judo
  organizations into the United States Judo Black Belt Federation.
- The person most responsible for introducing systematic weight
  training into Japanese competitive judo.
- The author of more than twenty books on the martial arts and ways.

I could go on and on; there was no end to the man. Sir Richard Francis Burton described a college friend who had passed away: "He was a good hand with his sword, always ready to fight, and equally ready to write." These words catch Donn as well.

I met Donn in 1948 or 1949. Johnny Osako of the Chicago Judo Club passed the word that a Marine captain back from the Pacific "holding a high judo rank" was coming to visit. The next afternoon a few of us were working out when in waltzed this big beautiful lug who looked like Randolph Scott's bigger brother and wore a uniform that had never been worn better, not even by John Wayne in films. And this is not just memory talking. Donald Richie, a respected authority on Japanese culture, met Donn once in Tokyo. Afterward, Richie said that Donn looked like a cross between Paul Newman and Mike Mazurki, the actor who played Moose Malloy ("You want I should bust this guy?") in *Murder My Sweet*, the fine film made from Raymond Chandler's *Farewell My Lovely* (1940).

The big one paused at the entrance, looked at us as if we were side dishes he hadn't ordered, and announced himself, "Donn Draeger, yon-dan." This was done with a panache I took for immodesty. I glanced at Johnny Osako who played it pianissimo, and then at Art Broadbent who arched an eyebrow before I could arch mine. After chatting for a half hour, Donn left, promising to return that evening.

Alas, Art and I had tickets for a Russian language film of M.P. Mussorgsky's opera *Boris Godunov*. (I was deep into Russian then.) So we missed the massacre. Back from messing with tough Japanese and Korean judoka, Donn probably expected easy pickings from our midwestern hicks. Instead, he was turned every way but loose by Osako and colleagues. It was a hot time in the old town that night and the pie poor Donn was made to eat was indeed humble.

Donn Draeger teaching the iron pill to all-Japan judo champion Isao Inokuma (r) and Jon Bluming (l).

After this, Donn returned to his hometown of Milwaukee and later opened the Detroit Judo Club. The latter had a wonderful sign on the front door reading, "Open 24 hours a day, seven days a week." Sometime later, Donn moved to the Washington, D.C., area. After Donn's death, Al Clifford, who owned the largest weights gym in the capital area, told me how Donn

Donn Draeger and two judo colleagues from Australia, Mrs. Betty Huxley (5th-dan) & Pat Harrington (6th-dan).

had walked into his gym in 1952 and become the star. He added that weight-lifting bigshots, possibly including Bob Hoffman of York Barbell Company, wanted him to enter the Mr. America contest. He would be a sure thing. Donn refused, saying that he wanted to continue full-bore on judo. And that he did, establishing administrative procedures, organizing the United States into several regional Black Belt Associations, starting a small magazine, and so on.

When Alice and I moved to the Washington, D.C., area in 1955, Donn was there to help us move in and get settled. For a year or so we were thick as thieves, practicing (a 1st-dan watching Donn and me randori at the Pentagon Dojo pronounced it the most stylish he'd ever seen – Donn made anyone look good); talking (about how the national judo effort should be organized); and scheming about future books we'd do. All too swiftly he was gone.

In 1956, on his last night in America before going to Japan, Donn and I had cheeseburgers in a small café near the old brewery on 26th Street in Washington. At the time, the CIA was still using World War II temporary structures as offices, and famed Kodokan 6th-dan Pat O'Neill was teaching his brand of rough-and-tumble to government personnel at the brewery and at the Marine Corps base at Quantico. That night, I recall playing Jimmy Dorsey's great number, "So Rare," on the juke box and talking with Donn for hours. Other than leading a 1970 visit by a top-drawer Japanese weapons group (it starred T. Shimizu and T. Kaminoda), this was Donn's last day on the mainland before returning home to die in Wisconsin on October 21, 1982.

Other than the amount of time we spent in the States, Donn and I were alike in many respects. We probably felt the essence of the Asian martial arts more and earlier than most exponents in the West. We abhorred commercialism. And we liked to read and write. Early on, the leading American martial arts magazine offered us its editorial slot but when we insisted that it be substantively sound and non-commercial, and that it be changed from a monthly to a quarterly format to retain quality, the owner lost interest in us.

We had two movie nibbles. On one, I read the existing screenplay that had a finale of two disembodied swords fighting each other, and pronounced anathema on it. Directed by John Frankenheimer, *The Challenge* was released in 1982 without the sword denouemènt. The other, a documentary, died when we insisted on quality and time. They told a lot of lies before disappearing to look for money elsewhere.

But we never did do our journal. During the 1970's, Donn put out several issues of *Martial Arts International* (MAI). While a good beginning, unfortunately, financial and other problems prevented it maturing into an institution. He asked me repeatedly for contributions, but my work, teaching, and family didn't give me the elbow room to help as much as I should have. I regret that now.

In Japan, Donn lived in a rambling house in the Ichigaya section of Tokyo. Big and well made, it nevertheless shivered its timbers when Wang Shujin, the *neijia* master, would visit and punch anything anchored. By the time of my six-week stay in 1961, Wang had taken the best that several high-ranking Japanese karate, kenpo, and other martial art experts could offer, and hurt the indestructible Jon Bluming with a no-inch punch that the film actor Bruce Lee would have envied. Bluming tried to get even by taking a free hit at Wang's paunch and only hurt his own wrist. In Wang's taiji classes (he would not teach his forte, *xingyi*, to the Japanese then, but did later), he had many highly placed Japanese executives and a handful of *yakuza* (Mafia-style low-lifers). When other warriors of the night stalked him for a short time (Wang himself probably never knew this), one of his yakuza godfathers got wind of it, Donn told me, and the stalkers disappeared into the night mists.

The author saying "hello" to Wang.

Donn Draeger (in the worst Hong Kong suit seen since the one I bought in 1962) with Dr. Gordon Warner, the one-legged ex-Marine kendo and sword expert. The two did a book on the subject published by Weatherhill in 1982 (*Japanese Swordsmanship: Technique and Practice*). Photo taken at the Butokuden, Kyoto, 1978.

While studying for my 3rd-dan in judo, I spent six weeks living in that storied house. Besides Donn, other residents included the afore-mentioned Jon Bluming, young Jim Bregman (the 1964 Tokyo Olympics 3-rd place winner), Doug Rogers (the Canadian heavyweight champion and a 2nd-place winner in the same Olympics), Bill Fuller, and a dyspeptic Japanese housekeeper with an expression stronger than Wang's punch. Her stony aspect was probably the result of the practical jokes this crew played. On anyone. I awoke my first morning there to find Donn holding a *shinai* one inch from my nose. Five minutes

later I was killed again. As I was returning down the hall from the toilet to my room, Bluming and Fuller fell on me from opposite rooms with *bo* and kiai. Alertness was all – no one could afford to completely relax in that house. The occasional prank involving girlfriends and water-filled condoms often breached taste and brought a guarded tension to the occupants. As far as I know, it never went beyond that. Nor could it afford to. With those heavy hitters, a punch-out would have severely tested the house, which had survived earthquakes, the massive firestorms created by U.S. bombing in 1945, and Wang's occasional beatings since then.

Draeger performs Tenshin Shoden Katori Shinto-ryu iaijutsu. Photo taken in Malaysia in 1972.

Jimmy Bregman was the youngest in that house. I had known him in the Washington, D.C. area since he was fifteen, when he tossed me with a shoulder throw to the merriment of Donn and others. He more than fulfilled his early promise by going off to Tokyo and placing third in the 1964 Olympics. Later, he returned to America and a lot of the contest promise died when a freakish accident on the mat injured his leg. At lunch in Washington one day, he recalled what I'd told him about his training at the Kodokan in 1961. I had called it, he said, the judo gray life: "Every day you came to practice in drab surroundings, the air almost astringent with sweat. You doffed your street clothes and winced as you tried to get into your limpid heavy judogi, which never completely dried out from the exertions of the day before. You walked toward the mat and there first up for some rousing randori was the monster you were happy not to see the day before."

I knew Donn well before that time in his house in Tokyo, but there I got to see him more closely. I came to admire not only his high skills, but also how gladly and patiently he assisted foreigners with their problems. It was said that he had more than a hundred black belts in the various martial arts. While that may have been true, it seems excessive. But perhaps not. Douglas Chadwick said in his seminal *The Fate of the Elephant* (1992), "I wouldn't claim that all elephant stories are true – but with elephants, you don't need to make up all that much."

What I do know is this. In judo when his knees gave out, Donn pursued groundwork. I learned from a good source that he was in the top echelon in Japan in that area. I also learned that Donn taught a few top Japanese swordsmen in a mountain retreat for several weeks each year. As for details, I was never able to corroborate these claims because of the bureaucracy surrounding such things in Japan. But the fact that Isao Inokuma, who won the 1964 heavyweight judo title, told Japanese television journalists that Donn's coaching was the key to his success – an unprecedented acknowledgment by a Japanese judoka – gives one pause.

Donn and the Ichigaya gang were on call for film producers in Tokyo who needed foreign extras. Big Doug Rogers told me he had played every type of foreign soldier in battle scenes. Donn's most lucrative film work was for the James Bond series. In *You Only Live Twice* (1967), Donn was a stunt double for an out-of-shape, obviously bored Sean Connery. Of the movie, Paul Nurse commented, "Hollywood trashes budo again!"

Out on the bustling Tokyo streets, we would walk, talk, and watch. There were the pipe dreams never come to fruition. Donn was forever urging me to join his weapons safari in Malaysia. Later we were to edit a real martial arts journal. Still later I was to join him on the faculty at the University of Hawaii. These things never happened because our paths diverged. But we did do a book together – this was *Asian Fighting Arts* (1969), later retitled *Comprehensive Asian Fighting Arts* (1980).

He wrote a lot, too, even more than me. In all, Donn wrote over twenty books. He pecked away at his small typewriter hours a day, instructing, clarifying, leading. His books were authentic, blending tradition and innovation. Though his prose was centered and vital, his inherent humor was absent.

Outside his books, which had all the wit and humor of Marine Corps administrative memoranda, Donn was always full of fun. I jumped him once for eating on the run. C.W. Nicol, in his excellent *Moving Zen: Karate as a Way to Gentleness* (1982), hits the same subject. Fourth-dan karate sensei Keinnosuke Enoeda grabbed a foreigner eating a banana in the dojo by the neck and set him down at a table. "You sit!" Enoeda was learning English. "Eat. No stand. Stand and eat no good. Understand?" Donn acknowledged that the Japanese had broached the matter to him before.

"What did you tell them?" I asked. "I told them I'd make a deal with them: we'd stop eating in the street if the Japanese would quit urinating there!"

Donn accepted the ribald as a valid part of life. His limericks and raunchy jokes livened up every party. Here is one he would have liked because it fools listeners into thinking they are ahead of the game when, in reality as in the martial arts, the words are only feints:

> There was a young lady named Tuck,
> Who had the most terrible luck;
> She went out in a punt, and fell over the front,
> And was bit in the leg by a duck.

Back during the early Fifties, after returning from Korea, Donn was second-in-command at the Inter-American Defense Fund housed in the pink Marshall Field mansion on 16th Street in Washington. He complained to me about the excessive social role he had to play help-

Donn Draeger,
a sword and a kiai from
a master of the Tenshin Shoden
Katori Shinto-ryu.

ing his colonel host parties for the Washington elite. "How do you stand it?" I asked. "Easy," he said. He padded his role and cheated by funning. In the reception line glad-handing the upper crust, when the mighty introduced themselves Donn said he would smile hugely and double-talk amongst the din, "Oh, Mrs. Whitney (or some such), you miserable wretch, still whoring I see." And get away with it.

While Donn played the diplomat role with panache, he could be brusque on occasion. Years ago, the chief editor for Tuttle told me that he once was delicately talking to a famed writer, a Jesuit priest, about publishing his book. They were in a sumptuous office with the door open while half-way down the large outer room Donn was arguing at the desk of an editor about some textual overhaul the editor wanted to make on Donn's book. Donn never took kindly to editing and he was cussing like a Marine as he demonstrated some fighting technique that he didn't want expunged by the editor's blue pencil. The din rose to a crescendo and at its zenith, Donn came down on the corner of the desk with the technique in question, breaking it off while expostulating, "That is how the [obscenity] thing is done!"

Not too many yards away in the chief editor's office, the kindly little priest looked at my friend with some alarm and asked, "Shouldn't we have some police?"

Red as a beet, my friend apologetically said, "Never mind, I'm afraid this is one of our own writers. You can understand, he is an artist and he feels more deeply than most people."

Another example of Donn's humor: one night at the 1955 Nationals in Los Angeles, during a hot-sake-in-a-saucer drinking contest with Kotani and other luminaries, he saved my life by showing me how to drink the stuff without letting too much go down. As in fighting, the trick was to fake with a lot of elbow and then shunt the liquor down your arm, sopping your sleeve and the floor. (But who noticed or cared?) Poor George Wilson, an old buddy from Seattle, never got in on the skinny. He held up magnificently all evening. Then he blinked once, widened his eyes, and fell over as though poleaxed. It took four of us to carry him off to bed that night and onto his plane the next morning.

Thanks to Donn, I escaped that fate. However, remaining sober and feigning tipsy presented another dilemma. The Japanese have the damnable custom of forcing everyone at a party to sing a song or declaim a poem solo. (I think I did James Whitcomb Riley's "Little Orphant Annie," on a previous occasion). Sloshing around on the floor feeling like Gene Kelly in *Singing in the Rain*, I told Donn I didn't dig that singing and was going to take a walk until it got over. Donn's brow furrowed. "You can't. If you don't show your ass, they'll lose face." I laughed at his attempt to impersonate anthropologist Ruth Benedict and turned to depart. He grabbed my arm. "Listen, I don't like it either. How about we do a duet?" So I sez how about "She'll Be Coming Round the Mountain When She Comes"? "OK by me." So we did, to tumultuous soused applause.

Donn loved to laugh. There was a time at the Meiji Club in Tokyo when we all told such stories that the waiters and other diners came over to our table, not to complain but to listen. At a corner table,

Partying at the Third Nationals in Los Angeles, 1955.

Circling, l. to r.: Donn Draeger, author, unidentified lady, Ken Kuniyuki, Ben Ishii, unidentified lady, Ken Yamada, unidentified lady, unidentified man standing center back, unidentified man seated rear, Ray Moore, unidentified man, F. Miyazawa rear right, Shuzo Kato, unidentified man, and completing outer circle, George Wilson. Seated in center, l. to r.: San Furuta, Tadao Otaki, and Sumiyuki Kotani.

the Deputy Chief of the U.S. Embassy in Taipei was host to a dozen party goers, out of earshot I thought. But a week later we lunched in Taipei and he mentioned that his group had enjoyed our party, even the dirty jokes told by the great big guy (Bluming). I told him that this was the expatriate judo crew and that, actually, they had been relatively well behaved that night.

There was another aspect of the man – his hyperbole. While his research was rigorous and abided no exaggeration, he would sometimes stretch a tale to make a point. His safaris into Malaysia and elsewhere were done partly to collect data on archaeological weapon finds. He was trying to correlate these with human migrations. From the jungles he would often write of defeating local champions in free fighting. Some of this may indeed have happened, but the embellishments gave me pause. His tiger stories he never told me (he knew he couldn't con an old storyteller), but did tell friends of mine. There are two versions. In one, he was treed by a tiger, while in the other, he was treed by one tiger in the morning and a different tiger in the afternoon. How could he know they were different tigers? Even this, of course, may be attributed to his ready humor.

Donn and Sir Richard Burton, the legendary English explorer and scholar (1821-1890), shared an expertise in weaponry and neither was a stranger to hyperbole. Burton carried an iron walking stick as heavy as an elephant gun to keep fit. They shared hoplology. Though Burton gave weapons research its name and was its first great articulator, he viewed weapons as an artifact, whereas Donn was the first to study man's use of weapons in a wider cross-cultural context.

Donn treasured Burton's *The Book of the Sword,* and during his last years he asked me to send him a reprint. (The 1987 Dover reprint is still available.) Like its author, *The Book of the Sword* was idiosyncratic, strange, and sound. I'm sure Donn was also familiar with Burton's *The Sentiment of the Sword* (1911), an equally fascinating book. Burton here quotes Arab sources to show the primacy of green work over gray words: "The lecture is one, the practice is a thousand." Here he tells that in teaching a new student, for the first month half an hour a day is ample, provided there's not too much to unteach. After that, three half-hour sessions a week are sufficient. This light schedule seems to contradict his own experience for he writes in the same book that he began sword practice at twelve and sometimes had three practices a day. But the apparent contradiction may simply mean that over

Sir Richard Burton.

the years he found that, with a proper focus, long hours daily weren't required. Germanely, Burton said that he never let the pupil continue once he saw that he was fatigued, but also never let him sit down until he required rest. Burton was cognizant of iaido: "The sensible Japanese, who, holding the scabbard in the left hand, draws his sword with so little loss of time that he opens his man from belt to shoulder."

Burton decried form or ritual when carried beyond reality. "Nothing is bad if it succeeds," said Burton in regard to proper form in fencing. He noted that an overly structured opponent often shouted loftily, "You touched my mask, my back, my arm!" without understanding that the mask touch could have gone through his brain, or six inches into his back. Therefore, he replied just as loftily, "I touch what is before me and I'm amply satisfied with the result!"

There was also a mystery to Donn Draeger. He almost never said anything about his personal affairs. Since I subscribed to Chesterton's philosophy that "the most sacred thing is to be able to close your own door," I never even thought of asking him. His past, his family – he never divulged anything of this, even when we'd sit around and talk about the halcyon past. And we did a lot of that. Almost everyone who'd gone through the Depression played the "Poor Game," for instance. In it, you let the other guy try to top your low-ball. I'd say that when I was a kid we were so poor we used water instead of milk on our corn flakes. To which Donn would say, "What's corn flakes?" So I'd counter that when he was a babe his mom used baby powder on him, but that my mom was so poor she used Old Dutch Cleanser instead. Then he would top it all by telling how one Christmas Eve, his pa hadn't a quarter for presents, so went outside in the dark alley with a gun. (Like Billy Conn, the great light-heavyweight of the 1930's, Donn was twelve before he found out there were streets.) Those inside heard a single shot. A few minutes later, pa returned to tell the family that Santa Claus had just committed suicide.

Donn's fighting priorities changed over time. Early on, judo and kendo were the objects of his effort. After 1965, however, weaponry

Master Otake Risuke
of the ancient Katori Shinto-ryu.

supplanted the judo. His mentor at the Tenshin Shoden Katori Shinto-ryu, Otake Risuke, said in an interview (Honolulu, November 2, 1981) that when Donn entered his school fifteen years before, he was already 5th-dan judo, 7th-dan kendo, 7th-dan iaido, and a 7th-dan in jodo with *kyoshi,* or instructor's rank. Once he started doing Tenshin Shoden Katori Shinto-ryu, he stopped judo and kendo, his old sportive favorites.

Around 1966, Donn relocated to Narita, an hour outside Tokyo, where he remained for the rest of his life. The main reason for the change was to be nearer his new training. I have heard that Kodokan politics and specifically the new director of its foreign section, I. Abe, with whom Donn and some other foreign judoka had problems, may have contributed to his move. Donn still collected his mail and touched base at the Kodokan twice a week, but gone was the historic Ichigaya house and its nexus with the fascinating judoka who lived there.

Illustrative of Donn's giving is this incident told me by one of his students, Canadian Howard Alexander.

In 1968, I went with Donn as a junior member . . . to Indonesia for the summer to study Pentjak Silat. It was a wonderful learning experience for me. Donn and I started out earlier [from the rest of the group] and went by freighter through Hong Kong and Singapore and Jakarta. During the twelve days on that ship, Donn decided to teach me the uke for kusari-gama, jutte, tanjojutsu, and various goshin techniques. We also did many hours of jodo. We practiced about fifteen hours a day, only stopping for breakfast, lunch, and dinner, and for a couple of hours at midday when the steel decks were too hot to stand on. Even now remembering those twelve days, my arms ache and pain shoots through my wrists and elbows. One dark night with no moon, he took me on deck to practice jodo. I thought it was far too dark since I could hardly see anything but a shadow. But in true Donn fashion, he said, "It will train your sixth sense and reaction if you can't see your opponent." Needless to say, I couldn't hit him, but got smacked a number of times myself.

Master Otake with *jo* (short stick) and his senior student, Donn Draeger, have at it.

Donn had women friends, but they didn't linger when they learned that his entire being was absorbed in the martial arts. I have it on good authority that he was married to a woman Marine once and that there was a son born before the union dissolved, but he never mentioned it.

I'd always thought of Donn the military man as being conservative in his politics. (We were both too busy to talk politics, though the few times we discussed Vietnam, he was as critical of U.S. policy as I.) Yet here he is on military procurement (November 13, 1976):

> Damn, when I think of all the taxpayers' money going into things like the new super-duper tank development, I could cry. We need that monstrosity like a spare bridegroom at a wedding. When is the U.S. going to get over its superlative complex – first, bigger, better? This damned tank [the future M1 Abrams] will only stimulate other nations to build a super-duper gun that will blast the super-duper hell out of our tank!

Like all friends, Donn and I had our differences. When Donn embarked on MAI, he began writing about overseas Chinese he'd met on his research trips throughout Southeast Asia. I did not think his articles and books on the martial arts and weapons of these regions approached his Japanese efforts. This had nothing to do with his branching into Chinese studies. In the past, we had cut the pie so that he took Japan and I, China. That specialization was not sacrosanct. I didn't believe he was encroaching on my preserve. Instead, it was that I believed that the men and systems he showcased were inferior to those I studied under in Taiwan. I had visited the other areas and met their leading teachers and found them lacking. These teachers' tendency to slander superiors ("beat 'em any way you can!") added to my dislike for them. Singapore, Hong Kong, and Malaysia all boasted boxers who boosted themselves by disparaging Zheng Manqing and other Taiwan luminaries I had known.

Sadly, after listening to enough of them, Donn became confused. In a letter (July 6, 1974), he questioned my objectivity. He just couldn't believe that tiny Zheng Manqing could beat people the caliber of the huge Dutch judo champion Anton Geesink, the German wrestling champion W. Dietrich, and other people we knew. How could I believe it? He added that Wang Shujin would not go onto a judo mat or into a sumo ring or in an exchange with top swordsmen. He then said that the Chinese weren't great fighters historically. He had fought them in Korea and they weren't great warriors.

Draeger and mentor Otake Risuke engage in Katori Shinto-ryu kenjutsu, at Katori Shrine in Chiba Prefecture, April 1978.

For Donn, this was an impassioned statement. It was certainly not consistent with his earlier remarks on Masters Zheng and Wang. (Although, with more than a hint of hyperbole, he told many, but not me, that he had taken Wang's punch even when Wang wore his big ring!) Away from the Japanese orbit, Donn was out of his element. The locals pushed their wares and Donn bought too quickly.

One ingredient in this bias was his personal animus against the Chinese as a military power. He gained this prejudice serving on the ground during the Korean War, and his many Japanese martial art friends probably reinforced it. But this anti-Chinese prejudice was too sweeping. For the period from 1830 to 1930, he was quite right about Chinese military frailty, "the weak man of Asia," and all that. But it wasn't a weak military power that pushed the United Nations forces from the Yalu River to the 38th Parallel. Further, one doesn't have to read Joseph Needham to know that during much of history the Chinese devoted more material and imaginative resources to war than anyone else. After all, the Chinese developed modern war from the fifth to the third centuries B.C., and then waged it on a scale that Europe did not achieve until the nineteenth century A.D.

Donn's protestation contrasts also with what he said during his lecture, "The Role of the Sword in Japanese Martial Arts," given in Honolulu on March 30, 1976:

> There is much development on ki studies currently. Not to slur anyone, but the Japanese know little about ki. The Chinese know, and the Japanese would do well to sit at their feet. This would take a lot of humility. No Japanese, including Mr. Tohei, claims to know how to use ki to absorb punishment. This is a significant Japanese failure, and they are still in primary school in this regard. The Japanese have their ethnic pride, of course, and they must suppress it or they'll never learn very much. If they were to develop some aspect of ki beyond the Chinese it would merely be by coincidence. Therefore, if you want to learn about ki find a qualified Chinese.

Puzzled, I wrote Donn to say that I too had believed as he did, even after being completely defeated in sensing-hands as well as in free and unstructured skirmishes. But the fact remained: Zheng had never been beaten in challenges. When I asked Zheng how he would have handled sumotori, judoka, and wrestlers, he acknowledged the physics

Shimizu Takaji in the early 1970's,
headmaster of Shindo Muso-ryu
and Donn's personal teacher.

problem. He said that he would tell a challenger that he could hit or kick, but if he grabbed his small body, Zheng would have to resort to *dianxue* (the art of striking vital points). I then suggested to Donn that he hop a plane down and I would set something up. Zheng had some tests such as turning his arm over while preventing the other from doing the same to him at which no one had beaten him, and I thought this would persuade Donn. If it didn't, Zheng would be amenable to a free fight.

As if his statements had been a momentary lapse, Donn wrote four months later that there was no need for him to test Mr. Zheng, though Jon Bluming might consider it. Then, ambiguously, he said: "Short of a fight to do somebody or myself in, I am not equipped to test anybody." Donn seems here to mix testing and fighting. Actually, he would have enjoyed the tests. Professor Zheng could take your hand, as in shaking hands, and turn it over or prevent you from turning his over, beating

Donn Draeger & Kobayashi Sensei of Shindo Muso-ryu jojutsu.
Photo taken May, 1978, at the Botokuden, Kyoto.

Another one of those
good looking *kamae*.

you without regard for your body weight or weightlifting ability. Or if you liked striking, he would trade chops on the other's arm. He had never lost in either test. Or in a fight.

I once asked a judo-cum-karate teacher who studied in New York City how he had done at sensing-hands with Professor Zheng. Alone of all Zheng's students, big or small, fast or slow, he told me that he never really tried to push Zheng in sensing-hands – "He was an old man" – but he was sure he could have pushed Zheng if he had tried. I bluntly told him that I and bigger and better guys than the two of us had thought the same thing and had been vigorously "managed" and handed our heads by Zheng. I added that in not trying, he had missed the biggest thrill of his taiji life. But he went away unconvinced. I even suggested a ready test. He should brace Ben Lo, who had just come to America. If he could handle Ben in sensing-hands, then perhaps he could beat Zheng. But if Ben beat him or it were a tie, he should forget it. Ben has great skill but never attained Zheng's level.

He never took me up on that test. Thinking about it now, I realize why neither he nor Donn – both fine fellows – would not pursue the test. Either consciously or deep down, their egos would not permit them to ever know that their years in the more or less "hard" arts availed nothing against a soft, old man. Ego, that monkey on all our backs, prevented them from ever knowing that Laozi was right in saying that the soft overcomes the hard. Sure, one finds it in the Gospels at a once remove, but where other than in Zheng Manqing did these friends of mine ever have a chance to see it physically demonstrated?

It remains a pity.

The mystery attending Donn continued to the end. We stayed in touch swimmingly until his June, 1981, letter saying that he'd just returned from two months in "Lulu" (Honolulu) where he'd worked on the Hoplology Center's legal status and International Jodo Federation matters:

> That was part of my time in Lulu. The other, which I'd rather not go into detail about, was the fiasco with the VA [Veterans Administration], Tripler [Army Medical Center], and my badly broken foot. Everybody decided it needed an operation but after the total time, I got no farther than a hospital bed; one hour before operation it was canceled and I was told to go now --
> Geeezzzzz!

That sounded ominous.

Eight months later in February, 1982, Peter Nichols, one of my taiji students, who was studying under Donn at the University of Hawaii, phoned me about Donn's physical decline. Peter was driving Donn to class and was mortified one day when, on an errand, he had parked some distance from the store to which they were going. They began walking and Donn, erect as ever, was struggling to keep up. Peter tried to get him to pause while he went back for the car. Donn would have none of it, and they made it to the store. Donn could barely walk and couldn't train. He told Peter that tests proved nothing and drugs, which Donn abhorred, had not helped. The brass at Tripler Army Medical Center now wanted to try a toxic drug, adriamycin, that might harm his heart. They gave him a week to decide. I already had been alerted to the problem by Donn's senior students and was working with a judoka, Dr. Tom Malone, acting head of the National Institutes of Health in Bethesda, on his behalf.

His May 11, 1982, letter was the last one I got from Donn:

Many, many thanks for your work on finding out something positive at Bethesda. Tomorrow I am on my way back to Tripler and after consultations I will know more and be back in touch with you again. At the moment I am in bad shape; hardly able to walk or stay up for long periods of time. Tripler's plans may well be to IV me with the antibiotic called adriamycin which in itself was ruled out earlier because they did not like my heart condition said to be either tricuspid insufficiency or mitral valve trouble. The biotic [sic] is famous for ruining hearts and without any guarantee of aiding my liver condition, I have held off until now. Wish I had other opinions for Tripler is all one opinion. The edema in my legs is now into my abdominal region to the point of bursting (no fooling) and I hasten to get back before some complication sets in. You'll hear from me after I consult Tripler.

I immediately phoned him. It was a sad thing. In a frustrated but healthy voice, he told me of the wards of the dying at Tripler and how humiliating it was to die an inch at a time. Dr. Malone had at last got the top man in the field to treat Donn, and an obscenity of a man he was, with all the warmth of an iceberg. But by the time I relayed word back to him through his seniors, Donn had chosen to return to a Veterans Hospital near his step-brother's home in Wisconsin, and died shortly thereafter.

Shindo Muso-ryu members in Hawaii, 1981. Left to right: D. Draeger Sensei,
Quintin Chambers Sensei, Pat Lineberger, Bob Valdez, & Peter Nichols.

Donn was a warrior on pain. He had to be. Pat Lineberger, one of
his *deshi*, tells me that Donn had severe allergic reactions to any type
of pain-killer. Which meant if he had surgery he could have no anes-
thetics. In 1978, while he was in Honolulu for a lecture series, he had
to have a root canal done. And did it *sans* pain-killer. Another time,
he was on the operating table for surgery on a big toe that had plagued
him for years. He insisted on no anesthetic and told them to proceed.
The doctors were stupefied, but when Donn stuck to his guns they can-
celed surgery! That toe was later caught in a door at Tripler Army
Hospital that another fellow accidentally slammed. Donn felt intense
pain at first, but then it disappeared. He laughed in recalling that the
door had corrected what the aborted surgery was supposed to do.

Back to the mystery. Death, of course, is the biggest one. We all
know that we must die but deny it will happen to ourselves, despite
Saint Theresa's "We are all going to die in a couple hours." In August,
1985, a Chinese-American Army doctor in Hawaii, a student of
Donn's, phoned me. His examination of Donn had revealed swollen
legs and a carcinoma that, as I recall, had metastasized from his
intestines to his liver. The doctor said that Donn thought he had been
poisoned during his trip to Malaysia. If true – Donn may have guessed
wrong – we will never know whether it was intentionally done or a
misadventure of diet.

There can be no mystery, however, in how he benefited America and the world by his contributions. He opened Asian combatives to the full view of the West. He was an authentic warrior able to blend the tough with the tender. He could fight the match, referee it, and then explain the mechanics of it later in his books. He was an unusual American – he never made a dollar with his incomparable skill. All of it went into the more than twenty books we have inherited. Hear his name. Donn Draeger: Don't nod in recognition; Donn Draeger: Bow with admiration and respect.

Richard Hayes, the hoplologist, said it for all of us in his poem:

> *Draeger no kami*
> *domiciled in that old snag*
> *high on the hill*
> *domo arigato gozaimasu.**

* "Thank you very much."

Jon Bluming

Dutchman Jon Bluming was an excellent judoka whom I first watched at randori with two spirited Japanese at the Kodokan. Bluming more than held his own. Returning from an errand, Donn Draeger joined me and watched. Later, as we walked away, I mused that the big guy wasn't bad. Donn nodded: did I know who the Japanese were? I shook my head. He told me they were numbers one and two of the current crop! If memory serves, one was K. Watanabe, 5th-dan; the other may have been Akio Kaminaga, 5th-dan, the 1960 all-Japan champ, whom I later learned Bluming had choked unconscious a week after Kaminaga won the championship. Bluming started looking even better.

Bluming damaging a dumbbell.

Above: Tadao Otaki, the samurai stranglee, throws a U.S. airman.
Left: "After Bluming, you needed a towel."

One afternoon at the Kodokan, two or three couples were scrambling around in groundwork in the foreign dojo. I was working with Shokichi Tanaka (7th-dan), a veteran who had been king before Masahiko Kimura took over after 1936. This one had done it, friends told me, solely with his uchimata. I badly wanted to ask him to do some standing randori so I could feel it, but the drill just then was only groundwork. He belonged to that group of hardy perennials with busted knees relegated to rolling around on the mats and embarrassing men thirty years younger. He looked to be fifty-five to sixty but completely dominated me. He toyed with me and as I tried unavailing, sometimes unorthodox, techniques he smirked, the closest he could get to a smile. Tanaka Sensei was a good guy but not much fun.

At one juncture we disengaged. When I sat up, I noticed him watching what was happening next to us on the mat. Bluming had gotten his hands in on Tadao Otaki's (8th-dan) lapels, but I thought his arms were too extended to leverage a choke. Still, Bluming stayed put while Otaki thrashed about trying to extricate. All at once Otaki subsided. He was out cold, but it wasn't all that apparent. Jon let go and asked him if he was okay. Otaki awoke, blinked, and announced, "Come on, I'm fine!" And on they tumbled the mats.

This really impressed me. These samurai not only never said die – they never even admitted to unconsciousness!

Jack Dempsey got hit a whopper of a shot by Gunboat Smith in the fourth round of a fight. Throughout, Dempsey functioned until the sixth round when he woke up enough to knock Smith out. Another

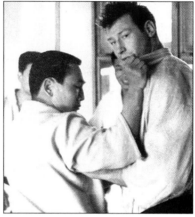

Top left: Bluming's last lesson from S. Kotani, the Kodokan's last 10th-dan.
Top right: Bluming practices with champion Isao Inokuma, 1961.
Left: Jon beats Kyoto champ Oda with his patented "sweeping loin," 1961.
Below: Bluming scores in red-white fall shiai with uchimata.

Bluming:
A punishing karateka.

Smith in a contest in Chicago, got choked so extensively and hard that, after escaping, he snoozed vertically during which time he did a dream of a tai-otoshi. He never remembered the actual throw. Coming off the mat after the throw, thinking he had lost on the strangle, he said to his neighbor, "What a choke!" That one replied, "What do you mean, choke? That was a helluva tai-otoshi!"

There was a tradition in Chicago before I arrived that one had to submit to being choked unconscious as one of the prerequisites for 1st-dan. (Another was that you had your hands trussed, and then were set upon a chair atop two card tables, the bottom one of which was boot-ed out from under you. How you fell in this disaster was a pivotal part of your grade.) I never submitted to a choke willingly.

T. Mifune (10th-dan) years ago fathered an idea he called "To win in one's dreams." If in a dream you are pursued by an ogre, even then in such a nightmare you must never run away. Even then you must win. Waking or dreaming you must constantly keep in mind that you will win. And though I had no dream on the mat that day walking around none too tightly wrapped, I still had some synapse or instinct functioning.

But to return to Bluming, who besides being a first-rate judoka, was also a punishing karateka. He studied under Mas Oyama in the Kyokushin Kai style, and was the first person anywhere to receive 6th-dan in the style. (He is currently ranked 10th-dan.) In 1966, he published a two-volume book with Kenji Kurosaki (10th-dan; 5th-dan then) called *Kyokushinkai Karate*, and he currently has another book at the printers. Some have asked me who would win an all-out go between Bluming and Mas. I don't know, of course, but breaking it down, I'd lean toward Bluming in judo, Oyama in karate, and all-in, old man ferocity, Bluming.

Germanely, Bluming once told Gogen "the Cat" Yamaguchi, "I want to fight your son." Yamaguchi looked up at Bluming (way up, since the latter was about a foot taller and a hundred pounds heavier than the former), and said, "No way. Too big!"

There are many tales of the man yclept Bluming, some of them true. He had an instinct for the jugular on the mat and rugged hilarity off. I wasn't with him when he put a fake spider on a woman's kimono aboard a train, then pointed at it, feigning fear and causing a near-riot. Nor was I there the time he emptied a small theater using a rubber snake in the same way.

But I was with him when a strapping 200-pound Korean carrying an umbrella approached us and tried to sell us some porn. Enraged that the guy would attempt to sell such vile stuff to us two boy scouts – the irony here is immense – Jon seized the man's umbrella and chased him down the street beating him about the head. I didn't see him again until later in the day. His first words: "Bob, do you want an umbrella?"

Then there was his first (and last) day on a job with his judo roommate, Bill Backhus, selling Bibles to U.S. military dependents in Tokyo. Bluming listened to Backhus make his pitch to some of the military wives, then asked Backhus if he could try the next house on his own. Backhus let him while he took another house across the street. Bluming knocked on his first door and a young American wife answered. Jon did his spiel holding the big gift Bible. He thought he was doing pretty good when she asked if she could pay the $30 in a couple installments. Backhus, sensing that Jon might need help closing the sale, dashed up and interrupted, waving his Bible. This rattled the woman and she hesitated, "I don't know, boys, with Christmas coming up and all, I better check with my husband tonight. Could I call you tomorrow?" The muscular Christian salesman, who even if he had known English better than he did would never have opened a Bible, disgustedly said to the smaller salesman, "You filthy [obscenity], I had the [obscenity] sold before you [obscenity] up the sale!"

Bluming and Backhus once spilled some newspaper clippings in front of me. These accounts from an English-language newspaper, garnished with photographs, described the exploits of these two brave foreign boys against the denizens of the dark. Their car had been burgled, their life possessions stolen. They got mad. And did something about it the next night. They set a trap by leaving some empty cartons in the unlocked car and then hid nearby. When three burglars came, they were met by these Kodokan-trained boys who apprehended them and gave them over to the local constabulary.

That was what the clippings said. Bluming and friend told me what actually happened. Someone had swiped a ripped and sweaty antique gi jacket one night. Hardly the Turin shroud, Bluming had been trying to give it away to judo friends for weeks and none would have it. But it was the seed of an idea. Why not plant some empty cartons in the back seat and get in some extracurricular practice?

Thus they cast their net and caught some fish. The newspaper was correct – they did apprehend the first three burglars they caught. And these three thieves, though bruised a bit, were intact when they were given to the gendarmes. The police thanked them and the paper raved. But it was too much fun to stop and so they did it again, visiting terrible trauma on the poor burglars. Unlike benighted America, there are no guns in Japan, so it was a fairly safe enterprise for the boys. One of the burglars in the first incident, however, brandished a knife but to no avail, and along with his partners in crime ended up unconscious and somewhat broken. (Bluming tells me that, though this had its farcical moments, these three were car thieves implicated in a murder and it had been serious business.)

Using their decoy, Jon and Bill turned those crooks they could catch in to the police. Injuries were common with the roommates competing over who could break the most bones. One thief held a club one night but seeing the desolation and overcome by fear, handed it to the boys who beat him nearly unconscious with it.

Mae West said that "Too much of a good thing is wonderful," but after a couple more incidents, the Tokyo police got grumpy and suspicious. Finally, they ordered the Kodokan pair to desist, at the same time giving Bluming and Backhus "the highest police gold medal" for citizen cooperation.

And one last story, one I heard rather than witnessed. Bluming was once approached by a Japanese autograph seeker. Could he get Mr.

Anton Geeskink:
The other Dutch giant.

Geesink's autograph? Imperiously, Bluming nodded at the real Geesink, surrounded by his fans. "Geesink I'm not," said Jon. "He's the guy with the gut." (Besides playing judo, Geesink liked to eat, ballooning past 300 pounds on the pro rassling circuit.)

Seeking photos for this chapter, I finally tracked Bluming down and received a letter in May, 1997, that began: "Dear Bob, What a surprise for I heard years ago that you had passed away. Welcome back you old rascal!" I paraphrase the rest of that letter and an even more lengthy one in June.

When he returned to Holland in 1961, he planned to participate in the World Judo Championships in Paris. Because of hate and bickering between the Dutch amateur group headed by Bluming and the so-called professional organization headed by Geesink, Bluming was sidetracked and not permitted to enter. Therefore, Bluming stopped competing and turned his energies into training future Dutch hopefuls, among them judo champion Willem Ruska and three-time world sambo champion Chris Dolmen. Bluming also got involved in free-fighting in 1966.

Bluming's move into free-fighting brought strains in his relationship with his mentor and friend Oyama. This was bound up in their temperaments and politics. Jon admits that they grew apart and is alternately critical and caring. At one point, Jon says Oyama never had a real fight in his life and rose through breaking things, though his breaking the horns off a bull was a scam – they were secretly loosened with a hammer before the demonstration. When Bluming told Oyama to try a small Spanish bull for an education on bulls, he was given a dirty look. But after receiving the news in April, 1994, of Oyama's death from lung cancer, he says he broke down as he had when his mother passed away: "I always admired and loved the old man as my father for all the good things he did for me in the old days and for giving me karate and a whole new meaning in my life."

Continuing, Bluming states that he introduced first karate, then kickboxing and Thai boxing into Holland. He pioneered free-fighting in 1989. His student, Chris Dolmen, was a star in this, winning the first World Free-Fighting Championship in 1993, at the age of fifty. Other martial art activities in which Bluming was a pioneer included bojutsu and iaido in 1962, kendo in 1963, and sambo in 1970. He established the Kyokushin Budokai in 1990, and by 1996 it was an international organization with many affiliated dojos and fighters.

Bluming says he personally challenged world judo champion Anton Geesink in 1962 and 1963 to a free-fight, but that his registered letters received no response. Since then, his mentor Mas Oyama, speaking for Bluming, challenged anyone in the world who thought himself unbeatable, "especially those big-headed karateka in the USA like Chuck Norris and Jeff Smith, and all the others in those days, but they never replied." He bluntly dismisses the American icon Bruce Lee with: "Bruce was a movie star who could not beat his grandmother."

Bluming's nearly sixty-seven now. While injuries have slowed him, he still teaches free-fighting. He adds that he can beat the youngster easily, and sometimes even the champions, especially on the ground.

He ends his letter by saying how sad he is over Donn Draeger's death (in 1982), for he was the man who "did so much to form me and make me what I am today."

Over the years, there have been rumors and gossip about Bluming's so-called misconduct on and off the mat. He was a fierce competitor in judo, and in randori, giving no quarter to anyone, not even his sometime roommate Bill Backhus. Anyone watching the two go at it hammer and nail (Bluming was, of course, the hammer) would swear they were enemies instead of best friends.

Even acknowledging Bluming's high-octane volatility, the rumors puzzled me. From his response to my inquiries, I now wonder if some persons or organizations, finding they couldn't beat him fighting, actively sought to undermine him with words. Reinforcing that belief is the fact that in 1996, Bluming was selected to be Prince Bernhard's bodyguard on the occasion of the prince's eighty-fifth birthday, as he had been several times before. Only a man with the cleanest record could receive such an honor, my Dutch confreres tell me.

Doubtless, Bluming mellowed with time from his earlier swings between ferocity and fun. Perhaps the answer lies in a story he told me once. During the Nazi occupation in World War II, he said, life had been a hollow affair. Deprivation, dreariness, and death pervaded everything. No one had much to eat and if you saw smoke coming from a neighbor's chimney, you knew that they were cooking their beloved cat. While he survived those hungry years, he evidently carried the cost with him for many years after.

Left:
Recent photo of Jon Bluming.

Below:
Bluming honored by Dutch Prince Bernard by being chosen as his personal bodyguard. Bernard, in the middle of this picture, sporting his trademark white carnation. Bluming is on the right, behind future king, boyish Prince Alexander.

THE
KODOKAN
CREW
CREATES
JOHN
GILBEY.

Bluming, ridden hard and put away wet, as monster Gilbey.

John Gilbey
& His Correspondents

John Gilbey was born in Donn Draeger's house in Tokyo in 1961. Donn hit on the idea of giving me a textile millionaire doppelganger. Then Bluming and Bregman got in the act, even getting up some photos, and in Bluming's case, posing for a drawing, to lend verisimilitude to the story. Gilbey was a joke, an exaggeration, a fantasy. He had money, time, and amazing skill in everything. We were sure that readers would be smart enough to realize this. We were wrong. Big writers fell like trees. John Gardner, who now writes the James Bond books, used a Gilbey technique that British poet Philip Larkin later quoted in an essay. William Burroughs, in his novel, *The Place of Dead Roads*, grabbed a bundle. Neither attributed their fictive use. Richard Heckler cited a Gilbey paragraph on the Vietnam debacle (*In Search of the Warrior Spirit*, 1985), and Michael Murphy, in *The Psychic Side of Sports* (1978), also used a couple paragraphs.

Given the enormous popularity of the Asian martial arts at the time, the idea was commercially a hot potato, but Gilbey himself mashed it by nixing the sleaze road. Early on, when the prestigious William Morris Agency knocked at his door, Gilbey only sniffed and didn't answer.

Jim Bregman working on qi.

He eventually published three books and a newspaper article on knock-knock jokes. ("Knock, knock." "Who's there?" "Gorilla." "Gorilla who?" "Gorilla my dreams, I love you.") *Secret Fighting Arts of the World* (1963) contained some truth, plus many whoppers. *The Way of a Warrior* (1982, 1992), contained more personal philosophy and some straight history. The chapter on savate and the descriptions of old Hawaiian martial arts, for instance, were as straight as I knew how to make them. And what John's old buddy R.W. Smith said about Tim Geoghegan in the Afterword of *The Way of a Warrior* (second edition, 1992) remains as true as the day is dangerous. Gilbey's third book, *Western Boxing and World Wrestling: Story and Practice* (1986), was almost entirely straight, and included most of the research I'd done for my long-promised *History of World Wrestling*. Perhaps because *Western Boxing and World Wrestling* was, unlike the others, mostly true, people seldom bought or quoted from it as they did Gilbey's less-reliable earlier books. Go figure!

Over time, Gilbey and I received many letters from people we didn't know. One of the strangest letters Gilbey ever got was from a Californication (oops, sorry) Dao school that snarled that since Gilbey knew seven languages, "Permit me to speak with you in classical Chinese – if you don't, then it's not worth my time." Well, despite a college one-semester course in classical Chinese that left me groggy, I couldn't handle his beautifully constructed characters even if I wanted to reply to rudeness. Then I had an idea. One of my students knew Tibetan, so I had him write a short reply in my name thanking the ultra-Daoist for his letter. In it, he said that, since almost everyone nowadays knows classical Chinese, could we add a little rigor to the discussion and correspond only in Tibetan, else it wasn't worth my time? Needless to say, that yahoo never wrote again.

Don Draeger as Don Eagle.

Perhaps Gilbey's best letter-writing story (and true!) is about a mother in Sweden who is concerned for her son. Sven worshiped the martial arts and particularly its king, John Gilbey, whose first book was Sven's Bible. One day at work in a machine shop, Sven's lathe happened to jounce him slightly. No serious bump and it didn't hurt when it happened. Yet, the next day he couldn't get up from his bed – in fact, one month later, Sven was still in bed telling his ma that it must have been a delayed-action death touch like Gilbey mentioned. So would ma write the Tuttle Company about curing it? Tuttle didn't laugh as I did – they were worried about liability: would Gilbey write the mother? Gilbey did, saying *inter alia:*

> Please tell your son that accident plays no part in the esoteric martial arts. The more secret tien hsueh [dianxue] start first with a good teacher (very rare these days), a proper system, and decades of work. There is a lot of nonsense written on these things nowadays – as though anyone can do them – done for commercial gain. Believe me, I cannot do these touches so how can these false kung-fu [gongfu] types? Answer: they cannot. Probably no one in the world can. Nor can your son. He could touch every inch of his body's surface every minute for a month and it wouldn't affect him at all. The book cannot harm him at all.
>
> This book is not a how-to-do-it manual. If you want a good one of these get my friend R.W. Smith's *Hsing-i.* Any of Smith's books are preferable for him than worrying about death in three months. It ain't going to happen. If Sven is not in a boxing mood, have him read Yeats, AE, or Gogarty. Poetry is better and much more powerful than boxing. I hope this helps Sven and that he recovers immediately.

And later, didn't Sven quit the machine shop and start writing poetry? And still later, didn't he win the Nobel Prize for literature? No, but he did get out of that blasted bed and throw Gilbey's book into the trash.

The worst part about the Gilbey books is that one soon finds far nuttier things in real life. For instance, there is a guy in England who really extends the variety of violence, claiming to be able to kill a man with his nose. Now this is no reversal of the Parisian Halitotic Attack described in Gilbey's first book. No, this warrior actually uses this bit of cartilage to put the quietus on his victims. I don't know the technique he employs with this member, but it's probably a doozy.

Remember the old story about the last fight you were in: how half the time you were on the bottom and the other half he was on top? And how your nose kept hitting his fist? Well, our British friend may be a master of strategically placing this nose against his victim's fist where the schnoz at the moment of impact generates a double-barreled (two nostrils, you know) charge of intrinsic energy that spurts up the arm, finishing the attacker. If this is the technique, it is not one I would recommend even to masters.

There was another correspondent who wrote to both Smith and Gilbey telling terrible lies and trying to set us against ourselves. To Gilbey, he offered a defense against mad dogs calculated to tear their jaws apart if Gilbey would provide him more data on the delayed-death touch. To Smith, he told how he could use psychic staring at the back of a person's head to make him move from his chair. A common attainment among on-beyond-zebra folk, debunked by Martin Gardner, America's premier debunker. About Uri Geller, the Israeli demi-magician who claimed to start stopped watches and make things move without touching them, Gardner said that if his gifts were real, he would take his bent spoons and iron rods and return them to their original condition. Johnny Carson, who was himself a magician, also put the quietus on Geller. Yet, he became more, rather than less popular!

Once at his office, this letter-writing chap said he used a "poison-mind" attack on a colleague who kept his window open on frigid days. Most of us would simply ask our co-worker to close or partly close the offending window. But our man preferred the mental mode. So he sat all day in the cold using his *qi* to force the guy to close the window. The upshot was that my correspondent caught pneumonia and was off work for a month.

Over time, I got many more Smith than Gilbey letters. In fact, in his survey of the fighting arts, *Mind Over Matter: Beyond the Bounds of Nature*, Glen Barclay accords top status to both Smith and Gilbey, and, at times, is hard put to choose between them. For instance, on page 68 of the Barker edition published in London in 1973, we read:

> Robert W. Smith found boxers in Taiwan who were perfectly prepared to let Smith punch them with all his strength in the testicles, for the benefit of photographers, thereby apparently proving that one can actually put chi [qi] in the groin, despite John F. Gilbey's assumption that one could not.

Gilbey also received a missive from a man who claimed Gilbey was his father, and several from applicants for a job at Gilbey Textiles Inc. Generally, though, the non-Gilbey letters were more interesting. For instance, Henri Plée was a prime mover in French and European martial arts. He introduced karate to a fairly strong judo base and had enormous influence. Early on, he published a French and English version of the Kodokan's monthly *Judo* (for a time, E.J. Harrison was doing the translation). A cryptic note from Henri, dated March 5, 1956, says:

> Thank you for the news. Here nothing new. Yesterday one Japanese has come in the black belt training. He was very high, judoka, karateka, aikika, sumotori, etc. . . . Arriving in the dojo he knock the walls with the fists and all the roof was trembling. Then he challenge the black belts . . . but nobody say a word. Awazu go in his corner quiet. [French judo champion Jean] DeHerdt say OK, and begin randori, but he did like with Daigo and did not attack quite crouch . . . After some minutes this Japanese look badly DeHerdt and put his fist in the face of DeHerdt cutting his lip. . . General stupefaction. He begin catch the 12 of this month.

There's a broken-nose charm about Henri's *patois* (and no ridicule is meant – Henri's English is now much better, and I had, and have, no French at all). T. Awazu, a high grade Japanese sensei visiting France, was the prize student of Tamio Kurihara, a 9th-dan from Kyoto who was famous throughout Japan for his demon groundwork. Jean DeHerdt was the French champion who, when faced with top-caliber opponents like D. Daigo, the All-Japan champion, and Johnny Osako, three-time U.S. champion, would go into *jigotai* (a deep squatting defense posture) near the edge of the mat in an attempt to stop their attacks. It hadn't succeeded with them, but may have with this impatient superman who beat on the walls with his bloody fists. Obviously, he got tired of trying

Bluming/Gilbey screws Bill Fuller's nose out the back of his head. (This was so bad even Gilbey refused to use it.)

Henri Plée (3rd-dan in 1953), teacher and promoter of the Asian fighting arts in France and Europe.

to pry DeHerdt up from his overly defensive stance and finally bashed him one in the mush. All this is pretty clear. But the ending is delightfully obscure. I don't think it means that he was going to begin teaching catch-as-catch-can wrestling on March 12, but rather that plans were afoot to show the visitor a darker French hospitality if the right assassin could be found. Alas, I never heard of the denouement.

Two years later, Henri wrote comparing different boxing methods:

Ideally, karate is superior for the numerous reasons you gave in your articles. But now that I am a correct 2nd-dan in karate (though I get a 3rd-dan for my success in diffusion of this sport in Europe; I don't believe it), I can readily speak about it. I have had three teachers (2nd-dan and 3rd-dan level) who stayed in my home for one year each. Out of curiosity I arranged private contests between karate and French boxing experts. Much to my surprise, after initial wariness over the naked hands and the stances, the French boxers won easily.

I can tell you that the Japanese karateka are proud to a fault of what they have, though they are only at the start of their potential. Many French boxing techniques are unknown to karate. When a famed karateka visited here recently I told him there were many methods he could borrow from French boxing which would make him superior to the other karateka on his return to Japan. Then we would randori and I would score with my favorite technique, a lead foot snap kick to the lower abdomen. This tactic is unknown in karate and while my opponent swore beforehand that it would be no problem for him, in the match he couldn't defend against it. But they make no attempt to learn anything except what they've been taught, so now I keep my opinion to myself.

I believe that when I blend the karate with French boxing, it will be superior to traditional French boxing. We've had two Thai boxers visit, anxious to move into western boxing and make big money. They were both more effective than karateka or French boxers, but soon left when no one would accept their challenge.

My hope is to bring in Chinese and Thai teachers and, using karate as a foundation, blend them all with French boxing for a rounded, more comprehensive sport.

Takahiko Ishikawa

Takahiko Ishikawa had considerable indirect influence on me. What a wonderful man and fine judoka he was! After drawing with Masahiko Kimura in 1949, Ishikawa won the All-Japan honors in 1950. He taught judo to U.S. Air Force personnel in 1953 and, with Air Force patronage, moved to Philadelphia in 1955. There he taught judo and served as technical advisor for various U.S. judo organizations. In 1967, he moved to Virginia Beach, Virginia, and opened his own school; and in 1984, at the age of sixty-seven, he became the youngest 9th-dan in Kodokan history.

We got on well. He was a wonder in randori, the only man who could throw you with only his hands (te-waza). Ishikawa threw a big lug once with *uki-otoshi* (floating drop), a hand technique seen in form displays but seldom in contest. The guy got up, said, "I don't believe it." Ishikawa did it again. Again the fellow said, "I don't believe it." A third time. "I believe it!"

On the ground, Ishikawa was just as deadly. John Anderson (6th-dan, Baltimore) tells me that when he first trained with Ishikawa, they were preparing to do some groundwork. Ishikawa had his glasses on. Anderson said, "Sensei, your glasses?" Ishikawa waved him in and left his glasses on: he was so good, nothing was going to disturb his glasses. (This recalls Benny Leonard, the impeccable lightweight champion boxer who never got his hair mussed.)

His heroes, he told me once, were S. Nagaoka (10th-dan), the most powerful judoka of his time; and Tsunetane Oda (9th-dan), the inimitable groundwork master. And he acted on his heroes as we all should. Like Nagaoka, he stood erect and reacted like a cat to any mistake: his counters usually scored. But let E.J. Harrison tell you how good Nagaoka was:

> During my active years at the old Kodokan, Nagaoka was, as already mentioned, judo instructor to the Kyoto Butokai. But I was fortunate enough to be present on one memorable occasion when he came up to Tokyo and paid his Alma Mater a visit. His appearance in judo kit on the dojo mat in the afternoon coincided with a swift line-up of perhaps twenty aspiring young yudansha ranging from 5th-dan to 1st-dan avid to test their skill and endurance against this famous master. Nagaoka made a swift survey of his

S. Nagaoka doing a hip throw on Kaichiro Samura (10th-dan).

prospective antagonists and then with a grim smile pointed a finger at Kyuzo Mifune, then a 5th-dan and generally rated as the most formidable of the black belts of that current grading vintage.

"I'll take you on first," he laconically remarked. It goes without saying that although, as was to be expected, Mifune put up an impressive showing, the finale was never in any doubt and ippon ensued well before the lapse of the statutory five minutes. After that Nagaoka went through the rest of the candidates like the proverbial dose of salts.

Like Oda, Ishikawa was relaxed and always in full control on the ground. Lecturing one day on *kami-shiho* (upper four-quarters holding) with me as dummy, as he talked, he intermittently forced air from my lungs. Every now and then he would look at me with twinkling eyes to see how I was faring. I was miserable. Another time some big boyo was atop the mighty one assaulting his neck in *shime-waza* (strangle). Underneath, Ishikawa undid his belt, adjusted it, re-tied it, and exhaled, throwing his foe into the air and extricating.

Born in 1917, early on his father wanted him to learn kendo. So he did, and eventually earned 3rd-dan. But he always preferred judo. It was said of Ishikawa that at school he never won at judo till one day, and after that, he never lost. That is something of an exaggeration; after all, he did lose to Masahiko Kimura during the finals of the 1940 Nationals. But it certainly gives an indication of his superior judo skills.

I knew Ishikawa fairly well, but time and distance precluded regular practice. If he had lived closer, my life might have proceeded differently. Donn Draeger brought him to dinner one night. As Ishikawa came in, a throw rug on a highly polished floor did what no one in Japan could do – it slipped rapidly and almost threw the great one. Catlike, he righted himself with a jovial smile. Donn said, "Bob, that was the closest anything associated with you will ever come to throwing this guy!"

For pure judo style, see the 1950 film, "The Art of Judo" (Tokyo, 1950), in which he throws a competitive five-man line. And he was obliging, too, even posing with Donn for the photographs in my first book, *The Complete Guide to Judo: Its Story and Practice* (Tokyo, 1958).

Ishikawa and I were alike on youth judo at a time when it had become an overly competitive Little League thing where whining kids got trophies bigger than they were. We believed that judo practice for children under twelve should be eighty percent fun and games and twenty percent work, and that contests should not be over-emphasized. At one time the area *yudanshakai* (black belt association) tried to divest local dojos of their right to give promotion belts to kids – effectively encroaching on the precious teacher/student relationship. I refused to comply with this absurdity and I heard that Takahiko Ishikawa did likewise.

I respected and liked the man and practiced with and knew many of his students. Among those who trained under Ishikawa was the late Dick Walters. This one was not fancy but strong as an ox. I remember him just starting out giving fits to black belts. He later did a stint in Japan and returned to grab a second place in the open division in the 1964 Olympic trials in New York City. Sans style, early on Walters reaped with his leg, approximating o-soto-gari (large outer reap) or ouchi (big inner reap), seldom achieving points but invariably spilling his man onto the mat. Then he piled into *kami-shiho* (upper four-quarters holding) and the unfortunate one moved nothing but his eyeballs. Later, in Japan, he developed an almost unstoppable osoto.

Ishikawa tosses Donn Draeger with "sweeping loin" and pins him with "upper four-corner hold."

Like Rocky Marciano, Walters was a bear on working out. He was lucky enough to be a live-in student under Ishikawa. One morning, Ishikawa started him on pushups, then was called to the phone. After taking care of the call, he remembered that he needed some items from the nearby mall. He walked there, made the purchases, and started back. En route, he met a chess friend who insisted on a quick game or two at his nearby house. Ishikawa enjoyed the chess so much that it took him an hour or so to remember Walters. He wound up his game, grabbed his bag, and went home to find Walters still doing pushups two hours later! The Chinese and the Russians have an expression, "You must eat bitterness." For Walters, endless pushup repetitions weren't bitter. He regarded them as butterscotch.

Malcolm "Kid" Gregory was another of Ishikawa's live-in students. Gregory was a prominent member of the British judo gang. He lived with Ishikawa in Tokyo during the early 1950's. I spent a couple days with him at the elite Los Angeles Athletic Club where he was the resident judo instructor, around 1954. Big, handsome, and rangy, he was a good judoka and a better raconteur.

Greg stood straight, eschewed anything fancy, and was a consummate attacker. In 1958, on a visit to Japan he revisited the Tokyo Police Dojo – you needed a 3rd-dan just to practice there – and won a bout against Miwa, a well-regarded 5th-dan by a score of two to zero. The throws he used on that occasion were o-soto-gari (large outer reap) and harai-goshi (sweeping loin). In a letter describing this match, E.J. Harrison said that the onlookers exclaimed while watching the points, "Ah, the Ishikawa technique!" Shortly before leaving Los Angeles, Greg took on a 317-lb. pro wrestler and actually knocked him out with okuri-ashi-harai (double ankle sweep).

As tough as he was standing, Greg was a terror down. In a letter to E.J. Harrison, I described his groundwork as being like wrestling with "an octopus with what seemed like four arms and four legs." When he was done toying with me, there wasn't a moving part in my body. And when he pinned you, you weren't just pinned – you were nailed to the mat. Greg was impervious to chokes and most pins. The only thing I could get on him was the old standby kata-gatame (shoulder hold).

As he did with me, E.J. had stimulated Greg in both intellectual endeavor and judo. There was a fine bond between them. Greg told me that the aging E.J. had thrown him with o-goshi (large hip throw) in an upstairs study, and the sound brought Mrs. Harrison running up the stairs to see if a part of the house had collapsed!

Greg's god was, of course, Ishikawa. However, he also was enthralled by Yoshima Osawa, the 160-lb. wonder – he died a 9th-dan – who punished the French judoka Maurice Gruel for punching a young Japanese 3rd-dan during randori. Gruel (4th-dan) was the top Frenchman at the Kodokan during the early 1960's. I worked with him once and found him awkward and lackluster. However, he was handsome and – tell it not in Gath or Paris – had an eye for the ladies. One time, he got frustrated when he couldn't muscle a skilled Japanese youngster and finally bashed the kid in the nose, bringing on the claret. Gruel then strutted off triumphant in the midst of bemused silence. Two weeks later, Osawa braced Gruel for some randori and he threw the Frenchman everywhere and often, even occasionally on the mat. The sequel: Monsieur Gruel, badly limping, had to be assisted onto the next ship back to France.

Greg told me a genre tale you hear in almost every athletic activity. He and Ishikawa were doing *uchikomi*. This is a repetition drill of a standing technique in which one does many reps using the *kuzushi* (unbalancing the body) and *tsukuri* (fitting your body to his) without actually throwing (*kake*). A fellow sitting on the edge of the mat inter-

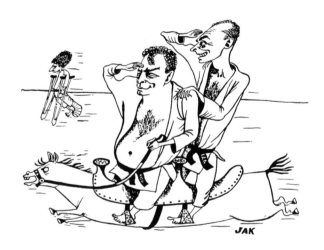

"JAK," staff cartoonist for the Budokwai's *Judo*, shows
Malcolm "Kid" Gregory, in front, and I. Morris galloping off to Japan in 1950.
For medical reasons, Morris was unhorsed and didn't make the trip.

rupted Ishikawa as he was going in and out on Greg. "Hey man," he said, "You're too high: he'll never go over unless you get lower!" Ishikawa paused, scornfully scrutinized the armchair warrior, then snorted and went back to his repetitions.

Another side to Greg was his wit, intellect, and mesmerizing way with words. He was quick with a limerick and his off-color jokes knocked me out of my chair. He could recite the whole (!) of John Dryden's translation of the *Aeneid*. E.J. once tested Greg, who reeled off some twenty or thirty pages word-perfect before E.J. cracked and called off the test. Nor was Dryden his only artist. He quoted the Bard by the yard and could perform prodigiously on other stars in the British literary skies.

Greg had written a script about the life of Alexander Pope. It was his own and he was proud of it, but acknowledged that it was not commercial, and that he would probably have trouble selling it. This was his tour de force and according to E.J., he had some nibbles. An actor friend of Greg's working on the film *Spartacus* discussed it with Sir Lawrence Olivier on the set and later told Greg that Olivier called it an excellent idea. Still later, his "Pope" was praised "in high quarters." Those were the nibbles, but as far as I know, there were no bites.

This left Greg, who went from the Los Angeles Athletic Club to the equally posh Jonathan Club as athletic director, working on commercial projects. The one that I thought had a good chance in movies or TV was his character Dyson San, an American correspondent who goes to Japan, where he studies judo and other martial arts. Greg made at least one major sale on this property well before Emma Peel and Bruce Lee blustered onto American screens, but I never heard the sequel.

During this period, Greg was able to train under perhaps the greatest fencer of all time, Aldo Nadi. That colossus I had wanted to see since watching a marvelous fencing display by Giorgio Santelli, one of his seniors, at the University of Illinois in the early Fifties. If Santelli were merely an ace student of Nadi (see Santelli's analysis of Nadi in the latter's *The Living Sword* [1995]), what must Nadi have been? Greg said he was merely magnificent. "To be lucky in the beginning is everything," wrote Cervantes. True. But here was Greg living and training with champion Ishikawa in judo and later coming to America to teach judo and meeting and training under another maestro, this one at fencing – Nadi. The gods were good to Greg!

Nadi came to the United States in the 1930's, but wasn't altogether happy with the experience:

> Little by little I was learning that except for love, health and death, or worse still, mutilation, nothing much is really important in life. Money the very least – and I am quite aware that those four words must not only shock, but be considered wholly blasphemous by all Americans almost without exception. And so be it.

Obviously, our charms – especially those of Hollywood, where he worked – hadn't impressed Nadi. Still, he remained thirty years in the place, dying there in 1965. For better or worse, America did give him the freedom to say such things

E.J. said Greg also had a fine baritone voice and a girlfriend who couldn't travel to Asia with him once when he wanted to go on a trip. This last didn't bother E.J. much. He wrote me on the subject of entanglements at crucial times, "A young man married is a young man marred."

After this, I lost sight of Greg. The last reference E.J. made to him was in October, 1959. He said Greg was still working on some TV series. Greg's mother owned the largest wholesale grocery business in north Wales and it may be he returned to the sceptered isle to follow the family fortunes.

Aldo Nadi.

I do know that he visited England in 1957 and stayed three months. E.J. hadn't seen him for seven years and several times in the interim wrote that he hoped he would last till Greg got back. He did last and a glorious time they made of it, the high spot being a trip to Stratford-on-Avon to see *As You Like It* with Peggy Ashcroft as Rosalind. Then Greg was gone. Said E.J., "If we do meet again, why we shall smile. If not, why this parting is well made." Greg himself died in Los Angeles in June, 1990.

To end, let me tell of Greg's trip to Cuba with Ishikawa. The great one had asked Greg to travel with him to Central and South America. Greg was occupied with pursuing his crust of bread, and couldn't make it. In June, 1956, however, the pair went to Cuba. The first week was interesting. At the start of a new class, it was Ishikawa's practice to "go," that is, to fall for any fairly correct throw. The Cubans couldn't believe it: they felt enraptured by their new prowess and cheated by Ishikawa's apparent inadequacy. Unknown to him, the Cuban black belts circulated a petition and telephoned the Kodokan to recall "this old man who can't throw us." Perplexed, the Kodokan phoned their man in Cuba. Enraged, Ishikawa asked that all the major black belts assemble on the mats in Havana. Out they all came. Greg asked if he could have a few, but Ishikawa looked hard at him and said, "They are all mine!" Ishikawa made twenty or so of the best black belts line up, and then proceeded down the line throwing each man several shocking times apiece before letting them limp back to the line. When he was done, he told them bluntly what he thought of them. He said that they did not deserve top-ranked teachers: in point of both technique and courtesy, they had all failed the judo test. Then he and Greg left the island.

Besides this cautionary tale, Ishikawa told me that Cuba was a dangerous place to live in those times. The dictator F. Batista was being opposed by Fidel Castro, a rich lawyer from the mountains, and everything was in turmoil. While he was there, a Cuban judoka, a doctor, was treating a wounded Castroite when Batista goons broke into the operating room and killed everyone there. Nor did one walk around aimlessly at night. Ishikawa made this mistake one night and found himself incarcerated by Batista militia who, in turn, found that a man they thought was a spy was actually a visiting Japanese judo champion!

Takahiko Ishikawa
doing tai-otoshi
(body drop)
on R. Smith.

Masahiko Kimura

Kimura: Never another like him.

When I lived in Seattle (1952-54), the old-time judoka there told me of Masahiko Kimura, a 7th-dan who had visited Seattle in May, 1952, as part of a pro rassling group. Although Kimura had been show rassling since October, 1950, evidently he didn't like it much, and he left the troupe soon thereafter. There are different accounts why this happened. One says that the promoter, a Hawaiian named Tetsuro Higami, felt that Kimura was too unreliable and did the rest of the tour without him. Another says that Kimura was so ashamed that he unilaterally returned to Japan in disgust. I like to think that it was the latter.

Kimura may have been the best judoka Japan ever produced, though Sakujiro Yokoyama might stir in his grave at such a judgment. But there is a saying in Japan that goes, "No one before Kimura, no one after Kimura!"

Something of a child prodigy, Kimura was already a 4th-dan as a high school senior in 1935. Then the Boy Wonder trained at Takushoku University under Tatsukuma Ushijima (9th-dan), and won the All-Collegiate championship at seventeen. Ushijima (died 1985, at 81) was a perfect complement to Kimura: one, the greatest fighter ever, the other, the greatest teacher ever. Tough as nails and charismatic – he looked like a muscular Omar Sharif – Ushijima was twice All-Japan Champion. He was perfectly poised between standing and ground judo, training summers at the old Kodokan at Suidobashi in Tokyo and winters at the Budokuden in Kyoto. Canadian judo instructor John Hatashita was at the Kodokan after World War II and saw Ushijima, then in his fifties, randori with the All-Japan contender that year. The young buck threw Ushijima, who, humiliated, rose and ripped the youngster apart, annihilating him without mercy.

Before World War II intervened, Kimura captured the All-Japan championships three consecutive times. After the war, the championships were resumed in 1949 when Kimura was held to a draw by T. Ishikawa, both being adjudged winners by referee Kyuzo Mifune. Ishikawa, who had been beaten by Kimura in 1940 and 1948, told me once that he was so frightened by the overwhelming Kimura in 1939 that he'd run like a thief. By 1949, however, things had changed and he chased instead of being chased. But he still remembered, John Anderson (6th-dan) of Baltimore tells me, the fantastic grip Kimura had on his jacket, "It felt like two steel I-beams." Yoshima Osawa (9th-dan), the great stylist, recalled that during practices Kimura threw him off the mat regularly. And everyone told me how people hid whenever Kimura appeared at a dojo. Paul Nurse adds that his own students dreaded him:

> His training regime was so severe that they feared every practice session. The only thing they were more afraid of was *not* showing up for practice. He was known to go to your house and tear the place apart demanding to know why you were absent without leave. So much for the old adage, "Those who can, do; those who can't, teach."

After his bout with Ishikawa in 1949, Kimura retired from amateur judo and tried to start a pro judo circuit. When this failed, he became a pro rassler. First stop Hawaii. A good source, *Revue Judo Kodokan* (Paris: January 1952) carried this brief report on Kimura's 1951 visit there:

> The gallant challenge of $1,000 to anyone who can beat him in judo garb that M. Kimura has thrown to the world has already brought him some surprises... Kimura has long been judo champion of Japan but has broken, amiably I believe, with the Kodokan in Tokyo. In Hawaii, Kimura's first opponent approached him and smashed him in the nose with a magnificent punch, and immediately jumped out of the ring to hide. The "spiritual pursuit" which then ensued amongst the audience lasted eight minutes, when at last Kimura caught his adversary and threw him into some chairs, and an atemi knocked him dizzy. Kimura's second opponent lasted fifteen seconds before a shoulder throw left him unable to continue. His next stop, the U.S., is preparing to welcome him.

Right:
R. Kano (left) presents
first-place plaque to
M. Kimura in 1949.

Below:
Masahiko Kimura (left)
and Takahiko Ishikawa,
All-Japan co-champions
in 1949.

This report reeks of the real. It is unlikely that Kimura would have accommodated the first opponent to the extent of letting him bash him in the nose. And, if it were show, the second opponent would not have been destroyed so quickly – the crowd wants more time than fifteen seconds. If a pro rassling circuit was involved, however, the report still must be taken guardedly.

In the same year, Kimura fought Helio Gracie in Brazil (see page 132). Then, sickened by show rassling, Kimura returned to Japan and became a coach at Takushoku University. Though he never regained his lost prestige at the Kodokan, he stayed fit.

Paul Nurse tells me that before the Tokyo Olympics of 1964, Kimura, then coaching at Takushoku, worked out with the Japanese Olympic team. This included Donn Draeger's weight-training protégé, Isao Inokuma, and Kaminaga. Kimura, aged 46 or 47 at the time, tore

them all apart. A week later, Doug Rogers of Canada (a student of Kimura and a silver medalist in those Olympics) saw Inokuma (the future gold medalist) outside the Kodokan. Rogers told Inokuma he'd heard about what Kimura had done to the Japanese Olympic team. Inokuma just shook his head in shock, saying, "Yes, amazing, amazing." Thinking to needle him, Rogers told Inokuma that Kimura was planning on coming out of retirement to try out for the team.

At this, Inokuma was visibly shaken, and told the Canadian that he had no doubt that Kimura could have any place on the Japanese team, including Inokuma's own, if he desired.

As a backdrop to all this, there is a poignant story of Kimura struggling as a young man. Quite poor, he never got food enough to feed his judo habit. During that period consigned to eating only rice, he would eat his bowl of rice while looking at drawings of fancy meat dishes. As he ate, his eyes feasted, and his whole being was the better for it. Able to dream into his wish for food, young Kimura was "dreaming true" (see George Du Maurier's use of this idea in his novel *Peter Ibbetson*, 1891). It would be nice to know the period in which Kimura was so destitute. Perhaps it was late in World War II, when the caloric intake of the Japanese averaged about eight hundred calories a day.

Nurse also told me a story about a middle-aged judoka, ex-Imperial Army, who, presumably because of war crimes, was thrown into solitary in Sugama prison after the war. He spent his six years doing ten thousand foot-sweeps a day. Released, he thanked his guards, returned to his family and judo, and reportedly went on to throw the great Kimura in practice! Don't ask me what throw he used . . .

Later, according to Wayne Erdman (6th-dan), Canadian National judo coach, Kimura, at 64 and weighing 165 pounds was still able to convey raw power into his judo. Rainier Fischer of Judo Ontario described this power following Kimura's visit to Montreal in 1980.

> Being an extremely humble and quiet person, it is hard to believe that he was responsible for ripping off an opponent's ear while doing o-soto-gari or breaking arms when applying *ude-garami*. But unless a person has trained very hard himself, he can never really appreciate the accomplishments of Mr. Kimura. Imagine bench pressing 80 kilos (176 pounds) for 500 consecutive repetitions! Imagine doing 1000 push-ups every day in your room after training! Mr. Kimura's judo includes no counter or combination techniques. His philosophy was geared toward ippon (full point) judo with himself attacking and his opponent attempting to defend. For him, there was no retreating. For every imaginable situation, the master had a specific technique. His ippon seoi-nage alone had a dozen different entries.

Kimura also visited North America in 1970, and attracted as many as 350 participants to his seminars. He died in 1993 at age 75.

Kimura
meeting
with Brazil's
Helio Gracie
in 1951.

In 1951, as part of a pro rassling tour, Kimura took part in an exhibition with Helio Gracie in Brazil. Since the Gracie family is all the rage these days because of the execrable Ultimate Fighting, it may be well to analyze the account by Don Beu, "Put to the Test: The True Account of Gracie Jujutsu's Toughest Proving Ground," that appeared in the February, 1990, issue of *Karate Kung-fu Illustrated*. Graham Noble sent me a copy of the article, adding that it was skewed toward Gracie. How right he was. It's "as biased as a scream from the dentist's chair," to borrow journalist Bugs Baer's famous line.

Before he could fight Kimura, Gracie first had to fight another Japanese named Kato, who purportedly weighed 180 pounds. Beu writes that they first went to a draw – Gracie had a broken rib – and so they went again. I have seen this bout in the film "Gracie Jiu-Jitsu" (1988) and it is underwhelming. Gracie towered over the short Kato, and though it is difficult to tell in a gi, I would say that Kato may have had ten pounds on the 140-lb. Brazilian, but certainly not forty.

They began with Kato being conservative, biding his time. Kato moved well; Gracie stood and moved like an amateur, foolishly picking his feet up. He tried a couple of weak sweeps, a knee wheel that wasn't even close, and then turned into Kato for an attempt at a frontal throw. When Kato didn't budge, he jerked back out of it. Just after this, Kato threw Gracie with what looked like a shoulder technique (*seoi-nage*), a beautiful throw that bounced Gracie off the ropes and back into the ring. A little higher and he would have been out into the crowd and in great danger. Kato then threw Gracie under the ropes using a scratchy tai-otoshi. After this, the referee brought the two men back into the center. Near the ropes, Kato nailed Gracie with another pretty shoulder throw. Here Kato made a fatal error. He should have continued throwing Gracie at will until the Brazilian quit. But on top of Gracie after the throw, he foolishly got into groundwork and was caught by Gracie's powerful choke from underneath.

Next it was Kimura's turn. Going into this match on October 24, 1951, Kimura was nine years younger and eighty pounds heavier than his Brazilian opponent. Given Kimura's unbeatable skill in both standing and ground wrestling, one could reverse those figures, making Kimura older and lighter, and he still would have prevailed. As it was, the greater mass and youth promised certain doom for Gracie. That's my physiological judgment. Philosophically, bear in mind that there is no distance greater than that between an accomplished amateur and an incomparable professional.

Kimura straight-away tossed Gracie with his famed shoulder throw and landed on top of him. Beu writes that Kimura stumbled and landed on top only because Gracie relaxed. That is analogous to saying that Max Schmeling's jaw beat the hell out of Joe Louis's fist during their second fight. The two men then rolled around a bit before Kimura secured *dojime*. (This is a dangerous pinning technique banned in judo; it involves encircling the opponent's body with the legs and squeezing.) This rendered Gracie unconscious. Then, says Beu, Gracie recovered, only to be headlocked so strongly that a blood vessel broke in his ear, causing it to bleed all over Kimura's sleeve. Three points in as many minutes, unconscious once, and bleeding from the ears – but no submission! So off they go again. Kimura gets an armlock that Gracie can't escape and finally the Brazilian's corner throws in the towel. The ever-credulous Beu then adds that since Kimura had never been extended beyond three minutes before and Gracie had gone thirteen, Gracie had held his own against the very best that Japan had to offer.

This is nonsense. Kimura nearly kills Gracie, yet Gracie is the "winner"? Among Kimura's many victims, I would guess that many went beyond three minutes. After all, this was pro rassling for a crowd that didn't like thirty-second falls. As for Kimura having never gone beyond three minutes, note that the bout in Hawaii lasted eight minutes, while his 1949 draw with Ishikawa went fifty minutes. That is the second-longest match on record. The longest match was an 1886 shiai between Sakujiro Yokoyama and Hansuke Nakamura that lasted 55 minutes. That contest was so fierce that in the end the officials had to literally pry the combatants' fingers off the other's jacket.

Now what does the Gracie film show? It shows professional doctoring. All the telling points Beu grudgingly acknowledges have been cut out. This is what I saw in the less than two minutes left in. Kimura and Gracie take hold. Kimura blasts Gracie to the mat with a large outer reaping (o-soto-gari). Unafraid of Gracie's chokehold, he follows him down and controls him the rest of the way. I thought Kimura could have ended it sooner, but "accommodated" by permitting some rolling. Of course, this could have been a function of the editing. But even in the bit that the Brazilian censors have left us, Kimura is so overwhelming that one can only shudder at the stuff left on the cutting room floor.

Another indication of accommodation is the first technique Beu mentions, the famed shoulder throw, after which Kimura lands on top of Gracie (significantly, not shown in the film). Donn Draeger once told me that, during the Thirties, Kimura would lie down on his back and let anyone in Japan have one of his arms – and still escape. Kimura was a bear down there. Therefore, with Kimura at 220 pounds, there was no 140 pound human anywhere in the galaxy who could have lasted – without Kimura's help.

I don't want to be too harsh on Gracie. I'll stipulate that, irrespective of rules, he would have beaten film stars Bruce Lee and Chuck Norris in a couple minutes, and the rest of the larcenous la-la land fighters from Hollywood (Seagal, Schwarzenegger, Stallone, ad nauseum) together in the same ring in under five. But, without jackets, let him face a freestyle wrestler like Dan Gable and he would fall fairly quickly. Give him a jacket, and he would have fallen for good sambo players like E. Chumakov, and did fall for a judo man named Kimura.

Nor is this to say that there weren't some competent jacket wrestlers competing in professional wrestling during the pre-television days. For example, in September, 1909, Takugoro Ito wrestled Eddie Robinson in Seattle. Both men wore judo jackets, and the rules prohibited striking with the clenched fist, gouging, biting, and kicking. Everything else went. "Robinson started out by jabbing Ito three times straight in the face," said a Seattle sportswriter the next day. In retaliation, "Ito locked his legs around the white man and began to 'scissor' him. Next he got a strangle hold, using Robinson's neck cloth as a tourniquet, and slowly forced the American into submission. The second round lasted three minutes. Again the Japanese tied on the tourniquet and Robinson's face went red and then black" (*Seattle Post-*

Intelligencer, Sept. 3, 1909: 6). In November 1909, Ito repeated the feat, choking out George Braun of San Francisco twice in less than four minutes of actual wrestling.

Another fine judoka involved in professional wrestling was Kimon Kudo (6th-dan) of Seattle. A former manager of the Seattle Dojo, Kudo was one of Jigoro Kano's demonstrators at the Washington Athletic Club in August, 1932. He began a professional wrestling career in 1934, published a book (*Kaimon Kudo Reveals the Secrets of Jiu-Jitsu*) in Los Angeles in 1935, and beat Scotty Dawkins, Dick Raines, and Danny Dusek during a regional tournament held in Bellingham, Washington in 1937. Kudo quit the game once television wrestling started in the early 1950's, finding that when he nailed a guy with his patented *hadakajime* (naked choke from the rear) too quickly, the promoters didn't like it. Gene LeBell, the 1954 AAU heavyweight judo champion, was another fine judoka who did show wrestling for awhile.

That said, this 1951 Kimura-Gracie episode reeks of the Mas Oyama claim of killing bulls with his bare hands and fighting more than 100 opponents full contact with no pads during an American pro rassling tour in 1952. Graham Noble has researched the matter thoroughly, and has great doubts. I agree thoroughly with Graham, and some of his data I incorporate here.

A year after the Kimura-Gracie go, Oyama joined a Chicago-based pro rassling group. His specialties included karate chops, breaking boards, and similar tricks. I read at the time, in the misnamed, now defunct, *True* magazine, that Oyama had defeated challengers from the crowd. Other sources adduced by Noble raise this figure to 240 in a seven-month tour. Because of its rassling milieu, this claim was suspect and I tried unsuccessfully for years to verify it. I never found one challenger or even one reliable press report.

Oyama copied Kimura, the one man he deferred to, in offering $1,000 to anyone who could defeat him. No one ever did; indeed, no one even lasted three minutes. There's that three minutes again. Much of this nonsense was the work of rassling shills and Oyama's students. One of these latter birds chided me for inviting Oyama to accompany me to an Iowa farm to see which of us could run faster than a mere domestic bull. Like Hemingway, Oyama's relation to bulls was less about fighting than about what the dead bulls left behind after they were dragged from the ring.

Kimura flexing muscles for his fans.

In his own book, *The Kyokushin Way* (1979), Oyama himself says that the 240 matches were only exhibitions, while in *What is Karate?* (1958) he writes that he had three matches with pro rasslers, gave karate exhibitions thirty times, and had $1,000 prize matches three times. Which beats 240 all-in matches hollow. I wrote in the Fifties that I could find no evidence that the so-called "triumphal tour" ever occurred. It was strictly a pro rassling charade. John Bluming (see p. 111, above) supports my skepticism. Alas, both the Kimura-Gracie bout and the Oyama visit are examples of the old line, "There's less here than meets the eye."

Oyama was admittedly quite a breaker of stones and bricks. I wanted to see him do some of these tricks, particularly the one where he broke bottles without upsetting them. Unfortunately, I never did. Hong Yixiang claimed he could break three real bricks flat unsupported while Oyama couldn't break more than two. Just now a student has brought me a 1-1/4 inch slab of granite which a 115-lb. French Canadian "breaks routinely." The legend on the bronze plate affixed to the stone reads, "This is a genuine stone used to set a new world record of 18 slabs broken by hand on May 3, 1996." Maybe when we get to the dojo in the Western Sky we can all break things together.

Getting back to Oyama, I don't mean to demean the man, a Korean who, until his death in 1989, was a powerful force in Japanese karate. I'm simply trying to reduce the public-relations hype that celebrities seem to attract. Donn Draeger took me over to Oyama's dojo one evening and we watched him and his top boys cavort for two hours. Donn and I agreed that his system, because it incorporated grappling in addition to striking, was the most functional we'd seen. We spent some time talking to Oyama, and he was agreeable and forthcoming, rather quiet-spoken in fact, and didn't deal in hyperbole. Still, as tough as Oyama's crew was, Donn wrote me later that his team had traveled to Thailand for a mixed contest and then came a cropper. All the team members were knocked out, the captain taking twenty minutes to come around.

Donn wrote an excellent article, "Karate's Man of Iron, Mas Oyama," in *Strength and Health* (July, 1962) which gives some balance to my appraisal. He told of Oyama's break with Goju-ryu karate to start his Kyokushin Kai system. His goal was to bring karate into the present, and away from the traditional jealousies and factionalism of the ancient ryu system. Oyama had even proposed a contest of the best fighters but other schools didn't pick up on the challenge.

As for breaking things, Donn wrote that Oyama believed that there was a small place for this in exhibitions, but that too much stress on hardening the body and breaking is "monkey business." A good karate man need not maim himself to impress anyone.

Oyama was a prodigious trainer and his hands were bruised and broken so badly that, when sleeping, the weight of the blankets on his swollen hands would often awaken him. Even Oyama admitted that this was excessive. He didn't say hardening must not be done, but rather it must not be done to excess.

Though he never achieved it, Oyama's ideal was for a more relaxed regime. Donn wrote, "Oyama uses the soft hands of the expert Chinese 'boxers' as examples. These experts are able to deliver amazing force with effective destruction."

Bill Paul

The late Bill Paul (he died in April, 1990) was a sometime student of mine in the Chinese fighting arts. He had a tough childhood, living in three group homes and attending four different high schools. As a teenager he studied jujutsu and judo with Richard Takemoto in Oakland. He started judo with Mits Kimura at the San Francisco Judo Institute in 1957, and the excellent instruction coupled with his no-frills childhood made him an instant success. He was west coast judo champion for several years, took 2nd in the nationals one year, was an alternate on the 1964 Olympic team, and captained our Pan-American team. Bill was one of those rarities, a fighting 5th-dan. In Japan, where he spent a couple years, he was liked and respected, All-Japan champion Toshiro Daigo complimenting his work to his teacher Mits Kimura.

Bill Paul exemplified skill and kindness.

Bright and an avid reader, after dropping out of City College San Francisco, Bill later enrolled at San Francisco State University and cut a swath through the remaining three years of undergraduate and two of graduate studies for an M.A. in thirty months. Later, he received a Doctorate of Education from Harvard – the street kid had made good.

He was whole-lamb on international pacifism, death on wars and stupid military expenditures, and, ironically, famous for his willingness to punch out Hell's Angels types who tried to rain on his liberal parades. Since he was raised without a father present (he died in World War II), I may have become something of a substitute dad for him in some ways. Off the mat, he had become excited over Chinese boxing and had studied some *wing chun* (Mandarin, *yong quan*). At the same time, he began reading my books and writing to me.

Bill would occasionally visit Bethesda and off we'd go to the high school running track three blocks away where we'd talk as we ran a half-mile backwards. Gene Tunney claimed that this practice saved him after he got up muddled from Dempsey's left hook in their second fight. Then we'd talk around the house, eating, and walking. And talk at a neighboring store with my daughter Annette Vivian in tow, so engrossed that we didn't know we'd lost her until the store's loud-speaker announced, "Folks, we have a little lost girl here who says her name is Annie-Bim." We never found her. Verily, excess of attention to the martial arts can sometimes cause loss, however transient, of something far lovelier.

Bill was a sponge on Chinese boxing: he couldn't get enough of it. Even at the 1964 Olympic judo trials in New York City, where he finished second to George Harris at heavyweight, he'd fight and rush back to our seats, oblivious to the judo, to ask more questions. On that trip, I took Bill round to see Professor Zheng, who hustled him hither and yon, manhandling him with yin, completely stupefying him in the process. On that occasion, caught by Bill's enthusiasm, I neglected to take Art Broadbent. Art was a pragmatist and I just didn't think he'd be interested. Moreover, judo had been displaced in me by things Chinese and I wanted to give the field to Bill, who unlike Art, knew and appreciated Chinese boxing. It was another of those things which, looking back, I would have done somewhat differently.

Bill was forever bringing back arcane tricks to test on me. He once asked me to palm chop his shoulder. I did so with my right. He seemed impressed, "Damn, that was good. In fact, the second strongest I've ever felt, next only to (he named some California Chinese guy whose name I've forgotten)." "But was that guy right-handed?" I asked. "Yeah, like you," he came back. "No, Bill, I'm left-handed." That silenced him (of course, I am right-handed but the name of the game in those days was one-upmanship).

When Ben Lo first came from Taiwan to San Francisco, Bill called and asked if I would introduce him to Ben. So on my next trip to the city (called "the city with the most character in the world" by poet Kenneth Rexroth), I took Bill to see Ben, telling him to be nice.

Bill tested everyone. When H. Nishiyama, the justly famed karateka, first came to America and, at a public demonstration asked for a volunteer, he had the bad luck to get Bill. Nishiyama asked Bill to throw him a punch. In the trade we call structured stuff like this "throwing balls." Bill accommodated with a slow right hand punch which the Japanese blocked, simultaneously doing a right wheel kick at Bill's midriff. Bill neatly grabbed Nishiyama's leg, pulled and got o-uchi-gari (large inner reap), held it, and then had the temerity to drive Nishiyama backward a couple steps to the edge of the platform before releasing him. Nishiyama was deeply embarrassed, of course, but he covered well. Straightening up, he moved to center stage adjusting his karategi, and said suavely, "Ah, I see we have judoka here tonight," and dismissed Bill with a wave of his hand.

Bill Paul
(right)
leading a
gang of
judoka at
Ben Campbell's
Camp Bushido
in mid-1960's.

Bill promised he'd be nice when I took him to Ben. No sooner had I introduced them, though, then Bill just had to ask Ben if they could move around lightly together. Ben looked at me and I nodded reassuringly, meaning that Bill wasn't a wacko and would keep the test gentlemanly. So Bill moved in with probing hands. He'd studied wing chun avidly until I told him that, because of overuse of arms and a static short-step movement, it wasn't regarded highly by boxers in Taiwan. While Bill looked for an opening, Ben bided his time. Bill suddenly took hold and launched a beautiful sweep (okuri-ashi). It almost got Ben, putting him up on swaying tiptoes, but not falling. The *Daodejing* says that you mustn't stay on tiptoe long, and Ben didn't. Down he came, down his qi went, and Bill was forever his after that. He owned him, neutralizing and pushing Bill all over the place. After ten minutes Bill halted the proceedings, telling Ben he was everything I'd said.

At the Fifth World Tournament in Salt Lake City in 1967, Bill introduced me to the champion, 6'7", 270-lb. Anton Geesink of Holland. I was badly tempted to test Bill and the Dutch interpreter by starting out, "Anton, Bill here tells me that you've been bad-mouthing me . . ." but wisely decided to talk to him on trivial matters instead.

Like me, Bill loved fun. Another time in Houston an oil mogul threw a party for the judo gang. One of the judokas, a buddy of Bill's named Jimmy, was a born mimic. So the pair of them schemed. And then sat down at the millionaire's table. Bill introduced his buddy as Oleg, a Russian judoka, and the Texan, who had never met a terrible Red during the Cold War, tentatively tried to be a good host.

"We are honored, sir, to meet you. You are an adversary but things are getting better between our two countries. Let's drink to better relations. [Everyone drank.] But leave us not backslide, because if you do, America is one powerful country."

"Oleg" (Jimmy) nodded his head, darkened his visage, and wagged his finger in front of Texas's nose and said sadly in broken English, "Yes, my friend, you are right, we must be brothers for the Russian Bear never sleeps and [wearily] many in the world will die."

On the mat, Bill was a fierce competitor. He gave as good as he got and, if he was fouled, he set Olympic records retaliating. At the Chicago Nationals in 1968 he was matched with a highly touted fellow from Japan (in those days the AAU permitted foreigners to compete). No sooner started than the son of Nihon wrapped his fist in Bill's jacket, pretended to lash out with a body drop (tai-otoshi), and bashed Bill in the jaw with it. This was a foul of the worst sort. A gasp went up from the crowd, but the Japanese referee and judges called it nothing. Having disengaged during this chicanery, when they took hold again Bill abruptly pulled his opponent to him and butted him in the face with his head. The guy fell over as though sledgehammered. The next gasp from the crowd was louder than the first and in short order Bill was booted from the tournament. Nelson Algren always advised boxers that, if they were going to foul, do it before the other guy did. If you react to a foul with a foul, the referee will invariably see only the second one. But Bill wouldn't have known about this. His judo was a gentlemanly thing: tough, unrelenting, stylish, but a thing of vigorous play. He fouled only to make for a rough parity.

Bill Paul (left) wrapping one up.

Later in life, after returning from Harvard, Bill simultaneously taught karate and his own brand of humane, non-violent self-defense at City College San Francisco. By brewing for them a broth of push-offs, distancing, and turns, this humane class, he told me, invariably beat his karate group in the final exam skirmishes. Bill claimed that I had been largely responsible for developing this non-violent form of fistics, but, while I may have contributed, the creation was his. He also had been influenced by a boxing coach at Stanford, the famed former pro Ray Lunny, who would let visitors mill and mix with him. No one ever dented his armor – all they got was tired. As a fighter, Bill worked in golden inches, recalling the old Chinese maxim, "An inch of time is an inch of gold." He would work you to a rhythm and then take you out of it. You were in a trance dancing to his cues, which meant you were always a couple seconds behind him.

Bill died before putting the system into a book, but his seniors tell me that there are plans to issue it one day. If they do, I hope that they capture his psychological insights, which are quite as important as his physical ones. Bill's excellent qualifying paper for his doctorate at Harvard was on this subject and appropriately titled, "Threat Potential in Body Cues: Nonverbal Communication and Aggression." He and his non-violent system I limned in a chapter, "The Master of Applied Cowardice," in John Gilbey's *The Way of a Warrior*. Bill himself wrote the outrageous "Mama Su" chapter in the same book.

Bill had helped out in mental wards and shaped some of his system to such circumstances. Randy "the Wild Man" rampaged there, sometimes getting out into the corridors and terrorizing even the muscular attendants. And of course there came a day when Bill and the head psychiatrist were strolling the hallway and, up ahead, here came Randy. The psychiatrist said, "Oh, oh," but Bill acted. Years later, describing the scene, he told me, "You don't let a dangerous patient have the initiative. But you don't oppose him with force, either. That's the Hollywood and Washington, D.C., solution. And it never works. Randy was focused on us and was at the top of his crazy arm-flailing form and voice. So I preempted him by speeding my stride and going into my act. 'Randy, old buddy,' I shout out in happy recognition, 'just the guy I want to see!' And as I casually walk up to him, I take the clipboard I'm carrying and I point at some of the notes I'd just made at a meeting. 'What should we do this afternoon, bingo or calisthenics?' I ask. 'My schedule's all screwed up.' Once he crooks his neck to look at that clipboard, he's no longer a threat, just a guy tickled to be asked a question. Oh, by the way, he wanted bingo."

Bill came to this synthesis of hard and soft through actual non-sportive fighting and his ability in applied psychology. He spent years as a bouncer, deepening his study as he insinuated miscreants out. One night he ejected Ray Nitschke, one of the most famous linebackers in NFL history; this one learned that there is ferocity beyond football.

A martial arts buddy was standing in his empty store once when he saw Bill's clunker die in the street outside. Instantly four thugs pounced on the car. Bill's friend rushed to lock his store and speed to Bill's aid, but arrived too late. All four thugs were down and uninterested in getting up.

His liberal politics and free spirits didn't endear Bill to the conservative Nisei. Though he stopped teaching judo because of the illness that eventually killed him, he continued his non-violent self-defense and karate classes until within a few weeks of his death. His judo students at San Francisco State University, however, never forgot his idiosyncratic judo which he taught as education first and contest second (as Jigoro Kano and – uh – I had earlier). Most of the reforms he advocated years ago and was excoriated for are now in place.

Bill liked laughter and a joke. As the Vietnam mess wound down he wired me once (April 1, 1975):

> Directions re light at end of tunnel   please advise   stop
> send most urgent   fresh Tae Kwon Do cadres at 300 million cash
> do not   repeat   do not route   repeat   do not route   Danang.
> – (Signed) W. Rostow

Finally, Bill saw a lot and did a lot. Like wonderful Alastair Sim in the hilarious British movie, *The Green Man*, he loved to puncture the pompous. A high-ranked competitive judoka on the west coast once bragged that he had never been choked out. His karma was so powerful, he said, that it prevented even the best ground warriors from squeezing his neck. Bill heard about it, sought the guy out, and tested the brag. Lo and behold, the Emperor had no karma! Bill's penchant for testing, however, was Bill at his least. At his best, he was a kind friend to those around him, an excellent teacher, and an indefatigable student. Like Donn Draeger, he shone as a light to those who came seeking advice.

With kiai,
Bill downs
another.

The fighting arts always need the qualities Bill had – a supple mind, ready wit, and an independent spirit – all integrated with excellent fighting skills. He was a man with whom you could roam a rough neighborhood, tire the moon talking Chesterton and Yeats, and have a spirited scramble on the mats. One can only hope there are other Bill Pauls in the pipeline, people who will garnish and grace the fighting arts, and protect them from the money-grubbers in Hollywood and Hong Kong.

Dermot M. "Pat" O'Neill

Donn Draeger first told me of Pat O'Neill (fittingly, the name O'Neill means "champion" in Gaelic.) This was in the mid-1950's. Later, when I queried him further, he wrote me the following letter on February 16, 1966:

D.M. (Pat) O'Neill is an approximately sixtyish man whom many people say was never deep in anything but wine, which can be said perhaps to be his only failing. I am of a different opinion.

O'Neill is a good man, a down-to-earth type of man who has a practical mind. Even at his age, he is vigorous, and has had a good background in combatives.

He is currently ranked *rokudan* [6th-dan] by Kodokan and is a contemporary of T.P. Leggett. O'Neill began his judo in Shanghai during the early 30's. As he progressed he gained the reputation of being an aggressive fighter and willing to take on anyone. In Japan, as a *godan* [5th-dan] he had the good fortune to study katame-waza [ground work] with Ushijima Sensei, the teacher of the famed Masahiko Kimura and perhaps the best katame teacher in Japan. O'Neill was especially known for his grappling skills.

During World War II he taught combatives to the British Commandos and U.S. Rangers. After his unit was assigned to the Aleutians, O'Neill insisted on going with them, declaring that after training his boys, he could not desert them; he could have remained behind.

O'Neill is reported to have had "kenpo" skills according to the Japanese who knew him. Just what they included is unknown, but he did study taiji in China and may have knowledge of Shaolin, bagua, or xingyi too. In Japan in recent years he was dabbling in aikido.

He holds no official ranks in other martial arts of Japan that I know of, which may be a sign of his superficial knowledge of other combatives: I do not think he has depth of knowledge in other than the usual "commando tactics" of the West. But, he is given to practical and functional approaches in combatives which rules out much of the fanciness which prevails in some formalized combative arts.

After these kind words for O'Neill, I have but one question. Why is it that our government has to go outside of its own countrymen to develop combatives? While O'Neill can unquestionably give us a good system [he was designing a program for the Marine Corps], I for one have more experience and a wider variety of techniques than he. Both you and I know that such as we could develop a damn functional program if our government would only support us on it. (I might even be coaxed to leave this land of the eternal smoke if I could get a good offer from Uncle.) My knowledge and skills now run from "empty-hand" to bayonet and I know I could do a good job. Too bad only foreign countries will ask me for training advice. Planned tour with Isao Inokuma [two-time All-Japan Judo champion and 1965-1966 World Judo champion] will include Thailand, Malaysia, etc. and have offers to teach combatives. Even Egypt has extended official invite to me via local ambassador!

O'Neill in background watching recruits practice his combatives.

Commenting on the letter, Donn writes that O'Neill is rokudan (6th-dan), but notes that he got godan (5th-dan) during his stay in Japan before World War II. This is not unusual – often ranks are honorifically upgraded for teaching and other services benefiting judo after one's fighting career is over. The puzzler here is that his manual, the official *U.S. Marine Corps Hand-to-Hand Combat* (manuscript draft, November, 1966), still has him 5th-dan. Perhaps O'Neill wanted to reflect only his fighting grade there.

It is true that O'Neill stuck with his boys in the Aleutians, almost to the extent of losing his life. He and a colleague paddling into Kiska against an outgoing tide never made it. The Navy picked them up the next day, drifting in the sea, so paralyzed by cold that they had to be hoisted aboard with a cargo net!

I cannot confirm that O'Neill ever studied taiji, xingyi, or bagua, the triad of Chinese internal boxing arts. Certainly twelve or thirteen years in Shanghai would have given him ample opportunity. As for Donn's complaint about the inability of the U.S. government to recognize its own resources, 'twas ever thus. Remember the esteemed Omar Khayyam saying, "I often wonder what the Vintners buy one half so precious as the stuff they sell." A stranger in his own land is always a stranger if that land is terminally afflicted by the bureaucratic imperative.

As a tall, 180-pound teenager, O'Neill left his native Ireland in 1925 for Shanghai. He joined the Municipal Police Force there and worked his way up until he became right hand man to the legendary

William Ewart Fairbairn. In his free time, following the lead of Fairbairn, he studied Chinese foot fighting and Japanese judo.

Fairbairn was O'Neill's mentor. O'Neill benefited from Fairbairn's experience and, when he took over as security chief for the British Embassy in Tokyo in 1938, he was off the mark early in his

O'Neill with mentor Fairbairn in Shanghai, 1939. O'Neill is sitting front right, and bespectacled Fairbairn is to his right.

hectic judo training at the Kodokan, achieving one of the highest ranks of any foreigner of that time.

Just before Pearl Harbor, O'Neill left Japan for Australia. In 1942 he went on to America where "Wild Bill" Donovan snatched him up for the Office of Strategic Services (OSS). What is amazing about these dates is that they suggest that he got his judo 5th-dan in less than four years. This meteoric rise – by contrast, Fairbairn took over twelve years to get 2nd-dan – was eased by the fact that O'Neill was already well along in his judo career. Training under Patrolman Yamada Shigeichi of the Japanese Consulate-General in Shanghai, he held a 3rd-dan in 1934 and may have been 4th-dan when he arrived in Japan four years later.

Be that as it may, he was a hard worker. He took on anyone and everyone following a preliminary warm-up of hundreds of deep squats and cat stretches (he probably learned these from the Sikhs in the Shanghai Municipal Police, as they are the traditional exercises of the Indian wrestler). He absolutely excelled at groundwork, said Donn, who was himself exceptional on the ground. Through this period he was averse to publicity and seldom got it.

During World War II, O'Neill left the OSS to act as a combatives expert with the U.S. Army. He served in the Aleutians, North Africa, Italy, southern France, and Okinawa. His exploits are enumerated in Robert Adelman and George Walton's *The Devil's Brigade* (1966). The book was later made into a film starring William Holden and Cliff Robertson. In the film, O'Neill is a Canadian fighting instructor who educates American renegade soldiers of a notorious U.S.-Canadian brigade in applied mayhem.

Captain O'Neill greatly impressed his charges, one of whom later said, "I killed a kraut with an O'Neill in the nuts." In Helena, Montana, the miners were spending their off-time hours beating up on the soldiers, especially the Canadians. Soon after O'Neill's arrival, the soldiers began whipping the miners – and the police. When the unit moved to Norfolk, Virginia, one of his men bet a Marine from a local detachment that he could take his bayonet away from him, and did, making five dollars in the process. Soon, all of O'Neill's boys were doing it. When "Wild Bill" Donovan tried to get O'Neill to come back to the OSS, he refused (doubtless he preferred having carte blanche with the First Special Service Force to serving under others). When the First Special Service Force was disbanded in Italy in December,

1944, O'Neill became Provost Marshal of Monte Carlo, then joined the advance party of the Allied occupation government of Japan.

After the war, O'Neill was a consultant in combatives for the State Department. He was posted to Florida for most of the time, until the mid-1960's when he retired and moved to the Washington, D.C. area. In retirement, he continued working part-time for several years.

During the 1960's, O'Neill taught his idiosyncratic method of hand-to-hand combat to Marines stationed at Quantico, Virginia. A judo student of mine was one of the senior instructors trained in his methods. From this student's description and the draft copy of *Hand-to-Hand Combat*, I was able to get a good idea of what the course involved.

The troops trained in mass formation on open ground. And trained quickly. Quoting from the manual's promise:

> The O'Neill system was easy to teach and simple to learn. There were no complicated movements which would be easily forgotten. Size and weight were immaterial. Flexibility, speed, and knowledge were important. Later, in combat, when this type of fighting was conducted by well-trained troops, it turned into a vicious form of hand-to-hand combat for which the opponents had no practiced defense. When combined with weapons, it was unbeatable in close-quarter combat. Every man was taught to be extremely dangerous, armed or unarmed.

Given the requirement to train large numbers of troops in the shortest possible time without severely injuring them, the system was only fair. My overall objection was that O'Neill's tactics were generally double-weighted, that is, the body weight was evenly distributed on both feet. This requires too much time in shifting and thus is inefficient. Watching a three-hour demonstration of the system by a top instructor, I was surprised and dismayed by its defects.

Reading *Hand-to-Hand Combat*, my concern grew. The most commendable aspect was O'Neill's use of the deep squat (*baitak*) and the cat-stretch (*dand*) directly from Indian wrestling as warm-ups. No set number of repetitions was suggested (this being left to the discretion of the instructor), but knowing the gung-ho Marines it was bound to be ample – though never at the level of Gama's 2,000 each a day.

The manual then goes downhill. In some of the tactics throughout there is a tendency to depend on diverting the enemy, much like a cheap Western. But in war, diversion comes hard and often doesn't come at all. Continuing, we are taught the on-guard posture showing the enemy a smaller profile by turning your side to him. The posture would be better if the front foot took forty percent and the rear sixty percent of the weight. The good points: elbows down and active use of shouting are mandated.

From this basic posture, the high and low parries are good. But against a rear bear hug over your arms, raising your arms to break his hold (A) will, in most case, go against his strength and leave him in position to strangle you. It is much easier to sink, turn, and use a fist to the groin or elbow to the solar plexus (B.)

The kicks also are awkward "spot-strikes" in which you simply kick with no control of his body (C). One longs to see a good old-fashioned knee or foot to the groin. The book has none. As shown in the photographs, the kicks used in bayonet fighting seem risky but technically feasible and useful. But, here again, the stance is double-weighted.

The sections on falling (using the basic judo chugairi, or shoulder roll) and "guard on the deck" (ground) are all right, but O'Neill should have warned the recruit to stay standing if possible and, if he goes down, to get back up again as quickly as possible.

Against rear bear-hug, don't go upward fighting
his strength and opening yourself to strangle (A).
Instead, bend your knees, turn and fist to his groin (B).

O'Neill's kick was merely a "spot-strike" (C):
his guard hands should have been intercepting.

Surprisingly, for a man of O'Neill's judo experience, his basic takedown is woefully inept. You kick the back of the enemy's knee, using only one hand on him, the other hanging uselessly (D). This is too loose, too long, and too slow. Even if it succeeds, it spills him onto the ground where you still have to follow and get a choke on him. Wrong! Put the choke on immediately, jerk him backward onto his butt and be done with the foul business (E and F).

Likewise, his defense against a club is chancy and built on questionable logic. True, as O'Neill writes, your leg is longer than his club (F), but only in the most structured, unreal, case: if both of you stand with feet on a line. In the real world, such theory doesn't put any butter on the spinach. First, he can still reach your body, if not your head, with the club (G). And if he takes his foot forward, all bets are off.

O'Neill's takedown into choke is too loose: both hands should be used or you lose contact on takedown (D).

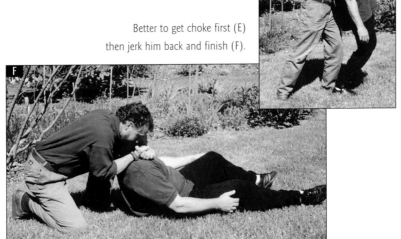

Better to get choke first (E) then jerk him back and finish (F).

O'Neill's defense against a club is awry. Your leg may reach further than the club if an attacker doesn't move his feet and only strikes toward your head (G and H). Better to step in, deflect, and attack (I).

Belabored by the blizzard of his blows as he advances, it would be stretching it to believe that even an expert karateka could stop the attacker with kicks. A general rule: bet the weapon. Your best bet is to counter by mobility, moving into and intercepting the club or club hand. Use your feet to move – your two can beat his one – and let your arms and body do the work (I).

All this ineptitude recalls a policeman student of mine years ago. This one was an exceptional wrestler whom I could lock and choke but not pin. Each week, at the end of practice, I'd teach him a new come-along. And he'd come back the next, telling how well it had worked in the mean streets of Washington, D.C. I'd ask him to show me the tactic he used. Proudly, he would do so. And every time he had it wrong. But it still worked! If he hadn't been so strong, however, he couldn't have locked the downtown thugs (now they call such cretins "urban warriors") and walked them a mile to the precinct house. The incident shows that everything works some of the time. Rudyard Kipling was cognizant of this phenomenon, "There are a hundred and one tribal stories and every one of them is right!"

The French have an expression, "The most beautiful woman can't give you any more than she has." O'Neill's system, as limned in *Hand-to-Hand Combat*, turned out to be only a tool for recruit training. It was probably designed to increase recruits' aggressiveness and confidence and to desensitize them to violence. The Army's current *Combatives* (Field Manual 21-150, Headquarters, Department of the Army, Washington D.C., September 1992), while flawed, is far superior to O'Neill's system in every area. Thus, O'Neill's Marine combatives system was short-lived. The Fleet Marine Force never accepted it, and during the 1980's another system with a more pronounced karate/grappling/striking system replaced it.

I never met O'Neill, though unbeknownst to me, he lived in my old neighborhood in Bethesda and died (August 11, 1985, aged eighty) at a hospital near my home. If I had known, I would have visited him and perhaps helped him in his last years. I may not have solaced him much, but I would have benefited greatly by learning more about the life of this reclusive, fascinating person.

The Legendary Fairbairn

W.E. Fairbairn,
first in the field, shows
excellent firing position with
a submachine gun. Note
similarities with front loaded,
cross-energy taiji posture
"Bow Step."

Captain William Ewart Fairbairn, with sobriquets like "Fearless Dan" and "The Shanghai Buster," was Sergeant O'Neill's boss in the Shanghai Municipal Police. Fairbairn had been with the Shanghai police since 1907, some seventeen years before young O'Neill came aboard. It was said that Shanghai in those years was so evil that is was impossible for a normal person to sin there. One evening, in leaving the red-light district (some critics say all of Shanghai was a red-light district), young Fairbairn was so beaten up that he awoke the next day in the hospital with a clipping advertising jujutsu instruction placed near him. He took the hint and started jujutsu training under Okada sensei. He also studied Chinese boxing under Cai

Jingdong. I've not been able to learn anything of Cai, though Fairbairn claims he was an instructor at the Imperial Palace. In judo, Fairbairn was graded shodan (1st-dan) in 1926 and nidan (2nd-dan) in 1931, and visited the Kodokan in Tokyo where he practiced with J. Kano's second-in-command, Y. Yamashita.

Fairbairn's first book, *Defendu, Scientific Self-Defence*, was published by the North China Daily News and Herald Ltd. in 1925. It was republished as *Scientific Self-Defence* in 1931. This edition contained a new note on page viii that said author Fairbairn had studied under Cai Jingdong. Fairbairn published three additional books in 1942. These were *Get Tough; Hands Off! Self-Defence for Women;* and *All-In Fighting.* The latter was a synthesis of his previous books. (See my bibliography in *A Complete Guide to Judo: Its Story and Practice, 1958.*)

I had several, perhaps all, of these books at one time. Although they have slipped away since, I recall well their practical aspect. I never met the man though I would have given my other shirt to do so. Reportedly, he was sardonic, humorless, and long on ego, but also long on expertise in weapons and unarmed violence.

After his retirement in 1940, he went to work for the Special Operations Executive (SOE – the British dirty tricks force in World War II). In a short time, the tradecraft in combat pistol and unarmed close combat of this organization and the American OSS were based on his teachings. The knife work, meanwhile, was built around the Fairbairn-Sykes double-edged dagger (Eric A. Sykes had worked with Fairbairn in Shanghai). Until 1942, Fairbairn was head honcho of these courses taught in the SOE schools in Scotland.

The Fairbairn-Sykes fighting knife.

In 1942, SOE established "Camp X" on the north shore of Lake Ontario in Canada. Its purpose was to teach American recruits of the Coordinator of Information (COI), which was shortly to become the Office of Strategic Services (OSS). Fairbairn was part of the original faculty of this school. He didn't hit it off with his British bosses and after only a few weeks, the SOE transferred him to "Area B" in Catoctin, Maryland (near what is now the presidential retreat at Camp David). While some recruits at Camp X recalled Fairbairn's explanations of killing methods as too long, too complicated, and too hard to remember, those trained in Maryland found him, despite being in his late fifties, perfect for his role. One recruit remembered that he had an honest dislike of anything that smacked of decency in fighting.

While in Taiwan, I sometimes shepherded VIPs from CIA headquarters. My most memorable group included the late Sherman Kent and two other top aides to the Director of Central Intelligence. After a meal one evening, my boss mentioned to the group my interest in the martial arts. Then everyone sat up. All these men had trained under Major Fairbairn in the OSS. All regarded him as a god. So I got two hours of their memories of him. We went around and back and forth. I asked one if he could remember any of the actual tactics he learned from Fairbairn. "No," he said, looking back twenty years, "All I can remember was the chief one – kick them in the crotch!" Another thought Fairbairn fair on the unarmed stuff but "absolutely overwhelming" at point-shooting with a gun or using a knife. I think it was Kent – the ex-Yale professor, erudite, one of God's own gentlemen, but who on occasion could out-cuss any man living – who got up, took out a newspaper, and demonstrated how Fairbairn would turn this innocuous paper by quick folding into a hard concentrated weapon with sharp creased corners that, in a pinch, could be used to injure or maim.

As a sidebar to this, Richard Helms, later Director of Central Intelligence, trained under Fairbairn in the Maryland mountains. He said that Fairbairn's favorite method for dealing with a hysterical woman was to: (1) grab her lower lip, and if fear of disfigurement didn't stop her, then (2) slap her in the face. This is curious and somewhat offensive. When would you use it? Why? Wouldn't she be able to bite your hand? Is this for enemy women only or our hysterical ones too?

Now away from hagiography, how good, really, were Fairbairn and his system? For this evaluation I rely on three of his books and the film, OSS Training Group, made by the Field Photographic Unit of the Office of Strategic Services and directed by Commander John Ford in 1942. Ford (The Grapes of Wrath, Stagecoach and other fine films) was a Hollywood giant who uncharacteristically downplayed his art, "It was just a job of work, nothing more."

The unarmed combat in the film starts with a little guy preventing a larger one from lifting him by applying nerve pressure on his lower jaw. I don't see the use for this. The enemy wants to kill you, not pick you up. I can, however, tell you a better way of preventing this lift. Simply drop one leg a short step backward while merely touching his

Fairbairn's vaunted chin clamp and knee-to-groin combination won't work unless you hold him with your left hand – he'll simply step back out of it.

left carotid with your right fingers. A lagniappe would be to simultaneously hold his right wrist pulse with your left hand. This is how Johnny Coulon, the former fly-weight boxing champ, at age 65 and under 100 pounds, could prevent any man in the house from picking him up. He used to travel to amateur boxing venues when I was training boxers and charge $100 an exhibition. No one could ever pick him up frontally, but Draeger told me that he heard that someone once snuck up on him from the rear, hoisted him, and ran around with him kicking the air and screaming bloody murder.

Given the need to teach simple effective tactics quickly, Fairbairn's system barely passes muster. Believing, properly, that it would take too long to train a man to a boxer's proficiency with fists, he felt that the edge of the hand chop and chin jab could be learned quicker and be just as lethal in combat. True, he often exaggerated the effect of these strikes, saying about the chop that, if the opponent grabbed you, counter by striking his wrist or forearm, as a fracture would likely result (it isn't that easy of course – but remember this was wartime). He "spot-strikes," that is, he strikes without using the other hand to pull or control the target to ensure that the strike will land on target. But many fighting forms, particularly karate, neglect this control feature even now.

Like others of that era, Fairbairn advocates shin scrapes by one's boot against the inner side of an opponent's leg. It's chancy: he has to stand still for it and if he does and is wearing boots, it doesn't hurt him that much. Ditto stepping on his booted foot – it won't hurt him and will unbalance you. He does his chin clamp/knee-to-groin combination fluently, but it lacks potency because his left hand does nothing. It is another example of spot-striking. For the tactic to work, his left hand must hold or control the enemy's right arm or shoulder (using both hands and a knee, you then have the same function as the taiji "Rooster" posture as shown above [A]).

Three awful tactics should be noted and given a wide berth. In one, Fairbairn goofs by having an enemy strangle you with one hand

THE THREE AWFULS

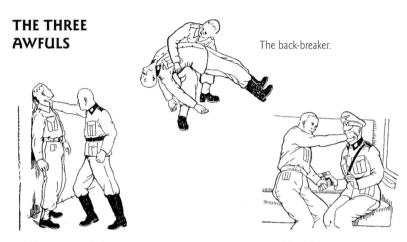

The back-breaker.

The one-arm choke.

Match box versus gun.

against a wall. For a trick to be credible, the initial attack must mean something. The one-armed choke doesn't. A frontal two-hand choke is hard enough – because of your vulnerability – but a one-hand strangle is impossible. Any old release will work here.

Even more ludicrous is his back break in which he bodily picks up an enemy, and then smashes him down against a waiting knee, commenting, "He cannot prevent you from breaking his spine." Crazier still, he later clenches his fist on a matchbox and knocks out the German who has a gun pointing at him, adding, "The odds of knocking your opponent unconscious by this method are at least two to one." How did he arrive at those odds, and why did he call the German an opponent? He is not an opponent: he is the enemy who will kill you with his gun if you ever try such an asinine thing!

The releases from the bear hug are spotty. Here, as in some other tactics, he overly relies on grabbing the testicles. This is sometimes difficult to do, and if you're in a good position to do it, you're probably also in a good position to use a more lethal technique.

Grabbing or even striking the genitals isn't as disabling as most people believe. During a major contest, judo champion Toshiro Daigo was once hit by an errant but powerful uchimata (inner thigh throw). Things ballooned afterward in the dressing room, but he was able to go out for the next bout and beat his man. I'm not saying that it's pleasant – only that it's survivable. Bill Paul and I used to argue the point, he thinking it not a particularly disabling strike. He kept offering to let me have a free whack at it but never quite found a good time for it.

Fairbairn's "hip throw"
takes too much strength (A).
A better choice: judo o-soto-gari (big outer reap)
with chin/spine articulation (B-C). The Grapevine:
A man's own weight secures him without a rope (D).

When the enemy has a front bear hug, Fairbairn advises you to grab his testicles. Wrong! Kneeing him is better. And if he gets a rear bear hug over your arms don't grab his testicles – you don't have adequate leverage or torque for this – use your open hand or fist, and guided by your buttock, glide it into his groin as you turn your waist. Or, you could raise your heel in a backward kick. Both are better than grabbing his testicles. Fairbairn might argue that the groin grab would make the enemy let go. Yes, and so you'd have to do something else – the cardinal principle in combat fighting is to make each tactic a killing one – while he's still behind you beating your brains out with his helmet.

The so-called "hip throw" Fairbairn espoused is unworkable against anyone of any strength. It goes against the two big considerations of self-defense: it takes too long and uses too much space. It is not properly even a hip throw – which in judo goes to the front. Here, Fairbairn would have been better served to use o-soto-gari against only one leg to the rear. That he did not puts his judo credentials in question.

A knowledgeable friend of mine used to laugh at some of Fairbairn's methods, remarking that with instruction like that it is a wonder the Allies won World War II! But we mustn't be too hard on Fairbairn. His good tactics included "the grapevine" – securing a man without rope around a pole by the force of his own weight – and his weapons work. The latter looks innovative and useful.

Let me simply record my notes of the OSS film cited above (p. 154). The masked instructor was obviously Fairbairn and the resonant voice sounds just as I thought he should sound. In offensive pistol shooting using a Government .45, the goal was to drop an enemy from a distance of up to 25 yards. One firing position with a pistol was like the taiji "Bow Step," your left leg anchoring most of the weight forward and, with cross-energy, the right hand fires. Fairbairn stressed safety throughout the session. An excellent touch was when he assembled his small group of operatives and fired several rounds over and to the sides of them, then making the point that it's easy to fire when no one is shooting at you.

On the live grenade toss, Fairbairn said that the small box target was seventy yards distant. It looked more like forty. He also said that throwing a grenade was like a shot put, but with more wrist action. Instead, it looked more like a baseball toss. The target was obliterated on the first and only try. Call me irresistibly skeptical, but I don't believe it. Like most things blurbed as too good to be true, it seemed to be exactly that. The target may have been detonated by some other agency than the grenade itself. There was too little bayonet work in the book (quite good) to judge a system by, but the knife fighting instruction for that period seemed top-drawer.

So much for his books and films. How did this stuff work off the page? Samuel Yeaton, a student of Fairbairn, wrote the following letter from Shanghai to his brother Charles on January 24, 1933. I've added numbers to the paragraphs so that I can respond to Sam's statements in detail.

❶ This man Fairbairn is beyond the shadow of a doubt the greatest of them all. I've had about twelve hours of conferences with him and done a couple of hours on the mats. His stuff is not jujutsu or judo – he gave us an exhibition of judo using five men, two third-degree black belts, two second-degree, and one first-degree, to prove it. He uses some of their falls and a few holds, but not over about twenty percent of it and most of it with variations. It's not Chinese boxing of which eighty percent is pure ritual. It's a collection of all the known methods of dirty fighting and it will beat them all. He knows it will. He's done it. Judo is too clean, he pointed out to us as we, with so little time as we've had, could beat a third-degree man and that's about the toughest working degree, when they get beyond that they get too old and slow up. Here's the dope: on every hold a judo man's eyes and testicles are vulnerable. But it is awful fast. Still it is not as fast as boxing. We proved that and to the Japs at that. Given men of equal speed, it's the one who is not surprised by the other's method of attack who will win. We put Sam T., who boxes featherweight now, against a third-degree judo man – the punches not to be delivered and the throws not to be carried out – and it was a draw, assuming both men stuck to their own rules. But we had a man hold his hand up and Sam put a one-two on it while the man stood beside the hand and tried to grab his hands. All they got was his necktie.

❷ So much for that. Fairbairn says that the average Jap soldier knows an amount of judo corresponding to the amount of boxing the average British or American soldier knows and he figures that the British and American would win on weight and elasticity of intellect. I believe he knows, I haven't caught him wrong yet.

❸ [Samuel writes that he will send Charles a copy of Fairbairn's book, and describes one trick not in the book, which ends with a knee in the opponent's face.] He uses that knee in the face for a lot of things. Just catch his head, hair, or the back of his neck (the same as in referee's hold in wrestling), pull down and jump up, and bang! They have even used it to dismount horsemen, and when I say used, I don't mean thought of its possibilities, I mean used.

❹ He [Fairbairn] says "I believe that a man who knows my stuff can beat any wrestler, boxer, or judo man because he knows their best stuff and everything that's dirty besides." I believe he's right. [Samuel then describes another tactic, a wrist throw.]

❺ When I come home I'll be set to beat hell out of anybody. He's promised to teach us all he knows, including practical gun fighting and last year's score was about like this, for armed conflict:

	Police	Criminals
Total Hits	700	8
Killed	150	3

One year they shot well over a thousand criminals, but the hunting is bad. Shanghai is getting shot out. I believe they are thinking of having a closed season next fall.

❻ The remarkable thing about Fairbairn is that although he damned near does know it all, he doesn't seem to think he does. If you've got an idea, he'll not only listen to your idea and point out what's wrong, if anything, but he'll admit it's new to him and that it's as good or better than the one he uses in the same spot.

❼ And how did he like Oscar [a cut-down revolver]? I took him down one and showed him and twenty-four hours later he showed me Oscar's big brother: a .45 New Service Colt, complete except for reblueing and putting the sight on what was left of the barrel, and he's got the gun and holster for copying the fit and hang of the thing. Well, it's quarter of two tomorrow and I couldn't get half the stuff I've got to tell you down tonight so, ...

Good night,
Sam

I comment on the numbered paragraphs as follows:

① Sam is young, impressed, and impressionable. Who are these black belts, two of whom are 3rd-dans, hence probably superior to Fairbairn who was only 2nd-dan at the time? Fairbairn tells Sam and the other students that they can beat a third-degree judo man. Beat them at what? Certainly not judo, when Fairbairn himself couldn't. And not wrestling, either: Karl Pojello was unconscious one minute, twenty seconds after meeting Mas Tamura, a third-degree man. No, he means beat them with Fairbairn's Defendu dirty tricks. This system, Fairbairn tells Sam, only uses twenty percent of judo and that modified. Fairbairn's claims suggest to me that his judo was not of a high order, despite his 2nd-dan.

Fairbairn adds that Chinese boxing is eighty percent ritual. Thus, presumably, it was of little use in his method. This tells me that his study of Chinese boxing did not yield him much. The "eighty percent ritual" I take to mean he studied a little taiji or other kata and didn't have a good teacher or, if he did, the teacher had a poor student. Yang Chengfu's school was going great guns in Shanghai just then and it's a pity that Fairbairn didn't meet him.

Sam's paragraph, though it talks of proof, gives none. It is simply broadcasting what Fairbairn claims, not what his students saw him do. There is one actual test – judo vs. boxer – but it was a draw, as it was bound to be when neither was permitted to fully use his own stuff. Nor should failing to catch a boxer's strike cast a stigma. Boxers themselves can't do it with gloves off – often they can't even block it with gloves on.

② Fairbairn is correct in asserting that the average Japanese knows about as much judo as the average American or Briton knows about boxing. And weight would be on the side of the American or Briton. But what is this "elasticity of intellect" favoring the American or Briton? Japan has universities, too; not to mention a warrior institution second to none.

③ The knee in the face technique, Sam says, has even been used to dismount horsemen! Pray, show me the photograph. Donn Draeger told me once that the absurd karate high kick originated in Japan by samurai, you guessed it, who used it to knock enemies out of their saddles.

④ Here is the heart of Fairbairn's claim: his boys will win because they also know each of these other things (wrestling, boxing, and judo), plus the dirty stuff they've mastered. This is utter nonsense. I would put my money on the skilled fighter any day. These boys that work to a system would make quick work of the junior Fairbairns. Face it: even if their killing punches and kicks were as effective as the teacher thought, how would they bring them off against veteran fighters?

The trouble with Fairbairn's system is that it is not a system. It is simply a series of attacks met by structured responses. In teaching with a time restraint, I agree, it is the only way. You don't have time to learn wrestling, boxing, and judo. Fairbairn was stuck with this fact and he simply put the best face on it by heroic hyperbole.

⑤ Throwing guns and knives into the mix changes everything. Regardless of how competent Fairbairn himself was with weapons, anyone with a gun or knife probably would defeat any wrestler, boxer, or judoka who faced them. I think Fairbairn unconsciously used such robust hyperbole because he was factoring in the weapon.

⑥ It all boils down to this: can green troops quickly trained in dirty fighting beat competent wrestlers, boxers, and judoka? I doubt it. Fairbairn conceived his student in the context of a combat zone with weapons available and concluded he was superior. He should turn his proposition point four around: why can't a wrestler, boxer, or judoka use their regulated skills plus dirty stuff also? Believe me, they know fouls that even Fairbairn had never dreamed of. That's the clincher. They will fight as dirty as Fairbairn's boys. Enough said.

I used to use the term "knife and gunner" for Fairbairn, O'Neill, and other golden oldies teaching and writing in the unarmed defense field. For such men as Rex Applegate (*Kill or Get Killed*, 1943), Colonel Anthony Drexel Biddle (*Do or Die*, 1937), and S. J. Jorgenson (*Thirty-Six Secret Knockout Blows without the Use of Fists*, 1930), the term seemed appropriate because their spotty unarmed tactics were compensated by a presumed prowess with a weapon. Although all were competent mixing unarmed skills with weapons, none of these "knife and gunners" could hold a candle in the unarmed arena to James Pilkington. All Pilkington did was win the national amateur heavyweight boxing championship and the national heavyweight wrestling crown in the old Madison Square Garden in the same ring on the same night in 1922 (John Kieran, *Not Under Oath*, 1964).

The quality of both armed and unarmed instruction has evolved greatly since the 1940's, and even considerably since the 1970's. For instance, the *U.S. Army's Combatives* (FM 21-150, September 30, 1992) is considerably superior to the work of the old knife and gunners, as are any number of self-defense books published since then. One of my favorites is M. Kawaishi's *My Method of Self-Defence* (1957), translated by E.J. Harrison. Ironically, this was during a period when, because of technological advances, improved weapons loomed even larger in the armed/unarmed equation.

On balance, Fairbairn was a resourceful pioneer. He was practical and tried to avoid the mumbo-jumbo. We should honor him for experimenting, innovating, and sharing his insights.

A Pause

In 1959 I was transferred to Taiwan for my work with the CIA. This presented a unique opportunity to see, feel, and learn Chinese combatives first-hand. I was to put judo on the back burner and give all my attention and energy to this new enterprise. "Jimmy's got a new goil" was the way poet e.e. cummings expressed it.

Taiwan:
A Martial Watershed

In the summer of 1959, the CIA posted me to Taiwan where I remained for more than three years. This was to be a watershed event in my life. I had heard and read and written about Chinese boxing for years and here suddenly was Taiwan chock-full of every variety hard and soft. I was determined to test Donn Draeger's contention that traditionally the Japanese had a paucity of unarmed fighting methods. And Donn said, "The Chinese had an ocean, the Japanese a lake." Ever pragmatic, the Japanese put their priority on weaponry.

My segue into Chinese boxing was made through Anderson Lin (then 4th-dan), Taiwan heavyweight judo champion in 1958 and runner-up in 1959 and 1960. Anderson was an amiable gent, in love with judo, and we had some great skirmishes. I worked out with Anderson of the round belly and marvelous smile that first night in an atmosphere much different from Tokyo. Here the summer climate was killing, and vigorous randori required more frequent rests than there. Ben Campbell, U.S. heavyweight champion, visited me once and the pair of us had a two-hour session with fifteen of Taiwan's best judokas. Going in, I told Ben that he would find his breath cut and not to be afraid of resting – it was a fact of the tropics. Ben scoffed but soon enough found he had to stop and rest in the searing heat.

Back to Anderson Lin, one of the finest gentlemen I ever met in a sport supposed to be long on such but which, in practice, often missed this ideal. Curious Chinese and Taiwanese crowded around the mat to watch the *waiguo ren* (foreigner) get his. And it looked like he would get it sooner than even he expected. Within thirty seconds of taking hold Anderson threw me with a splendid *hane-goshi* (spring hip throw). After that it got easier for me, and Anderson made do with stumbling me a bit. Later, I spilled him with o-soto-gari (large outer reap), but not cleanly. Then we were through. Later Anderson took me to his teacher, a 7th-dan in his mid-forties surnamed Huang, I think. Alas I've lost his name and he was by far the best judoka on Taiwan! This ace had lived and trained with the Toshiro Daigo crew in Tokyo a decade or so earlier and his skill reeked of it. He had an elegant touch but lacked versatility. He threw me with a left tai-otoshi (body drop) over and over again. Wherever I moved, whatever I tried, there came that damned tai-otoshi from the port side. To this day I don't know how he did it. I may have forgotten his name but never his technique.

In the sweat afterwards Anderson was anxious that we work out regularly together, but I told him I was more interested in learning something about Chinese boxing. He told me of Hong Yixiang and his judo/boxing friend Chen Meisi, and took me to them.

My first impression was disappointing. Hong Yixiang was overweight, unshaven, and had a cigarette dangling from his lips. But he brought me over the first time he fetched me up a blow on my shoulder; satori-like I immediately understood chaos theory.

I continued practicing judo with Anderson Lin for a time, but dropped away when I began to find other boxing teachers, the "monkey boxer" Liao Wuchang being next up. At first my teachers were Shaolin hard-school Taiwanese types, though Hong was expert in both hard and soft – also called the external and internal. I soon breached the mainlander boxing elite who came with gifts not for a Magi, but for an American. Their biggest prize was the soft triad of taiji, xingyi, and bagua.

I've detailed my encounter with these wonderful men in *Chinese Boxing: Masters and Methods* (1974) and don't want to repeat that. Its table of contents alone shows the coverage:

1. The Not-So-Little Elephant [Hong Yixiang],
2. The Monkey Boxer [Liao Wuchang],
3. The Guerrilla General [Yuan Dao],
4. Master of the Five Excellences [Zheng Manqing],
5. Master of Relaxation [Wang Yannian],
6. A Policeman's Bagua [Paul Guo],
7. Bonelocker Extraordinary [Han Qingtang],
8. The Wrestling Champion [Shang Dongsheng], and
9. Other Teachers.

A mere listing doesn't catch their essence and variety as fighters or their goodness as humans.

Liao Wuchang,
the marvelous Monkey Boxer.

Most of my teachers never charged me a farthing. To a man they would say, "This is for friendship." Among themselves, they swapped techniques as if they were money. Money per se never came up. Wan Laisheng mentions this sharing as a common feature of Chinese boxing a couple generations earlier (*The Essential Focus of the Chinese Martial Arts*, Beijing, 1929).

I revisited some of these boxers in films and old notes and will return to others later in these pages. There's a surprising freshness in them and even some nuances and insights missed before. As I said above, they changed the direction of my life from judo (though I continued teaching it until 1972) to the more sophisticated Chinese boxing. For the first year in Taiwan, Shaolin held sway, but as I dug deeper into the soft arts – xingyi, bagua, and especially taiji – the internal took over and I never stopped learning. Below I reprise some of the masters covered in *Masters and Methods*.

Hong Yixiang

Hong Yixiang.

Through judoka Anderson Lin I met Hong Yixiang who, in turn, introduced me to the wonderful world of Chinese boxing. I've described this worthy in *Masters and Methods* and elsewhere since I left Taiwan in 1962. He died in 1993 but I was able to have a good visit with him in 1983 when Alice and I traveled with Ben Lo's taiji push-hands team to Taiwan and Southeast Asia.

On that occasion, Hong and his older brother, Yimian, and family greeted us. Danny Emerick was with our group. We went to their home in downtown Taipei, and it was like old times, each brother vying to see who could make me say "Uncle" first, Yixiang's wife mediating the skirmishes. We were no sooner seated eating orange sections when without provocation (who would provoke him?) or much preliminary, Yixiang struck me with one big finger in the forehead, bringing a liquid river from my right eye. Looking at his big smile with my left eye, I asked, "Would you like to meet my wife?"

Yixiang's ability to isolate tear seepage from my one eye seemed to enrage his older brother Yimian, and he grabbed me and began a clinic on short stabs to foreign chests. And so it went. I seldom complimented a tactic of the two, sometimes even saying I didn't think it would work, and of course this only increased the intensity of the frenzy. I'd had masochistic fun with this tactic in the old days, and it still worked.

But it wasn't all pull-punch-push. We talked a lot. I told Yixiang that I'd heard he was now a great master like 50,000 Americans and he smiled. He admitted to having several thousand students. I asked if he had any good foreign ones. He waved his burly right arm dismissively. "I've had many foreigners," he said, "but never another one like you!" How come? "They don't want to work at it." Since Hong was always more direct and sincere than polite, I took this as a compliment. He also volunteered that I was the bagua fifth generation successor to the great Yin Fu (who had learned from founder Dong Haichuan), the lineage passing down through Gao Yisheng to Zhang Junfeng to Hong Yixiang to myself. As we took our leave, he invited me to a demonstration at his studio the following day and I accepted.

The next day, however, the many banquets caught up with me and I was flat on my back with an errant stomach. I urged the two top members of our taiji team, which had been prevailing over Chinese teams,

Author separating Hong Yimian on his right and younger brother Yixiang on left—they often needed separating. Yimian's forte was an arpeggio of open and closed hands, elbows, and feet – three hyenas closing in for the kill. Yixiang favored power punches, shoulder, and head – a bull elephant in musth (1983).

to substitute for me. Our heavyweight had already gone into the parks and thrown a Chinese teacher or two. One was nicknamed Xiao Xiong ("Little Bear"). Little Bear, with many of his students watching, sagged like a wet rag every time the big American tried to set him up for a push. It so frustrated him that he finally picked the smaller, older man up with what probably was a near *kata-guruma* (shoulder wheel) and tossed him. When he told me about this, I berated him for breaking Little Bear's rice bowl but he shook his head, "Bob, you had to have been there."

So, as sandbaggery, I suggested that these two substitute for me, and see a good show. The big one, worst luck, was doubtful, wanting to know about Hong. I told him Hong was a sentimental old man who'd first taught me Shaolin and the internal arts in the old days, that we'd visited the day before and that the clinic was in my honor. He didn't trust me, hesitated, and said he'd check Hong out. A half-hour later he phoned and said he felt sick, which meant this confident taiji expert had talked to the wrong person and would never fall afoul of Hong and his brutality. Nice try but no cigar. There was nothing for it but to call Hong and sincerely beg off. Sandbaggery hadn't worked.

At the hotel nursing my belly, I had time to think of Hong in the old days. At 5'7" and 220 pounds, he got every ounce of his body into his strikes. His toes were like spikes and he kicked as well with them as with the ball of his foot. His hands were worse, huge and misshapen. He was often hard put to pull his punches and once knocked me senseless with a chop to the base of my skull. To demonstrate hundreds of punches, he usually focused on my shoulder. He kindly told me that he had to do this so I could feel the power but that it was safe because the shoulder was the part of the body most impervious to injury. I've had bursitis in my shoulders ever since. Would I do it again? Yes.

An Asian friend and later a Chinese gongfu magazine, gave interesting particulars on Hong Yixiang's visit to the First World Congress of Karate held in Tokyo in 1969. One of his American students has translated the article from which I draw. His and my interpolations are in parentheses. Hong and two other top boxers from Taiwan were invited. The first, a Shaolin boxer, got a cool reception. After that, a taiji practitioner took the stage. Slowly and softly he moved through a long form, losing the audience's attention. They began to talk, open soda cans and drink, and generally raise a commotion. The audience was restless when Hong took the stage.

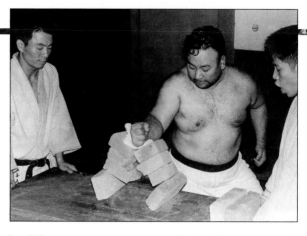

Hong breaks
three bricks.

Hong took off his gi top, got into a stake-hold posture, and did a breathing meditation for the crowd. His hairy and massively muscled, somewhat porcine body, relaxed and undulating with controlled breathing, deeply impressed and silenced the crowd. Then he did the *xingyi lian huan quan* ("connecting fist") form. He exhibited soft and hard, round and straight so that the audience could see both at once. They began to clap. Hong attempted to leave the stage but the chief consul of Taiwan in Japan encouraged him to do some more. Hong then performed more xingyi and possibly some bagua, ending to thundering applause.

Four Japanese *budoka* (martial experts) then approached the stage and said, "Hong Sensei, what you have just performed doesn't look bad, but does it have utility?" Hong had lived in Taiwan under the Japanese occupation, and had even been conscripted into the Japanese Navy and made to train in judo and kendo. He knew the Japanese quite well. So he told the four, "What you just saw was the tip of the iceberg. You haven't seen the essence of Chinese martial arts yet."

The four challengers then insisted on a lesson.

Hong agreed. The first man came forward saying that he wanted a free-fight. (Hong's training always stressed free-fighting, which he believed built intelligent reactions and lively, effective hands and feet.) Hong hit his first opponent with direct power and the man could not continue.

The audience was struck silent and awaited the next challenger. Again, Hong took his opponent out so fast that the audience didn't know what happened. The challenger asked, "Hong sensei, your technique was too fast; can you repeat it so we can see why or how I was struck by one palm?"

Again Hong shot out his fist. This time it was empty. (Hong often said, "If there is a bridge, take it; if there is no bridge, build it. Before people can fight there must be some contact. This contact is the bridge called opportunity. If you feign giving the opportunity to an opponent, it is called 'building a bridge.' If you take the opportunity given you by an opponent, it is called 'taking the bridge.'") Hong built a bridge. If the Japanese did not defend against the bridge, the fake attack would become a real one.

The Japanese defended and counterattacked. Seizing the opportunity, Hong took the bridge (that is, borrowed the energy of the oncoming attack) and struck with force. The opponent limped unsteadily and knelt down. The audience was dumbfounded.

The second challenger stood and said to Hong, "Hong Sensei, I'm defeated. But I am still not clear. Why have I been defeated? Can you show me slowly how I lost?"

Hong told him that Japanese arts like judo, karate, and aikido originated in China, and that the Chinese gave the Japanese only half the art. Compare a simple technique. The Japanese will practice in "one way" against one target. It is either an attack or a defensive maneuver. But when the Chinese use an attack, it can become a defense; or a defending hand can become an attacking hand – even attacking and defending with the same hand at the same time.

To show the difference, Hong demonstrated slowly for the second challenger. He faked a head attack and his opponent responded with a rising block. (As before, the Japanese response was single-directional and single-targeted. In defending, it could not attack; in attacking, it could not defend. All the energy was expended in the fist rising to defend; all other areas became vulnerable to attack.) Hong used his opponent's weak points, striking his stomach from an unimaginable angle. His opponent reacted by pressing down on Hong's hand. Hong took the bridge and used his opponent's power to strike him in the temple.

The audience was struck silent as the third challenger, carrying a bo (quarterstaff), came onto the stage. Bigger than Hong, he took his position in a horse stance holding the bo with his arms locked straight down, the staff's tip angled slightly up toward Hong. If he held this posture, he asked, could Hong knock the bo out of his hands with his own bo? Hong took a staff and cracked down smartly on the opponent's bo, numbing his hands. Almost simultaneously he circled the tip of his own bo, then snapped it upwards, knocking the bo from his opponent's hands. Again, this was followed by much applause.

Then the fourth challenger took the stage with a shiny *katana* (sword). Hong eyed it, apologized for having not brought his own sword, and said he'd use his bo. The Japanese raised his sword over his head and when Hong remained motionless, the challenger urged him to get ready. Hong didn't move. The Japanese kept warning him but Hong still didn't move. Suddenly, the Japanese realized in fright that the tip of Hong's bo, which had been directed at his eyes, was now aligned to his throat. Whereupon the swordsman aborted his attack and dropped to his knees in great respect – an instance of psychological rather than merely physical technique.

The upshot was that the Japanese hosts who had quartered Hong in a third-rate hotel moved him to elite lodgings and arranged for him to teach special classes for a month at the Tokyo Budokan. Finally, during this period, the All-Japan Budo Federation conferred on him the honorary rank of 9th-dan, its top rank, never before given to a non-Japanese.

This version of the events that day has been corroborated by the Hong family, though the bo incident probably occurred in Okinawa against a black belt karateka at a different time. I believe Hong referred to this episode in our meeting in 1983 but dismissed it with a wave of his hand as trivial.

Though he lived a quarter century less than his father, who died at 93 in 1985, Hong's life was full to the brim with boxing. His family was in the candle-making business in Taiwan in an era before electricity. They sold candles all over the island and often gangsters robbed their delivery men. Preventing this required strong guards, and his father, who trained in southern Shaolin White Crane boxing in his original home in Fuzhou, Fujian Province, hired the best boxers he could find to protect his product and at the same time to teach his five sons. I remember Hong telling me of some of these teachers. One was a great boxer but fancied himself a greater cook and wouldn't come out of the kitchen to train the boys until the father ordered him out.

Hong began studying boxing at age twelve. Besides his father's instruction, he learned Shaolin Luohan and *qinna* (seizing) from Gao Hejun of Jiangsu Province for three years. He trained in Monkey boxing and *wing chun* from Hong Chao for two years and Crane boxing from Chen Binyuan for three years. (Chen's teacher, Zheng Lijiao, had been a Shaolin Temple disciple.) Additionally, Hong studied Taizu Flowery Crane boxing from Lin Ju.

When the oldest Hong boy died from tuberculosis at age 28, the family became cautious about hard Shaolin boxing and brought in a taiji teacher. Zhang Junfeng, famed in all three neijia styles, was in Taiwan on business from Shandong Province and watched their practice. "The amateur looks at the smoke and fire, the expert looks for the way to the door." Zhang didn't like what he saw and said so. The resident taiji teacher called him on it. Zhang presented his belly and the taiji teacher took a free shot, which only hurt his fist. Taiji decamped. As this was 1949, Zhang was unwilling to return to Shandong because of the Communist takeover. So he settled in Taiwan and began teaching the Hong clan. He was 47 and Hong Yixiang 23 at the time. Hong couldn't speak Mandarin and Zhang knew no Japanese or Hokkien. But the chemistry between them was good and Zhang came to the Hong home for eleven years.

Hong's main internal teacher Zhang Junfeng, who studied under Gao Yisheng.

In 1951, famed boxer and hydraulic engineer from Henan, Chen Panling, visited the class. He singled out Hong Yixiang for special attention. He told his friend Zhang that Hong was extraordinary and asked that he too be allowed to teach him. So for the next four years Hong also learned the three neijia from Master Chen. These included Chen's idiosyncratic taiji which combined four major types of taiji, among them Wu Jianquan style and Chen-village style.

I was one of Hong's first foreign students, in 1959. The place was the gym of judo-cum-boxer Chen Meisi. In the next year or so, we began getting some U.S. Air Force students. One 1962-63 student who now teaches taiji in America wrote me of his experience in those days and of a fellow-student who continued practicing Chen's methods here. As a cautionary note it deserves mention.

This lad practiced with the other sporadically. Once the surviving chap noticed a red abrasion around the other's neck. He asked about it. The other reluctantly told him that he was working on chasing his qi up past the

Chen Panling, another of Hong's esteemed teachers.

neck. Because it got stuck there, he had devised a trick of hanging himself to expedite passage. My taiji friend was aghast and told him that it was foolish and dangerous and ended by making him promise to desist. His training buddy agreed. Alas, a short time later, they found the lad's body hanging in the local woods. Obviously, he had tried to get the qi up past the "jade pillow" one last time. Readers, take heed: do not constrict your carotids or injure your body in any way while trying to develop more qi!

Martin "Farmer" Burns, champion Frank Gotch's wrestling mentor, bragged that no one could choke him out and would even let himself be hoisted by his neck from the ground. Probably this was for no more than a few seconds. In the old days there was even a suspension device advertised in magazines that you could use to build your neck muscles. Young amateur wrestler George Loefler of St. Paul, Minnesota, read about the device, constructed it, and tried it out. When his brother found him later, "he was quite dead" (*Seattle Times*, January 26, 1912). Correct fighting arts essentially teach one to cross the street with the green light. Hanging yourself to strengthen your neck or to chase the qi up past your neck is crossing the street in Pamplona, Spain, on the day the bulls are running.

Hong's celebrated grandmaster in bagua, Gao Yisheng (seated), and student Wu Mengxia.

Over the years, Hong's fame soared and he trained hundreds of foreign students. Above we saw Hong demolishing several budo experts in 1969. He was so successful there that in 1982 he opened a Japanese branch of his *Tang Shou Dao* ("China Hand Way").

Both of us were born in 1926 and I knew him when he was formidable but not yet famous. We had a great, unmarred relationship. We both liked to train and we both laughed a lot. One night, Chen Jinsheng, the Taiwan national free-fight champion – who reportedly routed ten attackers in the street once with a sword – came around to watch us train. He politely challenged us on the spot. As

Hong deflects author's left punch and
counters with iron palm to the heart.

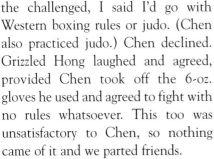

the challenged, I said I'd go with Western boxing rules or judo. (Chen also practiced judo.) Chen declined. Grizzled Hong laughed and agreed, provided Chen took off the 6-oz. gloves he used and agreed to fight with no rules whatsoever. This too was unsatisfactory to Chen, so nothing came of it and we parted friends.

Hong Yixiang was convinced that the Chinese fighting arts had been in retrograde since the Qing Dynasty (1644-1912). I thought about it at the time and concluded that the historical record is so meager and littered with clearly fictive figures with super-normal powers that it would be bootless to argue either side of the proposition.

Hong was such a pragmatist I doubt that historical hyperbole played any part in his belief. Rather, I believe it came from the few mysterious masters whom he would only mention sometimes when drunk. Even when I knew him he was traveling often to Taichung (Taizhong), the provincial capital, for secret practices with at least one master there who was a friend of Chen Panling. I've forgotten the things he told me of the man except that he could do a frontal break-fall and various locks unknown to other Chinese or to the Japanese. I urged him to do the belly-flop fall for me but he begged off, saying he had just begun learning it.

I believe that these "strange ones" had told him that persons such as themselves had become nearly extinct, but that in the Qing Dynasty times these *rara avis* were not uncommon in certain places. No one can know, of course, but some historians aver that the modern boxers are a considerable cut under the old-timers.

I would suggest that as the Chinese economy advanced with modern transport there was less time and motivation to continue the arcane practices of old. During the Communist period, after 1949, boxing was regarded as a waste of state resources and was at times attacked, notably in the Cultural Revolution (1966-1976). For several decades then, both external and internal boxing must have fallen in quantity and quality.

Which was the best boxing, the northern or southern (using the Yangzi River as the dividing line)? Even though he was Taiwanese, Hong would have picked the northern. On average, northerners were bigger.

Diet may have played a part. The Florentines of the Renaissance claimed to be smarter than other Italians because of the special quality in the white beans of Tuscany. So much for a thinking man's diet; what about one for fighters? There is none, or more correctly, there are as many diets as there are fighters. Northern boxers in China, who eat wheat, disparage southerners who eat rice, advising that one poke in a rice belly is sufficient to carry the day. This may be partly true – the north turned out the better fighters – but diet is only one of the variables involved. The most important is that all the major systems originated in the north, and the south merely copied or produced largely inferior offshoots.

I close again by citing the article above (p. 167).

In 1961, there arrived a naval commander, Robert Smith, who had studied judo and karate. Because of Hong's reputation, he "sought instruction" from him. During an exchange of blows, Hong locked Robert's arm. Robert resisted. Hong pushed and changed angle and broke Robert's arm at the hand. Hong was very embarrassed by this and since he knew bone-setting he offered to set Robert's arm. But Robert did not believe in Chinese bone-setting and went to the American military hospital. Two months later, Robert Smith appeared at Hong's doorstep this time really seeking instruction. He did not bear any ill-will about the broken arm and, since he was a trained fighter, viewed the episode as showing that Hong's skill was extremely high.

The reporter garbled some of this. The year was 1959, not 1961. I was a civilian, not a naval commander. Hong sprained but didn't break my arm. (Hong liked to stretch all my appendages. He just overdid this one.) I was gone only one month, not two, and on government business, not convalescent leave. Yet another version of this story sent me later is that when American doctors could not treat it, I returned to Hong and his ministrations cured it.

That version stoked the memory fire. Hong had trick stuff he liked to do. A stage trick was to stroke my armpit causing an electric shock to surge through my body. Other stuff was a bit more dangerous. One afternoon at practice, Hong told me that he had touched one of his student's knee-caps and "frozen" his leg. Did I want him to do this to me? "Can you release it?" I asked. "Yes, of course," he said, encouragingly, "That's why I was late for practice today. I was at the hospital releasing Du" [his afflicted student].

The word "hospital" was a red flag. I told him I'd mull on it (the Chinese and American way of saying "no"). The trust I had in Hong was not complete. It did not extend to leg-freezing or bone-setting, but to nearly everything else. He was friend and teacher, and he never asked a penny for his tuition. I honor him highly. He was the archetypal fighter who never stopped learning.

Yuan Dao,
a great teacher and
a better man (1965).

Yuan Dao:
Blending Tough & Tender

Most Thursday nights on Taiwan, Yuan Dao came to my home on Grass Mountain to practice and share dinner with us. He asked God's grace and was grandpa (*yeye*) to our three children, who were delighted with the slender gray-haired man at our table.

Yuan had won the 1934 Fujian Province boxing tournament. A gentle man and a Christian – I still have a scroll of his calligraphy of the twenty-third Psalm he gave me as a farewell gift in 1962 – he dazzled in that Taiwan sky of boxing stars. Nimble and deft, his fistic "touches" often left bone aches that not even bruisers like Hong Yixiang could. I wrote about him extensively in *Masters and Methods*.

Yuan's exquisite
Five Fists of Xingyi:
A) splitting, B) crushing, C) drilling,
D) pounding, and E) crossing.

I visited him a decade after I left. I think it was 1972. On the same trip, I remember finding a pirated edition of one of "Mr. L.'s" combatives books. This was delicious irony of a sort. L. had made his mark early on in the 1940's, when his boyish judo got him space in LIFE magazine. Though he never advanced much in judo after that, he did open a judo studio in Los Angeles that was deprecated by mainline judoka and started raining combatives books. After his first book on judo, he wrote successive books on self-defense – karate, gongfu, savate – you name it. His last two books emerged a year or so after I had written research articles on these arts, leading me to suspect that though he wasn't plagiarizing, he may have been taking his lead from me. I even thought of inventing "Ur-du," a Eurasian method, and writing an article with copious illustrations to see whether L. would emerge a month later with the seminal text on it (a seminal text is a book that one other university library besides ours has in its holdings). It would've provided me some laughs in my dotage, but, while I had the whim, I never had the time. (Urdu, is from the major language, of course, and John Gilbey had used it in one of his unconscionable knock-knocks, "Urdu, but her sister, her don't.")

Returning to Yuan Dao, his specialties were an idiosyncratic "short" xingyi; the rare *liangyi* boxing, a double-impact brisk method that only he and one other teacher in Taiwan knew; Yunnan Consecutive Step boxing and other Shaolin; and an athletic taiji using more shoulder in the "ward off, rollback, press, and push" sequence than I saw elsewhere. His stick work (which I learned) was first rate and his swordplay was among the best in Taiwan, but I was too involved in unarmed methods to take the time to study it.

Yuan made the arts he taught me into a grand synthesis of "invisible" free-hand and foot exercises. Showing no guard or posture, these were reflexes done immediately with an opponent's attack. He said top Shanxi boxers say that all correct striking or kicking is invisible. Such short boxing ripostes often started after an attack but "arrived before it did," as the ancient boxing classics say. When he attacks, a relaxed body, unhindered by tension, responds. The key here is speed, which is more important than power. The speed of the strike, not the speed of unnecessary body movement. (Jack Hurley, the great Western boxing manager, advised boxers that speed was detrimental. They should slow it down to one punch. "If you're moving fast you're also moving your opponent fast.")

That last visit with Yuan in 1972 was rewarding. Older and suffering from an illness, he rose from his bed as if he were trying to beat the count – despite my objections – and we had a pleasant and athletic reunion. (Taiji adept Wang Yannian once told me of visiting Weng Ruyuan during his last illness. Weng tried to get up and Wang tried to restrain the dying "Tiger of Shandong." Weng prevailed – he wasn't going to let Daddy Death beat him. And Daddy didn't that day. But decisioned him later.) Yuan punctuated the dialog by leaping from his chair to illustrate certain strikes. Nostalgically, they had all the old flair and pain. The gist of that rich two hours follows.

He told me he had prospered since I left in 1962, and now had over seven hundred students. During the decade just passed he had spent a successful period teaching in Malaysia. He reiterated that even as the Fujian Province free-fight champion in the mid-1930's, he didn't like to fight, the Army made him do it. Through all those years since with all his students, many of whom are now teachers, he taught boxing as exercise and self-defense, not as competitive sport. The so-called gongfu out of Hong Kong was silly and works only in stupid commercial movies, he added. It has nothing to do with real Chinese boxing.

Yuan teaching Alice
his type of taiji.

Our conversation turned to the tradition of challenges in old China. He told me that most challenges were caused by students and not by the principals themselves. The teacher grudgingly accepted a challenge not only because it was established protocol, but also to keep face with his students.

What about going to ground in a fight if one is a competent wrestler? He advised against this unless in a one-on-one situation. Generally, he believed it was best to remain standing so that your legs could work for you.

Yuan believed in holding xingyi postures but felt excessive standing stake-hold practice diminished qi and mobility. In this context, he mentioned the "hot-headed" Guo Lianyin who, I think, had moved to San Francisco by this time. Guo stressed the stake-hold, Yuan did not.

Xingyi is the premier boxing, he said. It used feet as weapons economically and wisely and merged striking and grappling as Shaolin failed to do. Do the postures slowly for precision, quickly for power. Hold them individually for up to fifteen minutes and then proceed. If the practice is correct, one hour is sufficient. For hand strength, especially in *qinna* (seizing), the best and simplest practice is to twist bamboo, the two hands going opposite.

Yuan Dao's
swordplay
was superb.

I left him and his wife sadly. We had memories to revel in, some stories and instruction for me to mull, and proximity warming us again after so many years. It was a meeting well-made, but our last. Some solace remains in his splendid teaching and the memory of his goodness, that quality in man Confucius sought but seldom found.

I may forget some of his teaching but I'll never forget the strong yet gentle man himself. In his last great adventure, detective Philip Marlowe is queried by a woman. She wonders how such a hard man can be so gentle. Marlowe responds, "If I wasn't hard, I wouldn't be alive. If I couldn't ever be gentle, I wouldn't deserve to be alive." Yuan Dao had those twin qualities – and in real life, when it is infinitely harder than it is in fiction. Yuan was the gent God meant.

Paul Guo

Nearly three years after I left Taiwan, I sent a copy of the manuscript for my *Pa-Kua: Chinese Boxing for Fitness and Self-Defense* (1967) to my bagua/xingyi mentor Paul (Fengchi) Guo. His response (May 7, 1965) reads:

> Things happen by chance mysteriously. Three years ago, 1962, when we were practicing our bagua, I hurt my leg in an accident and was confined in the Experimental Hospital of Taiwan University; and again, today, I was forced to go in hospital where I had the chance to read your book on bagua. This draft has brought very much happiness and excitement to a bed-ridden man.
>
> It is admirable that an American devoting himself to Chinese culture can digest and analyze so much complicated information about boxing – written, oral, theoretical, and practical – from which he extracts its spirit, and from the vantage of an American is able to introduce this healthful, protective, and complete bagua boxing.
>
> This is a seed of Chinese culture and you have sown it into the fertile soil of America where material development has reached its climax. I believe that the harvest from this culturation in America will be similar to that of judo in Japan.

I quote at length because Paul was such a tough taskmaster during our training, seldom praising me. Those sincere words, then, were a surprise and a joy.

Paul
doing xingyi
monkey style.

Paul had seen Sun Lutang and other greats. Sun was first off the blocks with his books on the internal arts in the Teens and Twenties. This brought him much fame and into contact with other boxers. One such was illiterate xingyi adept Shang Yunxiang, called "Iron Foot" because as an impoverished youth, to save wear on his shoes, he tied them around his neck as he "walked" his xingyi for miles every day. Shang, who would let a man stand on his belly and bounce him off with his breath, was never defeated.

Paul also told me of Wang Xiangzhai, famed but not totally liked in Hebei. Wang loved to fight and was beaten only once – by Shang Yunxiang. Paul taught me what he considered to be the strong points of these and other famous masters. I remember him showing me Shang's famed crushing fist (*beng quan*). As for Wang, the essence of his method was naturalness. It consisted entirely of circles. Every block was an attack. So, citing Wang, Paul taught me that when you block, you must aim at your opponent's head, not his arm(s).

I remember Paul as a no-nonsense man. He was upright and virile and married to a former "Miss Hong Kong," an actress. They had a daughter, a pretty young girl named Niuniu, who also became an

The author at Yangmingshan, Taiwan, with Yuan Dao and Paul Guo (1962).

Paul Guo, walking the bagua circle.

actress. I tried to contact Paul each time I was in Hong Kong, but without success. After 1969, he worked as an assistant pastor in the Evangelical Chinese Gospel Church in Kowloon, and in 1983 was said to be working as a Christian missionary among the tribal peoples in northern Thailand.

Once I had taken him to meet Yuan Dao, a long-time Christian. This may have propelled him toward Christ. Be that as it may, Paul gave his whole being to Him. The last letter I saw from Paul – to Christian friends of ours – suggested that because of some physical defect he only had a couple years left and that he had to work fast in order to accomplish the Christian work he'd set for himself. Given this and the galloping years, I suspect Paul has passed on. And done so as he did his beloved internal boxing – in style with a smile and Jesus helping.

Shang Dongsheng: The Grappling Boxer

Although we broke off our training relationship over his differences with Zheng Manqing, wrestler Shang Dongsheng and I remained friends. Several of his students over the years conveyed his messages and greetings to me. He died in 1986.

Shang Dongsheng practiced and taught the famed Baoding wrestling. This was one of the four major shuaijiao styles when the Chinese Martial Arts Institute was established at Nanjing in 1928. The other three were Beijing, Tianjin, and Mongolian. Baoding wrestling purportedly turned out a few wrestlers in the old days who could throw with nothing more than a touch. Indeed, Baoding is characterized by the words, "The moment you touch, you

Shang Dongsheng
at 160 pounds, the
undefeated heavyweight
wrestling champion
of China, 1933-1948.

throw." While this latter touch is probably short-hand for "taking hold," the lighter touch cited earlier may be simply a throw so skilled that onlookers failed to see it (of a piece with Yuan Dao's "invisible boxing"). In this old place of arcane marvels, it may have happened infrequently as claimed.

Judo masters such as S. Nagaoka or K. Mifune could produce throws seemingly without effort, but I doubt whether either could do it if he held his opponent's jacket with an intact robin's egg in each hand. Similarly, Hunter "Chip" Armstrong, a senior student of Donn Draeger, found in histories of the Apache wars and in anthropological papers of the Thirties some interesting things on Apache combatives:

> There is a kind of power used in wrestling, in which a man having it can throw down a man twice his size if he uses the power on him. He does not do it by his strength at all, but by his power. There is no name for this power at all, except for that known to the man who has it.

Other than the fact that the Apaches had this knowledge, this excerpt is not exceptional. It may refer merely to high and not supernatural skill.

Though not supernormal, Shang's wrestling combined an exquisite touch, lightning speed, and great power in tossing opponents. To round out his system, he added Shaolin strikes and kicks.

Shang was critical of judo, saying he had beaten the best judoka visiting Beijing. He had gone undefeated in *shuaijiao* (wrestling) from 1933 to 1948, and several of his biggest wins were over Japanese in the judo venue. (Though he provided no documentation, I didn't argue with him.) He was rough with me and said that I should drop everything else and go full-time with him and he would make me the best wrestler in the country. I told him I didn't want to be a champion; I only wanted to sample the best and someday write about it. I went against all his best wrestlers and prevailed even using their rules. No groundwork, chokes, or locks were allowed. And came to the view that judo, the offspring, had evolved better than Chinese wrestling and was superior to it in every way.

That judgment, however, does not diminish Shang one iota. He was a champion wrestler who, if he had chosen the judo road, would have been in the top ranks of that sport. Overall, he added considerable seasoning to my pursuit of Chinese boxing.

Wang Shujin

Wang Shujin, another of the estimable masters I wrote about in *Masters and Methods* (1974), lived almost another twenty years after I

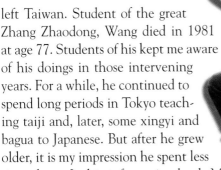

Wang in hawk posture of bagua.

left Taiwan. Student of the great Zhang Zhaodong, Wang died in 1981 at age 77. Students of his kept me aware of his doings in those intervening years. For a while, he continued to spend long periods in Tokyo teaching taiji and, later, some xingyi and bagua to Japanese. But after he grew older, it is my impression he spent less time there. In his informative book *Moving Zen* (1982), C.W. Nicol tells how Wang, while visiting Draeger's Ichigaya house, would make the edifice shake with his short punches and would hurl Donn from wall to wall. And if he let you, you could kick him square in the groin and he wouldn't flinch. (It's all in that first phrase. Did he ever let anyone? Nicol doesn't say.) But in *Masters and Methods* (p. 73), I described how he let me kick him (barefooted – we were in wrestler Shang Dongsheng's Japanese-style house where one left his shoes at the front door). I kicked him hard and often until both my feet were numb, but the agreement only covered his legs.

I used to tell seniors about that episode. Me blizzarding kicks on his legs for five minutes and him all the time smiling and afterwards when I asked how he did it, he replied, "qi." My seniors had read about this in my book, of course, and pretended interest. I told them that Wang left Shang's house that night a few minutes before I did. When I left I had to pass his house to get to my hotel. As I approached his house from still a block away, I saw a light go on inside and then heard the most anguished blood-curdling cry I'd ever heard.

Wang's bagua palm was like iron; his fingers fell on you like drills. An unlovely trick he liked was to pull you directly onto himself while he bumped you with his belly. This body attack was the harshest attack known to China and I seem to remember Hong Yixiang telling me that Wang had knocked him out with it once.

Zhang Zhaodong, Wang's superb teacher.

One of our sometime students whose character was of a low order came to me once and told me that my characterization of Wang as a religious man, indifferent to commerce and the ways of the world, was awry. Attempting to prove his case, he told me that his friend in Taiwan had just written him to tell him this story: His friend sought Wang out and told him he wanted to study under the great one and promised to work diligently and do anything necessary to become his student. Wang asked for his address and promised to visit him at noon the next day. On the dot, Wang appeared and the would-be student ushered him into his living room, seated him, and began to implore Wang to take him on as an apprentice boxer. He offered to scrub the floor daily, to pay Wang whatever fee he wanted, anything, to become his student. Wang smiled and looked around the room until his eyes settled on a brand new television set from the U.S. The set had cleared customs only the day before at a tariff of 100 percent, costing him upwards of $1,000.

Wang looked at the boy and said, "None of that is necessary. I'll take this set." The boy went into shock. He'd been a year without TV, the vilest drug of them all. He had counted the days until its arrival. And now to lose it. He tried to speak, shuddered, but the words wouldn't come. Wang touched his stricken shoulder commiseratingly on the way out.

Wang goes visiting.

My student stridently demanded to know what I thought of such commercial behavior. "You never learn," I told him stiffly. "Wang doesn't care for material things; his whole life is one of self-abnegation. He didn't want the TV set – he wouldn't have known how to turn it on. Your friend is too stupid to study under Wang, and you to study under me. The master was simply trying to discover how much of something that the guy really valued he would forego for his tuition. And he found it on his first shot. If he'd had half a brain, your friend should have jumped up and said, 'Done! Can I have it delivered right away?' Instead, he's probably still watching gongfu movies on that silly set."

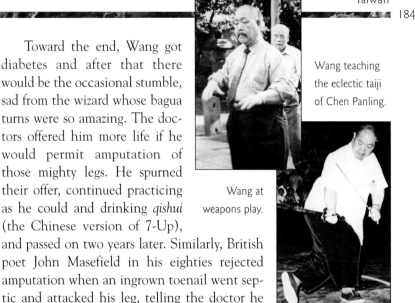

Wang teaching
the eclectic taiji
of Chen Panling.

Wang at weapons play.

Toward the end, Wang got diabetes and after that there would be the occasional stumble, sad from the wizard whose bagua turns were so amazing. The doctors offered him more life if he would permit amputation of those mighty legs. He spurned their offer, continued practicing as he could and drinking *qishui* (the Chinese version of 7-Up), and passed on two years later. Similarly, British poet John Masefield in his eighties rejected amputation when an ingrown toenail went septic and attacked his leg, telling the doctor he preferred to return to nature.

In *Masters and Methods,* I didn't tell of the afternoon Wang invited me to meet visiting Joe Brown, the Princeton sculptor and boxing coach. Brown fought as a pro boxer, winning his first six bouts, until a training injury cost him an eye, closing his career. Thereafter, he taught the finer points of the game to undergraduates and sculpted athletic subjects, earning critical praise for both. Personally, I don't think his bronzes of boxers have ever been equaled.

We had a pleasant time visiting with Brown and his wife that afternoon. Brown was erect and carried himself well. He also had very fast hands, as Wang was to learn. The physical part of the meeting started with Wang offering his belly to Brown's fists. Brown accepted and took several shots at Wang's ample frontage, but with no effect.

Brown wasn't overly impressed by this ability and told me later that he had known carnival types with "marshmallow stomachs" able to do the same thing. In the discussion afterward, someone raised the Harry Houdini case. Houdini reportedly had this ability. A young student once asked him in his dressing room to demonstrate this ability. Houdini rose but before he could get set, the lad struck him. At the time, Houdini carried it off without showing pain but later high fever and intense pain ensued. In a few days, Houdini was dead of a ruptured appendix. Researchers now believe that Houdini had been ailing with early appendicitis before that day and the blow aggravated an already existing condition.

Wang taking boxer Joe Brown's punch.

Be that as it may, Wang could see that Brown wasn't satisfied. There was nothing for it but that the two of them should get into a friendly scuffle during which Brown slapped Wang full in the face. Wang stood still and laughed. He knew something, and what he knew Brown had been using as a caveat for years with his boxing students (his best was Robert Cohn): "Boxing is risky business. In order to win, you have to get close enough to hit." Brown with his fast hands had slipped in a smart slap, but now he was close. So when they restarted, he tried again and Wang took over his body turning him hither and yon, manhandling and managing him exquisitely and totally. This really impressed Brown and he said so volubly. The meeting ended happily with *qishui*. Some years later, I read that Brown was attacked and robbed by five women in a motel down south and that he died in the Eighties.

If, as the Japanese believe, a teacher is better judged by his students than by his certificates, then Brown was a master instructor. Listen to his student, George Garrett, tell what he learned at Brown's knee (in "My One-Eyed Coach," from *Reading the Fights*, Joyce Carol Oates, ed., Holt, 1988):

> I tend to dismiss most comparisons of athletics to art and to the "creative process." But I have come to believe ... that what comes to us first and foremost through the body, as a sensuous affective experience, is taken and transformed by mind and self into a thing of the spirit. Which is to say that what the body learns and is taught is of great significance at least until the last light of the body fails.

Wang Shujin would have applauded those words as mirroring the internal even as he embraced Brown as a brother that day in Taipei. Master Wang was substantial – he threw a large shadow – in the essentially yin meadows of the internal boxing arts. He can't be replaced – only remembered.

Gao Fangxian

I wrote in *Masters and Methods* of the top northern Shaolin boxer, Gao Fangxian, and of his fine balance of authority and vitality with economy. For every attack I'd posit, Gao would have four responses. Here is a little background on that big smiling man – a smiling boxer is usually a secure one – taken largely from his obituary; he died at 64 in 1978.

Born to a family of scholars in Shandong Province, Gao was raised with six siblings in a troubled time. As a lad, he tasted Shaolin boxing and shuaijiao (wrestling), liked them, and made them a part of his life. We don't know whom he studied from but he was so proficient that he was made a coach at the Qingdao municipal *guoshu* (national fighting arts) academy sponsored by Mayor Sheng Honglie.

After 1937, Gao and his boxing colleagues were active in opposing the Japanese invaders. When Sheng became governor of Shandong, Gao became a professional soldier, rising to general in a succession of posts, and always in the thick of things.

In Taiwan, I used to see him refereeing boxing bouts and in other venues. He always had a smile and time to put at the disposal of a curious Westerner. I liked his wife, his son, and family. Like him, they were comfortable to be around. On one visit, I spent several hours with them questioning and snapping pictures. Most were functions of Shaolin's eight basic postures: (1) sitting step, (2) bow step, (3) crouching step, (4) lowering step, (5) four-six step, (6) standing step, (7) character "*ding*" step, and (8) horse-riding step.

Later, Gao became less active in Shaolin and began teaching taiji. This was after my time in Taiwan, so I don't know the type of taiji he taught, but I understand he became quite popular as a teacher.

Like Wang Yannian and so many other boxing greats, though he had been prominent in military affairs on the mainland, Gao never affected rank or displayed wealth. When I knew him, he lived in a modest house which doubled as a shop for selling tea.

Around Gao, one got the flavor of what old Shaolin in northern China was like. He had the body and mind for it. Unlike some other boxers who, while brilliant in person, never projected well (for example the younger Yang Chengfu), Gao's shape and flavor carried over into his photographs, some of which I'm privileged to show as a coda to this remembrance. So let's delineate the basic eight postures of Northern Shaolin.

Gao Fangxian in
Sitting Step (A-1).

In sitting step (A-1), you sit down putting most of your weight on your rear leg, just a trace on the front. This is an excellent blocking posture preparatory to an attack (A-2-4).

Bow step (B-1) puts most of your weight on your front foot. As an attacker strikes with his right fist, deflect and hold with your left hand while stepping forward with your right foot (B-2-3). At the same time, go into a crouching step while retaining your left grip and counter with your right fist and left foot simultaneously (B-4-5). Your left foot can kick out or, as shown, merely step down.

Bow Step
(B-1).

Lowering step (like "Snake Creeps Down" in taiji) retains most of the weight on the rear right foot (C-1). It must be used quickly since you are vulnerable if you stay in it for long. It can be used against foot attacks (C-2-3).

Lowering Step (C-1).

Crouching Step
(B-5).

The four-six step refers to the weight front to back (D-1). D-2-3 show functions.

Four-six (D-1)

In standing step (E-1), Gao intercepts the incoming right fist, and takes his left foot forward suspended while attacking with a short right hook to his opponent's temple (E-2-4). From here, the left foot can be used to kick or placed for a throw.

Standing Step (E-1)

Another example of standing step: Gao captures the attacking right fist with
his left hand (F-1). As he goes forward with his suspended left foot, he spears
with his right hand (F-2-4). Finding his spear blocked, Gao can use his cocked
left foot against his attacker's genitals or knee (F-5). Afterwards, he can rotate
his right hand into the genitals as he puts his left foot down and prepares
for an attack from the rear (F-6-8).

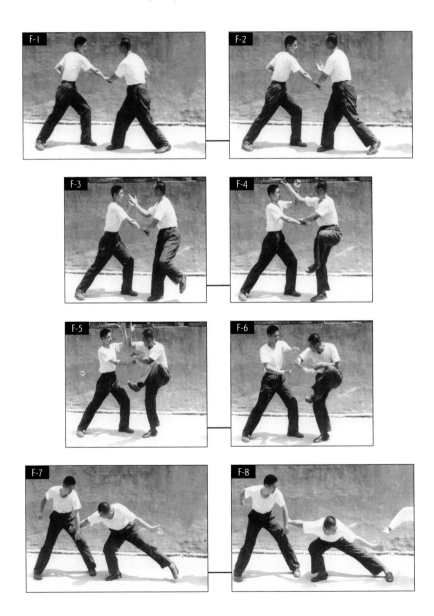

The character "*ding*" step (G-1) works well when one has no time to sit down into one of the other postures. Gao uses it next to deflect two fists (G-2) and a fist-and-foot attack (G-3).

Character
"Ding"
Step
(G-1)

Horse Riding Step
(H-1)

The last of the eight basic postures,
the horse-riding step (H-1), can be seen in H-2-3.
As the boxer shifts his weight to meet the
situation, one sees a mix of the bow, four-six,
and horse-riding steps (H-4-6).

Finally, from any posture, one must be prepared to modify to meet the unexpected attack. Here the attacker launches a feint with his left foot, which Gao guards against (1-1), whereupon the attacker uses a right wheel-kick. Gao responds by bending his upper torso downward to avoid, tearing his trousers in the process (1-2-4).

Without Gao, I wouldn't have been able to evaluate Northern Shaolin properly. With his superb body, he showed me its superiority; with his astute mind, he delineated its parts; and with his pleasant personality, he made its practice fun. I bow to him.

Zheng Manqing: He Proved Laozi Right

The inimitable
Zhang Manqing.

> The next best thing to a lie is
> a true story no one will believe.
> – Joe Palmer, famed turf writer

If Hong Yixiang introduced me to Chinese boxing, then Zheng Manqing illuminated taiji, which for me was its acme.

I met Professor Zheng in Taiwan over forty years ago. Before I met him, I was told that he was strange (*qiguai*), a versatile master blending painting and other arts with taiji. He sounded too dilettantish and I steered clear until T.T. Liang prevailed on me to go see him. Liang told me that the Professor had trained for seven years under the great Yang Chengfu and other luminaries in China and that he was not merely a soft exercise teacher. In fighting, he said, there was no one in Taiwan close to him. That got my interest. I knocked at his door seeking instruction and, in the accepted Chinese fashion, he turned me over to T.T. Liang.

After six months of learning the form from Liang and sensing-hands from Wang Yannian, one of the leading taiji teachers on the island, I again tried the Professor's door and this time it opened. For more than two years thereafter I was honored by being made a member of the advanced group who met at the master's home every Sunday morning for several hours. For me, it was an instructive and joyous time. People came from all over the island to try conclusions with the big-nosed foreigner, and I learned to relax while banging into the wall. In a way, this was analogous to falling in judo.

For the others, all Chinese, it was an opportunity to meet and know (I can think of nothing in life comparable to push-hands for getting to know someone) a foreigner. To a person they were a nice lot. T.T.

Wang Yannian, another of
the author's taiji teachers.

Liang kept me apprised on their feelings. Often he told me that they viewed me as a godsend. Before my coming, Professor Zheng had been preoccupied by his other activities with the result that the taiji sessions sometimes became perfunctory. My habit of asking questions, expressing doubts (as a foreign novice, I got by with things others couldn't), and, above all, drawing the Professor out on the celebrated boxers in old China helped make me a welcome member of the group.

Toward the end, they paid me the highest compliment by talking among themselves about the progress I'd made. "It's good for us that he's not going to be here another year," one told Liang. That was heady stuff but nothing to dwell on and, in any case, my progress since has been so modest that their concerns were not warranted.

Professor Zheng lived *hefeng xiyu* (literally, gentle wind, fine rain, meaning, "in a gentle way"). He was brilliant talking and not talking. Sometimes we would sit sharing the silence as if it were something precious, letting it go on for awhile. Christina Rossetti (1830-1894), living an earlier life, anticipated him:

> His heart sat silent through the noise
> And concourse of the street;
> There was no hurry in his hands,
> No hurry in his feet.

The Sunday bunch at Professor's house.

When I met him, Professor Zheng was already nearing sixty, but not showing it. I had been told that "his eyes were very high," that he was independent almost to a fault, and that he was a Chinese traditionalist, so I shouldn't have expected much from him. Add to the difficulty, I, too, was fiercely independent.

But what I got from the outset was the quality Mencius made so much of – *ren*, loving kindness. He could be impatient, he was never so with me; he could be angry, he never was with me; he sometimes could not suffer fools, he smilingly suffered me.

He knew I was studying not only his system of taiji, but him also. I used to ask the same question (how my questions must have tired him!) from a different vantage on different occasions. He would smile (probably thinking, "Smith and that same old question!") and answer.

The main thing I wanted to elicit from him was simply: what can taiji do for character? This, it seems, is the toughest question of all. He had waffled on this, I thought, in his *Thirteen Chapters* by saying that it depended on the person. I sought to draw him out on it and was able over the years to establish that yes, taiji – by relaxing not only the muscles, but the organs themselves – would quiet a person. That once quiet and secure (sinking into rooted centeredness), a person should be in a position where anxiety could make no inroads. This should then manifest in *ren*, loving kindness. In *Thirteen Chapters*, he was only citing reality: many do taiji as an exercise that, even if they become very skillful at it, is never carried over into their workaday lives. His message was that this is incomplete taiji.

Of course that wasn't the only question, merely the most important. I asked him endless questions on the postures and on pushing-hands (how I wish we could term this "sensing-hands"!). And he was always forthcoming.

Thank God for old notes. Here is the Professor, June 28, 1962: "Particularly toward the

Zheng's illustrious teacher,
Yang Chengfu.

Li Cunyi, famed for his
xingyi and bagua.

The legendary
Du Xinwu with whom the
Professor once "played."

last, all Yang Chengfu did was a little push-hands and some form, mainly endless repetitions of Single Whip, Guitar, and Repulse Monkey.
Yes, it was true that Yang's older brother, Shaohou, could extinguish a
lighted candle with a gesture from six feet. But this did not mean that
he could kill from a distance, it only meant that he had a special kind
of qi. Yang Chengfu was peerless with a sword; against famed Li Jinglin
in Nanjing, no sooner had they squared off than Yang knocked Li's
sword from his hand. Bear in mind that Li is renowned in our martial
arts, and especially for his swordsmanship."

Here are more notes, these undated, reflecting the Professor's kind-
ness to a crude unlettered foreigner on mainland martial art matters.
"Sun Lutang first learned xingyi, but when he was bested by Hao
Weizhen, he learned taiji from that esteemed master. The legendary Du
Xinwu was a close friend of mine who respected me greatly." Du creat-
ed a "natural" and highly regarded system of boxing called *Ziranmen*.
When Du was quite old, Zheng worked out with him and was exhila-

rated by his skill. "Li Cunyi was more
skilled than Sun Lutang." Historian and
xingyi exponent Zhou Qichun told me that
Li had the better gongfu, Sun the better
technique. While the Professor said that Li
Jinglin died of concubines, historian Zhou
put the blame on diarrhea and smoking
opium. I used Zhou to check the reliability
of the Professor's memory. For the most
part, their views coincided.

Wan Laisheng, Du's senior student, whose little
war with Zheng was prevented by the big war.

Digressing for a moment, Zhou moved in a circle (Chen Panling and Shang Dongsheng) antithetical to the Professor. I never knew the reason for the dislike. (Bertrand Russell once asked rhetorically why one never hears one Egyptologist praise another Egyptologist.) Years later, when the Professor introduced me to his students in New York City, he told them that he had defeated Chen Panling, whom I knew, in a challenge match during World War II. Later, I learned from Liu Xiheng, Zheng's successor as head of the Shr-Jung (Shizhong) Taijiquan Association in Taipei, that the Professor had also beaten Zhou Qichun's xingyi teacher in Chongqing during World War II. Shang Dongsheng may have been associated with the same xingyi teacher. These frictions that produce factions and ill-will are as old as the world and, alas, will continue as long as it does. Taking hatred as an evil, an Indian sage was asked how he accounted for evil in the world. He answered, "It seasons the stew!"

Back to our muttons. The undated note I was recalling above ended with Professor Zheng referring to Yang Chengfu. Zheng said that he had studied seven years under Yang. Zheng remembered Yang showing the students a few postures and then sitting down and correcting students from a distance. To my question of how Zheng knew then that Yang had such overwhelming skill if all he did was to sit around, Zheng replied that he had seen demonstrations in which Yang completely manhandled all who came forward, and did so with little effort. As an example, Zheng mentioned a famous boxer with the surname Wu who was among the victims. Unfortunately, I neglected to nail this down and get a full name for Wu. At any rate, Zheng said that these displays were public, not hidden, and from them Yang became so famous that he was earning $2,000 U.S. monthly from just two students whom he saw once a week!

Ah, the memories. Alice went with me once to a Sunday practice. After watching awhile, she asked the Professor to push her. He complied by lightly maneuvering her off the wall. She came back to me smiling but unawed, "It was OK," she murmured, none too enthusiastically.

Zheng's beautiful
"Squatting Single Whip."

Zheng defending against an attacker.

Professor uproots William Chen.

He watched well. And he was watching then, sensing her indifference. Walking over, he asked me her reaction and I told him. Whereupon he took her by the hand back to the wall and pushed her again. This time she ran back to me (one of life's sweetest pleasures is to have a comely woman run to you), her eyes sparkling, her words tumbling over each other.

"It was so strange," she said, "when he touched me I felt an electricity-like surge go throughout my body but without the shock."

He had followed her over and laughed at what she said.

"She felt that because she was relaxed," he explained.

That bothered me. "But I've practiced for two years and I can't feel it," I complained.

He laughed again. "Women," he said, "have an advantage over men. They are inherently more relaxed. You must work hard to get where they start from."

The master was strong on a sound foundation. A good teacher, a good system, and a healthy body could not but equal success. Lacking any of the these, the results would be less.

He had told me that taiji develops a tenacious energy (*jin*) quite different from the force associated with most fighting arts. This tenacity may be likened to a strong vine that is pliable force, in contrast to a stick that is rigid. Tenacity comes from the sinews; force from the bones.

Tenacity is always to be preferred over force because it springs from the qi. He said all this, but often my Western boxing background would obtrude and my faith would flee. I would dub all of it exquisite nonsense. Sensing my unbelief at times, he would flesh out the theory with techniques that stunned.

He pushed me around the room with just his two thumbs. Pushed is the wrong word. "Insinuated" is better but lacks the dynamic verve. Put it this way: he put you into the air, both feet off the ground, but without your feeling his hands. You really were pushing yourself. Your force was used by his energy to push you. Wang Yannian, the second-best taiji master on the island, would often come and he would be beaten worse than the rest of us: the Professor simply turned up the energy.

And he did all this manhandling without ever contracting his muscles. His hands weren't soft – they were nonexistent. For the most part he didn't push people. Instead he neutralized their energy sending it back into them and unbalancing them.

The Professor may have been something of a darling to Master Yang Chengfu in the old days after the young doctor cured Yang's wife. Most believe that this got him preferred treatment, windows and doors opened. But it didn't get him babied. Everyone else was afraid to ask the undefeated Yang questions. No one dared. But young Zheng did. He asked Yang a question on function. Yang put two light fingers on his throat and threw him twenty feet, knocking him out. When the memory of this faded, impetuous Zheng asked another question. This time, Professor Zheng told me, Yang put a hand that felt like cotton on his jaw and threw him, again knocking him out. In *Masters and Methods* (p. 38), I wrote of this and implied that these were the only two times Zheng pushed-hands with Yang. I was wrong. They pushed often. Rather, these were the only two times that Master Yang displayed his *sanshou* (free-fighting) ability.

Old judoka say that when you wrestled K. Mifune it was like holding an empty gi jacket. Pushing-hands with the Professor was a step up from that. With him you never had the sense that you were even in contact with his clothing. There was no place that you could put your hands that gave off enough substance for you to push on. You felt, reached, and eerily there was nothing. If you got devious – and with him I was pure deceit – and faked a push hoping you would contact enough of something so that he would fall for the feint and begin to neutralize while with the other hand you could try to lock his far elbow, he would get a look of utter disgust on his face, reverse the lock, and crack you into a wall. If you were good and patiently tried to find his center he would merely neutralize and unbalance you so that you stood on razor blades, letting him avoid the gratuitous push.

He was so soft and natural, so quiet and smiling, that between our practices my heart would go fickle again. If his touches were so soft and you couldn't feel them when they were occurring, how could I remember them?

So I showed up once at the private lesson, a mite more cynical than usual, and Professor Zheng, sensing it, invited me to attack him no holds barred in any way I wished. I complied instantly, faking high, going low, only to be bounced off the wall. I then launched a right haymaker. Midway through, though, I saw that his chin was too close and pulled the punch, which he neutralized and put me again into the wall, powerfully if a bit jerkily. He looked at me, his hands on his hips.

"What happened?" he asked.

"I thought I could've got you," I answered, "so I pulled it."

Again that look of disgust he used for those of little faith. "No wonder my push was a bit broken," he said. "Now this time hit me as if you hate me and if you can hit my head with either fist, then do it. This is no game."

So I tried again, this time full-bore. The same right fist but this time with his name on it. And I swear it was almost touching his jaw part of the way. He did almost a complete backbend to avoid my strike, his head near the floor. Then my head was close to the floor and, realizing I had missed and was hopelessly off-balance, I speedily tried to recoup and get vertical again. He was glad to help me and pushed me powerfully vertical and ten feet or so beyond it into the wall. His push this time was not jerky. It had been a sincere attack and the riposte was obligingly even more sincere. I had by that time in the training become accustomed to the wall, but this time it seemed to hit me rather than me it, leaving me befuddled and mute the rest of the session. But happy the man going home that night who had found that Laozi was right: the soft does overcome the hard.

After that, residual doubts fled. This was the multifaceted savant, the "Master of Five Excellences," famed as a painter, calligrapher, poet, medical doctor, and taiji genius on the mainland, showing forth his epiphanies on a skeptical American one afternoon in Taiwan, and owning his heart, mind, and body thereafter.

Historically, some Japanese samurai had trouble accepting artists in their midst. T. Yamamoto in his classic *Hagakure: The Book of the Samurai* (ca. 1716, translated by W. Wilson, 1979), reflects this:

> The saying "The arts aid the body" is for samurai of other regions. For samurai of the Nabeshima clan the arts bring ruin to the body. In all cases, the person who practices an art is an artist, not a samurai, and one should have the intention of being called a samurai.

Some Chinese warriors may have had the same aversion to artists messing with their matters. But no hard boxer in Taiwan voiced such a thought about Zheng Manqing.

During my final year in Taiwan, the Professor added time on Thursday afternoons for translator Liang and myself. During the instruction, we competed for his attention with a famed general who came to play chess with the Professor. This was to be a secret session giving me combat expertise, but mostly it was good old push-hands. In this venue, I learned much, and later forgot some and still later relearned it. So, in the 1970s when Ben Lo came to America, he explained the difference between his taiji and Zheng's this way:

> The Professor's form is smaller, more compact, and less defined than mine because he is working now with his mind [yi] while I'm still working with my body. Thus, in sensing-hands the Professor doesn't have to reach as far physically as we do because he can reach with his mind. He needs only one inch of your skin to control everything, so why should he reach so far?

I understood what I'd learned instinctively earlier.

During my final year in Taiwan, it gave more meaning to the words the Professor used to tell me how to react to a street attack:

> Don't over-analyze your opponent. Don't worry about his posture, his hands, which leg is forward, or things like that. And don't even think about your own hands. Instead, *keep your mind on your own legs.* This way, everything will work out fine.

Return to America & Judo

Returning to Bethesda in September 1962, I plunged back into work and judo. At the Betheseda YMCA, sandans Ken Hisaoka and George Inada assisted me with a large youth program (ages 8-18) and a smaller adult judo and self-defense program. Across fifteen years or so, we taught many students.

In these classes, we always downplayed judo's competitive aspects. At the outset of youth practice, I told their mothers in the chairs that I didn't invade their kitchens and they shouldn't hang around my mats. That if they could, they should leave their children in my tender care and go away. They wouldn't be harmed and, if we were lucky, some alchemy might occur and older yang and younger yang might coalesce and the kids be immeasurably enriched by the judo experience. The mothers were uniformly gracious, but the fathers, ah, there was the rub. They had been competing since first grade. They wanted their offspring to be winners, not players. I once told a particularly over-bearing dad that my fear for the boys was not that they wouldn't win, but rather that they would win too much. It was hard to lose, but it could be terrible to win. Like all good education, judo teaches you to lose with style and it prepares you for the awful wear of winning. After all, I told him even as he tried desperately to get out of the corner I had him in and away from this heresy, life is essentially about losing – no one but Christ got out of it alive. Judo simply teaches players to lose winningly.

Still, our students did fairly well in competition. I have nothing against competition – I just don't think it proves much. To expedite this philosophy, I wrote the following for our club during the mid-Sixties:

> We had a fine tournament this year and a good turnout. For the first time in seven years, however, we had some problems with overly aggressive parents. Be reminded that the Bethesda YMCA does not conduct judo on a Little League basis: we follow Jigoro Kano right down the line. Therefore, the parents' place is in the bleachers. If this kind of thing recurs next year, we will eject the son(s) of any offending parents and refund the entry fee. Coaches are asked to remind parents of what constitutes good judo behavior.

Besides the aggressive parents, the culprits included the big win-at-any-cost clubs along the East Coast. What really burnt these bozos was

Judo should be fun. Here Diane Tamura pins her father,
the late, great Masato, with scarf hold.

that in the seven annual invitational tournaments I conducted, we gave the biggest trophy to the player who did the best fall. We felt that winning always has its boosters and that someone should say a good word for second place. We taught each youngster irrespective of his or her talent or contest record. Each was promoted against himself. Thus he could theoretically lose every match and still progress.

We even tried to make junior judo fun. T. Ishikawa once said that kids' judo ought to be eighty percent fun and games and twenty percent judo (work), and I agreed. But almost no one else did. It was a real chore to keep judo fun in the face of excessive competitiveness. Many parents and most teachers conspired to make the sport overly competitive. There's a poignant sadness in the fact that I never heard a father say to his little tyke before a match, "Have fun."

I remember likening the competitive junior judo situation to the burgeoning gymnastics industry in which female gymnasts became mature without passing through a normal childhood. What a pity. Author George Gissing writes on this form of child abuse, "One of the most pathetic things I have ever heard: little Joseph Hofman, the nine-year-old piano genius, was working till he broke down. At a concert in America, he burst into tears and exclaimed, 'I'm only a little boy.'"

But in opposing victory at any cost, we were crying in the wilderness. I took a last stab at salvaging what Jigoro Kano had been after by writing the following words during 1965. While they were published in a judo publication, I don't think anyone was listening.

For several years I have not written on judo, partly because of the press of other things, but mostly because of a disenchantment with the art as it is presently lived. I have continued to teach, however, because here at least one can make and see his contribution. Some high-graded yudansha (none of whom agree with all of my ideas) have urged me to write an article appraising current world judo. It is true that internationally and nationally judo has taken giant steps recently. But it is also true that the old hurdles impeding judo growth – localisms, frictions, sheer unalloyed ignorance – do not seem to have diminished: we still risk rupture in clearing them. I wrote about these fifteen years ago without effect, but let me try one last time. One thing before getting to our muttons: some of my proposals may smack of an anti-Japanese orientation. It simply is not true. I have many Japanese friends. In what follows, I attack an institution and not the ancestry of any who people it. If judo came to these shores from Greece and developed here the way Kodokan judo has, I would be flailing at it with my lance and many Greeks would be displeased. So, if I anger any readers, let it be for reasons of substance and not for an alleged racism. Nor am I dogmatic on the substance. These are my views now, although I may be persuaded otherwise by you tomorrow. Therefore, I invite any and all to toss in their corrigenda, views, or mere thoughts. Together, perhaps we can make judo move.

Judo: Sport or Art?

Jigoro Kano envisaged judo as an educative process *for the masses of all countries*. Only the late G. Koizumi in the West correctly carried forward the idea. Perhaps someone in Japan is attuned to it: I have doubts about the Kodokan *per se*. Kano did not deplore competitive judo. Indeed, he began with this as the basis of the art he created. Later he saw that the thing which had him by the scruff of his neck had a larger rationale, one which might fairly be called a philosophy. He developed this into a system of physical and ethical education. His strategy embraced two ideas: (1) maximum efficiency with minimum effort, and (2) mutual welfare. We have forgotten that the first maxim covered life as well as sport judo and few of us seem to have ever learned the meaning of the second (which means simply *love*). The *nage* sequence *kuzushi-tsukuri-kake* and other technical prizes developed from sport judo are only *tactics* which are minor considerations compared with Kano's *strategy*. Van de Velde, the Dutch gynecologist, said a mouthful when he said that the preliminaries to love are as important as the main event. For without them you can't get there from here. The above had to be said as base for what we dive into now.

Competition

There is undue stress on contest judo. The art has something for everyone: young, old, male, female, introvert, extrovert, weak, strong, rich, poor, etc. But you would

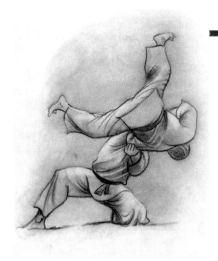

never know it. Judo today is strictly a varsity affair for the few who survive the bangings. For those naturally endowed with strength, agility and speed it provides technique and triumph. But what of the others? Judo can give those over 35 years of age a modicum of technique, a splendid self-defense, and a great deal of confidence. But if they are tossed to the wolves prematurely (I say this advisedly because often the light practicers develop, if left uninjured, into good contest men), they quit, a disappointment to themselves and a poor product of a system meant to improve them. Judo can give strictly self-defense built on Kano principles for those who don't want to wrestle. Similarly, it can provide for females and children, skills which will assist them throughout life. What I am suggesting is that we make judo meaningful for the many and not merely useable for the few.

To expedite the flowering of judo, I propose a few thoughts on the three R's: ranks, ritual, and rules.

Ranks

We can't kill old frictions. We can't tell X to make his peace with Y in a quarrel which has been 30 years brewing. We can only try to pre-empt the problem, stop the trouble before it starts. Because most frictions pivot on problems of rank, why not attack the problem? If we discard the rank system it certainly will kill much of the political warfare in judo. The reason given by most for preserving the rank system is that it provides a safety measure in that higher grades aren't matched with lesser grades. This implies, of course, that the lower grades will be injured by such mismatching. We know the truth to be otherwise. Most injuries occur in matches between like grades – the higher grades have the technique to avoid injury to those lesser grades running afoul of them. I urge that we eliminate all but two belts, an ungraded white and a graded black. (I would not quarrel with a teacher grade at, say, 4th- or 5th-dan level, but I fear that even this might become a political football.) The rank system, after all, is a Japanese institution pegged to that milieu. The art is now global – may we face that fact? Amateur wrestling – the fastest growing sport in the United States – neither has nor needs ranks. If we want to grow rather than to continue to stagnate, we perhaps could learn from our counterparts in that sport. To make this proposal a bit more meaningful, I cheerfully toss my sandan into the trashbin.

Ritual

Along with the above, I think it beneficial that we rid the art of its ritual. The
ritual actually contrives to rob the art of
the courtesy which it is meant to nur-
ture. By discarding this straightjacket of
obsolete forms, we can induce a return
to courtesy and with it an increase in the
popularity of the art. The Japanese ritual
injected into a foreign milieu too often
becomes mumbo-jumbo mystique for
the masses. To those who argue that the
mystique is pleasant and pulls those
seeking novelty, I retort that the art can
stand on its own feet without gimmicks.

Jim Bregman flips Goldschmid at the
1964 Olympics for a bronze medal.

All too often the novelty attracts sociopaths and, quite frankly, we don't need them.
Practically, I would replace the bow with a handshake, eschew most of the elaborate
procedures (who was it who thought Joseki was a town in Missouri not too far from
Peoria?), and – except for international matches – use the prevailing language rather
than Japanese. Two decades ago when United States judo was a mewling, puking
brat, I argued for retention of ritual and the use of Japanese primarily to keep the
growing core pure. But we need them not now. In a word, I am saying that their
retention now dilutes dynamism. I would urge retention, however, of the kata, for I
believe they have a legitimate role in the art.

Rules

The rules of judo badly need a thorough overhaul. Recent revisions have tended to
hurt rather than help healthy regulation of contest. I have in mind the OK recently
given throws off the mat. This is deplorable. Next we will accept tosses into the second balcony provided, of course, that the thrower remains in bounds. This is advertised to stop periphery paraders and to put the quietus on defensive judo. Whatever
happened to technique as a solution for this? The revision of the rules should be
done internationally and not in Tokyo alone.

This impetus provided by holds on the jacket and compounded by throws from
a standing position, plus the fairly free license given elbow locks and strangles make
contest judo a sport in need of rigorous control. If this sounds sissy, then let us
remove all restrictions, introduce striking and kicking, rename the thing "all-in fighting," and forget the educative aspects of the art. Give me a rule book and an audience and I could talk all day. Suffice it here to cite but a few examples.

- *Kani-basami* (crab-claw), a throw waiting for a disaster to happen, should be outlawed. Kano envisaged an ukemi for every throw in the repertoire. This throw often does not even provide the possibility of an ukemi.
- Tackling should also go. We have the throw *morote-gari*. But too often it degenerates into a driving tackle. Likewise, single leg pickups except where done as an immediate *kaeshi* ought to be expunged.
- *Makikomi* frequently prevents ukemi and invariably increases impact and the likelihood of injuries. Judo insists on technical excellence – why then permit makikomi, a technique born of an initial effort gone awry? Why not instead seek an improvement of the initial effort?
- The relationship of the judges to the referee needs to be clearly enunciated. Who has the last word? And, in the final analysis, do the judges have any word at all?

I fear I've tired the moon with my talking. Did you listen and did you hear? And what will you do?

Perhaps the greatest collection of judo skill ever gathered in one photograph. Taken in Kyoto, circa 1905, when Jigoro Kano was about 45 years-old. Front row l. to r.: Yoshitsugu Yamashita, Jigoro Kano, and Sakujiro Yokoyama. Rear row: K. Sato (?), Hajime Isogai, and Shuichi Nagaoka.

In 1967, while attending the Fifth World Judo Championships, I found myself in Salt Lake City. At the airport, settling back in the seat, I said to the cabbie, "There was a girl I once knew, from Tooele. Know where it is?"

"Sure," he grunted. "It's only 35 miles from Salt Lake. Wanna go out there?"

"Hold it," I said. "I knew her during World War II. But I never actually met her. We fell in love by correspondence. We did it all by letter."

He cut in. "I've heard of canoes and pogosticks – but letters?"

I overlooked his poor try. "To a teenager trying to ease himself across life's jagged edges, she was a godsend. The love was as genuine as a 17-year-old is genuine – how the hell old was Romeo anyway? I know it sounds crazy but it was a crazy war – though quite sane compared to today's imbecilities. When I returned from the Pacific in 1946, I chickened out and bypassed her on my way back home to the midwest. The reason is now fairly obscure, though it probably had something to do with not killing a dream. Actually, I probably choked up the closer I got to reality. Now I put it to you: here we are 21 years later and it's a beautiful morning. Should I go see her?"

Cab drivers are a pragmatic lot. He said with a laugh, "I wouldn't."

"Okay," I said. "Let's go out to the judo tournament on campus."

At Salt Lake City, to help create communication between quarreling team members and the coaching and administrative staff, I arranged a meeting. The coach initially thought the meeting a good idea, but later retreated, obliquely suggesting that I was creating more trouble than providing solutions. Reason didn't budge him. He and some others liked to talk, but they had never heard of Buber's "holiness of meeting" much less Kano's "mutual welfare," and so they huddled together for warmth in what Chesterton called "the clean well-lit prison of one idea." So we met without him. Here it was that I again met Ken Kuniyuki, a fine senior judoka to whom Bill Paul introduced me. Kuniyuki had given up smiling for the decade. Looking at him I recalled the words of an ancient Roman warrior, "I've seen friendlier eyes across the tops of shields." Kuniyuki muttered, "I read your book [A Complete Guide to Judo] – it was a fair book." And just as generously, I responded, "And I've seen your fair judo."

The meeting started with an administrator lashing out at the players for slander. I interposed that the charge was poor inasmuch as the person levying the charge had been calling the players "bums" for two days in his talks with me. After some more fruitless palaver, the administrators offered a couple egregious statements. (1) *"There was no Japanese bias in U.S. judo."* The bias was so evident that I had never heard such a novel thought uttered. (2) *"The Japanese team's teamwork, exemplified by the dives they took for each other, should be emulated by the U.S. team."* I told the top boyo who recommended this that I was glad Jigoro Kano wasn't alive to hear such nonsense.

It did little good. U.S. judo continued "dusty and divided," eventually splitting into two organizations. I found later that amateur wrestling politics was, if anything, worse than the judo politics. Wherever three or more gather in its name, you have the seeds of that social imperative called bureaucracy. However, the amateur wrestling experience taught me that bureaucratic disharmony can flourish without a racial component. This, at least, made me happy.

I was to remain active for a decade after my return from Taiwan, but the judo became increasingly sterile. The old zest was ebbing even as my judo back was going. At the same time, I was being reenergized by teaching something new, more subtle and sophisticated, and infinitely more satisfying: taiji. When I finally quit judo, I'd been at it twenty-five years, ten of it overlapping my involvement in the Chinese internal arts. But no regrets. "Jimmy had a new goil" was the way poet e.e. cummings expressed it.

Sometimes I'd meet old judo acquaintances and though cordial enough there seemed to be some separation. It was as if some were saying that I hadn't stayed the course. Why stop at 3rd-dan? If I would prolong the judo classes and help officiate at Sunday contests, the promotions would be forthcoming, the Association head told me. Nope, I replied, my family has loaned me to judo for too long – they were my first priority.

I would miss some of its aspects. For instance, the bow (never mind that I urged its replacement by a handshake years ago (page 208, above). Let me say a word on it that is seldom said. Judo has the custom of bowing toward the center of the mat when going onto it and leaving it. This is a macro, not a micro, bow; a bow to judo, the institution. It says, "You will be and have been my home for a time and I thank you for the education and community with which you have blessed me here."

The *tatami* came to have *baraka*, the blessedness that attaches to houses or objects after years of loving use by noble-hearted people.

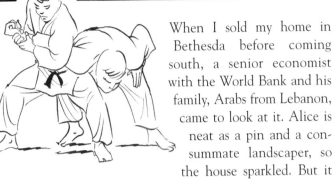

When I sold my home in Bethesda before coming south, a senior economist with the World Bank and his family, Arabs from Lebanon, came to look at it. Alice is neat as a pin and a consummate landscaper, so the house sparkled. But it didn't prejudice the thing when I asked the father if he knew what the Arab word *baraka* meant. His serious face brightened, "Of course." "Well," I said, "you may find some *baraka* here." The house sold the next day.

Richard Fukua, a classy California heavyweight who died early (all good people die too early whenever they die), told Bill Paul that the essence of judo was in the bows and the falls. That is, in the courtesy and the humility. Besides the bows to the mat, we bow to our partner. Many people can quote Jigoro Kano's principle, "Maximum efficiency with minimum effort"; but too often forget the other, "Mutual welfare," which means caring for your partner.

Similarly, if asked the most difficult thing in judo, most would answer that it would be acquiring techniques to win the struggle. Veteran British judoka Dicky Bowen a wrote me recently that, "I once asked a number of Japanese teachers what is the most difficult thing in judo – about half came down on *ukemi* (falling properly) and *kata* (traditional forms)." Not amassing wins, mind you, but doing two "lesser" parts of judo in good form. Something to think about.

Above (pp. 206-209) I commented on how I was viewed as a spoilsport and alarmist when I wrote long years ago of my concern for judo's future. At the First U.S. Judo Championships at San Jose in 1953, I congratulated the assembled officials on breaking down old localistic barriers enough to institute national tournaments, but in the same breath urged them not to become so enamored of contests that Jigoro Kano's educational/ethical base would be lost. My concern was justified. I wish I had been wrong.

The popularization and spread of judo has weakened Kano's base so greatly, I see no chance of it ever recovering. Judo is now merely a jacketed wrestling sport. The competitive has ousted the cooperative. Most judo publications these days are nothing but contest results and advertisements. Gone are the how-to articles, the biographies, the philosophical pieces, the textual acknowledgment of judo's combative roots, and the humor.

A European competitor and official recently wrote to agree that yes, "The stress now is on contest judo at all costs. To change this would be difficult as it allows for a host of referees, timekeepers, and officials to batten on to teams and travel, lodge, and eat free (only the best hotels) – some make a career of this, particularly in Europe. More or less all the income of the British Judo Association goes to big contests – and to hell with the thousand odd clubs struggling to keep going...."

Why this sad denouement? The lust for competition explains most of it. But there is also the fact that sport judo is easy to understand. It has definable aims and ends, and thus appeals to people who lazily don't care that this has killed the venerated teacher/student relationship, the small street (*machi*) dojo, and other elements of the judo Kano created. In short, a wonderful art has become a drab sport.

Once at a major tournament in Washington, I was one of two judges watching the top two players go at it. Both were good quality yudansha – the more yang of the two later went out to the West Coast and set fire to contests there. It was a fairly even affair until late when yang ran his partner off the mat and then, while off the mat, applied o-soto-gari (big outer reap), throwing the unlucky one into the chairs. In the fever of the moment, it is permissible to begin a throw on the mat that miscarries and spills over outside the playing area. But this wasn't that. Here, yang first ran his opponent off the mat and only then applied. I looked hard at the *nisei* referee and judge but their eyes avoided contact.

John Anderson (6th-dan)
of Baltimore
executes hane-goshi
(spring hip throw)
on some unfortunate.

Came time for a decision to be rendered. The ref called it a draw, the other judge gave it to yang, and I gave it to his opponent. We conferred and they both questioned my call. I told them that in my view, yang had the better of it until the flagrant foul. The rules expressly prohibited un-judo-like conduct, and if I had been refereeing I would have ejected him on the spot. Both were shocked. They seemed to be saying "Boys will be boys" and even yang's opponent (trying for samurai status) joined in the chorus saying, "Bob, he didn't mean it!" I stuck to my decision, and it was either adjudged a loss for yang or a draw, I forget which.

If your judo is only one of contests, you won't have much fun. Humor is the first thing to go when you fix on winning as everything. In the old days of small dojos, fun was more prevalent. One sees it in the old Budokwai bulletins and in singular individuals such as John Hanson-Lowe, who randoried into his seventies (he started judo in his forties and had a 7th-dan from the International Judo Federation before he died at ninety in 1995). This jaunty guy must have been lubricated by RU-420 and held together by Band-Aids.

Despite this, Hanson-Lowe, whom I never met (Donn Draeger told me of him), will live in infamy for the only memorable poem written on judo this century, "Rime of Winsome Winnie," which goes:

Oh, Winsome Winnie is my name
And though I'm not so tall
I love to smash the boys and girls
At the local judo hall.

My teacher said that if I win
The shiai in the spring,
I'll get the cup she's offering –
A lovely golden thing.

But, oh alas! a week ago
I took a nasty fall,
And breaking many vertebrae
Can neither walk nor crawl.

But I shall go and watch the fight,
With tears in my eyes,
And see a rival win my bout
And take my golden prize.

Judo and Taiji

I found that judo espoused softness and suppleness and geared its technique to these qualities. For instance, K. Mifune said that if your opponent pushes, you turn your body; if he pulls, you step out on a diagonal. Judo was the high school of soft. Taiji, I learned the first time I touched Zheng Manqing, was its college. Part of the difference is in the nature of the two. Judo is a grappling form where a strong grip is paramount; taiji an art that requires the hands and all else to be relaxed so that the *qi* can function through the fingertips. The difference definitely is not racial. Chinese jacketed wrestling (shuaijiao) is more forceful and far inferior to judo.

H. Nagaoka (10th-dan) once asked Dr. Kano to explain the meaning of the words *ikioi* and *hazumi*, one of which your opponent must have before you can throw him. Kano replied that setting up an impetus (ikioi) involves strength, but that establishing a momentum (hazumi) involves skill. A taiji player proficient at sensing-hands will catch that distinction about as readily as a judoka.

K. Kudo in his *Dynamic Judo* (1967) writes that the judoka should always carry his head so that he feels that it rests not so much on his shoulders as firmly on his hip region. Here, the taiji adept whose whole rationale pivots on keeping qi and mind at the dantian will grasp the idea even quicker than the judoka.

Finally, on spirit versus the use of strength, Kudo comments:

> By using one's spirit I mean keeping calm but alert and full of energy, relaxing your arms and legs, and being free but completely aware and responsive to what is going on around you.... By using your strength I mean exactly the opposite, that is, giving precedence to the power of your body and thus tensing your limbs and making your body heavy and hard.

Exactly. Chinese internal systems would subscribe wholly to this.

But when Kudo ends by saying, "In judo, from ancient times, use of the spirit has always had the upper hand over use of bodily strength," he may be a bit roseate in his recall. Certainly in the present age where the art has become merely a form of jacketed wrestling, where weight categories and weight training prevail, *wanryoku* (beef) takes precedence over *waza* (technique). His words no longer reflect Japanese thinking – if they even did in 1967.

Y. Yamashita, who won the All-Japan crown nine years in a row, scores with uchimata.

Yasuhiro Yamashita, who seldom lost (he won the All-Japan crown nine times in a row between 1978 and 1985), did lose on a decision once in 1977 against a man he'd beaten easily before. Off the record, he philosophizes in his book, *The Fighting Spirit of Judo* (1993:30-31), "While everything is going well, one can sometimes meet with an unexpected failure if one *relaxes* [my italics]." Without meaning to, Yamashita in trying to say that if one's attention wavers he risks defeat, pretty well expresses the gulf between the external and internal by demonizing the word "relax." With all his physique, drive, and dedication, I think Yamashita's technique would have been even better if he had relaxed more while, of course, keeping his attention focused. His judo was ultimate power judo, yet even here relaxation found a place. I've seen All-Japan finalists take twenty minutes to get a satisfactory hold – much depends on it. Their grips are like iron. Here is Yamashita's advice on gripping, "Put strength into your little, ring, and middle finger but keep your thumb relaxed or it will cause a stiff (less mobile) wrist."

Bill Paul used to lament that compared with other athletics, judo gave you less result for effort. I found taiji gave you even less than judo. Being equal parts external and internal, judo's contribution could be counted and weighed. Working through relaxation and jin (energy), and eschewing physical force, taiji was more amorphous. The synthesis I forged of reading/writing/practicing provided me a start, but alas I could never get to the end of it; or, for that matter, the half-way of it. However, there was solace in knowing that this mystery was real, if not realizable. Some students don't even reach that level.

Winning, Pain, & Gossip

Joe Svinth, an authority on the fighting arts, told me once of a judo winner from Seattle who was, "too much into winning for my tastes. He had never figured out that judo was about style, not strength, or that injuries were God's way of telling you that you were doing something incorrectly." Well said and from a non-judoka!

Why this furor over winning? Life, one long process of getting tired, is more about losing. In a worldly sense, the quintessential men of Zen were invariably losers: the great Go player Sekine in Y. Kawabata's *Master of Go* who loved to lose; the monk who mused, "Now that I'm enlightened, I'm just as miserable as ever"; and the master archer who never hit a bullseye, unlike Archer Yi who Zhuangzi tells us was skilled in hitting a minute target, but clumsy in stopping others from praising him.

It struck me early that the worst part about winning was what it does to your mind. You come to believe that success is your doing instead of simply what happens to you. Who gave you the genes and the energy and the mind? From whom did you get the money and time to practice? What exactly did you put into it? Really nothing other than showing up regularly for practice and persisting in contest when you were exhausted, vexed, and would have liked to quit. There is you in that, of course. Still, it's not your doing so much as what happens to you.

Scientist Benjamin Libet's experiments show that a half-second before you decide to flex a finger, say, an electrically detectable change occurs in your brain. The brain appears to have made the choice before you are even aware of it. This puts the very notion of free will in jeopardy. In the final analysis, acts that we think we decided to do are really things that merely happen to us. We are simply carried along by our brains and the world of which they are a part. If this development proves out, it will accord with Buddhist and Daoist teachings and, perhaps, make us a bit more modest.

As for pain, nature insists that nothing worth the doing is free of pain or the risk of it. All of us will be hurt at times. The mark of an intelligent person is how he or she handles the pain. American sports just now – pro football especially – are so dollar-infested and win-obsessed that many athletes play hurt much of the time. Really drastic opiates mask the pain so that they are not playing hurt so much as playing injured. This is business and not athletics and exacts a terrible toll on body and psyche.

I resisted George Orwell's 1945 comment on sport at the time as too harsh. I no longer do. He wrote, "Serious sport has nothing to do with fair play. It is bound up with hatred, jealousy, boastfulness, disregard of all rules and sadistic pleasure in witnessing violence; in other words it is war minus the shooting." If this sage were alive today, he would be harsher and just as correct. He would have to be: some 20% of National Football League players have been charged with a serious crime.

Lastly – in the error mentioned above that "I do it" instead of "it happens to me" – one sees the love of gossip in the so-called martial arts. The Chinese call such garrulous types, "boxers of the mouth corners." Pernicious gossip springs from insecurity, but even celebrated winners engage in it. Two friends, both fine judoka, suffered the injuries and gray tedium of the Kodokan – the soggy jackets that never quite dry out and the dull sameness of day following day. Both became champions, but this didn't stop their propensity to gossip about others. This shocked me at the time because I assumed (wrongly it turned out) that insecurity can't coexist with winning.

Ego survived, perhaps flourished, even at those heights. But of all the fine judoka I've known, I've never met one so egocentric as Aldo Nadi, probably the best fencer this century. My friends were exceptional at what they did, but a cut below in judo what Nadi was in fencing. Nadi's ego was staggering – this shouts out through his book, *The Living Sword* (1995). Egocentric perhaps, but at least Nadi didn't gossip.

Bob Goodwin, a taiji instructor in Los Angeles, was watching a xingyi class one night when he heard the teacher say that Bill Jones' xingyi wasn't very good. As Bob knew Bill, he asked the teacher if he could interrupt the class long enough to speak to him. The man excused himself and went into the hallway with Bob, who asked him if he'd ever seen Bill actually doing xingyi. The teacher said, "No." Bob then told him that he shouldn't judge someone he hadn't seen.

Bob continued, "I don't know xingyi but I have heard Bill say that his xingyi isn't very good. Trouble is, he says the same thing about his taiji, which I personally know is top-drawer. The moral is: avoid gossip and don't be confused by modesty."

Then Bob asked the teacher if he knew why he had taken him away from the class before chiding him. The teacher shook his head.

"It was because I didn't want to shame you before your class," Bob responded. "I had the courtesy to think of your feelings. Bill taught me that. You should give him the same courtesy, and not gossip."

The teacher reddened, apologized, and returned to his class chastened, perhaps now more of a real boxer rather than merely a boxer of the mouth corners.

I quit judo in 1972 and stopped cutting my toenails for the first time in twenty-five years. But as Willa Cather said of her beloved prairie, "If you come from there it never leaves you." Judo never leaves you. I don't mean the sore body parts that keep orthopedists in Cadillacs. I mean the memories of the kind people and marvelous places and the courtesy and the ethics which you tried to make a part of your self as assiduously as you tried to master tai-otoshi (body drop) or some other technique requiring hundreds of hours. So a last low bow to the *tatami* honoring the art and its devotees. And to its creator, Jigoro Kano, who after attaining its summit, discarded his black belt for a beginner's white one. This reflected judo's (and life's) essential circularity, humility, and irony.

Saturday Morning Taiji

Shortly after my return from Taiwan in 1962 I began teaching taiji to a small early-risers group at the Bethesda-Chevy Chase YMCA every Saturday at 7 a.m. This was to continue for 27 years and to expand from four or five people to a high of 125, when Kissinger and Nixon went off to Beijing to reopen a China the same two had been largely responsible for closing years before. The classes were gratis, a community contribution, and remained so despite some New York taiji seniors urging that I charge a fee, "If it's free, no one will regard it highly." To which I responded that I had so much and gave so little they shouldn't interfere with my trying to square the account.

The Saturday class, soft at it. Author leading; Alice at far left in first line behind Warren Conner.

Though it was mostly wonderful, the Saturday class seemed to attract a more dissolute bunch than the structured fee classes I began in 1970. It was from the Saturday group that we got most of the troubles we encountered – people starting to teach after a few Saturdays and so on. We nipped the teaching problem in the bud by issuing a guideline on teaching requirements that stated that even to be considered for a teaching post, five years in the trenches were required. This quickly cut attendance in both the free classes and later, the fee classes. So early on I was able to elaborate the first of my taiji laws, "Americans don't want to learn taiji, they want to teach it."

Alice and Bob.

Every man (or woman!) a teacher, yes. And beyond that, a master! Ah, what bliss. One of my first students quit after ten free group lessons (we had only eight students then) to teach taiji "to her church group." Shortly, she was teaching in county recreation classes. The last cash student I had after I moved to these Carolina mountains took ten lessons. After the last private lesson he asked for permission to teach. I didn't answer right away. First, I asked him why he wanted to teach. He didn't dissemble. He said that he often attended area taiji seminars at which most of the participants were "masters" with active classes. He believed that his form and sensing-hands were clearly superior to theirs. It diminished him, he said, to be better but not have a teaching credential.

His taiji wasn't bad, either. He had practiced for nearly a decade with several teachers, but sporadically at seminars. I told him that his taiji was improving but from what he said, his mind was not. We don't do taiji for honors or degrees. Laozi deplored competition. What others did was irrelevant to us. His job was to learn, mine was to teach. When, in a couple of years or so, perhaps, he was ready to teach, I would know. And tell him. Until then, he should empty his mind, relax, and go back to work. I never saw him again, but someplace in Tennessee there's a taiji teacher I want to tell you about....

There were all kinds of adventures on Saturday morning. We had visitors from all over. A Chinese chap came one day in full mandarin regalia down to the tin sword that he waved in our midst, doing his thing (and poorly, as the old French joke has it) as we did ours. When outsiders came I tried to tell them that in China when I visited other systems I followed what they did out of (1) politeness (*keqi*) and (2) a genuine curiosity about the system and a desire to learn it. But few of them listened, obstinately moving through their forms stiffly and double-weightedly. What a disservice to themselves – never to taste the new and possibly the real in their competitive assertion that they already knew it all.

If I sound negative, put it down to scrupulosity. Most of the time it was only wonderful. To start with, you leave a bed and its sundry delights at dawn to meet with other people. (Sartre said that hell was other people. If he had read Mencius, he would have known hell was only Sartre himself.) This may have been what Napoleon meant when he spoke of the rarest courage of all, "the courage of early morning." Anyway, during practice, Alice and I would sometimes walk in back of the YMCA building where peering through a fence we encountered a satoric vista of uncommon beauty and *déjà vu*. It reminded me of Alain-Fournier's story, *The Lost Domain* (*Le Grand Meaulnes*). And mostly the people were as good as gold and grand as a piano.

We had some fun with ads. The *Washington Post* wouldn't accept ads on meditation but we got them with "Discount Taichi: Beginning Levitation. Bethesda every Sat., 7 A.M." (Dec. 30, 1974). We got one call on that. Go figure. We ran another on "Mom and Pop Taichi" that also got little or no reaction from the hungering hordes. But that one did stimulate a senior later to make us a neon sign. In class I had kidded that the only prerequisite for being a teacher was a neon sign with that legend. It lay in our basement until a gauche big-footed baqua player stepped on it.

Saturday morning again, author illustrating "Fair Lady's Hand."

Still, there were times during that New Age period when a teacher earned his money even when he wasn't being paid. The swindle, *EST,* was in its heyday then and we had casualties, broken families and people, coming from this "Marine Corps Meditation" (so-called because you weren't permitted to pee for twelve hours at a stretch while these swindlers told their lies). Although I barred Transcendental Meditation (TM) people and others from proselytizing, I never mentioned *EST.* One morning, however, I did remark on it, urging the students that if they had a berth, to give it a wide one. After the class, a woman identified herself as the Washington contact for this spurious outfit and asked if I had taken its weekend. The least I could say was no, and she retorted, "Why then do you condemn something you've never tried?"

Though she was a contact person for this brutish bunch, the woman dressed well and seemed a nice enough person to cause me to be polite. Still, I knew that there were occasions when one must speak or be diminished. I responded, "My dear, I never had elephantiasis but to try it would be a drag."

I never gave permission to teach to anyone who attended just the free Saturday classes. They were meant to be mostly flow and fun. And they were. Still, their limited structure spawned some real yahoos, and several (perhaps many) unauthorized teachers bloomed from it. Too much, too soon, yet they aspired to get their own class and thereby become a master.

One episode I clearly recall. The nephew of the *Washington Post's* premier sports columnist phoned me to say he had been coming to Saturday class for a couple of years and was now teaching. "Teaching what?" I asked. "Taiji, of course," he replied. He then said he needed help with one section of the form and could he pay for some private instruction?

I knew most of my students. Certainly I knew my two-year students. This guy I couldn't remember at all. Ruthless, I told him that I knew him and that his form was deplorable. Arrogantly, he came back, "Well I think it's very good," to which I retorted, stealing from G.K. Chesterton, "You call that a thought?"

"What's the big deal?" he said. "I'll pay you whatever you want."

I told him that this wasn't about money, this was about special instruction, and he couldn't get it from me.

That left him sputtering.

The Roman Emperor Vespasian, who owned the concession on public toilets and used the collected urine in his dry cleaning business, told friends who sneered at such a low way of making money that *"pecunia non olet,"* meaning "money has no odor."

The hell it doesn't.

George Orwell said in 1940, "To say 'I accept' in an age like our own is to say that you accept concentration-camps, rubber truncheons, Hitler, Stalin, bombs, aeroplanes, tinned food, machine guns, putsches, purges, slogans, Bedaux belts, gas-masks, submarines, spies, provocateurs, press-censorship, secret prisons, aspirins, Hollywood films and political murder." To accept the money proffered by this presumptuous squirt would have drowned me in offal.

So I didn't.

What an absurd world! You flunk algebra and the next semester you teach it. You roll around a month learning judo falls and the next month you start a club. Much of the teach-at-any-cost fervor was caught in the following letter slid under my door during the late 1970s:

> Dear Bob:
>
> Namaste! (No mas, eh.)
>
> I really wanted to come to class during my visit to DC but just could not find the time. I also wanted to thank you personally for giving me my start on the road to spiritual (and shekelar) success, but these two months past just flew by. I cannot make the banquet either, but even tho' I could not give it to you in person, I wanted you should have this token of my success: my first neon sign.
>
> I don't know if you remember me but I was a student of yours at the BCC YMCA in 1977. You really are a great teacher as I learned the form so well in those nine months, I knew I must teach it to others. My job took me to Peoria, and when I remembered your suggestion that a Tai Gee teacher should use a neon sign, I got this one made and started in. Boy was it ever successful! Being in the Midwest the 'Mom & Pop' part worked for most of 'em, and the symbol brought in the rest (probably to see what it was). Pretty soon I quit my main job and later got so many students I built my own building with the profits. I also changed the name of my school and retired this sign. By the way, you should set up grades and belts and have uniforms and competition – people love it! Now with the school and my 'Personal Wealth Through Tai Gee' seminars I've made it like I always wanted. All thanks to you.

Just about the time I was getting bored with the same questions from new students, guess who visited my school? John Gilbey! He's quite a guy and I was surprised you two had not met. You'd like him. And he sure knows your work. Anyway John suggested I get in touch with an Apache shaman in Tijuana called Don Carlos. What a tip! He learned an ancient pure spirit Tai Gee form in a dream and has agreed to teach me (as his only student). This is why I was in D.C. – to get a grant from NEA (successful) and an advance from my publisher for the book (the fifth, two in their sixth printing). Off to Juarez and enlightenment.

So, I owe it all to you. Please accept this token as a sign of my appreciation.

Your boxing brother,
Grand Master Sifu Sensei
/s/ D. LeTant, "Squatting Bear"

There were always undertones of sadness, too. While we encouraged our students to keep such problems out of class, a pretty young woman once told me that her boyfriend was deep into a severe yoga system and had gone celibate. "Six months," she answered to my query about how long this situation had lasted. I commiserated with her and told her to be patient, that many of our students got into fads that they'd dropped fairly quickly. Maybe her beau would do the same. I cite this incident because it was unusual – most of our students' problems came from excess sex rather than abstinence.

After class some of us adjourned to a nearby Bethesda watering spot for breakfast. These breakfasts were sometimes as exciting as the taiji. So much so that some folks made breakfast who had never or no

Talking it up after breakfast at the Deli Den. Ben Lo second on right;
next to him, Denise Yver; and second down from him, John Johnson.

longer attended the class. Some strange ones came to that breakfast paradise. One man who didn't last – hell, few lasted, there was constant turnover – would come to breakfast at 9, order his meal, and let it sit in front of him until 10 when he'd eat it. Extraordinary. Turned out he used the "Hugo" eating system, which permitted eating at only 10 a.m. and 6 p.m. I never heard of it before, or thankfully, since.

So we got all kinds. Most we could help. People came and found a new way of being happy. Doing taiji in the half-light of dawn was like meeting old friends, breathing old air. One student told me it was like taking a shower inside your body. And, borrowing from poet Pablo Neruda, I would tell the group that if you let it, taiji will do to you what spring does to the cherry trees.

Taiji Takes Over

Through the years, students urged that I formalize the taiji by teaching structured fee classes. The Saturday morning free classes were, they said, full of flow and fun but they wanted something deeper. I agreed. As judo paled and became more sterile, the time might be approaching. But did I want to do it? Paul Guo, my internal teacher and one who wouldn't teach even Chinese students, told me when I left Taiwan:

> You are capable of teaching but my advice is – Don't do it! Don't teach. You will invest your time, energy, and love and usually nothing comes back. The students always think they know more than you. They don't believe you; they stop short; they are disloyal. They try to bend you to their own egotistic purpose. And in the end they disappoint you and end by breaking your heart.

A powerful man and a wonderful, sometimes acerbic teacher, his words hung heavy with me. They weren't to be taken lightly.

That "bend you to their own egotistic purpose" reminded me of Cardinal John Henry Newman's observation, "Those who think highly of me feel a respect, not for me, but for some imagination of their own that bears my name." Teachers who are warmed by some students' seeming respect should bear this in mind. These students often defend not the teacher or the teaching so much as themselves in their connection to that teacher. Mindful of Messrs. Guo and Newman, I nonetheless began to teach form classes in taiji in 1970.

Over the years we used several ballet schools for our practice sessions, so we were able to glimpse ballet up close. It was nothing I wanted to do. The toe-stances puzzled me since they seemed a sort of version of ancient Chinese foot-binding. I wondered why the ballet folks simply didn't recruit taller girls. Seriously, I thought it a contrived, unnatural ritual. Compared to taiji, ballet afforded no root, kept too much *qi* in the head and arms, and far too much èpaulement (expression in the upper body). Alas, it knew nothing of relaxation. It could be transiently beautiful to see and a discipline to do, but it was nothing to write home about. And going into the stuffy hall for taiji after fifty pretty young ladies had come out after an hour's exertions made me agree with the great Anton Chekov, "I don't understand anything about the ballet; all I know is that during the intervals the ballerinas stink like horses."

We practiced hard and true. And we saw America evolving from the frantic '60s – thank you Vietnam – through the '70s and '80s. Alice was gradually able to assume responsibility for teaching the beginners. The toughest job in the place, with her dance background and kindly disposition, she did well in giving me students with accurate postures and relaxed movements.

Pat Kenny, one of our best students, once wrote me a touching note. She wrote that if you want to gauge a teacher, watch him around his spouse. If there is discord there, then why should a student expect anything harmonious emerging from his relationship with that teacher? Thankfully, Pat gave Alice and me a passing mark on this rather than a revolver and an upstairs room. This pleased me; I'd always told my classes in judo and the internal Chinese arts never to sacrifice spouse and family for fighting skills. At best, they give you only a fraction of what a family does.

My family was always involved in my martial activity. I wrote above that I met Alice at a YMCA where I was training boxers. I was born in the year of the Tiger (1926) and she, the Horse (1930): the Chinese pronounced that combination a copacetic one. In Taiwan and America, Alice fed all manner of teachers and students including such greats as Yuan Dao and T. Ishikawa. She hosted Professor Zheng in our home in Bethesda; during his visit baby Christine sat on the great one's lap while the other kids gathered round awed by the Chinese sage with whiskers.

A female student of Liu Xiheng and teacher of taiji in Minneapolis

Left: Daughters
Christine and Annette
holding flowers.

Right: Author with daughter
Sue at taiji shindig.

Below:
Mom and Pop sensing something.

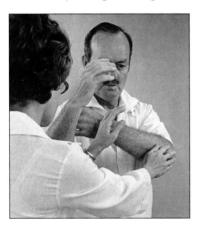

told me a while back that a too-yang male voice on the phone asked her, "Do you push?" To which she answered, "Not on the first date." Alice never did much push-hands, but has been my partner and vital helpmate down the crumbling years. While raising four children and minding nineteen homes in our nearly fifty years of married wonder, she learned taiji, taught several hundred beginners to consistently high standards, and typed numerous books and articles for me. So she figures in all I do, keeping me calm and civil. Though she now devotes her energies to dancing, she invests them with *qi* by doing taiji daily.

Occasionally we brought in excellent teachers from San Francisco and New York City for seminars. Among these were Ben Lo, William Chen, Tam Gibbs, Ed Young, Herman Kauz, and Maggie Newman. There are slight stylistic differences in how most teachers do the form and I wanted our students to see this diversity operating under one set of principles.

Artful repetition is not the all of education. We found and passed on sound counsel cognate to the practice to anyone who would listen. For instance, this advice from psychologist William James:

William C.C. Chen,
the soft pugilist, in
"Bend Bow & Shoot Tiger."

> Keep the faculty of effort alive in you by a little gratuitous exercise every day. That is, be systematically ascetic or heroic in little unnecessary points. Do every day or two something for no other reason than that you would rather not do it, so that when your hour of dire need draws nigh, it may find you not unnerved and untrained to stand the test.

Most taiji systems have no prerequisites for teaching. To prevent adulteration of the form, the Zheng school did. And it was fairly rigorous. In our structured classes, I required at least five years consistent training from students before putting them into the zone of consideration to teach. Then, if the student asked to teach, his/her form, practice teaching ability, and attitude were evaluated and a decision made. Most didn't make it. Of several thousand students across thirty years, I gave "permission to teach" to less than a dozen people. That didn't matter. Most of our students were content to practice taiji as a form of recreation, a hobby, a health/meditation, or social thing.

Tam Gibbs on right sensing-hands
with Ed Young in New York City.

Our students were varied, warm, and loving, in a way, our extended family. They often achieved the synthesis of hyacinths and biscuits that Carl Sandburg called poetry. They supported our frailties and overlooked our defects. Better yet, they were good to one another. Vic Crawford, charter taiji member, state senator, and tobacco lobbyist, couldn't quite dodge irony and contracted throat cancer. At taiji practice, he met Mike Pertschuk, who during his eight-year tenure heading the Federal Trade Commission had, among other things, forced the tobacco industry to put warning labels on their packs of poison. Taiji's proper timing (*shizhong*) attended Vic and Mike's serendipitous meeting. Mike encouraged Vic to go public with his story, and soon Vic was lambasting his former cronies on prime-time TV and in print media. He kept at it till he passed on, helping to put the tobacco monolith back on its heels – a posture it is still in. Afterwards, Vic's widow, Linda, wrote me a poignant letter saying that what distressed Vic most about the episode was that as his condition worsened, he was unable to do his daily taiji.

Pat Kenny was with us first and last. Walking to the guillotine, Marie Antoinette accidentally stepped on her executioner's foot and said, "Pardon me." Few of us have that kind of courtesy. Pat did. We learned from her that taiji was *"keqi quan"* (polite boxing). A big seven as a kid, Pat had had corrective surgery that left her small but still heart-big. Confucius said, "Men look for happiness in that

Pat Kenny, the perfect student.

which is above or below them. But happiness is the same height as man." So being little didn't bother Pat a bit. She told me once that when rain came, it hit her last. I kidded her, "But if the rain continues and a flood comes, won't it get you first?" Good people are sometimes too solemn. Pat would have none of that. "Pardon me, boys, is that the chap who taught you gongfu?" was a sample of her humor.

But we also had our share of doozies. Once a young woman paid the fee for the course of eight hours. She took her first lesson, moved in hyper-euphoria, and then told me that she had experienced a near-orgasmic satori over my commentary as we proceeded from posture to posture. She effused, exalted, exhilarated. Then left. Alice had heard her and wandered over with, "You've made a convert." "Nope," I said,

"We'll never see her again." And so it was, thereby causing me to establish another taiji law, "The Law of Early Enthusiasm," which said that the greater the early enthusiasm, the shorter the longevity.

Another under this heading was a surgeon and his family, a wife and three children. He came in, enthusiastic, saying he'd been looking for me for years. All five signed up and he bought four or five books from the book bag. I saw them after the beginner class and they were still smiling and perspiring. He told me it had been what they had sought all these years and the handshake he gave me was firm and genuine.

The "Law of Early Enthusiasm" got a workout here. They spent over $300 for an hour's practice and were never seen or heard from again. I phoned him to inquire, but, a busy doctor, he never responded. If his check had bounced, I would have understood – this was a thief. But it didn't and I was left with a puzzlement.

There was even occasional guidance from beyond. A Saturday student once confided in me that in dreams a Daoist master from a thousand years ago was teaching him. When I asked for an example of the Daoist's teaching, he replied that in the first taiji posture instead of keeping stiff knees, if you slightly bent your knees they will "disappear" as the junctions open and the *qi* moves through. We had taught this in class the week before. Periodically his Daoist guide would show him postural breakthroughs. In every instance they were things that had been taught in our class. Unusual, but I said nothing. I didn't care who taught it as long as he got it. Alas, neither I nor the Daoist could help him: his form remained stodgy and like a dream, he soon drifted away, perhaps to join his Daoist mentor in some nirvanic dojo in the sky.

One student from a class I gave at Haverford College in Philadelphia, a lazy, lackluster bozo, received a prestigious scholarship for two years taiji research on Taiwan and Mainland China. Later, a friend saw him for a month or so idling in Taiwan and asked why he wasn't doing any taiji. The bland but shocking reply was, "Oh, the scholarship hasn't kicked in yet." Damned diligent dude.

Another time, a wealthy Canadian phoned asking me to recommend a teacher for his son who was shortly off to Taiwan to acquire the real knowledge. I took some pains and drafted a letter to a taiji teacher asking for consideration of the young man. He went. Three years later he had still not contacted my taiji friend, but was studying taiji under the yardman at the CIA installation there, a non-boxer I knew but who now claimed to be expert in boxing. The lad was paying court to the man's daughter. Taiji had been compromised by love or what passed for love. It may have all turned out well – they went on gloriously together, etc. – but I am realistic enough to doubt it. At any rate, it made me leery thereafter of recommending anyone I didn't know well.

But that didn't always work either. I recommended a fellow I thought I knew to Professor Zheng. He went out and when put on hold for a while – a common practice that had happened to me – the guy hooked up with a teacher Laoshi had just booted for unseemly conduct. This wasn't calculated to please Laoshi. A few years afterward, when Zheng invited me to dinner in New York (and even brought a bottle of Napoleon cognac), I asked to bring this fellow along. At the outset of the meal, Laoshi addressed this man pleasantly but firmly, "Mr. Blank, you are Mr. Smith's guest and so we welcome you. But the others here [Tam Gibbs and a couple of other seniors attended] are teachers, and you are not. Be mindful of that." Later at sensing-hands, Laoshi, trying to remember the man, asked, "Weren't you in Taiwan for a time?" When the man nodded, Laoshi asked his teacher's name, and the foolish one named the dissident. Laoshi expostulated in disgust, "His taiji is terrible!" And proceeded to push him from pillar to post.

The man was beyond help. His kind of stupidity lasted like rust. I got away from him but did see him a few times after that. His ego reaction remained that Laoshi was a curmudgeonly old man, perhaps because he'd tried to teach this one twice: at the outset, when Laoshi asked him to wait (good pedagogy), and later when he implied that the guy was a fool in his choice of teachers. Some never learn.

Big Epiphanies From Little Kids

The occasional self-serving adult stupidity was washed out, happily, by the youngest among us, the children. In all these arts, not just taiji, the kids warmed us. While their parents toiled and trained, the kids copied. When they tired, they turned to their toys. We were better for the air of their tiny exhalations.

Because they were closer to *xian-tian* (pre-heaven) energy, the youngsters were always better at relaxation than we adults were. A little girl sat stroking a kitten. Why, she was asked, did she like to do that? She answered, "It softs me so." We play at taiji, stroking its postures, and, in return, it strokes us and softens us. Relaxation comes from imagination as well as touch. We know how refreshing a shower can be. Now imagine that taiji turns on an internal shower, the water coursing throughout your insides, revivifying all your organs. This idea/image too, is a stroking. Try it and see if it doesn't "soft you so."

Mike Ward recently sent me this vignette of his children.

> The other day my children Maya (six) and Colin (four) discussed how God made the world. (They haven't been to Sunday school so were basing their inquiry on family talk about God being everywhere, living in your heart, and being felt when you feel love.)
>
> So Colin said God made the world. Maya asked how he did it. Colin said, "God said the word and the world took it." God told the world what to put on it and the world took that. God was in the sky then. He came down to the world, buried himself under the ground, and became the earth. (I thought of the Apostles Creed, "And the world was made flesh and dwelt among us," and wondered how Colin knew about the power of the word.)
>
> Then Maya asked who made God. Colin said that's "the most serious question." They went on for a while and Maya said, "That's your idea, not something you know, it's your idea." Then they asked me how you know something. I said "you can know things with your mind and you can know things with your heart. You know that plate on the table is blue, but you know someone loves you in a different way."
>
> Colin looked at me quizzically. So, feeling increasingly less certain of what seemed like a good jumping off point to try to explain faith, I asked, "Do you know somebody loves you the same way you know the plate is blue?" Colin replied with an innocent smile, "Yeah, I know you love me."
>
> This reminded me of the Lakota Sioux remark in *Hanta Yo* (1978) about knowledge and mystery, saying something like, "What I know, I own; what I don't know, I call mystery."
>
> It made me happy to know that Colin "owns" my love for him.

Jim Grady tells me that his four-year-old son Nathan looked up from his macaroni and said, "When I was a young man living in Mexico…" (If I were still teaching I'd ask the class how to finish Nathan's phrase. Mine would be: "… I chanced to meet an old man named Señor Bierce.") Then Nathan went on to speak twenty minutes explaining why bees are more important than human beings.

Christ and Daoism urge us to become as children. We so-called adults are really just obsolete children. Gandhi said, "If we are to teach real peace in the world, we shall have to begin with children." The hope of this dusty old world has always resided with the smallest among us. Let's get back there!

Clockwise from top left: my son Dave doing "Press" of taiji; German baby and Chinese friend; quiet time during Saturday morning class; Julian Lowenthal practicing taiji sword with dad, Wolfe; Saturday morning kids join in; New York youngster at taiji.

Back at CIA

In a briefing I attended during the Nixon era, the CIA director likened us all to a character in a joke he told. A motorist has a flat tire beside a deep stream. He removes the wheel but accidentally kicks the hubcap holding the nuts into the stream. He is unsure what to do until a man behind a nearby fence tells him to use a couple of nuts each from two other wheels, which will get him to a garage. When the motorist thanks the man, he notices a sign on the fence: "Croydon Insane Asylum." Surprised, he asks, "You mean you're insane?" The fellow responds, "Yep. I may be crazy but I'm not stupid!"

We were crazy but not stupid. Most of the time. But serving at the pleasure of the President, the CIA at times did stupid things. Though its analytical role on major problems was generally praiseworthy, it often came a cropper on operations. I never believed that covert operations were productive in intelligence, and that was the area in which the CIA most often went awry.

On Vietnam, CIA intelligence estimates kept the war from being messier than it was. Still it was messy. As John Gilbey wrote in his seminal *The Way of a Warrior* (1982):

The United States' no-win grapple in Vietnam.

In the end we lost our butt. We lost because the guerrilla theory of the Viet Cong rested on a stronger base than our massive injections of men and materiel. The Viet Cong out-suffered and out-fought us. Their dead left little debris on the trails and battlefields beyond their bodies and occasionally some poetry; ours strewed cigarettes and condoms. The only solace is that we were wrong and lost. It could have been worse – we could have been right and lost. But, mind you, if we'd been right we wouldn't have lost. We wouldn't have been there.

A good friend at the Agency never forgave Director William Colby for his role in the Phoenix Program, an insane operation that killed 20,000 South Vietnamese, most of them innocents. The plan of several Americans, it was headed by the mild-mannered Catholic, Colby. (Torquemada, the grand inquisitor, was also a good Catholic and daily communicant.) Colby was one of W.H. Auden's "dangerous intellectuals" who muddle where they don't belong and end by mucking things up, cut from the same cloth as Graham Greene's naïve American meddler, Pyle, in *The Quiet American* (1955). (We spent billions visiting hell on this tiny country and all we had to do was read Greene.)

Under Phoenix, Vietnamese could finger as Viet Cong (VC) spies anyone with whom they had a grievance. These luckless folks would then be beaten or killed by joint U.S., Korean, or Vietnamese forces. The desire to obliterate Communist agents in the south made sense pragmatically – if you could have found a rationale for being there in the first place. But against a backdrop of a corrupt, muddling South Vietnam, it couldn't and didn't succeed.

Anyhow, Phoenix flourished and peasants and shopkeepers who had never heard of Marx or Lenin died. And Bill Colby returned to the U.S. and became director of the CIA. In 1939, as he was being driven to Lubyanka Prison in Moscow, writer Isaac Babel turned to one of his secret service captors and said, "You don't get much sleep, do you?" Colby may not have had sound sleeps, but he turned out to be an excellent Director.

But my friend brooded. He had fought against the war inside the Agency and in Vietnam. Substantively, it had been easy. The facts were on his side, so all he had to do was be honest. The South Vietnamese were natural heavies – they had, after all, supported the French against their own nationalists, then become a client state to France's imperial successor, the U.S. Our best and brightest, weaned on the gun and a khaki god, outdid themselves to go along with the ignoble thing.

My friend didn't. He succeeded as a moral being though his career languished. He didn't mind, though he was saddened when Catholic anti-war groups in the Washington, D.C., area called for a walk-out from Mass one Sunday, and only he, his daughter, and one small balding oldster out of 600 or so worshippers left the church they were in. Outside in the frost of early morning, he said to the other fellow, "Sort of lonely out here, isn't it?"

"Naw," the little big man responded with the hugest smile in Christendom, "Naw, it's wonderful!"

Some years later, my friend told me of being in downtown Washington. Crossing a street, he saw Bill Colby coming toward him. Things slowed, Phoenix returned, and he decided to give Colby some penance – he would casually clip him and keep walking. It would be safe for him – he worked so far down from Colby that he'd never be recognized. Plus, unlike Phoenix, my friend didn't aim to injure. Without breaking step, he planned only a short right hand to the shoulder, with only enough power to spill Colby to the pavement.

But as he neared Colby and got ready, a fleshy guy ran past him and all but embraced Colby, crying, "Bill! Bill!" The two started talking there in the middle of the street. My friend slowed, thinking furiously, but there was nothing for it but to abort. So he moved past the talking pair.

The stranger looked like the typical sycophant who crowded the halls at CIA headquarters. My friend told me afterward that if he had to do it again, he would have hit them both. While it wouldn't have been as neat, the sycophant probably deserved it more than Colby.

After Colby drowned while canoeing in May, 1996, my friend wrote that he was glad he hadn't punched Colby, who proved to be a good Director. Colby fired James Angleton, the weirdo at the CIA no one else would touch, and supported a nuclear freeze and cutting the defense budget in half. But being good is not career-enhancing in government, and maladroit President Gerald Ford eventually fired him for helping the press target CIA rogue elephants.

The drowning of Colby brought speculation in the press. Was it senility (he was 76), stupidity, or suicide? And, I would add, if suicide, what part in it was played by a Phoenix rising from the ashes?

This recalls a street incident in which I figured. Let me digress briefly. The sports editor for the student newspaper at the University of Illinois, *The Daily Illini*, from 1950-1952 was Robert Rice. (Concomitantly, somewhere in Champaign-Urbana there lurked another conservative, a pre-teen little boy who stepped on bugs, slept with a night-light, and would later prep a film actor for his debate with Jimmy Carter, then afterward as an objective TV analyst declare Reagan the winner.) Rice was a confused and dour chap, disfigured by egocentricity.

As company executive officer for the ROTC unit at the university at the time (I was poor as an Albanian and needed the overcoat it provided), one of my jobs was to ensure that Rice came to formation in some semblance of order. He was so unkempt he always looked like an unmade bed. Add to this the fact that he had a brain whose synapses weren't always sparking and that he wobbled instead of marched, never knowing the right shoe from the left, and unable to tie either one, and you had the world's worst soldier.

With exquisite irony, years later Rice became the Pentagon's leaky faucet writing for the *Wall Street Journal,* and later still, one of conservatism's chief voices in the media. I was walking one day on Pennsylvania Avenue in front of the White House, and here came Rice. ("… It was Caesar Borgia, and he was coming torgia.") He was strutting, not wobbling, now, and his head was up high so the commoners could see it. The khaki misfit had become Solomon.

Walking toward him, a whim hit me hard and fast. I'd brace him with, "Bob! Bob Rice! I'm Bob Smith. Remember me from ROTC at Illinois? I'm out at Langley with the CIA now. Done pretty well, heading up a Directorate. Hey, this is like old times." Then the kicker: "So, Bob, what are you doing for a living these days?"

Alas, by then I'd passed him. I actually thought of dodging across the street and doubling back to pass him again but the avenue was wide and filled with traffic, so it remained an opportunity missed. Conservatives have all the luck.

At the CIA, I heard of a sharpster on the staff easily the superior of James Angleton and other pathologic types. This one purportedly had no steady office but made a career of roaming the corridors and attending meetings. Poet Oscar Wilde didn't like socialism because meetings took all your evenings. The CIA also had a lot. So this man would go to a meeting and snooze with his eyes not only open but appearing interested (a technique he'd mastered in Himalayan yogic circles). When the briefer ended and asked for questions, his was the first hand up. And his question was always the same: "Where's the power coming from?" Think about it: his query was like the old lady's nightgown…it covered everything. It was an all-purpose, can't-miss query. Irrespective of what field the briefing was on – electric power plants, rebel activity, economic or political dynamics, or military order-of-battle – his question was always on the mark. He retired, I'm told, after thirty years still without an office, at full pension, and with a commendation for outstanding intelligence analysis: "Where's the power coming from?"

It wasn't all work. Humor helped us cope.

The stuff I wrote was classified, but getting it published was competitive all the way. To be printed in the top intelligence publication was a prize highly sought. Because of space limitations one's material sometimes went into "overset," often never to emerge as hotter news shouldered in. I had my say, of course, on this business.

The Kid in Overset

(To the tune of "Let's Go Gung-fuing Tonight")

Every night I fume and fret
Clocking time in overset.

Analysis apocalyptic they let
Sigh and die in overset.

I revise, improve, even stet,
Still I stay in overset.

Regardless of the strain and sweat
Can't get out of overset.

More than any guy I met
I spend purgatories in overset.

(Won't hide it,
Can't abide it;
A lousy scout,
Lemme out!
Said a prayer
But looky there,
A cinch bet –
I'm overset.)

Envoi

So call me by my sobriquet –
The forlorn kid in overset.

But later ...

Threw Mongolia into the fold
Got clobbered, cut me cold,
Talk about Russky roulette –
Now they've got me in underset.

Konrad Lorenz (*Civilized Man's Eight Deadly Sins*) seemed to catch the analytical life I lived in those years. He wrote, "Some formula of time unites passivity and aggression, a formula which is not the rhythm of time in factories but can be compared with more perplexing rhythms of bureaucratic work."

After a fairly brisk start at CIA, I grew bored with the venue and the actors. I lacked a sleepy conscience – this was the era of the Bay of Pigs and Vietnam, after all – and despised the evolving bureaucratic nihilism. I tried to steer a safe course between the Scylla of sycophancy and the Charybdis of unemployment, but after twenty-five years I tired of it and jumped ship with an early retirement.

Before I left, I agreed to a public display in the CIA library of my background in publishing combative and literary works. There was even a big color photograph of me with many of my books. It was all quite splendid and I should have been appreciative. But I wasn't: it wasn't enough. I had to have some fun. So I wrote a display summary that read:

> Robert W. Smith, an analyst in the Office of Economic Research since joining the Agency in 1955 has studied, taught, and written about the Asian martial arts for 35 years. Starting out in western boxing and wrestling, Mr. Smith later became a black belt in judo. For the past twenty years he has specialized in wushu (miscalled kung-fu in America), the Chinese fighting arts, on which he has written several books. A man of varied interests, Mr. Smith has also published poetry, is a frequent book reviewer for the *Washington Post* and *Bookviews*, and for a decade has been researching the internal dynamics of modern bureaucracies. He is currently editing a volume titled *Bureaucratic Success: Essays in Honor of C.M. Truckle.*

Despite the hundreds of brilliant minds in the Central Intelligence Agency, only one person – my boss, who knew me well – caught the chicanery of the last sentence.

To Teach is to Love & Learn: A Soliloquy

The teachin' an the learnin' is gotta mix.

– Uncle Remus

The greatest thing a person can do is to confirm what is deepest in another. This is the highest function of a teacher. Many may be able to teach the mechanics of an art – say taiji – but few can elicit that which lies beyond the obvious. Namely, the art of the art. All of us need help in dissipating the frustrating and futile, in letting our inherent goodness emerge. A good teacher can do this.

How do you recognize a good teacher? Simply by his behavior. He will be gentle, not forceful; he will be mild, not blatant; he will be moderate and modest, but courageous. He will hallow the everyday, touching everything with love. (Remember that line from Richard Llewellyn's *None But the Lonely Heart*, "Everything with a kiss"?) Knowing that a thought is a thing, hence on a par with an act, he will tend his thoughts. He will treat everything sacramentally, but not care for results.

But, because he is loving, he is too lavish to be conservative. His only technique is love, what he himself is. He knows that if he loves, everything will fall in place. It will be hard then for the bad to happen, and if it does, love will transmute it.

Don't pay much attention to what a teacher says. Instead, watch what he does. Many speak and write like angels whose actions are those of ego. Insist on looking beyond words. Watch how a teacher acts around the opposite sex and children. If he is indifferent to them, beware. A good teacher will be open to all and will bend his knee to play with kids.

Wherever love is, teaching occurs. All of us are teachers. The more we are unaware of this, the better teachers we are. Laozi once described three orders of teachers: the lowest is feared and respected, the second is loved and admired, and the highest teaches without being perceived as a teacher at all. He or she is only a friend.

To teach is to learn. That in a nutshell is my approach to teaching. I do not teach to build my ego, to amass students, or to make money.

Ben Lo teaching.

I teach to learn. "Teach" may even be a misnomer; I favor the verb "guide." I guide you to a position where you can operate on your own.

Each student is unique. My guidance tries to take this into account. What works for one will not work for another, so I adjust my methods accordingly. A constant in my technique is humor (there is an old saying, "You can tell a yogi by his laugh"). This may be disconcerting and even annoying to some. To them I respond simply that it is their hang-up.

Many years ago I taught in the samurai tradition, severely and unsmilingly. In the interim, I have learned at least two things: (1) Nothing quite offsets the burdens of life as a light heart; and (2) students learn more quickly when knowledge is imparted smilingly. Does it make sense to let heavy seriousness impede this?

One of our students once commented that I didn't discipline enough. This was in the context of the silent training we sometimes do. He liked this. It eased his meditation. I told him that silence was an important method but that we could not go exclusively down that route; that because we met only once a week, most of our time together had to be devoted to corrective work. Further, I suggested that his daily practice was the time for silent meditation.

He then argued that he wasn't able to be regular and often missed his daily rounds! This admission destroyed his arguments. You have to do the exercise yourself. If you habitually miss your daily practice, you should not talk of discipline. The art is saturated with discipline. It is not my job to bludgeon you into it. You have to do it yourself.

Why seek for gurus? Search instead for a way. When you find it, open yourself to it. Gurus have enough problems without you. To be a guru is to dominate and to dominate is to forfeit freedom. A guru can only introduce you to a way. You must take it. Or, better yet, let it take you. Now, some object to this, saying that this reliance on self is egocentric. Initially, it is true, we work with ego, but only to subvert it, to ultimately flush it down the spiritual drain. To perfect our training with a concomitant increase in our ego will not work. We will end up merely as skilled technicians. To such a one, the old Daoist saying applies, "When the wrong man uses the right means, the right means work in the wrong way."

Thus, let go of the guru-trips and grab hold of yourself. Where? In the dantian, just below the navel. And the next time you hear someone shout, "Call unto me, and I will answer thee, and show thee great and mighty things which thou knowest not" (*Book of Jeremiah*), go ahead and call and learn from him – but do not worship him.

Why, after all, do we seek a guru? Simply because he seems to give us the root we lack. But this is a dodge. Rather than work on ourselves, we extrapolate outward the inadequacy we feel, thus splitting our natures and cheating ourselves. For everything we need – our root, our security – is available within ourselves so that we can stand (in Emily Dickinson's fine lines):

> Adequate, erect
> With will to choose
> Or to reject:
> And I choose –
> Just a throne.

Xingyi & Bagua:
The Other Internal Arts

Along with taiji, I began teaching xingyi and bagua to a few students. Xingyi is a highly focused linear fisting form while bagua stresses the palm in an ambiance of circles. These two were relatively unknown in America in the early 1960's. (Culture critic Marshall McLuhan's words to the effect that in America if it hadn't been on TV it had never happened, applied: xingyi and bagua as far as I know had never made it to TV.) Despite that, over time a small solid core of students of these disciplines developed in Bethesda, several remaining for decades.

While not making it to TV, xingyi and bagua soon enough made it to the magazines. Where once there had been two or three teachers soon there were seeming multitudes in the country. Research grants were sought and granted.

A chap from Chicago visited us; he was in Washington, D.C., to secure a teaching grant in bagua. He showed up and glibly told us in glittering detail of his vast knowledge of the art. Catching him in a pause, I announced that it was time to go to work, for everyone to get on the circle. Puzzled he asked, "What circle?"

Author doing xingyi.

Another, more effeminate, signed up to join the class, plunking down fifty bucks for eight sessions. We worked less than twenty minutes when he stopped, out of breath and panting. He told me that I could have the money but he was withdrawing and wouldn't be back – this stuff had no functional use. I took him to a back room and told him that he was in dreadful shape and not to rationalize his inadequacies on the basis of bagua's and xingyi's purported lack of function. That he could choose the oldest man in the class (me) or the youngest girl (twenty) and attempt to make his case. He went to pieces but refused to take his money back. I forced it on him and away he went. I tried to figure it out later, but the best I could come up with was that he had never intended to take the course but did it to pad his resume, to say he had learned under me.

A couple guys would visit us occasionally spouting stuff such as Chinese boxing was taught only in the suburbs by some teachers who wouldn't teach it in D.C. because it was too tough a place for them. But these boys were paper dragons. The biggest one fancied taiji, especially push-hands, until the morning he was pushed too hard and tried to fight the wall. Veterans knew that when pushed against the wall, you had to relax and make it push-friendly. However, this one never worked hard enough to become a veteran. His ego was several sizes too big for his talent. Both men converted to bagua and xingyi but neither could last out the three hours of our monthly seminars. The last time I saw the big one, he said he'd made a breakthrough in bagua by looking at Sun Lutang's photo in a Chinese book. He said it was a great book. I told him to cherish it.

A Houston bunch invaded our turf once and even announced that their grand champion boxer had chosen me as his ultimate teacher. These people gave new toxicity to Texas, a place already choking in it. Anyway, this intergalactic champion enrolled for xingyi/bagua practice but couldn't stand the pace and dropped out. But before he did, he came to a taiji breakfast. In the voluble talk, this chap said that he could push a person without contact. Before he could continue we cleared the area and put relaxed Harry Johnston out there and invited Houston to have at him. He smiled and thanked me for the opportunity to show Texas esoterica. Then he held his hands on Harry's aura (I guess) and then moved them around in the air while asking Harry if he didn't feel an impulse moving him back. Harry encouraged him, "Not yet." Houston kept at it but Harry, now almost asleep, wasn't moving. After ten minutes I suggested to the chap that Harry's vibes may have gone negative and we replaced him with an older woman who was unstable in the posture at the best of times. She stood and Houston, intent, went to work. To no avail – she didn't budge, and after five minutes Houston gave up, ruefully saying, "I can't understand. We all do this in Houston!"

Another time the phone rang at 3:00 a.m. I picked it up reluctantly. A panicky chap at the other end said he was calling from San Antonio. He hated to call at this time, he said, but it was an emergency. When I asked the nature of the emergency he told me that he regularly "chased his qi" through his body, but an hour earlier it had become stuck in the back of his neck and now he couldn't move it up or down. The damned thing was stuck. What should he do?

I'd had a hectic day and to have my sleep stolen by a Texan didn't help my state of mind. I asked, pretending amiability, "You say it's right at the base of the neck?" He said, yes, yes, and again yes. My voice went cold. "Then there's not too much that can be done. That's the jade pillow area and once it's jammed there, it's hell to get it moving. If you're lucky it'll dissipate in a week. I'm sorry." And rang off. I went back to sleep instantly.

Though taiji had more flakes, xingyi and bagua had their share. A physical therapist visited me once. He plunked down fifty bucks for an hour of xingyi/bagua. As I got started, he interrupted to ask if he could show me what his teacher down south had taught him. I sighed and said it was his hour, show away. And sat down and got comfortable. I thought it might take awhile. It did.

He moved into a sort of eerie dance while hitting himself with a staccato of punches with light half-closed fists. He moved and rapped himself to no apparent purpose. It was agonizing to watch and I tried not to. On and on his form went, inexorably eating his hour. After about fifteen minutes he stopped. I tried quickly to rally us to reality. Too late, he moved into what looked like a repeat but which he announced with a superior air was a quite different form. The other had been Leopard, this was different. And on he went for another fifteen minutes. Finally, God is good, he stopped the moving and self-flagellation. And asked, "What do you think that was?" I wearily responded that I wasn't sure but it sounded like "Sweet Georgia Brown." He regarded me as the cretin I was and said, "No, it's Lion form." Like so many flakes in these arts, he could have whipped his weight in wildflowers.

He paused long enough for me to get him started on the xingyi "Five Fists." In the remaining half-hour, he only got to the first, *piquan* (splitting fist). He talked too much about his teacher and his systems to make much headway, often interrupting his own interruptions. As time ran out, I told him I hadn't really given him much, but he disabused me of the notion. He said it had all been instructive and marvelous and we had to do it again sometime. As he walked away I almost asked him how much I owed him. But he had taken my "Sweet Georgia Brown" remark in good grace, and I was afraid to rile him lest he turn on me and beat me senseless with that staccato of Leopards and Lions.

And every once in a while, there was truth. Ted Hillson, a karate instructor from Pennsylvania, came down often for xingyi/bagua workouts. After breakfast one Saturday, he blindfolded himself and challenged one of our students to punch him in the jaw. Each time from behind his blindfold, he deflected wicked shots, some of them quite close. Something of a magician – in a room in half-light he could levitate – his show pivoted on a trick blindfold. He said that if anyone offered to do the trick, don't let him use a blindfold. Make him squint his eyes instead.

Speaking of blindfolding, Johnny Osako at the old Chicago Judo Club in the 1940's sometimes had us do judo blindfolded with guards all round because in that smallish place the mats butted the wall. It was eerie. Eyes are not only the mirror of the soul but also are the big stabilizer. Try your practice blindfolded sometime and you'll see what I mean.

Staying with Johnny, the new boxing training didn't erase the old judo that sometimes came into play. In Chicago, Johnny Osako had taught me an ancient resuscitation method (*katsu/kappo*). I used it twice one afternoon in the 1940's to revive a woman at a beach near Quincy. Another time a woman with a stubborn nose bleed nearly caused the conductor on a train outside Champaign to pull the cord. I

Some of the xingyi/bagua bunch. Front row, L to R: Tom Skinker, Stu Scantlebury, Allen Pittman, Dan Egan, Dainis Jergenson; Back row, L to R: Paul Cote, Colin Wiltshire, Bill Ryechan, Jay Falleson, Irene Lee.

asked him if I could try to help her. He let me, and my massage of her carotids did the trick. I used the same technique for various boxers in those days and it never failed.

It didn't, couldn't, help the big young fellow just back from Vietnam, however. Delivering milk on my street in Bethesda one morning, his stand-up truck hit a dip in the road and threw him out the door. There he got whipsawed between the truck and a sapling, and ended up on the lawn near my house. I pulled a light bulb from the truck out of his neck and eased him a bit before the rescue squad came, but he died as I did so. I wanted to use kappo or at least mouth-to-mouth resuscitation on him but I didn't know mouth-to-mouth and the crowd that gathered made me leery of doing kappo. Feeling bad about it, I later queried the fireman who lived across the street who worked with the rescue squad. He quashed my guilt, saying that nothing could have saved the young man from the terrible trauma to his internal organs.

Along with the orthodox xingyi/bagua menu, I urged on my students the venerable practice of "stake standing." Quiet standing and sitting are not unique to Asia. Even Socrates liked to do it and reportedly did it once through an entire night in below-freezing weather. But the Chinese have had a corner on it in the last century. Americans and Europeans don't relish it. In fact, there is a Gaelic saying to the effect that an Irishman would rather walk thirty miles than stand one. It's a lonely business, but doing it enough, one can meet the meaning of Laozi's key maxim, "The way to do is to be."

This static work is boring to most people in our frenetic society. I agree with Irish poet AE (George Russell) when he wrote that will is the thing. Seekers for intelligence or beauty are easily accommodated. But work on the will is too hard. Therefore, few do it. Oliver Gogarty, poet friend of AE, nicely got at its reward: "...If but the will be firmly bent / No stuff resists the mind's intent."

Kenichi Sawai,
a Japanese exponent
of the stakehold.

One of my best senior students, Bart Ingram, started off boxing with a Chinese chemist in Ohio. The Chinese was lavishingly lugubrious and provided Bart with enough fantasy nonsense for him later to seek the core of truth in this blizzard of baloney. But his next foray into Chinese boxing was even worse. His second Chinese teacher (a 10th-dan!) purportedly communicated weekly with his own teacher in Taiwan using ESP. In those days, America was awash in such

Bart Ingram testing the Internal.

cretins; later with Bruce, Sylvester, and the other Hollywood fantasists it got worse. Anyhow, this 10th-dan told Bart that I had beaten five men in the street in Australia and another five in Taiwan. (I've never been Down Under and no such incident happened in Taiwan.) This story traveled quickly. Another version had the incidents occurring only in Taiwan. A third story brought back both venues but soberly declared that all ten of the muggers were drunk. I hear tales even now about the derring-do I did for the nefarious OSS and its successor CIA despite the fact that I was too young for OSS and I spent my time in CIA as a mere desk-warrior. Truly, a lie will be around the world before the truth gets its pants on.

Wanting to test the internal in actual fighting, Bart participated in five Golden Gloves tournaments in Atlanta, Georgia, and Auburn and Montgomery, Alabama, between 1979 and 1983. After losing his first bout to the local champion on a close decision – he had him stunned early but ran out of gas in the last round – he avenged that loss and won his next fifteen matches, four by knockout, and eleven by unanimous decision. Modest, he told me that he was lucky, for he never fought anyone really good.

He found that his biggest problem was breathing – each sport has its own rhythm – and so he devised a scheme whereby he ran like a thief in the first round, making his opponent chase him. With his great fitness, this was a breeze, and emboldened his antagonist to throw more than he should have. Then he'd start boxing in the second round and sustain a steady barrage for the next two rounds, winning easily.

If he could have whipped the breathing problem he could have got more kayos – but the respiratory rhythm is the last thing to come for a sometime boxer. As it was, my light heavyweight made such a point of comforting the losers afterwards, he was regarded strangely by the fight crowd. And by that time he had learned that the internal could prevail against beef, so he tired of the experiment and left off.

It was a diverse, happy group of people who met for xingyi/bagua. They gave their teacher nothing but attention. On the other hand, taiji seemed to attract some strange people. The xingyi/bagua students were sounder, more rooted, with hearts full of respect and heads focused on training rather than off-the-wall attitudes. We carried the odd ones that came, but the work was too hard for attitudes and they dropped away after awhile.

About 1985, one of my seniors, John Lang, circulated the following notes for his classmates:

To those who would learn bagua and xingyi: observations and suggestions after twelve years at the well with a leaky bucket.

♦ Come to each class with a learner's mind.
♦ Starters: pay attention to the feet – placement, stepping rhythms, and weight shifts.
♦ To do the forms correctly you must be able to stand on one leg. To obtain a foothold you must bend your knees, relax, and sink. Consecutiveness is the necessary ingredient.
♦ Heed Mr. Smith's invitation to work, relax, and cooperate. Work involves practice. To practice is often easy; to become one who practices is not. Nor will classes alone teach you the art.
♦ A beginner's task: Find a place to practice. Regularly.
♦ Read the books. Read them again and study the practice advice. Put them down and go practice.
♦ Circle walking in class –
   a. If you walk up on the student in front, increase your circle's size and step outside your classmate's feet.
   b. If a space opens in front of you, you are crowding classmates behind you – bend your knees, step longer, and close the gap.
   c. A circle only a little wider than that classmates are walking lets you work more – sink lower and take longer steps.
   d. Doing changes, the first step – the "toe in/out" – is most important; well begun, half done.
♦ Form Practice [on next page].

Form Practice.
First it is not how you do it;
but that you practice.
Then it's not that you practice,
but how you do it.
Later it's not how –
but that you not do it.
And when it does you
There it is.
~ J. Lang

Author walking
the bagua circle.

Over the years, new and old students still come to visit, practice, and reminisce. Some even come from abroad. Will Bibby, a xingyi veteran from England, stopped by and while here repaired a gate that had been waiting for him. And I occasionally visit Washington, D.C. Paul Cote told me recently that they had an "open arts" practice to which they invited any taiji student in the area, regardless of style, to come and try xingyi/bagua. There was a good turnout and everyone seemed to have fun. The most interesting discovery to come from the session, said Paul, was that those studying the Zheng Manqing form easily and fluently did these new internal movements. However, those from other taiji styles almost to a person were stiff and double-weighted.

Rose Li:
Cherchez la Femme

The best female internal boxer I ever met (and that includes the exquisite Jasmine Dong of Hong Kong) was Rose Li. I met Rose through letters and later visited her in England several times and hosted her for a week in Bethesda.

Rose Li at Dong Haichuan's tomb.

Rose has taught the internal boxing arts for over twenty-five years in London. A small, pleasant woman, her background in boxing is absolutely unique. She began boxing at age eight during the 1920s under the renowned Deng Yunfeng, a xingyi student of Geng Jishan and an associate of Sun Lutang, Shang Yunxiang, and other leading boxers. For a young girl from an upper middle-class Beijing family to take boxing was almost unheard of in those days. Her father actually made her take it for its health benefits. Her mother opposed it, fearing she would turn out like her uncle who had studied Shaolin from a well-known teacher, become an opium addict, and from age forty used his gongfu to exploit and terrorize his family.

Rose practiced with Master Deng for about fifteen years, from the time she was a tomboy eight until she was twenty-four. Deng came thrice weekly to her home and remained for dinner afterward into the evening. Thus the relationship went far beyond boxing. In some respects, "Uncle Deng" became an additional father to her, and her family became part of his.

Early on, Rose wrote me, "I could sit here and praise him for hours. He is still in my warm and living memory as a father, teacher, and friend. He enriched and strengthened my life and nothing – no fame nor wealth – thereafter could corrupt me. Thus I sometimes became known to clever people as a failure."

Rose Li (on right, first row) as a youngster standing with Master Deng Yunfeng's internal group in Beijing, late 1920's or early 1930's. Deng (arrow) is smiling in second row. Famed taiji master Liu Fengshan is slightly back of Deng's right shoulder. The mustached man on his left in a silk brocade jacket may be Deng's teacher, Geng Jishan. Rose's father is back and slightly right of her, next to the mustached man.

Rose graphically described part of a training session at home this way:

> He sat and watched me as I walked through piquan ['Splitting,' the first of the xingyi Five Fists] for 15-20 minutes without stopping. Then "Stop and rest," he'd say and walk to me to adjust my knee. "Doesn't that feel better? It wasn't quite right. You didn't harmonize your knee to the toe. A posture wants to be alive, not dead." Then we would continue. Later he would correct my taiji form. As he sat he would smoke his pipe and eat watermelon. His eyes missed nothing. And, though he was kindly he made no concessions for my age or sex. I did it until it was right.
>
> He used to say, "True humility is not feeling that you know nothing; rather, it's to know what you know and don't know." He didn't negotiate in his teaching. He once shouted at an uppity influential visitor. "Just do it. If it's xingyi I'll tell you. If it's not I'll also tell you. So don't argue!"

Besides private instruction in her home, Rose also regularly went to Deng's training center at the inner court of a Daoist temple. Many students came there. Master Deng was kind to most of them and there was much good social interaction. For instance, one of his students was a prominent banker who helped Rose raise money for her father's funeral. Although Deng had many students, he remained poor.

Along with the students, Deng's kindness and skill also brought many famous masters. Liu Fengshan (a.k.a. Liu Caizhen), a famous student of Yang Banhou's pupil Wu Quanyu, came regularly to teach taiji to Rose and other interested students.

An old photograph Rose gave me (p. 252) shows a smiling Master Deng flanked on his right by, I believe, Master Liu and on his left by a mustached man in a brocade jacket who might be the famed Geng Jishan, Master Deng's teacher. Rose didn't recollect his name, and I am guessing from the picture of a mustached Geng in *Asian Fighting Arts* (1969). Negating it being Geng was the fact that Rose would surely have remembered her grandteacher, if it were he. Also, for it to be Geng, the time would have to be 1929, the last year of Geng's life. But Rose would have been only ten years old then – whereas she looks closer to fourteen as she stands first in the front row on the far right. Be that as it may, the man standing to the left of the mustached mystery boxer, in back of Rose, is her father. Rose has another much better quality photograph of a group of masters with Deng and the mustached boxer in it. Other than Deng, she knew nobody in that one.

Master Deng had two sons adept at boxing, but I don't know whether they are in the photograph here. He hailed from Shandong and his wife remained there except for occasional visits to Beijing. One of Deng's assistants, unidentified but in the photograph, ended badly in Mao's Cultural Revolution. The young Red Guards invaded his home, seized his weapons, and ridiculed him. This was a common occurrence in that troubled time. As was the sad denouement – Rose's boxing brother died of a stroke as a result of the assault.

Some visitors taught Deng's students in their own specialties such as bagua and taiji. Others came less frequently just to chat with the amiable, winning Deng. Rose told me that as a youngster she once heard everyone at the center talking of the impending visit of a great taiji teacher. (Alas, she either forgot or never knew his name.) The day arrived and an old man presented himself; everyone including Deng treating him deferentially.

Sun Lutang, a colleague of Master Deng.

The little girl watched as the old man strode to the center of the practice area and began his exercise. He stood and seemed not to move and yet everyone oh-ed and ah-ed, swept away in admiration. Rose was mystified and a bit bemused. She looked again at the man doing almost nothing and then at her older classmates and still could not connect their admiring sighs with the barely moving oldster. When she asked Deng about it, his eyes sparkled as he told her that he was too great for a child to understand.

Master Deng was a friend of Sun Lutang, but that worthy, famous through his books, now was a darling of the warlords. Deng believed that Sun neglected his share in furthering the wushu spiritual heritage. When Rose was accepted as a member of Deng's wushu family, Deng invited Sun Lutang to attend the ceremony. When Sun failed to appear, Rose asked the reason. Deng told her, "Your father is not famous, otherwise Sun would have come." Rose didn't understand. Her family was not rich, but well-educated and upper middle class.

Though never defeated in a fight, Master Deng had a circumspect view of challenges. "When a tree grows too high it gets too much wind," a favorite saying of his, catches his feeling on the subject. The fact that he always insisted that you lost if you bloodied or damaged an opponent in a fight – a good boxer should be able to defeat a man without hurting him – also showed his style. Two expressions of Rose's are also germane, "As a result of my training, I am better for me. To compare with someone else is irrelevant. I don't live their lives: I live mine." The other, "Skill is secondary, a good master is one whose character is stronger than his fists," neatly rounds out Deng's and Rose's attitude on fighting.

By the time Rose came to America in 1949 she had earned an M.A. in ethnology at Furen University in Beijing (1947). In America, she received an M.A. in educational psychology at Columbia in 1950. She lived in America (San Francisco, New York City, and Ann Arbor, Michigan) until 1967 when she went to Durham, England.

I originally heard of her from T.T. Liang, whom she had met in New York City. Liang had urged her to come with him to see Professor Zheng. She resisted, saying that Zheng with his association with Madame Chiang Kai-shek was too grand for the likes of her.

This sprang from her detestation of the corruption of Chiang's Nationalist government in China. Though she was sympathetic to the Communist's anti-feudal campaigns, she opposed the Maoist ideology.

Only her Deng Yunfeng boxing family with its mutual affection and loyalty sustained her.

When I first knew her, Rose was teaching Chinese language class-es at the University of Michigan. She remained several years and even attempted at one point to start a taiji class in Ann Arbor, but it didn't last. We developed a friendship through the mails, each being warmed by the other's experience and words. We didn't meet for several years, however, and then it was in England where she had moved to accept a job teaching Chinese at the University of Durham. She told me there that my written support of her had contributed to the success of her teaching internal boxing.

I visited her several times in England, twice helping her with her summer camps. I lectured and gave classes on sensing-hands. Before one visit, I had written Terry O'Neill, captain of the British karate team, that I would see him at Rose's studio where he was learning taiji. I met him outside the hall. He told me that he couldn't hear me speak that day because Rose had banned him. He had missed taiji practice one Saturday when he and the British National karate squad were off fighting in France. (She could be a tough mentor.) I interceded with Rose and she grudgingly admitted him.

Rose had learned taiji from the renowned Liu Fengshan, who reg-ularly taught at Uncle Deng's. (Her students had to earn their spurs by first learning taiji and bagua for two years before being accepted for xingyi.) I got to see and feel much of her form, which came from the rarer Yang Banhou side of the Yang lineage. She told me that she did-n't believe in molding the student postures, that everyone had a differ-ent psycho-physical makeup that correct practice would take care of in the end. This hands-off pedagogy seemed awry to me. I do not think a person can learn taiji without being molded continually. Even prac-ticed eyes cannot detect what sensitive fingers can.

So while one of her seniors did the form and she praised him to me, I asked if I could touch him. She assented. He stood tall, but tense to my eyes. I felt his lumbar area, chest, and shoulders. He was stiff as a board. I told Rose that he needed to relax more. After doing this to sev-eral others, I concluded that this form was often double-weighted and not relaxed. As it was a long form, the students were repeating basic errors. I believe this was the result of inadequate learning or dilution of Liu's original form by a young woman whose overwhelming first love was xingyi.

This may seem a harsh judgment, but it is the way I learned taiji. It is no bowl of cherries, but an exacting business. Nor is it gratuitous. I am not trying to hurt or offend, but when I write I teach – or try to – and teaching takes precedence over ruffled feelings. Those who are piqued by it should do as Zheng Manqing advised – check their taiji against the Classics. If they still think they are doing it correctly, then perhaps I'm wrong.

In 1980, Rose came to Bethesda and stayed a week with us. Here I got to really see and feel her xingyi. Her form was profound, absolutely exquisite, with body and mind coalescing perfectly. I watched in awe and she corrected my form. She attended some of our classes, endearing herself to all the students. They found her, as I had, a singular person commingling skill and spirit.

We got in many sessions of xingyi work. She was indefatigable and thrived on it. In London, she would lead classes hours on end. And when we rested, she would talk of the old days. During the 1940's war against Japan, she once was with a group of several hundred missionaries and Chinese fleeing the approaching Japanese. I can recall two tales from that grim exodus. In Henan Province, their group came upon gaunt, starving villagers who seemed to be surviving (barely) on taiji and opium. As everyone in old Hawaiian villages knew and did the hula, here everyone young and old, male and female, spent their time blending the internal, taiji, and the external, drugs. She traced the journey – over 800 miles – and it was through the area in Henan of Chenjiagou, birthplace of Chen-style taiji. Until she told me the story, she seemed unaware of the Chen village's location or its contributions to taiji.

She told me that on that same sojourn when they were descending a mountain, they encountered a strong odor of orchids where there were no orchids. A bit later when they came into the valley they found the orchids but smelled no perfume! It was a rare mountain variety noted for its perfume – only at a distance. We spoke of this in boxing terms. Some students, I remember saying, could only appreciate a teacher from a distance. If they got too close and sat too long at his feet, after a time the feet began to smell. I even had a senior who told an out-of-town student that he was lucky that he lived away from us – presumably, so that the teacher could never see his warts. Another explanation of this perfume-from-a-distance is that students fail to see the obvious. They will believe a highly publicized stranger instead of their own teacher. For them, the perfume is in the lure of the thing rather than the thing itself. Oblivious to the obvious, resistant to reality, these students remain forever blind. Didn't Mencius warn us to forego the distant for the near at hand?

I told Rose of Professor Zheng's response to a question raised in New York City. Observing flowers while out for a walk, a student asked Professor why few flowers in America had odors. Laoshi, twinkling, answered with a question, "Could it be that they're offended by you?"

Rose's views on boxing were similar to her iconoclastic anti-traditional political views. She advocated honesty and openness and deplored kowtowing and secrecy. She'd often cite Deng quoting Sun Lutang's and Shang Yunxiang's criticism of the traditional method of teaching bagua, with its insistence on an overly twisted body and staring at the index finger. The first was bad because it could hurt your back or spine and the second could make you dizzy. One should stretch the arms only as far as is comfortable and look past the hand at the surroundings without staring at anything in particular.

According to Deng, Sun Lutang's taiji was not too good, but his xingyi and bagua were acceptable. Some other boxers were just as good, but they lacked his scholarship and literary ability. Unlike the largely illiterate boxers of his day, Sun could write excellent essays and books, and thus became famous. Some leading boxers – Yuan Dao for one – and historians in Taiwan had made similar observations to me regarding Sun.

For Rose, Master Deng was the greatest boxer of them all. Seeing him through the prism of a young girl growing to adulthood, this is understandable. She had much emotion tied up in him. But she eschewed warmth to analyze Deng from his xingyi boxing and teaching ability. Here she was coldly factual.

In Beijing in the 1930's, she recalled, it was not customary for boxers to distinguish different schools of taiji from each other, for instance Yang Style, Wu Style, and so on. Rather, it was generally accepted that each master assimilated the traditional teachings and adapted them to his own needs and physique. Deng believed that following his discipleship, a boxer could and should adapt the principles of xingyi to develop his own forms and stylistic variations of other systems, for example, the bagua free-form.

That is for the teacher or senior, Rose said. But learning xingyi is another matter. For the student, there are no two ways. Unlike taiji or

Rose's old bagua group is still active. She is in foreground (ca. 1985).

bagua, in xingyi it's either right or it's wrong. (I disagree: the all-or-none principle applies to all three internal arts.) Xingyi pivots on mind and spirit. These must be developed by continuous guided practice while young. One book she cited as embodying the letter and spirit of xingyi, though she couldn't recall the author, was *Xingyiquan Shu Jiangyi* (*Illustrated Lecture on Xingyi Boxing*, a small edition only for private circulation, probably published in Beijing in the 1930's).

On the difference between internal (*neijia*) and external (*waijia*), Rose was forthcoming. Some say that all boxing is external – only sitting meditation or *qigong* are truly internal. As soon as there is movement, the practice becomes external. Rose disagreed. Her view is that internal refers to the inner self and is used to distinguish boxing for self-cultivation from boxing for display. External boxing is impressive, flamboyant, often very acrobatic, and always practiced for an external purpose – sport, self-defense, or demonstration. However, the internal can never be a sport since primary emphasis is placed on mind (or intent, *yi*) with which the body harmonizes and which it follows. The internal has no physical culture (i.e., bodybuilding) aspect and no intention of affecting anyone else. From the health standpoint, the external may offer initial advantages, but by age thirty one's body begins to change and health will deteriorate. The internal, on the other hand, can be practiced throughout life.

The internal and external each has its own teacher/student relationship. Because external boxing is mainly interested in technique and outward effect, the student needn't respect the teacher's character to learn from him. Inner attitude makes little difference. However, to learn the internal one must harmonize mind (*yi*) with the teacher. Of course, genuine respect cannot be forced on anyone. By its very nature it has to come spontaneously from within. No amount of outward formality can compensate for its absence. Lack of love or of deep respect for one's teacher – or worse, actual hostility – causes inner disharmony that is reflected outwardly in the boxing. To cultivate harmony between inner and outer, there must be harmony between teacher and student. Then one becomes a disciple, not just a student.

Thus, one cannot evaluate an internal teacher merely in terms of physical skill. His character and level of spiritual development are more important and should command even greater respect. A good teacher won't dazzle students with promises of supernormal powers or lure them in other ways. This only distracts attention from the here-and-now and creates over-expectation that obscures mind. Only when the student himself reaches a certain level of attainment can he see the value of higher *gongfu* (achievement) and advance to it. A good teacher always relies on his own experience as final authority. Many inferiors try to climb on a teacher's reputation. But it is irrelevant who taught you, if you don't have "it."

Master Deng once told Rose, "Never use my name, or anyone else's, to justify your own beliefs." She could call him teacher and be of his xingyi lineage, but what Deng meant was that the student must work so that later her teaching, while reflecting the master's, was her own. The student, turned senior, justifies herself by her own achievement, not by her teacher's name.

Another time, Rose told me that most seniors, after several years should, like fledgling birds, be turned from the nest, so that over-reliance on the teacher doesn't take hold and stultify. But she told me once that across two decades or more of teaching, she still has more than a dozen students who have been there for the entire journey. This suggests that certain students are not pushed from the nest, but rather sustained for as long as they care to stay.

What does Rose regard as essential in xingyi? I list some of her principal beliefs:

♦ Xingyi movements should all be as simple, direct, and natural as possible. Do not waste time or energy. Aim for maximum efficiency. If you do not always feel comfortable, then it's wrong.

♦ It is quite easy to learn the Five Fists, but they require years of practice to master. You only learn through continuous guidance by an expert. Most corrections, though seemingly small, are basic, hence important.

♦ The legs are all. Without *tuijin* (leg energy), you have nothing.

♦ At first, practice quietly and slowly with no sudden exhalation or noisy feet. Without this easy beginning manner you can injure your insides. After a time, when coordination has improved, you may use a more outward energy, breathing in deeply through your nose, gently tensing your lower abdomen, then releasing your energy all at once as you exhale sharply through your nose. Rose observed that while she was watching a xingyi group practice outside a Beijing temple, she actually felt the ground shake under her feet like an earthquake!

♦ Xingyi can't be taught to old people, though it can be continued through old age. By middle age, the body processes – breathing, for instance – change too much. If learned late in life, it will lack xingyi spirit.

Finally, let me detail the first of the Five Fists, *piquan* or splitting fist. Though called a "fist," this action uses the open hand as the striking member. Splitting's most important moment is half-way through, just before the release of energy. If your arms are very long, the strike doesn't have to come out in front of your nose. More importantly, always keep your arms as close as possible to your body. Never lean left or right: your body is always centered between your two legs. Lean slightly forward, spine erect, shoulders rounded and sunk, and chest hollowed.

Keep your fingers relaxed and lightly touching, the tips bent a little, and the palm hollowed. Do not exaggerate your "tiger mouth" (*hukou* – the area between the thumb and the index finger). Rather make it like Zheng Manqing's "Fair Lady's Hand." Here Rose is contrasting Master

Rose's bagua brother, Gao Zeying (on right of sign) had a special touching ability. Rose is on the left of sign.

Deng's natural "Tiger Mouth" to that of some teachers who stretched the thumb away from the index finger instead of letting it stand naturally.

Always keep your feet flat on the ground, whether full or empty. Step onto the whole sole at once, not heel-to-toe as in taiji. Point your front foot straight ahead a little to the side of your back heel. As your front foot withdraws to the rear, rest it on the ground by your

Sun Jianyun (on left), daughter of Sun Lutang, here does a wushu set with friend Rose.

rear foot, the whole foot flat but empty. Sit down into the posture and hollow out the inner thigh/groin (inguinal) area. Keep your lower spine straight as the upper torso leans slightly forward.

Bring your arms back as close as possible to your body, elbows in to sides, fists lightly balled fingers up, facing each other and cupping under your navel at the dantian. Your fists climb your body leading your empty foot forward to toe-out. Now take your body directly forward facing straight ahead. Your opposite hand and foot attack in unison, releasing simultaneously both the energy from the base of the spine and the qi from the navel. Use your whole body – your limbs are merely extensions. Your waist pulls your torso slightly to the side as your body falls forward and down onto your "enemy." Come down firmly onto your front foot, follow-step with your rear foot, shifting sixty percent of your weight to it, ending up in the "on-guard" position (*santi*).

In 1982, Rose left Durham and bought a new house in London, where she established Chinese language and cultural arts classes. Though she attracted even more students and visitors, she often was vexed at their behavior. These quick-study emperors quickly knew – or thought they did – more than she and went off teaching. And in her several trips back to Beijing to renew relations with Deng's old wushu group, she met and learned of Chinese so-called teachers going to America for the fast buck. In 1986, her bagua brother Gao Zeying told her that so-and-so was leaving to teach bagua in America. Rose objected, saying he knew relatively little. Gao answered, "Most Chinese going there have only a 'quick-learn,' and then they earn a lot of money. The Americans only hear what you say, but they can't see."

Gao's father had been a xingyi classmate of Deng Yunfeng, presumably under Geng Jishan. Gao was an accomplished bagua master and Rose told me startling things about his ability to touch her and raise her from the floor with no muscular effort and to completely manage her. Another of her classmates was the son of famed Liu Fengshan. I was never able to visit the group to meet these stellar men. Liu died in 1985 and Gao, if alive, is nearing ninety.

In 1990 and 1993, Rose spent much time visiting with Sun Lutang's daughter, Sun Jianyun. They became great chums. Sun taught taiji and was gaining fame as a painter. By 1994, her growing prominence obscured their friendship and it waned, somewhat reminiscent of what had occurred between Deng and Sun Lutang years before.

Sun's daughter told Rose how a Japanese fighter had once issued a challenge to her father. In the week or so awaiting the challenger, Sun Lutang nervously walked around the house trying to distract himself from the coming combat. He didn't talk much to family members and remained aloof from domestic concerns. Finally the challenger arrived and Sun speedily beat him and returned to his usual equable state. This story smacks of realism in contrast to many that invariably show the master imperturbable before and after the conflict.

Rose continues to teach her devoted followers in London. Though age cannot wither nor custom stale her, she sometimes rebels at the commercialization of her beloved internal arts. In 1993, she wrote, "Everybody teaches taiji. Everybody learns qigong. Everybody gets sick. What a mad world!" All who teach these arts sympathize with her sentiment. But mostly, Rose is Rose: good-hearted, patient, and giving. We all want the secret. Here it is from Master Deng Yunfeng, passed through Rose Li to all serious students:

> The heart knows,
> The mind understands;
> The form follows;
> Words can't convey it.

A Word on Weapons

I decided early on that I didn't care for weapons and so, other than some staff work under Yuan Dao, kept strictly to the unarmed side of the arts. Of course I had been trained in the M-1 Garand and bayonet, but that was a World War II necessity. Like other kids I loved the six-shooter and Winchester of movies and literature, but I grew up and past these childish things.

My older brother Leo, an accomplished hunter, took me out after quail one frosty morning just after World War II ended. He hoped to convert me to the manly practice. The dogs flushed a covey and up came the birds and his gun. Some quail fell and he called me to fetch them. I found one and started to put it in a paper bag. It was dying but not quite dead. I hollered, asking him what to do. Back came the reply, "Sack it and crush it." I did that and can still feel the tiny bones give to my grip. I remember that more vividly, in fact, than I can remember how my brother looked in those years.

Kevin Roberts (l) and Doug Perry at weapons play.

I can almost understand why some like to hunt. What disturbs me though is the nonsense they invoke to ease their consciences. First, hunting is not a sport: hunters are sportsmen in the same sense that pro rasslers and Ultimate Fighters are. The hunter does not participate in nature. He hunts to kill. He does not love what he kills; if he did, he would not kill it. If he regards animals as beautiful, to kill that beauty marks him as a victim of soul-blindness. To kill beauty is to kill the thing in us that responds to beauty. The animal is made to suffer because he is "inferior" and incapable of thinking as we do. Whereas the question should be not whether he thinks but whether he suffers as we do.

Before getting a license, every prospective hunter should be made to read the following words by Walter de La Mare:

> Hi! Handsome hunting man,
> Fire your little gun.
> Bang! Now the animal
> Is dead and dumb and done.
> Nevermore to play again, creep again, leap again,
> Eat or sleep or drink again, oh, what fun!

In other words, I do not think that a sportsman is a man who "every now and then simply has to go and shoot something" (Stephen Leacock).

My hunter friends attack that argument by urging me to pay more heed to humans than animals. But I do. What I don't understand is why the hunters turn tail and run every time I point out that in the past thirty years firearms alone have killed 100,000 more Americans (750,000) than died in every war in U.S. history (650,000). So why not save some human lives and ban the damned things? The carnage resulting from our continuing to ignore the problem is costly and tragic, and besides killing so many innocents, kills our prestige in the world.

The National Rifle Association (NRA) and its chief booster, the Republican Party, prate on the inherent goodness of guns. The NRA spends millions crying, "We must have them for self-defense." Nonsense. The Department of Health and Human Services and FBI data (1993) put the lie to this cant. They state that for every criminal shot and killed in self-defense, 130 other Americans are killed by guns for other reasons.

The NRA speaks with a forked tongue, our streets swill with the smell of cordite, and our metallic society is alive with youngsters killing one another with handguns and rifles. It shouts out about a so-called constitutional right for citizens to own handguns. Once and for all, there is utterly no such right.

George Bushnell, president of the fairly conservative American Bar Association, on December 8, 1994, definitively said, "The Second Amendment was included in the Bill of Rights to provide the states the ability to maintain a militia. The Supreme Court and other federal courts have been unequivocal in every case they have considered in adopting and supporting this meaning. Those who would construe a different definition cannot find a single judicial decision to validate their claims."

A 1996 New York study inquiring why policemen committed suicide contained some surprises. We all know why – the stress of their job. Wrong! Among the factors studied, job stress came last. Relationships with others ranked first as a factor but was closely followed by the availability of guns. That is, police commit suicide because a gun is always at hand. Another datum discovered by the study that buttressed the conclusion was that firemen don't commit suicide.

Pardon my rant on cant. Here is a simple test for you gun buffs. The prelude is from Zhuangzi:

> The accomplished man uses his mind like a mirror: he neither pulls nor pushes, he responds but does not take hold. Thus he is able to bear things but not harm them.

Niels Bohr, the great Danish physicist, loved American Westerns though he never learned English. From watching so many he formulated "Bohr's Law," which stated that in gunfights the man who drew last would invariably win because he didn't have to think what he was doing. This seems to contradict the rationale of the fast draw artists Hollywood loves to portray. Bohr claimed to have proved the validity of his law, however, by staging dozens of mock fights. Does coming last work for anything other than gun fighting and love making? (As I remember, George Washington married a widow.) Although there is Biblical writ for it ("The last shall be first"), few in our present frenetic culture would buy it.

My Writers: An Interlude

Out of judo and more fully into internal boxing in the early 1970s, I began writing on subjects besides martial arts and intelligence. In late 1974, I read Dashiell Hammett's *The Continental Op*, wrote an appreciative article on it, and sent it to the *Washington Post*. In due course, I got a letter from the editor saying that they seldom took "unassigned" reviews, but this one they liked and would accept. I was off and running.

Across the next twenty years, I wrote more than 240 reviews for *The Washington Post*, the *Chicago Sun-Times*, the *Cleveland Plain Dealer*, the *St. Louis Post-Dispatch*, *The Guardian* (London), and many other newspapers and magazines. The editors treated me well, even permitting me to refuse an assignment without prejudice. I never won a Pulitzer, though my mentor at the *Post* did. He was an interesting guy whose dad had worked in a steel plant in Akron. He took a hankering for literature and went to work for the *Post*, nailing a Pulitzer years later for his criticism. He told me once that he met a girl who knew the only nine words remaining of Pictish (the language of a possibly non-Celtic race who merged with the Scots in the ninth century). I asked him whether she was the one who didn't know how to say "no" in English. That amused him. After he won the Pulitzer, I wrote facetiously warning him from my own experience of winning two Pulitzers that he needed to "stay young and humble and beautiful" (*à la* a song of the Thirties) if he wanted to be loved. He may have been less amused by that, for I never heard from him again.

Despite its great work on Watergate and other issues, I thought *The Washington Post* choked often in its political coverage: in fact, was downright illiberal. I said so in a letter to the editor published in Fall, 1976:

> I am finally heeding the advice of the Irish poet, AE, who likened newspaper readers to "…starving men who come at last to gnaw their boots." I am divorcing *The Post,* stopping my subscription of two decades, save for the Sunday issue. A big and sad step for a guy to whom reading has been a life-delight and who still reads matchbook covers. Why? Heed and mull, old omniscients. I'm quitting because you no longer touch me. You are too fat and comfortable. I applaud your work on Watergate, but it's almost as though you use that triumph to avoid a sustained involvement with other

Truths. You were dead wrong on Vietnam and McGovern, and continue so on Kissinger (whom you adulate egregiously) and the huge defense dollar drain. On the last, you seem unaware of the extent to which these needless and expensive arms fuel inflationary fires, enhance the militarists, and guarantee continuing paranoia. The prophet, Georges Bernanos, once wrote: "All the ideas one sends alone into the world, with their pigtails hanging behind them, and a little basket in their hand like Little Red Riding Hood, are raped on the first street corner they come to by any old slogan in uniform." As Mark Twain put it: "I would rather go to bed with Lillian Russell stark naked than with Ulysses S. Grant in full military regalia."

But I could even abide that. I shouldn't expect you to have the courage of my convictions. What is worse than your straddling and waffling, though, is your marketplace orientation. Your editorial page writers are so balanced they are woefully unbalanced. Your movie reviewers' shill for the inane violence of our *Godfathers* and *Kung Fu's* and your movie advertisements look like the wallpaper in a Mexican brothel. Plus your society writers give me the snew.

I may come back, sweetheart, but you're going to have to straighten up.

On the morning my letter appeared, a woman interrupted my breakfast by phoning to commend the letter, adding that there was one thing she didn't understand: "What's 'snew'?" "Not much," I answered. "What's new with you?" She got it but humor came hard at 7 a.m. in Washington, D.C., in those days and she hung up quickly.

The *Post's* fetching style – compared to which I found the lumbering *New York Times* waterlogged – led me to cheat. I kept peeking at it till I left Washington in 1989.

In any case, my differences with the paper didn't stop me from reviewing books for it. I learned a lot and had fun. To be paid for reading a book – I thought I'd died and gone to Heaven. Fasten your seat belt and I'll let you taste, if not savor, my romp through reviewing.

First off, Hammett in my first review. The Op confronts a

...big, red-faced, red-haired bale of a man – big in any direction and none of him fat. Ordinarily I am inclined to peace. The day is past when I'll fight for the fun of it. But I've been in too many rumpuses to mind them much. Usually nothing very bad happens to you even if you lose. I wasn't going to back down just because this guy was meatier than I. I've always been lucky against the large sizes.

> The guy wants to try conclusions outside where there's room enough.
> I got up, pushed my chair back with a foot, and quoted Red Burns to
> him: "If you're close enough there's room enough."

After this quality, Tom Clancy reads like an insurance salesman and
Elmore Leonard, a used car shill.

Hammett was out of Baltimore but San Francisco was his literary
home. Ray Chandler, from the sceptered isle, bedded down in Los
Angeles. Chandler influenced me morally as well as literarily. When
asked about the secret of writing style, he shrugged off pretension with,
"It just happens – like red hair." Here is Chandler as Phillip Marlowe
bracing Moose Malloy in *Farewell, My Lovely*. Moose wants Marlowe
to go up the stairs into the beer joint with him (later, as boxer Hong
Yixiang groped me, it often brought this passage to mind), "He reached
for my shoulder again. I tried to dodge him but he was as fast as a cat.
He began to chew my muscles up some with his fingers."

Since Mae West warned us that too much of a good thing is wonderful, here is another excerpt of Chandler we all can delight in:

> I got up on my feet and went over to the bowl in the corner and threw
> cold water on my face. After a little while, I felt a little better, but very
> little. I needed a drink, I needed a lot of life insurance, I needed a vacation,
> I needed a home in the country. What I had was a coat, a hat and a gun.
> I put them on and went out of the room.

George Orwell was a writing colossus with a conscience. An artist
who couldn't be bent or bought, his books *Animal Farm, Burmese Days,
Down and Out in Paris and London*, and *1984* are classics that will
endure. His essays are even better. Everyone who wants to learn to
write should read his piece on gobbledygook called, "Politics and the
English Language." Orwell was honest and decent, always on the side
of the underdog and against cant. Above all, he was no whore. He
attacked America's consumerist imperative (TV, computers, shopping)
as presciently as he did Russia's totalitarianism. He was devastating in
his essay on the American comic book whose ideal was the tough guy
who specialized in the "all-in-jump-on-the-testicles style of fighting.
The gorilla who puts everything right by socking everybody else in the
jaw." Thank God he can't see how low American culture has deteriorated since he wrote those words fifty years ago! His whole message: if

people could behave decently, the world would be decent.

Writers are of all varieties. I picked those whose books I reviewed and interviewed those I liked. After writing a review of Sir Victor Pritchett's, *The Mythmakers*, and knowing the body of his fiction and criticism fairly well, I went to London in 1979 for *The Washington Post* and interviewed him. Over good biscuits and tea, I found a genial wit, a towering man of letters superbly secure in his genius (he would mitigate it by saying "talent"). He loved words and chose the good ones. And he was a tough taskmaster in how he arranged them:

> I suppose I got regular habits of work since I was put into the leather works at 16. I have written as many as ten versions of some of my short stories. A story has to be springy. It must be kept on the move. One must cut out anything essayish – the structure won't accommodate it. Thus I find that reworking is mainly refining sprawling previous drafts.

Pritchett worked to a dogged discipline at the desk, but like Wordsworth he met his muse walking. He never achieved Wordsworth's road mileage, but when young averaged over twenty miles and old ten miles daily. Unlike Wordsworth, Pritchett's passion was for short stories ("The Sailor" and "Blind Love" are among his best) and essays (all are good: those on the great Russian writers, best). The greatest critics put him at or near the top in both forms.

Sir Victor Pritchett, master of the word.

What attracted me to Pritchett was his assured but modest approach to his work. Like Chesterton, he was masterful enough at his craft to be egotistic, but wasn't. It never occurred to him to be. And like Chesterton, he had no malice, wasn't personally competitive, and knew no enemies. Like Orwell, he was against pudder (the gobbledygook of the media, academics, and government), against the banality of television, and for love as a matter of the heart, rather than the Anglo-American obsession with the genitalia.

Finally, he didn't talk kindness: he was kind. He took the draft of our interview, rewrote whole sections, enlivening it enormously, and then apologized for doing so. As for the world's likelihood of muddling through its problems he said he saw "a sporting chance." With authentic people like Pritchett around, I'd agree with his prediction.

Perhaps the greatest influence on me of all was exerted by the bulky, genial, G.K. Chesterton. I believed him when he wrote that humans must have a moral slant. And when he said, "My country right or wrong is like saying my mother drunk or sober," it led me to leave the Roman Catholic church when it supported the ignoble war in Vietnam. Thank God he'd died in the Thirties and didn't see the abyss our church helped create. A fine man and writer, one the phlegmatic Orwell would have hugged if he could have got his arms around him. Here is Chesterton, reeking of Orwell, "Christian charity is something as special as the smell of onions."

Kay Boyle risked being more message than artist but managed beautifully. She combined an enduring social activism – show her an outcast and she would go there – with fine fiction, poetry, and nonfiction. Premier critic Clifton Fadiman said that Boyle was a more serious, more moving artist than even Scott Fitzgerald. Running afoul of the McCarthy witch hunt, she was blacklisted and spent her last years teaching at San Francisco State University. Her last brush with her beloved America was over Vietnam, for which the local yokels tossed her into jail. I chatted down a sunny afternoon in New York City with this gracious, grand woman, and we corresponded until her death.

John Sanford has been writing fiction and idiosyncratic history since the Twenties. Past ninety, he continues to write with a brilliance that, compared to most writers today, is like a lantern on a dark lawn of lightning bugs. He once called Wobblie leader Eugene Debs that "rail of a man homely enough for two – who didn't have the right kind of knees for begging." No one since D.H. Lawrence (*Studies in Classic American Literature*, 1923) and William Carlos Williams (*In the American Grain*, 1925) has limned the American experience quite so well. Alas, he wrote too well and Americans didn't buy his books.

The world is cluttered with amateurs. The fighting arts exert a powerful attraction for them. Of this situation, my favorite humorist, Kin Hubbard, who died in 1931, said, "I believe there's more difference between an amateur

Kin's character Abe Martin muses on Occam's razor.

and a professional than any other two things." Kin was as good a philosopher as a humorist. Even his contemporary, Will Rogers, conceded the field to him. Kin was succinct ("Trouble prefers blondes"), loved women ("I don't know o' nothing better'n a woman if you want to spend money where it'll show"), had problems with feminists ("Never marry a girl that's sore 'cause she's not a man"), and was as philosophical as Rochefoucauld ("It's kind o' fun these days t' plug along an' wonder what you're going t' git stung on next").

Here's a sampling of Hubbardisms to brighten your day:

♦ "You can't git away from yourself by walkin' out in th' country."
♦ "Don't worry about trouble, it never broke a date yet."
♦ "The odor o' buckwheat an' sausage can't be counterfeited."
♦ "Th' word 'slob' sounds just exactly like one looks."
♦ "Between those who toady after 'em an' those who hate 'em th' rich have a plenty hard time."
♦ "Nobuddy is ever ready for company."
♦ "What's become o' the beautiful early pink rhubarb complexions the girls used to have?"
♦ "It's pretty hard to tell what does bring happiness. Poverty and wealth have both failed."
♦ "Envy an' malice tell on you quicker 'n plowin'."

The great English poet, Ralph Hodgson, was reared with little schooling. He became famous for his brilliant poetry, "The Song of Honor," "The Mystery," "The Linnet," and especially "The Bull." The last is a wrenching lament of an old sick bull banished from the herd he led. He remembers his youth when he was champion of all – even the lions feared him. But life is change and in the end he turns from memories of his splendid yesterday to meet the "… loathly birds / Flocking round him from the skies, / Waiting for the flesh that dies." At the height of his fame, Hodgson left England to teach at Sendai University in Japan. On his return years later, he had nearly been forgotten and his muse was only a sometime visitor. There were still little epiphanies such as, "Some things have to be believed to be seen." But the towering poetry had already been written. From "The Song of Honor": "The song of men divinely wise / Who look and see in starry skies / Not stars so much as robins' eyes"; Or from "The Linnet": "It may be even as my friends allege. / I'm pressed to prove that life is something more / And yet a linnet on a hawthorne hedge / Still wants explaining and accounting for." But quite enough to stand on. He moved to Minerva, Ohio, in 1941 and died there in 1962 at the age of ninety. In 1983, I visited his grave (in fact, Alice said I inadvertently stood on it) with his widow, Aurelia. And bowed to the man who loved poetry, nature, boxing, and one woman.

Edmund Blunden, a gentle and giving poet-writer of World War I (his idiosyncratic classic, never superseded, was *Undertones of War* in 1928), also spent time, like Hodgson, teaching in Japan. He was alive to his students' sensibilities, urging them never to have bad dreams over anything he told them. He questioned every rationale for the war, implying its profound idiocy with, "There seems to be something amiss / When twenty million funeral urns are called for. / Have you no hypothesis?"

Frank Waters:
writer and friend.

Frank Waters was one of America's top novelists and was nominated for the Nobel prize several times. His fiction was not commercial and though he had an avid readership, he got neither Nobels nor riches. His greatest novels were *People of the Valley* (1941) and *The Man Who Killed the Deer* (1942), works so good that even commercial Hollywood couldn't manipulate them into films. They and his nonfiction works are the finest written on the uneasy interaction of the Anglo white with his Hispanic and Indian neighbor in the American Southwest. More than any other American writer, Frank has lived with silence. Not silence, the negative absence of sound, but silence, the crucible of positive possibility. To sit with him as I did on three visits was "to be quiet together." This silence is the ground of being from which all great writing comes. It gave him a thinking or apperception that sees.

Frank's other abiding theme was the sense of place (the relationship between people and place that in taiji is called rootedness). He believed that the world and all its forms are alive, the rocks and trees as much as the people. He was a wholly integrated writer and man. I saw him as a master mystic, a Daoist who had come to it through life, not books.

Here is Frank from *People of the Valley* (1941):

There are many earths, and each has its own irreconcilable spirit of place. Now what is a man but his place? It rises in walls to shelter him in life. It sinks to receive him in death. By eating its corn he builds his flesh into walls of this self-same earth. He has its granitic hardness or its soft resiliency. He is as different as each field is different. Thus do I know my own earth; I can know no other.

Frank told me of seeing Jack Dempsey at the Colorado Springs railroad station when Frank was a youngster hawking food on trains. This was when Dempsey was just getting started as a boxer and called himself "Kid Blackie." He had seen Charley White, the great left hooker, lose in a lightweight championship bout to Freddy Welsh in 1916. So he liked boxing. When I knew him, though, he was more interested in taiji, which he'd seen in China. I showed him and his pretty wife Barbara some movements and explained the correlation of body and mind undergirding them. Both were more than open to the internal ideas – they were congenial to them.

He died in 1995 just short of 93. In *The Woman at Otowi Crossing* (1970) he wrote, "So when your time comes, Jack, don't be afraid." "Be glad! It's our greatest experience, our mysterious voyage of discovery into the last unknown, man's only true adventure."

He and Barbara basked in a love beautiful to be around. They allowed me to come by and bask several times with them. Such splendid times with such splendid people. I'll never forget all that goodness and warmth.

Fred Manfred wrote *Lord Grizzly* (1954) and over twenty other exceptional novels. He was a giant man and writer with powerful energy and beautiful rhythms. Big (6'6") and well past 200 pounds, he once knocked out a sparring partner of Joe Louis and hospitalized a New York City mugger. But as gentle as only very big men can be, "It has always been my belief that if one wishes to speak with truth in the brain one must speak with love in the heart." I spent half a day with Fred interviewing him, drinking a tea made from weeds at his doorstep (it tasted like shellac the first glass, and the finest cognac thereafter), helping him eat a robust dinner, and swapping salacious jokes.

I interviewed Farley Mowat, the plucky little Canadian explorer/writer (*Never Cry Wolf*, 1963) at his home in Windsor, Ontario. He took on his own government time and again over environmental issues. And he collided with ours when the Reagan reincarnation of Joe

McCarthy banned him entry to the U.S. during a planned book tour. This free soul had gotten into a State Department register of suspected Communist sympathizers when he visited Siberia. When writers all over America (I among them) complained of the silliness, Mowat was okayed and the Big Bad Book disappeared, though I will bet you that it is even now inside some bureaucrat's desk waiting for a more bare-knuckled conservativism to return.

Mowat was a lulu. After a fine meal at his home, I excused myself and went to use the bathroom at the corner of the large eating area. There was only half-light in the place and as I started to do my verti-cal business I sensed the presence of someone else in the room. I looked around into the shadows and saw a nun in her habit standing nearby. She said nothing, nor did I, but when my fumbling hands had arranged myself, I looked closer and found she was a full-sized mannequin. When I returned to the table there ensued general hilarity – Mowat had told the other guests of the "nun." When I joined in, he told us that one friend hadn't come out for half an hour. He goes through life laughing. It is a good life.

I also interviewed Richard Adams of *Watership Down* (1972) fame at his home on the Isle of Man in the Irish Sea. Like another I inter-viewed, the New York novelist and nature writer Edward Hoagland, Adams was so caught up in his own wonderfulness that he was a better writer than a man. In fact, when I was visiting xingyi boxer Rose Li in London, her students drove me out to Newbury to talk with the youngest daughter of famed poet Edward Thomas, killed in World War I. When I mentioned that I had seen Richard Adams, the daughter, Myfanwy Thomas, made a face and said she'd heard him on the radio a fortnight before and found him one of the most pompous persons she'd ever had the displeasure to hear. So my reaction to the man prob-ably was not an unusual one. But I'd been warned: Raymond Chandler wrote that if you like some writer's prose, avoid him or her at any cost, the idea being that, up close, all feet are made of clay or at least smell a little. Chandler was wrong for my lot of writers – only two failed to hit the mark as fully human beings.

In contrast to those two, R.B. Cunningham Graham, writer and traveler par excellence, shines. He believed that there are only two classes – the genuine and the humbug. This man's man and writer's writer was as genuine as Jesus' smile. He had been in jail on three con-tinents, was a master fencer, an even better horseman, and absolutely fearless. He even took pains to attack his readers in print. Success he viewed as accidental, usually illusory, often stolen, and always ephemeral. His calligraphy was execrable (friend Joseph Conrad couldn't read it to proof it), and he didn't write like any angel I know, but thank God, his paper accepted his ink. His best short stories stand tall in world literature, chief among them, "Beattock for Moffat," "The Gold Fish," and "Calvary." If you read one of these, you will thank me; if you read all three, you will bless me.

The late Sydney Harris wrote pithy little columns that were syndicated in over 200 American newspapers for almost forty years. Living in Galesburg, I caught him five times weekly in the *Chicago Daily News*. Out of Robert Hutchin's old Great Books gang at the University of Chicago (though he never graduated from high school), he was erudite, witty, and a wonderful earthy speaker. At the University of Illinois, I heard an academic heckler who ranted on about the defects in Harris' argument. With a smile, Harris deflated him, "You've made a poor inference...."

His daily non-didactic stint of eight short paragraphs provided me much intellectual sustenance. Here was a philosopher for the masses. When I wrote asking for an interview, I quoted a favorite jazz singer of ours, Lee Wiley, "Any time, any day, anywhere / Say the word, you'll be heard / I'll be there." Back Harris came, "Come on: if you like her, you can't be bad!" I had two of my most marvelous hours with him. In 1986 I had submitted my review of his latest book, *Clearing the Ground*, to the *Chicago Sun-Times*, but before it could run he was dead from heart problems.

Harris helped untold thousands to think and feel. He once wrote that the three hardest tasks in the world are neither physical feats nor intellectual achievements, but moral acts, "To return love for hate, to include the excluded, and to say, 'I was wrong.'"

Another Chicagoan, Nelson Algren, wrote splendid "insider" stuff on boxing, fiction, and nonfiction. You could learn more about boxing from Algren's, "The Dark Came Early in That Country" (he even taped this one), and others than you could in many gyms. Through mutual friends – mainly Kay Boyle – Algren and I corresponded for awhile. After he left Chicago for New Jersey, I spoke with him for a half hour one evening on the phone. He was active then trying to get boxer Reuben "Hurricane" Jackson out of the jug, where he was spending life for murder (much later, Jackson was pardoned). Our talk concerned only boxing and we didn't discuss the case. We gave boxing a workout, however, and before it was over, he suggested that we make a day of it in New York City: take in a couple gyms, eat with his friend (famed trainer Freddy Brown), visit a gallery specializing in boxing art, and cap it off by seeing two good heavies go at it. He would call me when a good match was made. We had taken turns deploring the poor quality of post-war boxing; it took a while before two good heavies appeared. For us, it went forever. Algren died of a heart attack, and we never kept our date.

In "Dark Came Early in That Country," Algren has his fighter reminiscing on a bus at twilight. He thinks about what he had to show for getting his face punched in for fourteen years – a swab stick, the cardboard core of a roll of gauze, the top of a Vaseline jar, and half a bottle of liquid adrenalin. He is unable to image most of the guys he'd fought but has better luck with the places:

> I remembered the Camden Convention Hall in South Jersey, and the Grotto Auditorium in San Antonio, and the Moose Temple in Detroit, and the Marigold in Chicago, and the New Broadway in Philly, and the Norristown Auditorium, and the Arcadia Ballroom in Providence ... and the Rainbow Garden in Little Rock, and the Garden Palace in Passaic, and the Armory A.C. in Wilkes-Barre, and the Fenwick Club in Cincinnati, and Antler's Auditorium in Lorain, Ohio. Then I went back to Detroit and remembered the Grand River Gym and the old Tuxedo A.C. on Monroe Avenue. Just before I fell asleep I knew those were the names of the places where I'd used up my hostility.

Hearing this litany again on the taped version, I really taste the regret of never getting Algren all to myself that day in Neurotic City. Two old Chicagoans would've made it shine.

"Ray Bradbury published his first piece, a poem, when he was sixteen. He's been at it ever since, for over sixty years, happily trudging a path that has produced such classics as *The Martian Chronicles*, *Fahrenheit 451*, and *Dandelion Wine* (my favorite by far). Plus he's written plays, poems, movie and television scripts, and articles in a quantity and of a quality to exhaust any five normal professional writers." That was how I began my interview with Bradbury titled, "Ray Bradbury: Literature as Lark" (published in *Whispers*, October 1983). Bradbury behind that desk with its big vat of dandelion wine was as excited and exuberant as his office in Beverly Hills was rumpled. His ideas awed you and his voice – that of an exceptional actor – did justice to each one. We corresponded for a few years, but he, a registered Democrat, was too tolerant of Reagan's policies. He had gotten cozy, I thought. Later, downstairs having a beer, I was telling him this when our black waiter heard and heartily joined in on my side, and we had a warm old time. Though I never got any more Christmas cards from him after that, I get vitalized just thinking of this great storyteller.

I recall the worst joke of 1934 – "A lot of men smoke, but Fu Manchu" – but I don't remember much about the evil doctor since his creator, Sax Rohmer, had him most active from about 1912 or so through World War I. Thin and tall, he was "evil, immutable, apparently eternal." In a fine review in the *London Review of Books* (Sept. 4, 1997), E.S. Turner wrote that he exuded wickedness as other men exude body odor and his enemies were "sucked empty" by his green gaze. His chief antagonist was Sir Denis Nayland Smith, a smooth bird as long on ego as Dr. Fu himself. This Britisher once apologized for a discourtesy with "Forgive me – the fate of millions was at stake." Shades of Herr Kissinger, the Nobel laureate for peace, whose word, you will remember, was good until sundown. Anyhow, Warner Oland played Fu Manchu and did a very good job of it for a Swede.

These are but a few of the writers I read or interviewed. All affected me deeply. I even learned from the two I found weighed down by ego to keep the ego behind, as Nietzsche warned, and not to let it get out ahead where it starts leading you. There were so many others reflected in my reviews who influenced me, too many to be mentioned in a book ostensibly about martial arts. This group suffices, I think, to show the places I came from (there is a "there" there) and the biases with which I'm stuck – or blessed.

Zheng Manqing:
The Last Decade

Laoshi watched and
saw more than we.

Ah, did you once see Shelley plain,
And did he stop and speak to you?
– Robert Browning

By 1965, Professor Zheng was ensconced at Riverside Drive in New York City and teaching at a studio on Canal Street. When his local Chinese sponsors, who didn't cotton to the hippies he attracted, locked him out, he led his multi-ethnic tribe to a large loft three flights up on the Bowery. Wolfe Lowenthal's charming and insightful two books – *There Are No Secrets: Professor Cheng Man-ch'ing and His Tai Chi Chuan* (1991) and *Gateway to the Miraculous: Further Explorations in the Tao of Cheng Man-Ch'ing* (1994) – catch this time brilliantly. I visited Laoshi as much as my work and family permitted and, while I never learned to like New York City, that nickel town, I enjoyed the small oasis over the Bowery.

Let me dilate a little on Professor's toleration of the dirtier and wilder fringes of America at that time. Long hair, drugs, and bad manners – he accepted it all and converted it into a fine respectful following. That he lost some, not all, of his Chinese students wasn't as important to him as was his conviction that taiji could work for the low as well as the high and for the Westerner as well as the Chinese. Zheng had been poor and knew empathy.

He loved the lotus, the pre-eminent flower in Chinese culture. For the Buddhists, it symbolized spiritual purity. Poet Dao Yuanming (367-427 A.D.) used the lotus to represent a man of honor in a famous poem, saying that the lotus rose from the mud but remained unstained. For Laoshi, the lotus was an enduring subject in his art and poetry. And well it should be. A poor boy, fatherless from an early age, he struggled through hardship at a chaotic time in China's history, becoming its most Olympian man in recent history. For we in the fighting arts who know well the meaning of Belloc's phrase, "the wear of winning," it is all the more perplexing that he came to many-faceted magnificence – like his beloved lotus – showing little wear.

Part of it, of course, was the path he chose, the internal. A struggle is a struggle, however soft or hard. How he pulled it off without wear while balancing those other excellences, was that he had a mind (yi) that made taiji principles work for all the others. So there was no balance needed – one size fitted all. Paraphrasing Indian sage R. Tagore, his center was still and silent in the midst of an eternal dance of circles. His accomplishment was all the more singular in that he nurtured the internal while staying in society amidst the stress of work and family. There was only one way to look at him and that was up.

He made one week-long stay in the Washington area where he appeared on television. He and I demonstrated taiji and he the inner and outer aspects of brush painting. It was a full fun week, and my students got to see Shelley plain and he did stop and speak to us. And eat with us, too.

Luncheon Incident

Ten of us gathered that day at a Chinese restaurant in Washington, D.C., to pay homage to Professor Zheng, newly arrived in America. The group was an elite combatives group – judo, karate, aikido, and wushu – all seniors in their respective disciplines. Zheng's nephew from nearby Silver Spring, Maryland, acted as interpreter.

I reserved a secluded table so that the Professor could demonstrate as he wished in response to questions. But when we arrived, the waiter took us to a table in the midst of a few other Sunday diners. I asked him if he hadn't a more private table and he went surly and told us to sit down. Meekly – so as to keep the occasion happy for the Professor – we did as we were told.

While we were having drinks, the waiter returned to say loudly that he'd found a private room but that it would cost $25 extra. We were comfortable by then, so I thanked him and told him we'd stay where we were. Making an expression implying that we were too stingy to pay for the private table, he left us.

In those days the Washington area had only three northern Chinese restaurants of any worth, and the repast we had was excellent. However, it was marred by the antics of our waiter and two others.

Obviously seeking to embarrass us in front of our Chinese guest, they took to spilling sauces and deriding us. By now entranced with our dialog with Zheng, we paid this little mind.

Zheng spoke on a variety of subjects (qi, relaxation, one-legged weighting, and the like). In that context, the maladroit actions of the yahoo waiters seemed more amusing than mean. But as the party was breaking up, the jokers spilled beer on one of us. My patience at an end, I passed the word that this had gone beyond silly and that no one should tip the waiters. I paid the bill and we lingered over our drinks.

In a few minutes, two of our group came back to the table agitated. The manager at the cash register wouldn't sell them cigarettes, saying that we had refused to tip for an excellent meal. After urging the group not to touch the waiters and having two of them escort Zheng outside so he'd be clear of any untoward developments, I bearded the lardaceous manager at his money machine. To my query of why he wouldn't sell us cigarettes, he screamed that we'd had excellent food expertly served and then insulted his waiters by denying them a tip.

I lectured him as his face alternated between red and livid. His waiters, I said, had been terrible, careless, and childish. The food (I fibbed a bit here) was not fresh, had been poorly prepared, and atrociously served. He was fortunate, I said, that we hadn't deducted something from the bill for the food spilled on us. At this, he so completely lost face that his words wouldn't come. But three cooks and galley workers did come from the kitchen, cleavers in hand.

I swaggered away disregarding the cleavers. The anguished manager shouted after me, "The next time you go out for Chinese food, try People's Drugstore." I returned to him and retorted, "Yes, we'd probably get better food and service there." That tore it. He turned apoplectic and I turned and walked out.

A day later, two of our group, aikido students, phoned to tell me that two of the waiters had followed them in a car and actually attempted to force their car over to the side of the road. When I asked how they responded to this, they answered that they hadn't.

"Why the hell not?" I asked.

"You told us not to touch them," they replied.

Quite right; I had. But that was to spare Professor Zheng, I told them. Away from the Professor, and after being attacked by their car, they had a positive obligation to educate the bozos. Instead, the waiters got off scot-free, though their manager did lose face.

Had Professor Zheng known about this nonsense, it might have been interesting. When angry, he burned with a deep steady flame. So it is just as well that he never knew.

Some of the guests that day. Laoshi, author, and Bill Neisler, seated; standing at my left shoulder, the late Vic Crawford, a real fighter who battled the tobacco industry. The man beside him is unidentified.

"Mystical" Taiji

Some of Zheng's bedrock ideas are derided by some Westerners who label his taiji "mystical." By "mystical" they mean that his taiji could not be learned and mastered without recourse to such basic ideas as *jing* (essence), *qi* (intrinsic energy), *jin* (tenacious energy), *shen* (spirit), and the *Dao* (path). Despite my earlier skepticism on these ideas, I believe that to discard them would be disastrous. In fact, toss them and taiji ceases to be real – it becomes merely calisthenics. The form becomes low-impact exercise suitable only for oldsters. The sensing-hands becomes shoving, and free-fighting (*sanshou*) remains a kata, a pre-arranged two-person dance.

I go part way with the critics. To assimilate these ideas in your form, push-hands, and free-fighting takes a long time. And, other than the form, if you get something you usually don't get much. Happily, if you practice the form correctly and long, making it an integral part of your life, you will have a pearl beyond price. The body and mind will benefit greatly. But the functional returns on push-hands and free-fighting for the average person will be far less. It may give you an edge in the street with non-fighters, but beyond that the yield is questionable.

The progression in the internal school is that as you limit your spending of sperm (*jing*), this will enhance your qi and open your body to it. When the qi is stored, nourished, and moved, it is capable of becoming tenacious energy (*jin*), which protects your body and focuses intense energy on an enemy. As for spirit (*shen*), this is a spiritual dimension few if any have achieved, certainly no one I ever met. It is beyond our ken so we need not discuss it.

But let's look at the other ideas briefly.

Conserving Sexual Essence

Essence, a distillate of most body fluids and substances – blood, marrow, and bone – is largely sperm. All the Asian fighting arts subscribe to the notion that excess "spending" is bad for one. Indian and Pakistani wrestlers still follow the regime of Brahmacharya (celibacy and self-control) rigorously (see Joseph Alter, *The Wrestler's Body: Identity and Ideology in North India*, 1992.) Zheng Manqing said this on the subject, "'Promiscuity shakes the universe' – When one is young one tends to spend, heedless of the reckoning ahead. The promiscuity of youth must be paid for in future coin."

Chinese practice drawn from sources such as Sun Simiao's *Qianjin Fang* and the stricter Daoist regime (Wang Yannian conversation Sept. 24, 1984) on the daily intervals between spending follow.

AGE	CHINESE	DAOIST
20	4	7
30	8	14
40	16	20
50	20	30
60	avoid	49

Invariably, when I asked various teachers whether this tradition was being observed they would say yes, but that it depended on the individual boxer. Uniformly, though, they thought the Daoist regime too harsh and that one shouldn't try it.

One finds this idea of conserving semen in many activities, even literature. The great French novelist H. Balzac is a case in point. Believing that every man had a finite store of vital fluid and that the secret of a creative life was to hoard one's energy, he forsook women to write his masterpieces. Thus, he regarded sperm as pure cerebral substance. It is written that once after bedding a woman, Balzac ran (slowly) to a friend's house crying, "I just lost a book!"

The great American boxer Sam Langford put it equally succinctly, "You can sweat out beer, and you can sweat out whiskey, but you can't sweat out women."

And here is Saadi, the Muslim poet, seven hundred years ago:

I asked a scholar the meaning of the tradition which says, "Your most subtle and deadly adversary is the sexual energy in your loins." The reason is this, he answered. "Any ordinary enemy that you treat politely will begin as your friend, except that lust-energy. The more you indulge and placate that, the more powerfully it drags you both down. Strong discipline needs to be brought forward to stop that bully from killing you."

So we can say that the idea of sexual excess is not restricted to Asia nor to the fighting arts.

Qi: The Thing That Moves

The subject of qi is vast and has been studied for centuries. There are many analogues. The Sanskrit *prana,* the Greek *pneuma,* and the Latin *spiritus* have the same meaning as *qi.* The Sioux Indians called it *skan,* "something that moves." Poet Robert Penn Warren once wrote of the Eskimo concept, "*Sila* for the Eskimo is the air, not the sky; movement, not wind; the very breath of life, but not physical life. It is clear-sighted energy, activating intelligence; the powerful fluid circulating 'all around' and also within each individual."

The animating principle, qi is the vital energy by which we live, move, change, and think. We breathe in the qi of heaven (yang), blending it with that of earth (yin). Qi is breath, air, soul. Even its pronunciation – "chee" in Mandarin and "hay" in Cantonese – is aspirated like exhalations. Many modern words use it; for example, "*qishui*" means carbonated water (7-Up soda, etc.)

The philosopher Mencius pithily observed, "If men concentrated their will, they would have more command of their qi. If they concentrated their qi, they would have more command of their will."

Teaching someone about qi is like teaching blind children about colors. Seeking and chasing qi are not altogether good. Excess qi is bad. When a Chinese wants to calm someone down, he or she says, "Don't qi" instead of "Don't get angry." If a Chinese baby wakes up crying from a bad dream, its mother strokes its chest downward so that the excess rising qi may sink to the dantian (center).

Qi is both vital and subtle. The ancient battlefield warrior was vitally filled with it. The same qi, now subtle and quiet, is used in meditation, special breathing, and creative work. "[Qi] fills the stillness of the undistracted heart-mind and hence the whole being and ends in the stilling of the heart," writes Si Maimai in *The Way of Chinese Painting* (1959). So, in external boxing, qi is sought for forceful strength; in internal boxing, it is cultivated for a more relaxed but still powerful energy.

In taiji, "relaxation" is the key to moving the qi. Everything is relaxed inward to the bone. Not collapsed, which shows a lack of mind (*yi*), but relaxed that is led and suffused with mind.

Laoshi had five main principles:

- Relax (incorporating "sink") everything.
- Hold your body erect by imagining a string suspending your head from above.
- Keep the waist flexible without twisting.
- Let only one leg at a time take most of your weight.
- Hold a smooth, straight wrist throughout.

Relax is the prime rule; without it, the others avail little.

In our classes, we insisted on relaxation. When we corrected pupils, we used soft hands to detect tension and to correct alignment. This we called "molding," and students' bodies required it. The eyes can be fooled (Harpo Marx put it, "Who do you believe, me or your eyes?"), the hands cannot. Lay on the hands and most students will benefit.

It isn't easy to mold. First of all, you yourself must be relaxed. Next, some students don't know where their bodies are and don't believe it when you tell them. Others complain that they are being molded when they don't need it – they're already relaxed. Their minds need to relax so they can quit competing. One student, a university professor, announced to the class and me that since he started taiji six months before, his taiji had actually worsened – he was more tense than when he started. I replied that no, he had become more relaxed: now he was able to feel tensions he was oblivious to before. I think he understood, but his mind needed to relax before he could figure out such things on his own.

Relaxation is anathema to most Americans. Tension is a way of hanging on to something that isn't there. Put another way, relax is who you are; tense is who you think you are. Alas, relaxation is tough for us. Our economic and social structure would suffer if we relaxed. Selling products works best in a tense competitive milieu. If people relax they become more rational and they consume less and better.

Marilyn Vos Savant, who claims to have the highest IQ in the world (228, which would top Goethe), was once asked (*Parade*, July 15, 1990), "Is discipline important to the thinking process, and if it is, will deep meditation help one to be a wiser person?" She answered, "I think that deep meditation may help you to be a more relaxed person, but I doubt very much that it will make you one whit wiser."

Laoshi: the best way
to extend qi is with a smile.

Take your high IQ if it results in such ignorance. Each of us knows intuitively and pragmatically that we perform better at nearly everything if we are relaxed. If the task is becoming wiser, it seems to me that to be relaxed would be a requirement. The things that I remember doing well in life were invariably done in an easy, relaxed way. The things I have done poorly I recall as things done hurriedly and tensely. (These adverbs naturally go together, don't they?) If I remember, Buddha made no headway in his physical and mental exercises until he sat under a tree and relaxed. I think that to want to be relaxed is already to be a wiser person, and that to be relaxed is to be an even wiser person.

You can have Marilyn.

Tenacious Energy (Jin)

Just as qi cannot be cultivated if one spends one's essence (*jing*) excessively, one cannot achieve a tenacious energy without a great qi such as Mencius claimed to have.

I told how Laoshi described the tenacious energy (*jin*) developed from taiji. He likened this energy to a strong vine that is pliable; force, to a stick which is rigid. Tenacity, he said, springs from the sinews, force from the bones. Chinese boxing claims to have all kinds of energies. I recall a half dozen associated with striking for example: trembling, laughing, and coughing. All of these were associated with the internal school, though external boxers sometimes claimed they were able to come up with similar techniques.

By mastering your essence and qi you become capable of tenacious energy. Most of us get some of this but can't replicate it at will. We could call this the "Law of the Magic Moment" because it's usually transient. For more on this, your best guide is always translations of taiji classics. I recommend *The Essence of T'ai Chi Ch'uan: The Literary Tradition* by Ben Lo, Martin Inn, Robert Amacker, and Susan Foe (1979) and *Cheng Tzu's Thirteen Treatises on T'ai Chi Ch'uan* by Zheng Manqing, translated by Ben Lo and Martin Inn (1985).

The Dao

The old writ runs, "To know the Dao [path or way] is not as good as loving it; to love it is not as good as practicing it." A cornerstone of Professor Zheng's belief was the idea of following the Dao, the Path that leads to wherever love is. This path not only moves but stands. It lies on the ground (is still) and leads somewhere (is moving). It is not only circular (linearity is merely a portion of a circle) but also concentrated. The moving Dao is external and spatial (action); the standing Dao internal and fixed (meditation). Both are forms of walking.

And to take the Dao you have to walk. It is the only way. Before Edmund Hillary and his Sherpa companion conquered Everest, I read a story of a Texas millionaire who amassed thirty climbers and the latest technology and attacked the bloody mountain. On the eve of the assault, he met with a famed monk in Darjeeling at the foot of Everest. As Texans will, he talked and talked, vowing that neither human defects, rock, nor weather would stop his small army and big ego. "Everest," he blustered, "must fall." To which the tiny monk replied sunnily, "Good luck to you, sir."

In the 1940's:
Laoshi in "Single Whip."

Three weeks later, the Texan reached the top of the world. Half-dead from the climb that had killed his entire team, but still exalted, he strutted about lording it over all creation. But then, in the swirling snow of twilight, he saw ahead of him a small campfire and near it a small figure. Upon closer inspection, the Texan recognized the monk he'd met in Darjeeling. The fact that he had come second failed to diminish his joy, and he shouted to the monk, "See, I told you that I'd make it!" To which the monk rejoined, "Yes, but you walked."

It is charming. But it is a story. Until the Dao takes us, we must walk.

Language, by its power to refer to things, is part of the Dao. However, it cannot substitute for music, dance, taiji, or other systems of being. As dancer Isadora Duncan put it, "If I could tell it to you, I wouldn't have to dance."

Zheng: Maestro in Manhattan

During and between visits to the studio, I kept in touch with how Professor Zheng was getting along. The students loved him and they and others tested him. There were stories galore. He gave a big black belt judoka ninety percent of an o-goshi (large hip throw) and the man couldn't bring it off. Then the judoka dove in with uchimata (inner thigh throw) and was repelled fifteen feet away at great speed. Another time, a weirdo somehow got through the seniors and attacked the old man with a knife, only to be thrown across the room. Laoshi then tossed the knife on a table and sent a scathing look at the seniors who were supposed to buffer him from that sort of thing.

In sensing-hands, he handled everyone easily. When I wasn't being handled, I intently watched him with others. As always, he advanced into and softly disposed of his partner. Years later watching Babe Ruth on old film walking into and blasting the ball into the stands, his stepping into the ball reminded me of Zheng at push-hands. His soft pushes, of course, were not at all like Babe's hopeful swings (he struck out a lot) but the step forward prior to the coup de grace was similar. In fact, Laoshi advised us to step only forward, never backward, and I never saw him do otherwise.

Besides his elegant forms and overwhelming sensing-hands, Laoshi tended to the medical and other needs of his flock. For example, he thought that we all sleep too much. His genius resulted from his easy blend of reflection and doing. Lying abed in the dark watches of the night was not for him. He was more concerned that we slept too much than that we didn't sleep enough. He believed that we need but four hours of sleep a night and these need not be consecutive periods. His routine was to sleep only from 11 p.m. to 1 a.m., rise and spend two hours on restful purposes such as poetry and the like. Then at 3 a.m. he slept for two more hours before he rose for the day.

This seems impossible for most of us. Few will practice it and probably few should. Professor Zheng never advised us to follow this. However, the principle that we sleep too much is probably valid. One sees it in Asia (Tohei and others inveigh against it) and Europe. Lord Wellington, who snuffed Bonaparte at Waterloo – a great victory that only made page fourteen of the *London Times* – advised that, "when one begins to turn in bed it is time to turn out."

A fable. A fellow goes into a pet store and sees three parrots priced $50, $500, and $5,000. Why the disparity in price, he wonders.

So he asks what the $50 parrot can do. The shopkeeper says, "He is quite charming. He can recite the New Testament in English."

How about the $500 parrot? "Ah, he is brilliant. He can recite the whole Bible in the original Aramaic and Greek."

Impressed, the man asks, "And what in the world can the $5,000 parrot do?"

The proprietor replied, "Oh, him. He can't do anything – but the other two call him 'Maestro.'"

In orthodox boxing terms, Zheng Manqing was nothing, a slight man about 5'5" and weighing perhaps 120 pounds. He stood easy, usually with a half-smile on his face. He needed no snarl to feel secure. He never used force. Everything he

Laoshi in "Shoulder" (1960).

did was soft. He seldom made a fist; when he did, it was so light it looked like a child's half-open one. Yet none could withstand his swinging hand against their forearm. Or hurt his thin arm when the roles were reversed. He didn't need to contract his muscles to get either power or protection. Plus he was a celebrated artist in several disciplines antithetical to even the idea of fighting. Still the Chinese boxing community called this man "Maestro."

How was this possible? He never tired of telling his secret. His *Thirteen Chapters* delineated the process fully. As a start, he advised us to do taiji as though it were a common everyday thing and something we did very well. Don't posture and don't pose. Do it as though you were walking. In fact, he liked to quote the ancients' words, "Fighting is like taking a walk." Relax and sink, stand erect, and keep your qi at your dantian. He believed and practiced such principles throughout his life. Others couldn't or wouldn't do this. And so they and we call him "Maestro."

Speaking of confidence, all of these martial systems – not just taiji and the internal ones – bring confidence after a time. A quiet confidence not associated with competition. Without speaking, it says that this is a person committed to a discipline. And passers-by "hear" and respect this. Here is someone who has no fear and this sustains him. If someone does attack, no harm comes. Gandhi's great disciple, Lanza del Vasta, says of such an event, "When a man is afraid of nobody he finds it trying to have to be angry with someone who is vainly attempting to harm him."

Four of us couldn't budge him.

T.T. Liang & Tam Gibbs

They say you never forget your first lover. I never forgot my first real taiji teacher.

His name is T.T. (Tongcai) Liang. He has just recently turned one-hundred. He owned to having fifteen major boxing teachers. Zheng Manqing, the master others measured themselves against, he put at the top. Liang was as good an enabler as he was a taiji teacher and he introduced me to other top teachers in Taiwan.

Like the Professor, he came to America in the mid-1960's. He was unfortunate in some of his students. Once I even called him offering to rid him of a few of those albatrosses. He laughed and said something to the effect that it was all right; he needed them as a penance. I never understood that fully, but it did remind me of writer Nelson Algren asking an addict friend why he kept killing himself with cocaine. To which the snowbird from Tacoma replied, "Nelson, a man's got to have something to belong to."

In America, Liang deservedly drew quite a following. His English was natural, witty, and urbane; and he wore a perpetual smile. After several years, I got a letter from him in which he said he'd made a significant advance and now could hurl people easily and far, much as Professor Zheng did. The next time I was in New York City, moth to flame, I stopped at his apartment. Two of his students sitting there precluded my usual pragmatism and I made do with light touching and no

Laoshi and T.T. Liang
showing taiji function.

pushing. He pushed and I obliged, neither resisting nor neutralizing. But for me the earth didn't move. Alas, for he was my friend, it was the same as always. Poignant in a way, recalling Nathaniel Hawthorne's, "The Great Stone Face."

He later relocated to Minnesota, then to Los Angeles and New Jersey. I visited him in Minnesota a few times. He always welcomed me with an embrace and a story. This centenarian now lives in a nursing home in New Jersey.

In my time with Liang, I learned much about taiji and those who practice it. My teaching and writing, whatever their quality, owe much to him and his ideas.

He had had problems with Professor Zheng in New York City over working conditions and never got over them. I tried to patch the problem up with the principals and was making headway when Laoshi died in 1975.

Liang had to make a living for himself in America. He began teaching on his own. His place at Zheng's side was taken by an amiable and bright Tam Gibbs. Tam followed Laoshi, acting as an aide, in America and Taiwan until the Professor's death. He loved him and was loyal almost to a fault.

Tam's taiji was top-drawer. His form was excellent and his sensing-hands delicate and soft. He had a good root and neutralized force easily. Where he came up a bit short was that he lacked the explosive final push. He'd pull you around neutralizing you all over the place, but would then let you off the hook. He never seemed inclined to finish the action; he totally lacked the killer instinct.

Nothing propinqts like propinquity, and his nearness to Laoshi helped Tam learn quickly. But it also had a downside. Once he rushed down to Bethesda for advice. Professor Zheng had hinted to him that he might be called on to erase an old adversary of his from his dance-list. Although he could be New York abrasive at times with students, Tam was good-hearted and had no desire to fight anyone.

Tam wanted advice: he had a dilemma. He didn't want to fight this old boxer, but if he refused Laoshi, it might cost him favor or even his position with him. It was a no-win situation. What should he do?

I told him, no, that it was a great opportunity for him. When Wan Laisheng challenged Yang Chengfu in 1924 on the mainland, young Zhang Qinlin intercepted him, took the challenge for Yang, and beat Wan. From a window, Chengfu's father Jianhou watched and appreciated Zhang's courage so much he gave him special instruction secretly. I told Tam that if he agreed to Laoshi's request, Laoshi would be in his debt and that Tam might get special training. If Tam refused, he might be kept on, but I doubted the Professor would ever give him special treatment.

Tam said he knew all this, but he just didn't like fighting.

"That's the beauty of it," I told him. "You can get special stuff on the cheap by agreeing energetically. You will never have to fight anyone.

First of all, Laoshi may just be testing you with no intent to consummate the thing. You agree to a phantom fight and you win favor. If it goes further, the odds are still in your favor. This boxer is an old man, but if he knows anything of you, the one thing uppermost in his mind is that while you are young, you are close enough to Zheng to have gotten a lot from him. Though a tempestuous type, it's a safe bet that he would not accept your challenge. So go back to Laoshi and tell him you hesitated because the boxer was so old, but that if he really wants to frolic, you will oblige him. You can't lose. I almost envy you."

Tam Gibbs, the devoted confidante, doing taiji sword.

Or words to that effect. Tam seemed comfortable with my advice and went back to Manhattan. Strangely, I never heard how this turned out. Perhaps Tam didn't take my advice or Laoshi decided not to press the boxer. It's queer that I heard nothing more of the matter. Why didn't Tam tell me what happened? If the boxer had refused the challenge I think Tam would have told me. If Tam had shied from the match, he probably would not. It's really of no importance except in the context of whether Tam ever got special instruction from Zheng. We'll never know.

Laoshi's Friends & Irish

During the 1970's, there were many New Age feel-good philosophies to inebriate minds and empty wallets. One such was Arica, spawned by the Chilean, Oscar Ichazo. Popular in New York City, Ichazo cultivated Laoshi, once even purring, "I am your worst student." Zheng rejected Ichazo's overture, saying, "No, I am my own worst student."

There was a beautiful Indian yoga adept, Swami Bua, visiting the U.S. during the same period whom Zheng liked – and liked to bedevil with Socratic irony. Bua was given to verbal excess. He would say, for instance, that in India he had a friend who would stay underwater for two days. Zheng would arch an eyebrow, smile, and respond that such a feat could not be surpassed – he had known a man in China who could stay underwater, but only for one day! Not suspecting that Zheng was pulling his leg, Bua would then tell of a chap in Bombay who could jump from a six-story ledge and land intact. "Oh," Zheng would say, "this sort of thing was not uncommon in China, but the best I saw was a fellow who jumped from five stories up." And then, as Bua would start to blossom, Zheng would add that the Chinese made utterly no sound landing and he supposed that the Bombay man also made a soft landing? A bit startled, Bua recovered quickly, "Yes, of course, soundless."

Returning to Ichazo, several of Zheng's students trained in the Chilean's enterprise, and a few taught taiji there. In Bethesda, we had twenty or so Arica graduates studying taiji with us and regularly beating us out of the tuition. To minister to the poor, I had a rule that we would waive tuition for those who did a weekly stint helping to restore and maintain a low-rent apartment house for the poor in the Washington, D.C., inner city. So ten or fifteen of the Aricans agreed to do this work for their brethren. A few months later, I chanced to meet the church member who was managing the project and asked how my group was getting on? Mystified, he asked what group I meant. We booted these birds. Later, when the New Yorker who was responsible for teaching at Arica branched out to Washington, promising that he would make students into teachers in five weeks, we lost the rest of the Aricans. It was no loss to us; in fact, we saved money.

One of the drop-outs, Stan Swartz, years later wrote me a long letter apologizing for leaving. We met in San Francisco one day between trains. He told me that when he did taiji, he heard my quiet voice. Further, he said that, even while training, the teacher who spoke to him internally was always me. Seeing the other teacher, he went on, was a mistake, but a necessary one because it gave him an opportunity to see two different approaches and to see that mine was the only one that spoke truthfully and without fanfare. The sinner can repent, the sick can recover, but stupid is forever. Stan Swartz was not stupid and the last time I heard, he was teaching successfully in Pittsburgh.

In a world of zanies, this particular New York teacher Stan spoke of was a beaut. His method deserves some space as a cautionary thing. He's passed on now so I'll just softly call him Irish. He was full of blarney and fooled a lot of people. Alternating absurdity and charm, as they said of Henry Kissinger, he lied even when he didn't have to.

Irish was seldom at the New York club when I visited. We met there one day for some push-hands. He was a wonder. Not his push-hands – his humbuggery. We moved a bit and I started to go in, and he unhanded me saying, "You're against me, Bob, no use going any further." So we reconnected and circled hands some more. He didn't try anything so after a while I insinuated myself toward him. Again he quickly disconnected, saying that I was too forceful and that he had me, therefore it was pointless to continue. With that, he grabbed his coat and was off into the night. Afterward, I often mused about the incident and even partly persuaded myself that this fellow was the most sensitive person, excepting Professor Zheng, I'd ever met.

Years later in San Francisco, I was chatting with Martin Inn, a fine taiji teacher, and out of the blue he asked me if I'd ever pushed with Irish. I told him my story and he roared with laughter: Irish had pulled the same swindle on him! The sequel: years later in London, Irish wandered into the studio of a Chinese student of Laoshi, said to be pretty good in push-hands. He and Irish began their session and, sure enough, Irish turned away the first time the Chinese began to maneuver in. "No," Irish said, "You're against me too heavy, I've got you." The Chinese teacher nodded, "Yes, it's true, I can never get rid of strength. But [and here the Chinese reconnected] bear with me and I'll try to get softer." For Irish there was nothing for it, nowhere he could go, he had to stand and try to deliver. He tried but that was all. The Chinese teacher pushed him all over the studio, and then his students got in line to capitalize on Irish's non-existent soft artistry. It is said that a man kicked by a mule gets an enormous amount of information in a very short time. So Irish found out that night that there is a difference between taiji soft and taiji soft-soapery.

Unfortunately, the lesson did not last. Rushing all the way from New York City to Bethesda one Saturday morning, Irish showed me a photograph of Ben Lo pushed into the air by himself, our son of Erin. I'd never seen anyone push Ben, so I congratulated him. Still, anything associated with Irish was suspect. So I went home and phoned Ben in San Francisco. Had Irish visited him recently? He had, so I told Ben about the photograph. This left Ben puzzled because Irish could not and had not pushed him.

Intrigued, I asked whether Irish was alone when he visited? Ben said he brought a woman with him. Did she have a camera? She had, and saying that, Ben understood the scam. Irish had asked Ben not to neutralize but to stiffen so that Irish could see if he leaned while push-ing. Ben fell for it and even jumped a little, as Irish's continuous chat-ter diverted him from noticing the flash of the camera. Now Ben was angry. And Irish caught the fury of it. He called me from New York that afternoon saying I had misunderstood: the shot was staged by him and Ben for some educational purpose. And could we have dinner the next time he was in my area? I told him forcefully that we had broken bread together for the last time. That was the last time he came into my ken.

Ben Lo: Modest Man, True Taiji

Not all – indeed few – of Laoshi's friends and students were of this questionable type. Ben (Pang-jeng) Lo certainly was not. As Laoshi's first student in Taiwan (1949), Ben was trained in the old-fashioned way – he earned his taiji. This, despite the fact that Ben was very ill at the time. Posture by posture, no moving to the next movement until he got the present one down 100 percent. Because each movement alternated solid and empty in the single-weighted stances, there was pain involved. Ben suffered pain as Laoshi suffered Ben's mistakes. Thus teacher and student made progress together.

Professor Zheng didn't baby Ben and the slender man with what Zheng called "the monk's face" ate bitterness and stuck it out. Zheng could be short while Ben wanted long. Zheng showed a movement once and Ben tried to imitate it only to be shot down as Professor would list a dozen errors he had made.

Like Oliver Twist, Ben asked for more, "Could I see the movement again?"

Sarcastically, Zheng, "I've shown you once. How many times do you need to see it?"

"Just once more," the student who had been in such poor physical condition before that he couldn't walk fifteen consecutive steps would plead, "Just one more time."

Professor's first student in Taiwan, Ben Lo.

Of course, Laoshi would show him again but not without a weary sigh and a glaring glance at the importuning student with the downcast eyes. Ben watched solemnly and saw something he hadn't before.

Laoshi then said, waxing wroth, "Now you do it." And Ben did and Professor snorted again and scrupulously corrected him again. But this time there were only eight errors. Progress came hard but it came.

As Ben improved, he began to assert himself, to take the initiative. However, this was not without its dangers. Once, Professor Zheng was conversing with a friend while doing single-hand sensing with Ben, who had his back to the wall. Zheng got so animated and involved in the talk that Ben thought he saw an opening, and he launched an attack. From another world, Laoshi responded like lightning, catapulting him into the wall. Ben told me that it was all so fast and powerful that he suffered massive shock and was stuck to the wall and bereft of breath. He felt a rising gorge within his body and, as it rose, he thought it was the bloody mass that would accompany his final breath. All this time, Laoshi was frantically massaging his arms. Finally the gorge came up and the breath came out, fortunately without blood. Obviously, Zheng had been distracted and only became aware as an outside force attacked. He responded with a massive over-reaction.

I wrote the following article about Ben when he first came to America in the early 1970's. When I sent it to him to check for accuracy, he responded by asking that I not print it. This in contrast to the more than a dozen martial art students who have written premature memoirs and sent them to me, hoping I'll publicize them. Ben now permits me to print my piece, not because he's turned from modest to ego-centric, but rather because he's older now and tired of resisting.

Ben with Laoshi in the
Botanical Garden, Taipei, in 1951.

Pang-jeng (Ben) Lo is small and thin – weighing less than 140 pounds – and teaches taiji quietly and unobtrusively in San Francisco. Twenty-eight years ago, Zheng Manqing began teaching the art to Ben, then an emaciated, sickly student. After a rigorous apprenticeship under the demanding Zheng (who died in 1975), Ben has come to be the best example of Zheng's teaching in the U.S., and possibly the world.

Yet Ben demeans his own ability, saying, "I only got a little." This modesty is the mark of the man. And it's not something he puts on like a shirt. He stands up in nothing but character. He does what all of us should: he *lives* his life.

A refreshing change from the prevailing pattern of warrior-gurus, Ben wouldn't know how to be anything other than what he is. He isn't flamboyant. Teaching, he wears street slacks and shoes, whereas every American master of the art knows that Chinese regalia is a must if you're going to get it up and across.

This 49-year-old master is different in another way – he holds nothing back. Everything is trotted out for the newest tyro to examine and test. When I told him he was giving too much out too soon, he wryly rejoined that the nature of taiji is such that oral teaching will not help without the student putting in the decades of work. What he was giving the students could not be mastered by the ears. The whole body had to work it out with that old gypsy, *time*.

He freely shows actual evidence of the qi. He can:

- Withstand chops on his arm until the chopper's hand goes numb.
- Make you feel like a bridge has fallen on you by chopping you once with a relaxed hand.
- Drop you to your knees by pressing his wrist against yours or – worse! – by sawing on your wrist.
- Putting a hand on your stomach (you likewise), push you backwards irrespective of your weight or strength.
- Bring the qi to the palm of his hand, creating a small lung there.

These are not skills, only manifestations of his skills. It is in *tuishou* (push-hands) that one is astonished into an appreciation of his great craft. Other than Zheng Manqing, he is the only one I have pushed with whom I could not push even a little. He is always there but you can't bring any energy to bear on him. A neutral-izer *par excellence*, he sticks to you and ends by uprooting you.

He cannot be armlocked. Mr. Chee, an excellent Shaolin boxer in Malaysia, I could not armlock either, but there was a quantum difference between the two. Chee's qi was somewhat forceful in frustrating me while Ben's is elastic and what-ever technique I essay he neutralizes, at the same time locking or pushing me.

Ben Lo's beautiful
"Squatting Single Whip."

Though self-effacing and mild, Ben in the old days really epitomized the *wu* (martial). Where situations tended toward the physical, he was a terror. Boxers in Taiwan wanting to compare themselves with Professor Zheng often tried their wares first on Ben. After this "Lion Who Guards the Gate" completed their education, few of the challengers went on to Zheng. Ben was discouraging.

After the birth of his son, Danny (his wife, Pat, was trained by Professor Zheng in New York City), Ben told me that he realized the beauty and creativity in life and vowed never again to be destructive. He keeps to that vow despite being tempted by various yahoos.

Recently in San Francisco, a hardhead came calling. (The infinite variety of weirdos in California, a friend tells me, is accounted for by the fact that America topographically tilts downward to the southwest, causing everything loose in the country to settle there.) This one had a reputation for slapping women and strong-arming men in push-hands and was spoiling for a fight. Ben took him and smiling-ly neutralized him for half an hour, until, exhausted, the cretin slunk off, perhaps smarter.

Like Koichi Tohei of aikido fame, Ben regards challenges as stupid. Because another occupies a toxic space is no reason for you to occupy that space. So he rarely accepts one. Several months ago he phoned me: did I know a 5th-dan karateka who had told Ben that he had challenged me? "Never heard of him," I responded, "but how did I do?" Ben said the guy hadn't told him, but had come there to challenge him. Ben promptly and properly turned him down cold.

Not that he will not let good boxers try their best against him. He only asks that

The author sensing hands with Ben.

the best be controlled so that serious injuries are precluded. This for the other's benefit: uncontrolled, Ben's potency makes one wince. When I took Bill Paul, former west coast judo champ, to him for a skirmish, Ben so completely managed him that Bill, impressed, took Ben down to San Francisco State University where he demolished the whole football team, if only one at a time.

Despite his skill and pragmatic ability, Ben is still largely unrecognized. He doesn't advertise and will not even paint a sign on the window of his studio. Word of mouth brings him students. Far inferior teachers get and keep more students through commercial promotion and fancy rhetoric. But where inferior teachers do little but explicate, Ben teaches. There's a difference, old cobber.

After a brilliant period in college – Ben emerged with an M.A. in literature – and a rise in the Chinese civil service for twenty years, Ben gave up his career and pension to carry the taiji gospel to America. A man so modest that we may undervalue his great ability. A soft word of advice: don't.

Heavy Hands

There were all kinds of fighting specialists on Taiwan. One I remember would use the "tiger mouth" of one hand's thumb and index finger palm up, to grab your throat. It was so fast and he had perfected the vise so that, once bitten, you surrendered. The trick with this bird was to keep him away from you and try to destroy him from long range.

The top "heavy hand" on the island had trained his hands so that he could chop down a (small) tree barehanded or, at least, chop the bark off it. Ben, who liked to try these specialists, braced the champion and this odd couple took turns whacking each other's forearms. Soon enough they found that neither could "suffer" the strike of the other. It was a tie but the fact that Ben struck with a relaxed arm while the champ used all his force spoke loudly.

Ben told me once that during this period of heady success, our classmate Weng Ruyuan, a famed boxer/wrestler, invited him over to his house for tea. Once Ben was inside, Weng locked all the doors and windows, pocketed the key, and announced that he wouldn't let Ben leave until he had shown Weng his "secrets." Ben laughed and told his old friend that there weren't any secrets. Progress was only a function of practice. Then they practiced and had tea and talked into the night.

In Bethesda

To the dismay of his American students, Ben Lo insisted on the necessity of a strong deep foothold. You rooted into that one leg and then you held the posture until your body began to shiver and shake. With Ben, you got a root pretty quick or you quit.

Before he disappeared into Mexico, Ambrose Bierce wrote outstanding literature that included this vignette:

> A drunken man was lying in the road with a bleeding
> nose, upon which he had fallen, when a pig passed
> that way. "You wallow fairly well," said the pig, "but,
> my fine fellow, you have much to learn about rooting."

Rooting teaches one how to separate the weight quickly and facilely, but it ain't all good. Too much reliance on it in push-hands – which itself is not the street – may mean that you develop a good root but one so deep you can't respond except defensively to an attack.

Masochists all, our students enjoyed when Ben visited in Bethesda. After an hour, we all limped. One fellow at practice said that the best way of characterizing Ben's taiji is, "Sink, sink, sink." John Murphy mused, "Gee, that's the same as Benny Goodman's." To which the first guy said, "Oh, where does he teach?" At this, a third jokester started singing, "Ben Lo, sweet chariot." Other aphorisms Ben used before the media did were "No pain / No gain" and "No burn / No learn." (I suggested "No hurt / No yert" – a Mongolian abode – but it didn't sell.) My favorite of Ben's, though, was, "Hate me now or hate me later."

Here is how he summarized taiji practice for all of us, "First you do it wrong and don't know it. Then you know there's an error but not what. Then you realize what the error is but you can't correct it. Then you correct it."

There Ben caught everything. But he could also nail the thing down for you. Asked by an earnest student about the precise timing (*shizhong*) of pushing, Ben observed quietly, "Once you've learned to yield, it's always your time."

He Meets a Master of Yin

Many students love one thing better than enlightenment – they like to argue with teachers. (Arguing is only a way of resisting in your mind.) This is vexing and Ben would attempt to curb their doggerel by asking, "Do you want the truth or what?" When one such arguer resisted his corrections by saying that another teacher had said that his postures were okay, Ben told him with a smile that if one teacher says your form needs work and another teacher says your form is fine, only one is being helpful.

Ben was approached by a well-known Chinese taiji teacher from Chicago for some sensing-hands. Ben agreed, and instantly the other was at sea drowning (one of British poet Stevie Smith's poems was titled "Not Waving, But Drowning"), completely out of his element. Ben lightly pushed and pulled him all over.

Frustrated, the man yelped, "What in the world is this?"

"This is called taiji," Ben answered. "This is how yin and yang interact in tuishou."

"But," Chicago says, "I have many students. I owe much of my reputation to my lectures on yin and yang!"

Ben said that might be so, but talking was not doing. On yin and yang in the real world, Chicago hadn't a clue.

So the defrocked professor asked Ben if he would teach him if he moved to San Francisco. Ben agreed. And give the guy credit: he went out there, enrolled, and exposed to the real, may have learned a little.

But not much. In a few months, he quit the rigorous training and began his own taiji class in which San Franciscans could now learn the truth of yin and yang shorn of work. I could comment on this with the old country tune title, "It Ain't Love, But It Ain't Bad," but it is bad. It stinks.

Like all good things, taiji is a kind of loving, an art of being genuinely and totally real. In Margery Williams' *Velveteen Rabbit* (1922), remember the skin horse's answer when the rabbit asks him, "What is real?"

Real isn't how you are made. It's a thing that happens to you. When a child loves you for a long, long time, not just to play with, but really loves you, then you become real. It doesn't happen all at once. You become. It takes a long time. That's why it doesn't often happen to people who break easily or have sharp edges, or have to be carefully kept. Generally, by the time you are Real, most of your hair has been loved off and your eyes drop out and you get loose at the joints and very shabby.

"Get real," yes. Real resides in our relation to our bodies. Institutions (taiji, yoga) and individuals (Freud) realize this and teach this truth. However, most of us do everything we can to avoid Real. Where we want wings and stimulation, Real plods along. It sometimes seems uninteresting, but Real is under no obligation to be always interesting – it simply is.

And where Real is, that teacher from Chicago isn't.

William Morris wrote that if a man is good he imputes goodness to another. That is a risky business among the denizens of these so-called martial arts.

Ben Makes It

Ben hadn't seen Professor Zheng for several years when he saw him last on Taiwan. Ben was visiting. A little boy came to his home in the afternoon with a message from Laoshi – "Come on over." Ben went hoping to get some sensing-hands with him so he could see if he had progressed. He did and all Ben's efforts for all those years apparently went for naught. Everything he tried was neutralized, including his neutralizing. Laoshi pushed and threw him with abandon. At the end Zheng chided him.

"What's the matter? Did you forget everything I taught you? This just won't do!"

Ben went home crushed. He thought of quitting taiji and sat morose and shaken. Later that evening, his anguish was interrupted by the same little boy bearing another message, "Come on over."

Back he went to Laoshi's house. With penetrating eyes, Professor told Ben he'd been too harsh with him earlier.

"Actually, you've improved greatly. I had to stay alert to handle you. Keep up the good work!"

They sat and talked. Later, a different man walked Ben's legs back to his lodgings.

Guo Lianyin

Years ago, I got a letter from a columnist for a popular martial art magazine, one which paid large sums to find out what kind of cover sold the most magazines. The experts analyzed the question and told the owners that sales were highest when the cover depicted (in descending order of sales): (1) a male foot in another male's mouth, (2) a male fist to another male's nose, (3) a male foot to another male's torso, (4) a male fist to another male's torso, (5) a female foot to a male's head, (6) a female fist to a male's head, (7) a female foot to a male's torso, and (8) a female fist to a male's torso. Apparently there was utterly no market for a female to kick or hit another female in any locale. Alas, this was a long time ago. Nowadays females get a more (ouch!) equal billing.

Like film star Bruce Lee, my smallish correspondent was photogenic but couldn't fight a little. He wrote that I had wasted my time in Taiwan. That none of my teachers were first-class. That he alone knew proper wushu, and listed two pages of methods he learned. Then implied that Zheng Manqing was an inferior taiji teacher. He had the gall to end his letter by graciously inviting me to his gym whenever I was in his area.

I nearly jumped a plane. And would have if it hadn't been for the long catalog of swindles he'd cited as part of his arsenal. Even real masters didn't know that many methods. This obviously was another Cantonese "boxer of the mouth corners," clearly not worth anyone's time. So I put the letter away.

A few months later I was visiting Ben Lo in San Francisco. Walking the streets, I remembered the letter and asked Ben about the fellow. Ben was surprised. "That little guy? He knows nothing." I gave him details of the letter including his put-down of Professor Zheng and asked him what I ought to do.

Incredulous at the little guy's effrontery (bear in mind Ben is only about 140 pounds himself), Ben smiled and said, "I know him real well. Here's what you do. Write him back and thank him for his valuable wushu information. Then ask him how

Guo Lianyin
in "Universal Post."

he'd rate me, and let me know what he says. If Professor is no good, I must be terrible – but I want him to respond and I want to hear what he says."

The denouement? The jerk had done nothing for me or, in his articles, correct wushu. He deserved nothing; I owed him nothing. Then why did I do him the biggest favor of his life? Why did I never write him that letter Ben suggested? He probably wouldn't have answered it but he was a foolish fellow and may have. If he answered positively, rating Ben above Zheng, he would be displaying karmic or at least cosmic foolishness. Worse for him, if he was his usual negative self and criticized Ben's boxing as low order stuff, he would soon enough have an opportunity to eat those words sans soy sauce. But I went Daoist and let the fish off the hook. I'm sort of sorry. Later that day in San Francisco, I made up for it by bringing two enemies together to renew friendship in an ambiance of possibility. Here is how that one played out.

Guo Lianyin I met in Taiwan and years later visited in San Francisco. He had been in the movie, *The Killer Elite* (1975), and the resultant publicity made him well-known. Just before leaving Taiwan in 1962, I had visited his class where he treated me cordially. Though aghast at the lack of relaxation and the fast tempo of this taiji, I said nothing. I was more interested in seeing his xingyi, but he begged off showing it, probably because Paul Guo, my xingyi/bagua teacher, was with me. He made a point of inviting me to see the xingyi at his house the next day, but I was returning to the U.S. then, so had to refuse. Paul hadn't been included in the offer, and he reacted to the lack of courtesy by asking Guo with a sneer where he'd learned his taiji? Guo named as his teacher, an old monk who'd studied under Yang Banhou (died 1892). Paul reacted by telling Guo that he would have to be over 100 to have done so. Guo fell silent and didn't answer Paul, though I knew he raged inside. Paul's brazen assertion threw a pall on things, but I got a kick out it. Paul and I made our escape shortly afterward, agreeing that it was a good place to be leaving. It had information of a sort but no knowledge.

Anyway, I stopped to see Guo Lianyin later in San Francisco. His pretty 39-year-old Taiwanese wife, who taught taiji on local TV, greeted me with their little boy and called her husband down. It was an agile family. The boy, the momma, and the eighty-year-old teacher in a sea-captain's hat all could lean over and kiss their feet. I couldn't kiss mine and wouldn't kiss theirs, but they were most gracious and treated me well. Guo had apparently forgotten the embarrassing incident with Paul Guo in Taiwan, and was cordiality itself.

'Twas not always thus. A hoplology student of Donn Draeger told me that he interviewed Guo for a local newspaper. (This student later turned out to be a total disappointment. But that is another story which I'll forego – this book isn't long enough to include so many dis- appointments.) Starting out, he mentioned to Guo that he'd seen an article on him the week before that perhaps contained some hyperbole. If so, how could Guo and other teachers control such writers? The old man went into an instant rage. His eyes flashing and his face flushing, he shouted at the interviewer, "What do you mean, that I tell lies and exaggerate when I talk to reporters?" The bewildered reporter aborted the article and returned to his weapons play.

But I was Guo's buddy, in spite of Paul Guo's impertinence, and, apparently, in spite of Zheng Manqing. To put it mildly, these two didn't hit it off. I was unaware of any friction between them in Taiwan. But on his way to New York on his first visit to America in 1964, Laoshi stopped for a few weeks in San Francisco. While there, his chap- erone was an overweight American who later followed him to New York City. This chap is my source for what happened. Not too credible on many things, he was so self-interested that he would not have fol- lowed Zheng to the East Coast if the story had not occurred as he reported it.

During a social function in San Francisco, Professor Zheng was sit- ting conversing with other guests when fiery old Guo Lianyin approached him and challenged him to a fight. Zheng rose, faced Guo, then disdained him by turning his back to him and walking over to his chaperone, my source. Professor told him that Guo obviously was out of his gourd and did the chaperone know of an available lawyer? My man did and dashed out to find him. It was a freeze frame for twenty minutes or so. My man and the lawyer returned on the run, Guo fum- ing with a couple allies, Laoshi talking pleasantly with other guests. Laoshi and Guo then huddled with the lawyer, Laoshi taking the lead. He pointed out to the puzzled lawyer that Guo, an old boxing adver- sary from Taiwan, had insulted him in public and challenged him to a fight. He was new to America, Zheng continued, and wanted to stay within its laws. However, he would agree to the fight if Guo would sign a waiver relieving Zheng of any liability for injuring or killing him.

At this, the shocked lawyer (a first for this breed), looking from one elderly Chinese gentleman to the other, said, "This is crazy! You're in America. You can't have fights to the death here!"

The chaperone jumped in at this point and told the lawyer that this was no lark. Though old, these men could and would fight unless some solution could be reached. So the lawyer took it more seriously. Addressing Guo, he asked him if he would sign such a waiver as Zheng demanded. Guo shook his head and stalked out. That ended the incident.

Bob and Ben, ol' buddies.

So while Guo and his family sat smiling and drinking tea with me that morning in San Francisco, he knew that I was a student of Zheng Manqing, yet still treated me as an old friend. Dale Carnegie (*How to Win Friends and Influence People*) had taught me well. We had a good chat that ended with them inviting me to dinner later at a nearby restaurant, an invitation I accepted with alacrity.

Walking back to Ben Lo's studio for a workout, I met Ben en route. I told him of my visit with Guo Lianyin. On a whim, I asked Ben if he'd like to join us at dinner. At first he couldn't believe that Guo had been so nice to a student of Zheng Manqing. When he saw I was serious, he said that he'd like to attend, but that it was unlikely Guo would have him. I told him I'd ask Guo, and returned to Guo's place.

His wife smilingly admitted me and I explained my return. She called up some stairs and down he came, smiling. I told him I'd been staying with Ben Lo and since it might be impolite to leave him to go out and dine with my friend Master Guo, was it possible that Ben could be included in the invite? Without hesitating, he said he knew Ben and that he was welcome to join us.

The dinner was delightful. Our hosts included Guo, his wife, and two of his seniors. One was a tempestuous type I'd heard of who later fell to Chu Hongbing in Taiwan. The other was an American who had studied xingyi eight years under Guo. It was all entertaining and pleasant and, as I remember, Laoshi's name was not even mentioned. In the end, the lure of the meal, its possibilities of combustion, was better than the excellent repast itself. The fact that nothing dire happened didn't matter. The excitement of the suspense was sufficient. Ben and I got off with our skins and full bellies. If I remember, neither of us partook of the world famous maotai liquor from Guizhou Province, preferred by our host, of which a Chinese friend in Taiwan told me once that you had no hangover from it when you woke up – if you woke up. Two pints of it made one cavort, and that night we needed clear heads.

Southeast Asia Revisited: Laoshi's Other Top Students

I visited Asia in 1983 – my second trip there since leaving in 1962 accompanying Ben Lo's team on a three-week tour to Taiwan, Malaysia, and Singapore. I wrote the following article on it in *T'ai Chi Player* (December 1986).

Generally, the senior cadre was competent and the overall quality of the membership fairly good. I was disappointed, however, to find that in many places the form has been externalized by music and uniforms. No big thing perhaps but anything that detracts or diverts from an individual meeting on that narrow ridge – the ultimate internal path we call taiji – probably ought to be avoided.

Music is an externality. Since it has a beat, using it may subordinate taiji to it, making this moving meditation merely a dance. There is an innate rhythm and beat to taiji but it derives from an internal alchemy of breathing, movement, and self rather than externally "manufactured" melody. Years ago I experimented with music and though Bach soothed and Beethoven was pleasant, no music was quite so good as that music taiji itself was producing from deep inside me (though I must confess I still occasionally do part of a round to Don Redman's jazz classic "Chant of the Weed").

Uniforms are less of a problem. Like music, they may help stimulate a social collectivity in the group – plus promote revenue – but for me it seems all too homogenized and external. Because the art is essentially Daoist, I think it is best done by de-emphasizing externalities of a kind that dilute the uniqueness of each individual.

Among the long and short forms of Yang, Wu, and Chen derivation I saw many interesting things. And call me a traditionalist but I shuddered at a couple of systems that mixed taiji and bagua. One doesn't mix – it usually dilutes both and results in no satisfying synthesis. I saw a slender cheery oldster at one village do the Chen Panling eclectic form. Happily imprecise, he was oblivious that his fly was open – an ominous thing since this form requires several high side-kicks – but he made it through without mishap.

The level of push-hands was lower than I expected, the procedure used far different from what we followed in the old days. Then, one pushed with sundry partners in an ambiance where as many as fifteen or more couples simultaneously played at interpreting energy. If the going got too forceful Professor Zheng would chide the miscreant that the Classics insisted on relaxation and, to show the efficacy of his words, he would introduce the chap to the real softness of his hands and the resultant hardness of the wall.

At the Annual Push-hands Tournament at Taoyuan, however, four-ounce touches had deteriorated into pushes and pushes into frantic shoves. Here, bureaucratization brought together men and women in fixed weight categories in a contest with all the hoopla of karate or western boxing matches, but sadly with little of the skills. Participants rushed around shoving in a mad milieu in which a small sumotori would have cleared the decks in fifteen minutes. Before my eyes push-hands had reverted to *jiao-di*, the earliest Chinese fighting form in which men butted each other like bulls. One tall American even attempted to surprise his opponent by leaping into the air and twirling a full circle. Some root. Women in t-shirts struck others with piston-like arms in the bosom, and so on. Something was amiss. Did I have a hypothesis?

Sure. The major wrong was first of all forceful strength. An uproot done with *ti-fang* is not even given a point – one must simply push the other past the boundary. Yang Chengfu said that we don't progress because we use force instead of technique. We must become softer. The taiji I saw was much harder than twenty years ago, a function, I think, of its growing popularity (Gresham's Law) and the proliferation in the quantity and a dilution in the quality of teachers. Plus it is difficult to remain soft in a private setting. How much harder it is to relax before crowds!

Add to this the fact that competition is anathema to Daoism and the problem is compounded. Taiji is cooperative rather than competitive. In New York City a person got three pushes before he had to turn around and take the defensive role with his back to the wall. (I think the wall is indispensable for focus and as a deterrent to grappling and forceful strength.) In our classes in Bethesda we insisted that if someone successfully pushed a partner he must then tell him how he did it. What is softness if not cooperation?

Chu Hongbing: The King of the South

Chu Hongbing lived down-island, so I couldn't remember him from my early stint in Taiwan. Like so many taiji brothers, he had become wealthy, having a factory making sugar cubes for export. I watched his form and it was superlative. He and Ben Lo were quite close. It was Ben, who liked to put people together to see what would happen, who rushed to my room in our small hotel in Taiwan to ask me if I wanted to push with Mr. Chu. Chu's push-hands was top-drawer and he had soundly defeated Guo Lianyin's senior student when that worthy had challenged him in Taiwan. Because he was the only one I hadn't practiced with in the old days, I jumped at the chance. I told Ben, "Darn tootin'," an idiom which Ben might have had trouble understanding (he was still struggling with English then, telling some of us once that we were small buildings but Professor Zheng was a "sky-crapper"), but when I jumped up and followed him out of the room, he saw I was elated. Mr. Chu was Mr. Big in taiji circles in south Taiwan, where he had trained most of the teachers.

As the author pushes Chu Hongbing, Ben Lo picks his pocket.

The crowded corridor outside his room was the venue. Mr. Chu was a smiling handsome man and shook hands with me warmly. We began by crossing arms and, always impetuous, I straightaway attacked. His concentration may have been lazy, for he was unable to neutralize and fell back against the wall. It was a mental error on his part, but as we continued, I became aware that most of the people watching were his students and I felt bad about the embarrassment I was causing.

Then, in trying to redress the situation, I made it worse. He was superior to me, I was sure, and if I'd just continued normally he would have taken me down a peg. Instead, anxious to make amends, I tanked for everything he tried, falling this way and that. Later, Mr. Chu asked Ben Lo why I had attacked him like that. Ben, who really enjoyed the incident, answered, "Because I signaled him." When Ben found out that Alice had a snapshot of the incident, he had a dozen prints made for happy distribution. Since they were great friends, this didn't bother Mr. Chu. But, as for the foreigner, Mr. Chu was cool toward him the rest of the trip.

Liu Xiheng: The Soft Buddhist

Liu Xiheng – he got the soft.

On a more pleasant topic, I was able to renew acquaintance with the incomparable Liu Xiheng. I couldn't remember Mr. Liu – though he said I had visited his home in the old days. I put this down to his modest self-effacing ways.

At the time of my visit, Mr. Liu was a retired civil servant, a 72-year-old Buddhist with a Catholic wife. Quiet natured, Mr. Liu's push-hands was incredibly soft and he used his waist to maneuver one into a cul-de-sac, thus foregoing the anticlimactic and unnecessary push. Mr. Liu had a large following of Chinese and American students, all of whom I found warm and intelligent.

In just a couple of days, Mr. Liu tried to correct my form (a Herculean task), taught me a new single-hand form in which the weight stays in the rear leg, and cleared up many difficulties. Some of our dialog I record below:

◆ In learning taiji, is it best to use hard at first and progressively soften, or should one always use soft?

❖ Always use soft. Always have mind [yi] but don't think of qi: if you do, it will impede the natural flow of qi. Don't use force [li] in the beginning, lest it become a habit. So, disregard the li or qi and think only of the yi.

◆ Should we stick slavishly to Professor Zheng's teaching or should we modify?

❖ Follow his teaching precisely. If in doubt, seek the most natural way. Adhere to the taiji principles, because if you pick up a bad habit and continually practice it, it will make the error natural after a while. And of course, this is wrong.

◆ In the Yang family, why are the Banhou and Jianhou styles so different?

❖ Time and innovation brought changes. Even in the Jianhou transmission, Wu Jianquan changed the style. However, change is not necessarily dilution, and we mustn't criticize without knowing the reasons. The important thing to remember is that which one sometimes gains from intense study or long practice. *Gongfu* is time, *xinde* is awakening, but your xinde can only come from correct principles and not just from yourself.

◆ Of what use is sensing-hands?

❖ Its most important use is that it corrects and reinforces our form which is the basis of taiji.

◆ Why did Professor Zheng favor fixed-step over moving sensing-hands?

❖ Because fixed-step forces us to use our waists whereas moving sensing-hands exercises only the legs. Zheng of course followed his partner. He said that when he engaged senior Chen Weiming, Chen would begin moving as soon as they touched and so Professor accommodated him by doing as he did.

◆ Where should we put our minds in practice?

❖ The two hip joints are very important and you must be conscious of them in practice – but use only one joint at a time. Relax the other hip completely – if you think of both joints at the same time you will be double-weighted. I asked the Professor about these two points and if in practice one should think of them. The Professor thought awhile and finally said, "No, you should only think of moving the waist."

Usually Mr. Liu mentioned these two points in connection with his idea of "the rectangle," this being the shoulders and hips connected by imaginary lines on the torso. He had his students practice for 100 days, thinking of the four points (hips and shoulders). This helped them be conscious of moving all parts of the body together. Later, he had them think of the vertical alignment points – *weilu* at the tailbone and the "jade pillow" at the base of the skull – which helped them stay straight.

◆ **Professor Zheng taught us to do the form as with an opponent in view. Mightn't this result in an alertness that triggers tension?**

❖ If the form is done softly this visualization is all right. It may help concentration and can't harm your form. After a time you can discard this idea and concentrate only on your yi. Once, as Secretary of the Food Bureau, the demands on me became so hectic I wrote to Professor Zheng in New York City seeking help. He chided me in his reply: "In practicing taiji, you don't have trouble sinking your qi to your dantian. Now you must do it in your workaday life and you will be all right." The Professor is gone, but this advice lives on.

◆ **Is taiji for everyone?**

❖ Yes, we must teach it without distinction. If you refuse entrance into taiji they may never have another chance to learn the taiji way and change. You can only try to help someone after you accept him or her into the class. Professor always told us to embrace everyone and to exclude no one. We must yield first or it's not taiji.

◆ **What has been taiji's most important value for you?**

❖ Its most important use is in daily life where it taught me to make yielding a habit. This becomes a way of dealing with friends and events peacefully, accepting everything in a relaxed way. Eventually, this changes your character.

That was the account of Mr. Liu I wrote for *T'ai Chi Player* (December, 1986). But the man needs more ink.

Mr. Liu was Professor Zheng's second student, starting in January 1950. Young Ben Lo preceded him by four months. Mr. Liu saw the Professor in all settings. Having a high post in government, he could assess him intellectually; being a devout Buddhist, he could evaluate him from the philosophical vantage. He never consciously did either.

We visited
Master Liu (l. to r.):
Terry Lee, Martin Inn,
author, Liu Xiheng,
Alice, Danny Emerick.

Instead, he listened to and learned from Laoshi and tested him through his system. Laoshi would rise or fall on that basis. Laoshi rose.

Only after Professor Zheng's death in 1975 and his own retirement from government service the next year did Mr. Liu begin teaching. About the same time, he became a vegetarian given to regular fasts. His personal progress accelerated from that time. Gone was the busy and plagued government worker of thirty years before who smoked two packs of cigarettes daily. Now there was time to focus, and with time, focus. Soon he had a faithful following. The ten or so foreigners who came to him for instruction were so fervent that they urged him to formalize their taiji relationship by making them avowed students in a kowtow ceremony having obligations on both the teacher and the students. Pleased with their practice, Mr. Liu complied. The group was an exceptional one.

In old China, it was common for a teacher to take disciples bound by tradition and ritual. But it was a hard system. The student listened and guarded the teacher's words. He was expected to accept everything the teacher said. Ben Lo tells me that in the Qing Dynasty if a student did great wrong, his teacher and his teacher's family could be forfeit. Professor Zheng accepted disciples carefully, but still had some bad apples. Liu Xiheng's use of the disciple system in Taipei involving several young Americans, sadly, was not an unalloyed success. Even in China, Time, that old horse, gallops along and institutions change. I think discipleship will be modified to a teacher/student relationship making it easier on both parties. In America, neither Ben Lo nor anyone I know supports the old disciple system. I think that is as it should be.

In contrast to Ben Lo's students, Liu's group comprised persons who seemed non-assertive and almost timid. Without choosing between these two seniors, Laoshi had once commented that Liu had inherited his softness, Lo his fire. This apparently carried over to their students.

And this difference was seen in their teaching. Where Ben Lo seldom deviated from the intense and painful "holding" postures that he had been taught by Laoshi, that produced pupils able quickly to root, Mr. Liu stressed shorter holding and more adherence to the waist than the root. Ben stuck to form practice to bolster his students' sensing-hands. Mr. Liu followed the principles of the form, but also created different patterns that in repetition would complement regular form practice.

The author and Liu sensing-hands.

As shown me initially by Danny Emerick (the class "character" – when his congenitally flawed hips failed, Mr. Liu created a "Danny's Form" for him), Liu's Eight Basics come from an off-hand remark Laoshi made once to Mr. Liu. The "Five Animals" form was gleaned from some notes left by Laoshi and given to Mr. Liu by Mrs. Zheng. These simulate Hua To's ancient Five Animals exercise:

- Ward Off, Rollback, Press are Dragon.
- Push is Tiger.
- Fair Lady at Shuttles/Repulse Monkey is Monkey.
- Cloud Hands is Bear.
- Brush Knee (with adjustment step) is Bird.

Mr. Liu sprinkled his instruction with Professor Zheng's words, "Many teachers say relax, stand erect, and don't use force, but the most important factors in taiji are honesty and sincerity. For without these qualities one can't advance."

"Taiji is simple but not easy. It is hard work, but it is eased if you always maintain harmony with nature. Yield and never go against it."

And Mr. Liu added his own wisdom. Laoshi had once chided Liu for not working hard enough, for resting too much, "If you want to go down the road, you must walk." Another time Liu complained to Laoshi about his lack of progress in taiji. Laoshi replied, "So, what do you want me to do about it?" Such remarks cut to the quick, leading Liu to really apply himself. From that work came advice such as this:

- Yield first, then turn, then attack.
- If you are not relaxed, you are crooked. If you are crooked, you are using force.
- To be nothing is good (see Emily Dickinson's words on page 242).
- The Daoists still have an idea of self; in taiji you must lose it.

Mr. Liu often told his students Buddhist stories. Here is one, a cautionary tale on anger: A terrible ogre, ugly and mean, terrorized the people of a small village. They hated and feared him. One day a monk, traveling through the village, came upon the ogre blocking his way. The monk ordered him aside, and when the ogre refused, he became very angry. But the angrier the monk got, the bigger and uglier the ogre became. Then the monk began to pity the ogre for his ugliness and mean disposition and, as he did, the ogre became smaller and smaller until he was but a speck in the road. The monk fed him, put him in the shade, and walked on. The moral, Mr. Liu said, is to avoid anger, "If you become angry at someone, they will only become angrier at you. If someone is angry at you, then it is best not to become angry at them."

Though Mr. Liu wasn't given to hilarity, his soft humor is seen in, "If you double-weight, you haven't a leg to stand on." Finally, sensing-hands with one of his pupils one day, he yielded to force and twirled him around in a circle. Then with a subdued smile he said, "disco."

Mr. Liu and Ben Lo still believe that I was the American at a beach in Taiwan one summer day who entertained Professor Zheng and others by picking up a case of beer (24 bottles) with one hand, thrusting it out and holding it out at the shoulder. Alas, it wasn't me. Memory isn't even a factor. Tim Geoghegan might be able to do it, but not this little old Who from Whoville. Ben thought I was being coy at first, even pressing me with more information, "You remember, it was the day Professor Zheng lost his bathing trunks!" I told him that I sure as the devil would've remembered that, even if I lapsed on the beer case memory. The moral of this story is that Laoshi, Ben, Mr. Liu, et. al. got me and let a real powerhouse get away! Do you suppose the mystery man could have been that ever elusive engineer of esoterica, John Gilbey?

Chen Weiming,
Laoshi's old friend.

Shouzhung in Hong Kong to ask if he endorsed this outburst, he disavowed it, answering that he didn't know the Australian and, in any case, shouldn't be held responsible for what students of his students said.

Yours is the bigger fault. So in the spirit of the Bard – "Use all gently" – I urge you to be more responsible in what you print. All too many of the martial arts magazines print letters and articles of the My-teacher-can-whip-your-teacher, My-style-is-better-than-yours ilk. This is childish and silly and divisive. And it leads many subscribers to become only sometime readers, who attack you all too often as being sociopathic. Most of us are trying to spread these arts as systems of physical and cultural education, not methods of savagery. If you had simply stopped with the writer's corrective, that would have been sufficient, but to indulge his wild and whirling words on Zheng Manqing only encourages such gossip-mongering.

Poor Professor Zheng. On the one hand, we have persons who swear they saw him levitate and, on the other, bozos who get caught up in ambiguities such as he was too soft and he'd fight a bear and give him first bite! There is too much documentary evidence that Yang Chengfu's teaching began and ended with softness for your correspondent to disparage softness; surely Yang Shouzhung (your writer should sometime learn to spell and pronounce his grandteacher's name, incidentally) knows and teaches that.

Ditto on fighting skill. There are far too many boxers who bit the dust before Professor Zheng – I was in that number – for anyone to be confused about that. Anyone, I should say, but enemies. Therefore, I can only remind them that Zheng was eminently available, and only fear and ego kept them from trying conclusions with him. Though Professor Zheng himself ranked taiji lowest of his skills – he even tried to keep knowledge of his boxing prowess from his artist friends lest they regard him as a low-class brawler – but he was of a fighting tradition and willing to accept a worthwhile challenge.

Professor Zheng didn't always do his best to assuage the enmity caused by the envy of others. His "eyes were very high" and he brooked no nonsense from boxers generally, regarding them as inferiors. Plus he didn't look like a boxer: he was small, gentle, and appeared to be what he regarded himself – an artist. When I first met him I didn't think he could fight, but I learned otherwise, and after a lifetime spent practicing with and analyzing boxing, wrestling, and judo adepts, I have to conclude that Zheng Manqing was superior to any I met. (Because your pages are often exploited by self-serving Walter Mittys, let me note that against the top rankers I was a "second eleven sort of chap"; I am modest and, as the man sez, have every right to be!) Among these worthies I list Jack Johnson, Joe Louis, T. Ishikawa, M. Oyama, and M. Ueshiba. They would beat you, but only Professor Zheng could beat you without hurting you. That, friends, is body management.

So, people who have never met or touched this man continue to berate him. Some, including this same Australian, pass on stories implying that Zheng was never a student of Yang Chengfu. This, the most ridiculous cut of all, has been refuted by Ben Lo in the *Journal of the Taiwan Taiji Association* (volume 92, October 30, 1975). Professor Zheng was one of Yang's few seniors and the one (with Chen Weiming) who was used by Yang to explicate his teachings. He and Chen wrote Yang's *Complete Principles and Applications of Taichi Ch'uan* and when it appeared

in 1934, it had a Preface by Zheng Manqing. If Zheng were not a senior, how did he come to write this Preface? But ancient quarrels set in (I could dilate on these but since they do not dignify Yang Shou-zhung and might put me in the position of gossip-mongering, I won't) that are best forgotten by all of us. To cap all this, the youngest of Yang Chengfu's students, his nephew, the late Fu Zhongwen, has gone on record certifying Zheng as an active member of Yang's inner circle, remembered chiefly for his exceptional push-hands.

While I'm sweeping out this debris, let me say a word on Zheng Manqing's death. A Chinese man wrote in his book on taiji boxing that Zheng died from a heart attack brought on by alcohol. This couldn't be more wrong. Professor Zheng actually died of a burst blood vessel in his brain, caused, many think, by a chunk of masonry falling on him at age ten which left him in a coma for a week.

Laoshi in "Step Back and Repulse Monkey."

Laoshi
does
"Lotus Kick"
in Taipei.

Zheng did drink as have nearly all Chinese painters and poets since Li Bai, but not to the excess of his eminent predecessors. Traditionally, artists used wine to forget the world. Bo Juyi in ten years reputedly wrote over a thousand poems and drank several thousand gallons of wine. Xie Lingyun (385-433), a devout Buddhist, liked to sit semi-nude and drink in public. The Daoist Tao Yuanming (365-427) substituted wine for immortality therapeutics, but another Daoist wrote: "Drink is no elixir of life; but how can one bear to stay sober in a drunken world?" Against these, Zheng was a piker. In the sixteen years I knew him, I saw him drinking only twice and drunk never (though he was about the only person sober at a party I attended in New York City just before he went back to Taiwan). The author then misquotes Zheng's *Thirteen Chapters* (1946) to try to make his case. Why? Even if Zheng were a rip-roaring, downfalling, upchucking drunk, why such pernicious revelations after his death? Will the author next provide us with a sequel describing how Zheng abused his wife and children? In the West, our betters tell us to speak softly of the dead. One would expect that the author, being of China – a much politer civilization than ours – would be even softer.

Suffice to say that taiji is or should be a gentle art, practiced nowadays mainly for health; for constructive purposes, not destructive. *Sanshou* (free-fighting) and even tuishou (pushing-hands) have deteriorated, but taiji for health is more popular than ever. And that is, it seems to me, a proper denouement. There are, however, several Zheng seniors who are excellent exponents of tuishou and your writer may want to further his education by trying some of them on for size before he again shoots from his lip.

Zheng Manqing:
A Summing Up

Then came the phone call from Ed Young in 1975. Laoshi was dead at 73 in Taiwan. The news numbed and saddened me. Others it shocked, often almost seeming to anger as though they were saying, "How dared he?" The masterless, the invincible, had fallen. Everyone phoned everyone else saying good and courageous things about passing on his message of quality and relaxation, but the words didn't change the fact that he had "changed," and returned to nature.

Although I respected Zheng Manqing enormously, I did not regard him as a god. Certainly his array of excellences awed me. Of old it was said, "Bow to genius, but kneel to goodness." I both bowed and knelt, but the bows predominated. Zheng was always good to me, but I heard from other insiders that he could be short-tempered and didn't always suffer some students gladly. This was natural. He was an artist with constant demands on his professional time and with normal family obligations. When some students did things he considered disloyal, he let them know it. Even then he never scolded, simply informed the transgressor of his error.

For years, I've written much on Professor Zheng. I didn't want to particularly, but was driven to it by attacks on him by envious others, including some former students.

I don't know which is worse: those who never met the man, or those who did but didn't listen to what he said. For instance, we hear that Professor Zheng never studied under Yang Chengfu. This was a lie begun in Southeast Asia by malicious types too stupid to know that Zheng wrote the preface for Yang's 1934 book. Here he explicitly states that he began training under the master in Shanghai in 1932. Zheng signed the preface with his birth-name Zheng Yue. He and Chen Wei-ming probably wrote the book itself, as Yang was not a literati. As stated earlier, some of Yang Chengfu's top students have stated and/or written that Professor Zheng was indeed an active member of the Yang inner circle. Zheng's exceptional attainment in push-hand skills left an imprint on many of the time.

As for Zheng's very real fighting ability, an American-Chinese historian for a martial arts magazine once phoned me to carp about

Zheng's taiji not being functional. I replied softly that he could say that and other foolish things in a magazine that delighted in showing a foot in someone else's face each month, but that as far as I was concerned, Zheng had time and again proven that Laozi was right – softness can overcome hardness. I then added that whenever forced to conclusions, Zheng's high skill never deserted him. At that, the man blustered, "Yeah, that's another thing – Zheng loved to beat up people!"

In *Masters and Methods*, I told of another dubious type, a karate 2nd-dan, whom I invited to attend class with me one day in Taipei. He wanted to try the system out combatively. Zheng had him attack Ben Lo twice. In a flash Ben blocked the offending foot or fist and lightly touched the guy's heart each time. This one realized it not and went away mumbling about how old Zheng was. As he wanted something harder taught by someone considerably younger, I sent him to Hong Yisheng. A bit later I saw him again. "How is it going?" I asked. "I quit," he replied. Why? "Those guys really wanted to fight."

So much for Professor Zheng's bonafides. He was the only person I ever met in any martial art who could defeat you and not hurt you because he only knew the soft. Therefore, it is not surprising that such unworldly skill would induce jealousy.

After saying this, then why do even his students foul up? Paradoxically, for much the same reason as his adversaries. The misbehaving students don't really know Zheng. Sure, they can recite Laoshi's ideas about contacting the four jin or lecture on his five excellences. But if they really knew him, then the ends they seek (money, ego, prestige) could never make their disloyalty worth the candle. Zheng Manqing is the towering figure in taiji since Yang Chengfu's death in 1936. To cheat his memory is to not understand reality.

Fencer Aldo Nadi says in his autobiography, *The Naked Sword* (1995), that his fencing master father had a sallè whose sign proclaimed the celebratory words, "Honor the teaching [traditions]; respect the teacher." Just so. And why should Italian fencing outdo an internal art such as taiji when it comes to courtesy?

Happily, measured against the number of his students and grand students, the miscreants are few. And I am not talking about nuances of posture, either. (How many taiji teachers does it take to change a light bulb? One hundred: one to change it, 99 to say he didn't do it quite right.) Nor am I scrupulously insisting on the traditional teacher-student relationship. Modern life has diluted, sometimes for the better,

the scope of this ancient institution. No, such changes can be understood and perhaps even applauded. But when former students try to
impeach Zheng's honor, it is sad no matter how few the miscreants.

Anyhow, this is why I write often defending Zheng Manqing. We
all are keepers of his flame. In my taiji classes, I often asked seniors
questions. One was "why does fire burn?" Not how, but why. One
answer – there are several – is focus. Like a child with a magnifying
glass focusing the sun's rays on a dry leaf (this concentration of energy
ignites the leaf and releases the heat), we must focus on the teacher
and the teaching. The best prism is constancy and love. It wants only
a keen eye and a willing heart and, if persisted in, can dissolve somewhat the mystery of taiji.

Laoshi easily balanced and reconciled his many excellences. If his
combative artistry had come from the hard Shaolin side, that would
have contradicted his other arts, preventing an easy synthesis of all of
them. But, it came not from the hard but from the soft qi of taiji and
so blended easily with the rest. Even his simultaneous supporting of
Daoism (that nature mysticism) and Confucianism (what Joseph
Needham called "this worldly social-mindedness") was done lightly,
without rancor, as a complement not a contradiction. In his book on
Laozi, he noted the lamentable lack of an ethical base in Daoism and
left it at that. (His remark to me – "I am three-fifths Confucian and
two-fifths Daoist" – said everything.) Without taking sides, I note these
lines of L. Giles on Confucianism, "Unlike Christianity and Muham-
madanism, the Way preached by Confucius knows neither the sanction
of punishment nor the stimulus of reward in an afterlife. Even
Buddhism holds out the hope of Nirvana" [plus I would add that
Confucius never gave a lecture].

One of Laoshi's little tricks, using that word non-pejoratively, may
illustrate this synthesizing theme. In taiji we are taught to stand erect,
but in his insistence that the principles ought to be applied to everyday
life, Zheng stood among the greats. If in conversation, say, you slumped
in your chair (only your lower back should touch the chair), he would
playfully stand in front of you and lightly hold your shoulder down and
you could not get up out of that chair. The Daoist would support the
straight but relaxed back (Laozi would have starved at West Point),
and Confucius would have been more interested in the conversation.
Laoshi balanced both interests.

Professor Zheng once told a top senior, "My gongfu would be higher if I didn't paint or write poetry. But my artist friends don't regard taiji as a very great art. They want me to paint or write poetry because these arts are higher." After Laoshi passed sixty, the same senior asked him how he would compare himself to Yang Chengfu and got the answer, "I'm almost as skilled."

In writing about him, I've tried to do as Einstein urged, to make things as simple as possible but not simpler. Laoshi, with all his good and great gifts, left us a wonderful legacy. The pragmatic among us might demur, saying that he was an exceptional student but a limited teacher. After all, none of his students remotely approached his ability. The same, of course, could be said of other, even greater teachers, say Jesus or Confucius or the Buddha, or even in a boxing context, Yang Chengfu and his father Jianhou. But such a complaint puts the onus wrongly, namely on one's teacher rather than on oneself where it belongs.

We come from Laoshi and his teachers and taiji brothers. They now are gone: the Yangs, Zuo Laipeng, Zhang Qinlin, Chen Weiming, and other Yang seniors including the fine Sichaun master Li Yaxuan. And we derive from his earliest students, notably Zhang Zigang and Guo Qinfang (Guo was the Western boxing champion of China during the late 1930's). Most are gone, some dying miserably in Mao's insane Cultural Revolution. But we who still live walk their Dao, gently guiding others in this great enterprise.

I'm sure our students see us and wonder what fierce alchemy conspired to keep us so bereft of Professor Zheng's abilities. We know and can do more than the student. Not all, of course. Some left the living Zheng for far inferior instructors. Some others who knew him only through films or pictures in books believe they are superior to him. They are wrong. I know no one who can do what Laoshi could. Does this, should this, diminish us? No.

Zheng was unique, a happy aberration. He was able through tedious practice (much of it so arcane that it is a safe bet that it resides now in no living person) to take an intelligent and creative mind and to soften, reduce, and even empty it in the service of a none-too-robust body. From this synthesis came an absolutely unparalleled art of health and protection of health.

In the old days, we used to say of a unique girl we'd met and if we were lucky, married, that this mysterious thing only happened once in a lifetime "when the moon was blue." Laoshi's widow, Mrs. Juliana

Laoshi and some of his senior students in China (1943): Center front, the lightweight western boxing champion of China, Guo Qinfang (rear row, far right with scarf) and Zhang Zigang (behind Laoshi). In 1960, Laoshi told me that Zhang, if still alive, was probably the most skillful master on the mainland.

Zheng, had that experience. Over twenty years later in son Patrick's restaurant in Asheville, she told me how it happened:

"My father loved to play chess with the young man who had been a painting prodigy since he was twelve. Father was prominent in society – he headed the Chinese Air Force – but was fascinated by his chess partner. Zheng was smart, spirited, and very gifted. My father liked the cut of his jib. They were playing chess one day when I chanced by. Father called me over and introduced us. He looked up, smiled, and said hello. And my life changed forever.

"Although we only had one date, we were married two years later. My mother and two older sisters were cool to the marriage. They didn't consider an artist without money nearing forty much of a catch. But father was adamant. He insisted that he was so sure of the union that if it turned out to be a mistake that they could come to him dead or alive and scoop out his eyeballs! Father prevailed."

So, she married the multifaceted man of many excellences but little money in 1939. And lived a long and happy life with him. The moon had been blue for them.

As it was for us lucky enough to meet Laoshi. A Zheng Manqing appears rarely. The chance to learn at his knee was so remote that we who knew him and call ourselves teachers of taiji should be overcome by joy and grateful beyond measure for such luck.

It's in the blood.
The new
generation:
Laoshi's
daughters,
Ellen
(in "Brush Knee")
and Katie
(in "Wave Hands
In Clouds").

For myself, Zheng Manqing brought me a new lifestyle (to use Adler's term) by which I could rediscover my body as a tool of expression. It is as no other. Other fighting arts brag they are defensive: taiji asserts that it is yielding. When others miscall their systems soft, taiji responds that it is softer – it is nebulous. When others with fire in their eyes say theirs is masculine and powerful, taiji is off somewhere doing its postures, breathing in life.

The taiji mind is turned toward something infinitely greater than fighting, namely living. But it pursues its "meditation in movement" blithely unafraid. For no one will attack.

Professor Zheng was the most creative man I ever met. The great mystic, Simon Magus, said that all of us have the latent powers of the high gods, and by creating, we grow like them and into their being. Zheng did that all his life. And masterless man that he was, he knew that there is no creativity without love.

Finally, an old line from Chinese tradition rampages back from memory, "I would not have you monks of whom there are many, but men of whom there are few."

Laoshi was a man.

Tam Gibbs Again

Professor Zheng's passing had shocked and dismayed Tam. Add to this the fact that his return from Taiwan – he had accompanied Laoshi on his last trip in 1975 – occasioned jealousy on the part of some of the regulars. What he needed was love and sympathy. What he got was a struggle with egotistic persons who feared his ascendancy.

In a 1973 letter to me, Tam kidded about the ego types abounding in New York. He said they were the opposite of what Confucius called benevolence (*ren*); instead, they stand for "All for one, and that means ME!"

True, Tam did not help his case by trying to out-arrogant his opponents. He had identified so closely with Laoshi (his mimicry was first-rate, every gesture timed and toned to near perfection) that he represented a threat to these few. An embarrassing schism occurred that I think it best not to revisit. Suffice to say the dissidents refused to accept Mrs. Zheng as part of the hierarchy, believing that she would favor Tam's case. So the club broke up, the teachers going separate ways.

All of this took a toll on Tam. With the help of his friend Filomena and taiji, however, he was able to resolve Laoshi's death and his own subsequent bout with alcoholism. He began a new class in New York City and asked me to come lecture. Which I did, learning in the process several of Zheng's "Eight Ways" of exercise for oldsters that Tam had down beautifully.

New York City was hell on relationships. Three other seniors had broken away even before the schism over personality differences. I had closed my obituary article on Professor Zheng with the thought that we should welcome back those who had left. At the time, Tam and another senior resisted this, saying that, since the strayed had had the chance to return and hadn't while Zheng was alive, they had forfeited any right to reconciliation.

That last night in Manhattan, I urged Tam to visit and reconcile with T.T. Liang – the two had been estranged for years – to add impetus to his new start. He agreed and had a happy reconciliation with a grateful old man.

Alas, the new start with all its promise wasn't to mature. On Tam's return from that visit, he got acute appendicitis. He unwisely tried to treat it with herbs from a Chinatown quack. Appendicitis is relatively easy to diagnose: the quack should have noted that the distended right lower quadrant of the abdomen was painful to the touch and sent him to the emergency room, where an intern could have cinched the case with a white-cell count. As it was, the herbs only masked the pain and Tam collapsed a few days later from the spread of peritonitis. He was rushed to a hospital where he died shortly after. Besides Filomena, his only solace at the end was Professor Zheng, whom he claimed to see in the room as his body processes shut down.

The Weird and Wild

> When the going gets weird,
> The weird turn pro.
>
> – Raoul Duke

I've met many fine men and women in the fighting arts, people who trained and taught and loved with superb style. My belt of memory is studded with these jewels. From them I learned how to study, to be patient, and to be gracious. I learned how to win occasionally, to lose a lot, and to teach a bit. I wish that these people were the totality. Alas, the field has crabgrass as well as flowers.

Without being overly didactic, much of what I write concerns behavior. I try to teach as I write. I tell of many persons who displayed good behavior and these I have identified to the sound of my two hands clapping. Alas, there were others whose behavior was otherwise. Sometimes attention should be paid to poor conduct. I could simply say, "Do this," and I will. But these little vignettes put meat on the didactic skeleton and, while they may not be entertaining, they may be instructive.

Generally in my life and in this book I try to live by the maxim "Everything with a kiss," seeing the therapeutic utility of letting bygones be bygones. Yield, yes, but sometimes stay attached and deal with the behavior. Some bad or weird behavior cries out for citation as cautionary cases. Mostly I don't identify these persons, being interested more in showing their poor behavior than in attacking them personally. I believe that every person is capable of redemption and that this can be done more easily when the person recognizes his deceit and is allowed to act on it anonymously. The ancient emperors of China concluded their edicts with the words "Remember This!"

Below I limn several wrongos who collectively sum much of what is wrong with the fighting arts. Their swindles characterize the sort of behavior any long term worker in this vineyard will, with dismay, remember seeing. None of them was unique or even singular. Most regarded themselves as consummate masters, legends in their own minds. Neurotics to a fault, there was simply too much ego in their cosmos. Niezsche said that God died when humans lost their roots. These poor souls had no inscapes or roots. They were externality incarnate.

Not grounded, they floated hither and yon attracting others of like dispositions. They then formed organizations and scratched one another's backs trying to make the strength of a group of zeroes more than zero. But zero, however added or compounded, remains zero. And though they issue magazines and write articles and make movies about subjects beyond their ken, they come to prove the old Daoist aphorism, "No matter where you go, there you are."

Terms of Endearment

These types prospered because of American ignorance of *wushu*, the fighting arts. Take the term gongfu – please. Bruce Lee not only got the fighting wrong, he also loused up the label. When the first Chinese wushu teams came to the U.S. in the 1970's, one of their coaches asked me where we had gotten the notion that gongfu meant a combat system. He said it means not what, but how fighting is done. And not only fighting, but math and music as well. You can say that a person's skill (*gongfu*) in Shaolin is good but not that Shaolin, xingyi, and gongfu are all fighting arts. Only the first two are.

I thanked him and told him to blame it on Hong Kong movies and Cantonese film actors who themselves had not known the difference. I corrected the major U.S. magazines but they resisted corrigenda from a Caucasian, siding with what G.K. Chesterton called the Heresy of Precedent:

> This is the view that because we have got into a mess, we must grow messier to suit it; that because we have taken a wrong turn some time ago, we must go forward and not backwards; that because we have lost our way, we must lose our map also; and because we have missed our ideal, we must forget it.

Chesterton's words are such good counsel that I've quoted the entire passage for the reader's use.

Throughout this book I call our subject either fighting arts or martial arts. "Martial" seems to soften the more sanguinary "fighting." Fighting can only be pain but martial can be parades and John Philip Sousa, painful only to those who abhor march music. "Martial art" can also be pretentious, sort of like Mike Tyson chewing Red Man tobacco at the opera rather than opponents' ears in the boxing ring.

The only alternative to these two terms I can think of is "combatives." It is more compact and describes the things without forcing in the questionable second word "arts." Are these fighting systems arts? Or are they simply skills of varying levels, which on the higher levels sometimes become artistic? It is a helluva stretch to connect fighting or martial to art. We don't add an "art" to music, history, philosophy, medicine, and other occupations.

As bad as "martial art" is, "martial artist" is worse. Through the magic of euphemism, even the garbage collector or hauler can become a sanitary engineer, or more concisely a garbitian, but he would never call himself a garbage artist (a term already descriptive of the celebrity industry, the media, and the U.S. Congress). The wince I wince when I hear the term is akin to hearing a stick being scraped across a blackboard. Baseball, football, and other sports have simply players. We have artists. Western boxers and wrestlers were never martial artists, and even in Japan the judoka plays, the sumotori wrestle, and weaponry experts do their thing. Why not call martial artists "marticians"? Wouldn't that make morticians die?

So there's nothing wrong with us except we don't know what to call what we're doing. Fencers fence, boxers box, and wrestlers wrestle. But we haven't a clue.

While we're at it, another law, "Whenever you hear someone calling him or herself Master, protect your southern regions and padlock your wallet." In the martial arts, masters outnumber students. They are everywhere and you'll meet many in these pages. There's none in my house, but there is a buggerly monster. He makes me shave him every morning.

Masters

I've found so many teachers (invariably they crown themselves "masters") of taiji who are wrongos of the worst stripe. Sometimes I rationalize this as some defect in myself. But listen then to Joe Svinth, a Seattle karate teacher whom one would not expect to have much familiarity in the area, "Why is it that so many taiji teachers project this weird, almost angry energy? It's as if they want to fight but can't or won't. It's not supreme self-confidence or a challenge. Instead, it's an unpleasant, almost contemptuous energy. I don't receive such energy from tournament fighters or battered old pugs. Serenity? Is that what they're missing?"

What so many have are big egos and great insecurity. Like much of our spendthrift society, these little emperors want too much, too soon. They want it all and right now. They should heed – if they could read – Leo Tolstoy's words that the greatest warriors of all are *Time* and *Patience*. If they don't dig literature, they could give an ear to the country tune recorded by Little Jimmy Dickens, "Take an Old Cold Tater and Wait." This was one of the great lightweight Lew Jenkins' favorites. (Lew was an aberrant case: other than Jack Johnson from Galveston, I can't think of another Texan who could fight as big as he talked.) The words derive from what feasting parents tell their youngsters who are anxious to get at the victuals.

These wannabe warriors want to become masters to avoid that bane of our existence called manual labor. The word "work" sinks them into the deepest of depressions. Most of them still live at home sponging off their parents. They have little sweat equity in combatives, and get most of their information from Chop Sockey films. They are dirt lazy, unaware of the old western boxing line, "You never learn anything until you're tired." Never short on stupidity, they think that Arnold and Sylvester can actually fight, and, worse, that as actors they are on a par with Ronald Colman and Clark Gable.

Back in the 1970's, a man wrote me singing the praises of a so-called neijia expert in Asia. Later, on a business trip, I stopped and had lunch with this "expert." He was undersized and, like so many runts, densely packed with pseudo-pugnacity. We had no conversation at the table. He did all the talking.

He told me he had been rigorously trained in taiji by famed Dong Yingjie, a senior student of Yang Chengfu. I broke in, doubting. He was too young to have trained under Dong; didn't he know when Dong died? He obviously didn't know, but my question led him to think he'd died long ago instead of just six years before (1964). He paused, thought quickly, and then told me, incredibly, that he had been only a baby then and that the training consisted of Dong holding him and putting his tiny arms into taiji postures.

The good food started tasting bad.

Nonplused, he resumed his lecture, all the while talking about himself or taking oblique chip shots at Zheng Manqing. He said that some people believed that in painting he was on a par with Zheng. He also mentioned that Zheng had never studied under Yang Chengfu. I started citing chapter and verse to correct him. He just kept talking.

"When does your class meet?" I finally broke in. Without exhaling, he said, "Tonight."

I asked him if he did sensing-hands in his class. This time he paused and inhaled. Then he said that they'd done it in the past, but he had hurt so many of his students that he had to quit! Did he have any good push-hands people? He allowed as how he had quite a few. Could I visit? He was amiability itself, "Sure, I'll pick you up at your hotel at seven." We parted.

I never saw him again.

Such a giant ego for so small a man whose fondest dream was to die in his own arms. I'd lost the letter from the guy who'd suggested the meet. If he wrote again, I wanted to do to him what H.L. Mencken threatened to do to God for all the world's miseries, "Give him a good talking to."

But I never heard from him either.

Even before Professor Zheng moved from Taiwan to New York City in the mid-Sixties, a New Yorker wrote me, fluent to a fault. He said he had developed a new "soft" approach and successfully tested it for several years against wrestlers, judoka, and Western boxers. I was hopeful that perhaps he had found another softer route and invited him down. There in my basement he asked me to push him as hard as I could and he would neutralize my energy. I pushed and he crashed through a shoji screen and came up stupefied. He would, he said, go back and work on it some more. I felt no elation but a real sense of being cheated. And of fear: Alice stormed downstairs not at him but at me. After the Professor settled in New York, I would see this fellow there, searching always, but practicing seldom.

The Women's "Gongfu" Champ & Self-Defense in a Car

The women's gongfu champion of Ohio visited me in Bethesda one Saturday. She swaggered up with her swashes buckled and began lying about her exploits. She didn't like me as a man and was letting me know it. It was getting tiresome when Sidney Tai, my old translator from Taiwan, showed for a visit. (Sidney later became curator of Rare Books at the Harvard Yenching Library in Cambridge, Massachusetts.) Winking at Sidney, a non-boxing scholar, I introduced him to the woman as the highest ranked gongfu master in Taiwan. She instantly forgot me: her eyes were only for the new "champion." She barraged him with questions and he handled them fluently, all the time gesticulating with boxing movements he had seen. They were awful, strangely reminiscent of the Kama Sutra, but to her, divine.

After a while, Sidney reluctantly – he was getting to like his role – departed for another appointment. Sadly, she watched him drive off, but soon was again bouncing the words off me. She could escape, she said, from any man. My son Dave came out (she was a pretty thing), so I told him to get a standing choke on her. She roiled and throve but could move nothing but her eyes. I suggested to Dave that a man would have trouble extricating if he let you get the choke, so for him to try something easier like a simple bear hug. She gave me a dark look when I mentioned a man might have trouble, but she submitted to the bear hug. Here too she died, until I gave Dave a mean look and he caught on and loosened up to where she broke free. Telling her it was a good escape, I still worried aloud that Dave wasn't a big fellow. What would she do if a 250-pound bruiser took it into his mind to rape her in a dark isolated dead-end alley?

She brightened and said, "It happened. I took him out with two fists and a foot." She had lost her swagger when Dave was crushing her. Now it returned.

"Okay," sez I, "Let's try another scenario. He's still bent on rape but he's got a club-foot and the alley has an exit. And he's now 300 pounds. What then?"

Pert as you please she came back, "I would stand and fight no matter his size. I'd rather die than run from any man."

Decades ago, when road rage was in its infancy, I taught that all bets were off in how one treated misbehavior in a car. The faster one drove, the more the driver came to resemble the car. And while a person who you accidentally brushed in a crowd was unlikely to go ballistic over it, the same Caspar Milquetoast in a 150-horsepower pile of metal might seek to retaliate. And so I advised that in a car on a road one should shift into a bland cowardly mode: do a St. Francis of Assisi toward all the animals in this high-octane kingdom. It's even better counsel today – of 42,000 fatalities on our highways last year, some one-third were caused by road rage.

I once agreed to teach self-defense to a group of girl students from a Quaker (!) high school in Maryland. However, I found soon enough that the standard stuff wasn't what this group of delinquents wanted. And they weren't bashful about telling me.

"This is okay," their leader said, "but what we want specifically from this course is how to defend against a guy in a car. We all hitch-hike and when they get you in a car, it's pretty difficult." I told her she didn't need a self-defense course to handle this. A simple home truth would suffice: female hitch-hikers are being foolish. Don't do it!

The girl replied that they were going to do it. That was a given. They had a right to do it. (Excessive feminism as well as situational idiocy doubtless figured in this.) Plus, they had paid for it and I had to teach them.

Briefly, I told them it couldn't be taught. To enter a car of a stranger was worse than silly, it was masochistic (in the old joke, the masochist says, "Hurt me, hurt me," to which the sadist replies, "No-o-o.") The same zany group also wondered what they could substitute for the groin grab or strike against a female attacker. There was a raunchy reply having to do with a bowling ball, but I didn't make it; I was more a gentleman than they were ladies.

At any rate, they finished the course and, strangely, wanted another. Not so strangely, I was too busy to provide it.

Our "Shaw Desmond"

In old newsreels you can still see Frank "Cannonball" Richards stand in bathing trunks before a cannon. The charge is ignited and the ball propels Frank pell-mell into a large net. I can still hear the commentator's words, "Mr. Richards is the only man in the world able to do this stunt." Then, wryly, "And, after all, Mr. Richards is the only one in the world who wants to do it." Frank moved fast when hit. At the opposite pole, in the 1930's, Al D. Blake, known as "Keeno, King of the Robots," held the record for standing absolutely motionless for one hour and twenty-seven minutes. Both stunts were achievements, if sort of weird. Unlike some yahoos in the fighting arts, though, Frank and Al could do something besides shooting from the lip.

I can never forget an Asian I came to know in the period 1963-70. He wrote me lengthy letters, telephoned, had Alice and myself out to dinner, and worked out with me in my basement. He was intelligent, handsome, and seemed anxious for my imprimatur. Small and looking to be under thirty, he was glib as all get out. Infrequently, he interrupted the torrent of words to show his wares. His forms struck me as neither substantial nor malleable, neither yang nor yin; indeed, too hard to be internal and too soft to be external. Essentially, epicene. But gad, he could talk, reminding me of Dashiell Hammett's lucid line, "The cheaper the crook, the gaudier the patter."

He claimed to have been boxing champion of his homeland in 1950-52, and had had sixty-six total bouts including Western boxing; sixty-three he won by knockout. The three losses were all to the same man, his teacher. He was especially pleased with his "midget" and "cobra" punches, which "did the job" when he fought "three so-called experts in Chinese kenpo, gongfu, and Shaolin boxing during the last three weekends in Cleveland and Pittsburgh" (letter, March 21, 1968).

Before that, in spring 1966, he wrote me saying that he had a challenge with a Thai champion slated for June at the Thai embassy and requested that I be his second or act as referee. I agreed to help. He said he'd get back to me on the details. Two years later, he wrote telling me that he'd won by a K.O. and was sorry I couldn't act as second or referee (!).

But now, he said, he had a bout coming up with William Chen, a taiji teacher in New York City. He wrote asking if I would act as his second (March 21, 1968). I phoned him to tell him that William Chen was a close friend, so I couldn't be in his corner but that I would referee. He agreed. I then called William in New York. Had he heard of this guy?

"Nope."

"Well, he claims he's got a fight coming up with you and wants me to referee."

"Sorry, I never heard of him, but have him call me up. I'll oblige him whenever he says."

So another putative fight was never joined. Which didn't mean our boy was not keeping busy. Though he was having trouble getting "friendly" fights with Japanese, Chinese, and Korean fighters, some black boxers and Thais were accepting. (Corcoran and Farkas state that this chap was respected as a tournament official during this period, but make no mention of his ever competing.) He wrote me that he'd been thrashed by blacks Foster and the middleweight from the West, Heyward. Bob Foster, the light heavyweight champ, was active then in Washington, D.C. In a fight with the Asian, Foster was dropped early on with a knee to the kidney. After that, Foster stayed away and bombed him with long rights, finally dislocating his shoulder. Even this defeat doesn't pass muster. One of the best light heavies of all time, Foster was so good he couldn't get fights at his weight and had to fight heavyweights. The weight discrepancy proved too great and three good heavies (Doug Jones, Ernie Terrell, and Joe Frazier) kayoed him. But Foster did well with others. My midget puncher was asking me to believe that at 130 pounds he would match up with powerful Foster at 175 pounds. And that Foster, making big bucks professionally, would fight free against an Asian who might knee him in the kidney in a mixed combat.

Though I avoided him after that, I met a few of his students down the years. They also liked to talk. This was not the end of Ricco though. Just recently a correspondent friend of mine revealed that in his research he had seen articles written by our boy's students that said he had: (1) won a silver in the 1956 Melbourne Olympics; (2) kayoed James "Buster" Douglas' son; and (3) been a Gurkha in World War II. My friend wrote our principal for verification and met only indignation from him. These were new ones on me.

Which event in the Olympics? Whichever, it seems to have been omitted from the record books. Who is Buster Douglas' son? And a Gurkha in which war? While he likes saying that he served with Merrill's Marauders and the OSS in Burma in 1944, Corcoran and Farkas' *Martial Arts: Traditions, History, and People* (1988) gives his birth date as 1933, making him only ten or so during the war. Corcoran and Farkas are good for pointing one in the right direction, but are not always reliable. Following our own Civil War when thousands of men claimed to have been veterans and became suspect because of tender ages, they claimed they had actually served as drummer boys! But the Gurkhas had no drummer boys (maybe mascots?). My correspondent writes that our boy, in an attempt to redo history, now says he was born in 1926. This is my birth year – though I only had four days in it before 1927 barged in. So he is now saying that he is older than I. This is nonsense: when I knew him, I took him to be at least fifteen years younger.

I never really knew how good a fighter this curious man was. What piqued me more was his obsession with romantic invention. He was utterly charming. As a boxer I'd rate him at 1st-dan or 2nd-dan, but as a tale-spinner I'd put him at 10th-dan. Truly, he was our version of Ireland's Shaw Desmond (see pages 62-67).

Mr. "X"

One particularly noisome chap gained notoriety by challenging weak teachers, always in good supply. Many teachers either can't or don't choose to exercise the combative aspects of the internal arts. So this bird went around embarrassing them in front of their students.

I had heard about his manic antics for years. Some of the stories from good sources indicated that this boyo not only preyed on the weak but also liked to insult real experts. At the Kodokan some years back, wearing an unearned black belt, he was doing randori with a nice mild Texan (a contradiction in terms?) who happened to be a top contender that year for the U.S. heavyweight championship. As they began, X started talking.

A short digression: in the 1940's, I was doing randori at the Chicago Judo Club with a young chap terrified for some unknown reason – there were far worse monsters than me in that venue – and trying to overcome it by talking. Nothing profound and I grunted answers as we moved, the conversation impeding the play. He took a breath and I prepared to attack. But just then, his voice again, saying these words, "Do you like buttermilk?" I walked off shaking my head.

X was also a talker. He asked his opponent where he was from. "Texas" came the polite reply. X was curt, "Texas sucks." Before Texas could react, X took off on judo. "It's overrated," he ranted and continued that it had no combat value, and on and on. X's opponent loved only one thing more than Texas, and that was judo. Enraged, he proceeded to thrash the living daylights out of X, throwing him with the forty basic throws (*gokyo no waza*), hard, fast, and frequent. And only sometimes on the mat. After fifteen minutes, X could no longer rise and it became bootless for Texas to pick him up just to throw him down again. So he let X crawl off – onlookers said that even his crawl had a limp to it.

Another time, X bearded the California judo champ at a party. The latter was a street fighter par excellence – in peace parades in San Francisco in the 1960's, this one marched with homosexual groups and, when the jerks from Hell's Angels reached into the pack for easy pickings, this was no plum they pulled out and they got their comeuppance instanter. X told him he'd heard of him and that he didn't look so tough. "I put him through a plate glass window," California told me later, "and I'm still not satisfied. If you ever meet him, tell him that if I ever see him again I'm really going to break him up."

There were myriad stories about X from Taiwan. Wang Shujin reportedly floored him for discourtesy, and a famed mantis boxer whom I had never met was once the target of X's crotch-kick. The latter tale probably is dead wrong: if it were true, X would have gone to the hospital.

All this suggests severe psychological problems. When a man goes around insulting top fighters into assaulting and hurting himself, it reminds one of the so-called "dump women" of whom Nelson Algren wrote. In Chicago in the old days, Algren said he knew such a woman who for $60 a night would let a deviant beat her terribly. This was sado-masochism with a vengeance but, for the woman, partly exculpated by her economic need. For X, however, money didn't figure in the trans-action – only some weird pathology gone berserk. Stupid, he didn't seem to know that there's no education in the second kick of a mule.

Then, out of the blue, one day I get a call from him. He introduced himself as a person following my earlier path of seeking out and learn-ing from great boxers. I was, he said, his idol, he respected me greatly, and so on, ending with a request that I let him visit me. I refused politely, telling him that I'd heard stories reflecting him as a loose can-non. He denied it, but "no" remained no. Later that day, a taiji acquaintance from New York phoned to plead his case. This bird was a glib talker and soft-soaped me on X's sincerity. I relented and told him to tell X that he could come down.

He visited my xingyi/bagua class on a Friday evening and a taiji class early on Saturday morning. He was young and unremarkable, someone meant for the anonymity of the crowd. The only thing stamp-ing him as a bit unusual is that he had one of his arms in a traveling cast. When in the course of instruction I'd mention that it was too bad that he couldn't participate in a certain movement, he'd pull the arm out of the cast and say it was okay to do the move – his arm was get-ting better. Friday evening in a restaurant, he expressed hatred for Wang Shujin – that story about Wang flooring him was probably true – but great enthusiasm for Hong Yisheng. He told me that he had been knocked about by Hong's sixteen-year-old son, after which he trained there for several years and became a star pupil. Later in a magazine, Hong responded to X's mischief by writing that X practiced with him only for a year and then was booted for bad behavior.

The next morning at our free taiji session, I lost track of him as I moved among the small groups. Later, after I learned that he had been bad-mouthing Professor Zheng, I told him that his behavior stunk and that he should return to New York immediately to start working on it. He didn't argue and he didn't challenge me. Maybe his arm had turned bad again. (In judo in the old days, we had some players who wore bandages and pads over presumably wounded parts, which permitted them to avoid tough partners. We derisively called these folks "bandage athletes." X's cast reminded me of them.) I phoned his New York sponsor and told him that if he ever saw me again in this life, to give me a wide berth. For once in his benighted life, this New Yorker wisely kept his trap shut. The last I heard of this one, he was giving seminars on the subject "Money Has No Odor." Stupid me, I'd always thought money was all odor.

Just before I retired to these mountains, a visitor to one of our sensing-hands classes gave a bit more on the execrable X. The visitor was a taiji teacher from Colorado, and long on theory. He asked if I knew X and I responded darkly. "Well," said Colorado, "he came by my class a while back and challenged me. I simply told him I taught taiji as life cultivation, not fighting. He smirked, turned his back, and swaggered out of my club. But not before I gave him a double-whammy: I took my special American eagle feather and gave his departing back an ancient Indian curse, coupling it with a Daoist one."

"And?" I said, not wanting to encourage him, but knowing there was more coming.

"And," he went on, "he came to see me a week later, apologizing profusely, and telling me that after he'd left me he'd had some kind of satori which shamed him to his soles. He said he was giving up his noxious ways and would now teach as I do, for life cultivation."

So maybe X is reformed. And fishes fly and forests walk and circles have no centers. And Richard Nixon was honest and Dan Quayle knows all the alphabet. Miracles sometimes happen.

I wouldn't bet on it. But ever a believer in humanity's redemptive qualities, I hope that he has grown.

Anyone Want to Buy a Bridge?

Not so long ago, a well-known xingyi boxer from China visited San Francisco for six months to show his qigong. He was 82 at the time but never made it to 83. He boasted that he could knock down from a distance and proved it by publicly pushing his wife down without touching her. A friend of mine described it thus: "As the qi hit her, she made several stuttering backward steps and flopped on her back. There, her body writhed for twenty seconds and then the convulsions stopped. Finally, she let out an enormous belch and the show was over." (I'm glad I missed this, though I've seen similarly horrendous happenings.)

Ben Lo, who was also there, properly asked if the master would do it to him, but was rejected, "It works on my wife because she has qi, but it won't work on you because you don't have it." Ben responded wryly, "Then you're saying that it's better not to have qi than it is to have it!" For which, of course, the old man had no answer.

He died the same year. I just read an account of his ninety-year-old widow throwing a 300-pound man around the mat and stopping a mass attack by others with a wave of her qi-filled hand. She held people down on the mat sans touch and made others bounce with one gesture and stop with another. The description reminded me of a story by wrestling adept Tim Geoghegan. When he trained rasslers for the pro circuit in Canada and the U.S., Tim said he'd tell an aspirant to get down on all fours. Then, he'd say, "Raise your left hind leg," and the bumpkin would do it. And Tim would then say, "Nice doggy!" When everyone laughed, the guy realized he'd been had.

This is funny business, but there are so many bumpkins around nowadays that we must take it seriously. Most qigong experts cannot extend qi. It's carny stuff. One fellow, quoted in an article, said he'd been taken with the taiji master in Beijing whom Bill Moyers showed on TV a few years ago. That guy put his qi through one man to throw a third. Moyers should have interposed his own body into it instead of letting the guy off scot-free. There used to be a Singapore taiji teacher fond of this kind of malarkey. It's all "park nonsense." I scorned it thirty years ago, and still the U.S. media wants to believe. Next thing you know, there will be people believing that Scotty can beam you up!

As bad as the how-to aspect of the article was, its history was worse. The same woman claims that she got Yang Chengfu's "complete transmission." Yet according to Chen Weiming, Yang's senior student, the only one to ever get it was Professor Zheng Manqing. She got it, she says, by practicing three hours daily for five years under Yang, who had board, room, and salary at her family's wealthy digs. I told this to Ben Lo and he roared, "No one got three minutes a day from the great Yang, but she got three hours, or over 5,000 hours, in five years!" Nor is there any mention of her in any Yang record. The sad thing about the business is that her husband did have a reputation in xingyi (he may have practiced under the great Wang Xiangzhai), and for him to get mixed up in such nonsense is sad.

Taiji & Other Contests

Taiji contests are another kind of fraud, though not as disgusting as show wrestling. The very term is a contradiction, what writer Hilaire Belloc called a confusion of categories. Taiji can have no contest. It is Daoistic, against competition. Chesterton put it properly, "All competition is a furious plagiarism." So, while I have attended a few such contests, the advertisement detracts from the performance. There was contest but there was no correct taiji. It was hard force and fierce shoving in which qi never figured nor would ever have a chance of appearing.

Some taiji contests I saw in Taiwan were frightfully embarrassing. More temper tantrum than anything resembling taiji. The key idea of taiji – no resistance and no letting go – was alien to the proceedings. I went to watch but was immediately tabbed as an official with decisions to render. I delegated that function to Alice and went walking out by rice paddies redolent of night soil, excreta smelling sweeter than the noxious odor within the gymnasium. (Entertainer Bob Hope, visiting Taiwan years ago, stepped off his plane on a hot day, inhaled and gasped in olfactory anguish. His host smiled and said, "Bob, it's only shit." "Yeah, I know," answered Hope, "but what the hell have they done with it?")

I concluded publicly that a young sixteen-year-old sumotori would have cleared the gym of the shovers in five minutes. Just where then in the annals of human endeavor did that put taiji?

If grandma had wheels, she'd be a wheelbarrow. Taiji is. If we must have something to publicly gauge sensing-hands ability, perhaps the method used by the Wu Style Tai Chi Federation of Australia would be acceptable. Says one of its teachers, Gary Hartmann:

- The Federation holds annual push-hands meetings rather than annual push-hands competitions.
- While recognizing the martial aspect of taiji, ego aggressiveness is discouraged during push-hand exchanges.
- Students from different clubs are put together in mixed teams. This reduces the obligation to uphold club honor.
- Pairs from different teams push together and are awarded points based on taiji principles.

- Referees control the proceedings and stop the use of force.
- If the pusher loses his balance the point does not count.
- A round-robin pairing ensures that every person will push with everyone outside his team.
- Points accumulate to a team. The team, not the individual, wins or loses.
- Special prizes are awarded to persons displaying taiji essence, regardless of whether they win or lose their matches.
- Non-participating students applaud and encourage those displaying taiji principles and essence.

I applaud this effort to get ego off our back. Most taiji contests are a contradiction in terms. They violate the basic principles of the art barring exertion and force. They encourage competition and its products – violence and ego – all of which Daoists and Buddhists deplored.

Professor Zheng always emphasized the primacy of the form, where you learn about yourself; and of sensing-hands, where you find out about others. Admittedly this might have been stimulated by the fact that he himself was a genius at push-hands. From that vantage, the form can be seen as selfish, even (if one strains a little) as egocentric or narcissistic. On the other hand, push-hands gives us community, Martin Buber's "Meeting With the Other."

Even the harder external systems such as judo and karate, though controlled, concentrate too much on competition and winning. Thus they destroy their original motivation and rationale.

Why fight? We practice fighting so that we don't have to fight. If there is a secret in these arts, it is that. Primarily they are taught and learned as defenses against personal attacks in the street, and not to help us compete against expert fighters in tournaments. To insist that they develop champion competitive fighters is to misunderstand their nature. The fact that such contests are applauded and sanctioned by a bellicose society doesn't excuse them. If we participate in this commercial swindle, we are no better than the street thugs who motivated our practice in the first place.

In fine, we learn these arts so that we may live well, doing good to ourselves and others. To contest them for commerce or ego harms us and diminishes both the hard and soft fighting arts.

The Bogus: Hollywood

So much of what passes for the fighting arts in America and Asia is bogus. Except for judo, which has fairly consistent standards, one is lucky to get the authentic in a sea of chicanery. Always and everywhere it is hard to distinguish the thing from the version of the thing. A good deal of the blame for this is the media. Magazines increase market share by using covers showing foot against face. Hollywood is even worse. Here, with moneyed thoroughness, they show these arts in vile socio-pathic ways. All are screened for savage effect – none are realistic. G.K. Chesterton's retort covers this insanity, "The definition of decadence is to do a wrong thing carefully." But, because some fighters participate for the filthy lucre and others see its absurdity but think the glamour reflected from the Sylvesters and Arnolds and Stevens and Bruces (Lee and Willis) makes them bigger warriors, the martial arts community doesn't protest the awful offal.

The thing and the version of the thing, yes. Lincoln once queried that if you call the tail a leg, how many legs does a dog have? When folks answered five, he'd give them a scathing look and say, "Four. Calling a tail a leg doesn't make it a leg." Correct. And calling the version of the thing the actual thing doesn't make it so.

T'was ever thus. Actors always acted awesome. And sometimes even authors joined in the fantasy. Writing in *Esquire* in 1970, George Frazier told of taking Bogart and John Steinbeck to see the great Lew Jenkins fight. In the locker room afterward, Bogie tried to tell Jenkins how to fight. Lew casually bundled Bogie up and put him under the shower. Later, Steinbeck claimed *he* put Jenkins under the shower because he didn't want to hit him and said that he had once killed a man with his fists!

As annoying as they are, the weirdos cited above are small pota-toes. Far bigger frauds make movies. They fake sex and violence in order to make money for Wall Street tycoons too greedy to care what or whom they hurt. Unbridled greed has turned television and the movies into surreal activities.

The several thousand people throughout the world who produce this rot are, at bottom, too stupid to be ashamed. The money they make dulls their already neurotic minds and creates sleepy consciences. As a result, their product defies reason and responsibility. They do it for money of course. They don't seem to know that that kind of money costs too much. They would retort that they're only being good Americans. Like poor old America, they have so much but control so little.

TV and movies reek of sewers rather than mean streets. Plots are shallow and mindless. The big bucks go to special effects: bombs explode, cars always catch fire, everyone shoots everyone else. To hell with the story – there is none, save the same wretched formula of kill and screw. It is impossible to tell hero from anti-hero except that the latter usually gets the best lines. For his part, the hero has none of the humanity of Philip Marlowe or the Continental Op. He is only a kill machine with sophomoric sound bites ("Make my day") and endless sexual couplings. He loves to hate and hates to love. The pimps who produce and push this profitable bilge sell a violence that is soul-numbing, and claim that the result is cathartic and fun.

Sylvester's *Rambo* series is comprised of adventure films for an immature generation of young American men who can't even venture from their parents' home where sixty percent of them still live. This psychological/sociological datum tells it all.

Earnie Shavers, who won forty of his first forty-three fights by knockout, was a rarity among modern heavyweights – he actually had a punch. Sylvester auditioned him once for a role in *Rocky II*. The two of them were scuffling with the gloves and Sylvester thought he was doing pretty good. So he told Earnie to punch him harder, to make it look good for the cameras. Earnie tried to beg off, but Sylvester insisted. Finally Earnie gave in. "I gave him a little one in the ribs, then another little one in the liver. He stopped the workout and the camera and went to the bathroom for a little while." Twenty minutes later, he sent one of his dog robbers back to tell Earnie they couldn't use him.

"People come up to me now, they know who I am, and they say, 'Hey Earnie, think you could beat Rocky?'"

A few years back, one of the brightest stars in the Hollywood galaxy, a man who had studied aikido, challenged an ex-judo champ and stuntman. In less than a minute, the celebrated icon was unconscious from a choke. Moral: life is not a movie.

As for Arnold, here is Canadian judoka Paul Nurse:

Many weight and body trainers succumb to the "Conan mentality." After gaining weight and strength they subconsciously feel they have increased their fighting capability. Thus they equate physical conditioning

with carefully acquired bio-mechanical skills. This mentality is
media-generated for the most part and sucked in by people unwilling
to do their homework, or more precisely, pay their dues. Rule #1:
There are no shortcuts. Rule #2: It never happens overnight. Rule #3:
Assume that you know nothing, and you'll probably progress faster.

There are many problems with Hollywood violence. Here is one. In
1964, three six-year-old boys were suspected of kicking a younger boy to
death in Oslo, Norway. The mother of one of the offenders said, "This
is terrible, but my boy suffers too. He believes that people can get back
up after being beaten down." She is right. Little kids think a victim will
rise because the media shows it that way all the time. I would hate to be
a producer facing this fact. One can avert his eyes and conscience only
so long. God may forgive them, but their nervous systems won't.

Along with violence, the media has recreated sex into a surreal
thing bearing no resemblance to reality. The thing that requires the
least time and causes the most problems of anything in life is glamor-
ized ad nauseam. If you are not a fourteen-year-old boy, the sex shown
is boring beyond belief. It isn't down-home sex in a marriage or the
back seat of a car, where two persons seek solace from the day's
onslaughts, and sometimes find love and security. I'm not condoning
promiscuity (nor was G.K. Chesterton when he wrote that the boy
knocking on the brothel door is also seeking God), but simply giving a
picture of the thing as opposed to Hollywood's false version of the
thing. Hollywood portrays a competitive gymnastic sex in which all
men are studs and all women multi-orgasmic harlots.

It simply won't do. Critic George Steiner says it succinctly,
"Despite all the lyric or obsessed cant about the boundless varieties and
dynamics of sex, the actual sum of possible gestures, consummations,
and imaginings is drastically limited." The media hopes you won't hear
this truth. Memorize these words, teach them to your children, and you
should be okay: sex sells things.

Although other cultures have a considerable literature on the dangers of sexual excess, until recently we had only the repressive Puritan
legacy of our forefathers to keep the brakes on. That teaching has collapsed, though the Southern Baptists keep trying to spoil the fun.
(Down here in the Carolina jungles, it is said you can't have standing
sex with your spouse lest the Church-folk look in your window and
think you're dancing.)

The excellent autobiography, *The Living Sword* (1995), reflects the great skill and world-class ego of fencer Aldo Nadi. It also makes him out to be quite a Lothario, but on the evidence, I'd put several fighter friends well above Nadi on that score. (Nadi would have disdained Ming Dynasty (1368-1644) poet Meng Jiao's, "Keep away from sharp swords / Don't go near a lovely woman.")

One fellow who fancied himself a world-class stud argued with me once in a Tokyo cafè about the ancient wisdom that as you spend sperm, your energy diminishes. He thought it nonsense, and to cap his case, he told me that he often took down a line of ten 3-dans in monthly contests. En route on his walk to the Kodokan he had four girlfriends, never missing a stop. And still ran the line. How could I explain that? I told him that of course the old wisdom was true. Why else do you see it in many sports in nearly all countries, even in sex-obsessed America? Freddy Brown and other top boxing trainers proscribe their charges from having sex for up to six weeks before a fight.

Then I fought dirty. Had he ever tried to run a line without female help? As he paused to think, I went on. If you can beat ten 3-dans when you're sated and drained by sex, isn't it likely that you could run ten 4-dans if you kept your zipper up? He never answered, but sat deep in thought as I left.

You may not be wiser after our foray into sexual excess but you'll be older. I end by quoting Anton Chekov who mused, "Sex is the remnant of something that was once magnificent, or a foretaste of something that will become magnificent, but at present is disappointing." And that was before Hollywood!

On violence and sex in the media, oh I could write a book about it, as Clark Gable keeps telling Claudette Colbert in, *It Happened One Night* (1936). (Though he was talking of subjects such as dunking doughnuts and hitchhiking.) But for now I'll just say that, though the times are vulgar, we need not be. Say no to movies and TV, grab an old book or hug a young child, and do something creative.

Bruce Lee

The child actor out of Hong Kong, Bruce Lee, has been lauded for bringing science to Chinese boxing. Nonsense. He introduced to Seattle and Hollywood a minor boxing method (Wing Chun) that he later personalized into his own *Jeet Kune Do*. Far from revolutionizing Chinese combatives, his creation is not even practiced in China.

Lee's only formal instruction began at age thirteen and lasted at most five years. Wing Chun, a short-stanced system featuring excessive arms, is almost unknown on the Chinese mainland, though it may still linger in Guangdong and a few other southern provinces. Bill Paul practiced it for a time until he learned that movement, body weight, and kicks would go right through it. So how much of this thing did Lee get? Because the average thirteen-year-old can't mow lawns, trim hedges, or do homework, I'd say his first three years were a wash. Which means that with two years training in an obscure system under a relatively unknown teacher (Yip Man), this actor and purported cha-cha dance champ of Hong Kong became the greatest fighter in the world. Get real, please.

To cinch this, in 1961 Lee returned to Hong Kong to visit his parents and to show his Wing Chun teacher Yip Man how far he had progressed. "His progress was zip," said Lee's student James DeMile in a published interview (*Washingtonians,* edited by David Brewster and David M. Buerge, 1989). "He came back from Hong Kong shattered. He could hit the good Wing Chun men maybe once out of every three times they could hit him. He thought seriously about giving up martial arts." Donn Draeger told me years ago that he'd examined Yip Man's roll book and found Lee inscribed at the bottom in point of quality.

Lee never studied orthodox Chinese boxing of either the "hard" Shaolin type or the more scientific "soft" taiji, xingyi, or bagua. He knew no wrestling or judo, nor was he privy to the more esoteric dianxue (striking vital points) taught to more senior boxers.

Although in his early years he made a mania of training, he entered no tournaments – either contact or non-contact – and fought no verifiable fights. Former karate full-contact champion Joe Lewis said in 1975 that Lee was a great theorist but "there is the fact that he never fought in competition, so you can't really tell how he would have done." Ironically, his widow, Linda Lee, wrote that one of Lee's favorite sayings contradicted his unwillingness to compete in karate tournaments, "Knowing is not enough, we must do," she quotes him. "Willing is not enough, we must apply" (Mike Chapman, *The Toughest Men in Sports*, 1984). The inevitable, obligatory stories told by his students and fans about his street fights are anecdotal at best.

If Lee was not quite a warrior, he was handsome, martially prepossessing, did forms (kata) well, and had been acting since he was a toddler. But everyone who's snuggly wrapped knows that acting is not living, much less fighting. A film boxer doesn't have to be a real boxer any more than John Goodman has to be a baseball player (Babe Ruth) or Lionel Barrymore a doctor (Doctor Kildare) to play those parts in movies.

So Lee got his unearned reputation as a fighter from the movies. A.J. Liebling, a helluva writer, thought we'd all do well if we rejected everything connected with the damned things. Writing in the 1950's before the Lee era, writer V. Nabokov noted the inanity of the "ox-stunning fisticuffs of the movies," and remarked how the hero invariably recovered from a "plethora of pain that would have hospitalized a Hercules." But this mythic manslaughter sold well, and so, as Michael Medved wrote in his classic *Hollywood vs. America* (1992), "Hollywood made films lower than life with violence that most Americans didn't want or like." That last is encouraging – it's good to know that most people don't like this drivel. But I'd like to see more proof of it.

What Lee had going for him was that his Chinatown stuff was a gimmick, something new to American movies, which could produce big bucks for our film magnates as it had millionaire producer Run-run Shaw in Hong Kong. The fact that Lee couldn't act was no bar – it has never been in Hollywood. U.S. martial art magazines, lusting for dollars, also rushed to join in the creation of the Lee myth.

In the early 1970's, when Lee was making the transition from Asian to American film, I was asked to critique his first film. I went to Nickel Town and watched this atrocity – I forget the title – in company with a dozen top executives from an American film corporation. The film honcho sitting next to me told me to review it candidly. Was it a credible representation of wushu?

The execs looked uncomfortable before the screening and even more so as it continued. For me it was anguish. I recognized nothing from Chinese boxing; it was all Hollywood special effects. Lee was an even worse actor than a fighter. As the tomcat said of his love affair with a skunk, I enjoyed as much of it as I could stand. And stand I did twenty minutes into the film. The honcho looked puzzled and protested. In the half-light of the room I tried to keep my words sotto voce, but he got loud. (There was a fee I was forfeiting, but that consideration didn't have a chance against my disgust.)

So I made a short farewell address to the group, most of whom stared fixedly at the floor as soon as they got my drift. It was directed at the honcho but was mainly for their ears. I told them that the film was not credible, but a total distortion of wushu, and that while it was so bad and so nihilistic that it would find a ready audience in America, they should be ashamed. And then I stalked out.

But they were not ashamed, and soon Lee was a commodity being sold. He never quite got over Caucasian David Carradine being chosen to play Kwai Chang Caine in the television series *Kung Fu*. Given the plot requirement that Caine be docile and long suffering before getting condign satisfaction finally over his tormenters, Lee could never have managed it. In fact, Caine was so servile that half the audience wanted to put the boot to him. At the end of each episode, he got his revenge with a flurry of fist and foot techniques invented – you guessed it – in Hollywood. Never before had the hero of a Western spent so much time kicking his enemies in the stomach.

En route to this grand denouement, the audience salivated to sayings by pacific sages (they live near the Pacific in California). These howlers were usually something such as "Fear is the only darkness" and "Men do not beat drums before the tiger hunt."

While the series got most things wrong, because of the cultural vacancy of America, no one ever knew, much less cared. And this chop-suey Western soon outdid the awful spaghetti Western.

Since then, the bandwagon has careened down the road. It's still going. Carradine claims to teach taiji on videotape, and Steven Seagal, who claims he trained in aikido, a Japanese non-contact form, is the rage just now. A *New Yorker* article in 1992 caught this boyo true. "Maybe he's so popular because he answers the need of a volatile confused age: he can symbolize nearly anything while embodying next to nothing." Jackie Chan, Lee's successor in Hong Kong, makes even more gelt than Lee did and does his own stunts to boot, if you believe his PR flacks – and no one does. I'm sure Jackie will invent his own boxing system, if he hasn't already, and someone someday will be lauding his science and innovation. Technology tears along. In recent films fists and swords have given way to explosives as a way to suck customers in. The assessment of the ghastly psychic and physical costs of this bilge on our culture I leave to sociologists.

Most Asian combatives are taught as non-contact forms (kata). I am not knocking them. I've learned and taught some of them, as well as contact methods such as judo and western boxing. They are good exercise and most have a fighting use. In fact, some are so lethal that they can't be contested even in a contact venue in which few tactics are barred. Ironically, unarmed lethality itself can't stand with assault weapons on our streets. You can be barehanded Dr. Death himself and some TV-poisoned punk with a gun will honor freedom of choice by plugging you with it.

The problem with forms is that they often deteriorate into dance that dilutes the fight component. The fighting arts are littered with kata collectors who can do hundreds of forms but can't fight a little. Bruce Lee danced his jazzed-up jig and the Hollywood fantasy factory went to the bank.

My analyses of these arts in such books as *A Complete Guide to Judo* (1958); *Secrets of Shaolin Temple Boxing* (1964); *Asian Fighting Arts* (with Donn Draeger, 1969); and *Chinese Boxing: Masters and Methods* (1974) tried to put a factual floor under these arts (no American, certainly not Bruce Lee, was cited in these books). Lee brought nothing of substance to America. He merely let himself be packaged and sold by Hong Kong and Hollywood. The lords of la-la land choreographed him in a meretricious way calculated to dazzle kids and bored adults but having no relation to real Chinese boxing. They used trampolines and special camera angles and sound effects. Reportedly, the sound of a fist breaking a jaw cost $100,000. The result was that, instead of capturing the moves of a good athlete, they created a martial superman.

Though Lee won all his film fights, he lost everything to unreality. His films were worse than the egregious TV rassling. He made big bucks, but as the late great Donn Draeger said of him, "He's the richest guy in the graveyard." His excessive energy burnt out early.

Lee made high kicks borrowed from Chuck Norris fashionable, even though they are of no use in the street. (Don't believe the story that samurai used them to unhorse their foes.) In a word, you can't fight on one leg. And you can't fight without relaxing if you believe in qi. Or, if you've never heard of it, like Joe Louis or Ray Robinson, but do believe in efficiency, watch those Western boxers and revel in their relaxed artistry. Then watch a Lee film (I saw half of one once) and you will see that even in undangerous films he can't relax. Overfighting is as bad as overacting and Lee was guilty of both until the day he shuffled off this mortal coil.

Awed by the special fighting effects – unreal but carefully choreographed to make them seem super-real – one reviewer commented on the menace Lee projected in the 1969 U.S. film, *Marlowe*, made with genial James Garner. He erred: Lee portrayed the same spoiled, pouting, adolescent brat throwing a tantrum that he played until he died. There was no menace; the reviewer was fooled by chop-socky trade-craft into confusing rant for menace. An old Chinese saying covers Lee's acting and life well, "There's noise on the stairs, but no one enters the room."

Immortality was in the marketing. But all too soon Lee could no longer balance over-stimulation with depletion and he passed from the scene. Gone is that pout of a little kid denied his ice cream. Gone the shocking power of 130 pounds created by Hollywood. Gone the guy pain couldn't hurt and for whom life didn't matter.

If only he could've learned to relax.

Novelist Blasts "Gongfu"

One of the few articles to attack bogus aspects of Chinese boxing appeared in *The Nation* some years back. Titled, "Magazines: Kung Phew," it was written by celebrated novelist Timothy Mo. Himself of Chinese extraction, Mo scored some telling points while erring on others. He started off by recalling in the mid-1950's watching a Hong Kong master in a horse-stance resist a small car. "Without difficulty, in fact without any perceptible impediment," the Morris Minor rolled over the master and dragged him a few yards before he was disentangled. This, Mo said, had affected his view of the Asian fighting arts ever since.

He spoke of strutting masters, "some of whom (not necessarily the most modest) look in need of a good work-out." They teach pigeon-toed, knock-kneed, hands-stuck-out-in-front, methods: "in short just asking for someone to knock you over." He ends by noting that, unless you are very good, karate and kung fu (sic) are not effective fighting methods compared with international methods.

The contingent, "If you are not very good," is controlling. Apply it to international boxing or even wrestling, and you could make the same judgment. Instead, one must make the assumption that the protagonist of a given fighting method is first rate, and then you can dig into the mechanics involved. At this point I will stipulate agreement with Mo's view that inept and silly masters abound and that southern Shaolin stances with small bases are vulnerable.

Judo and wrestling he seems to have no quarrel with, and he beams on Western boxing. He notes that Asian combinations lack the subtlety of boxing, where a light (sic) blow can set up the opponent for a heavy one. (Apparently he is talking about a left jab/right cross basic combination.) The jab, though, has to hurt; if it's light, the opponent will cross over it with his right. So I think Mo means "lighter" rather than light. True, Chinese boxing and Japanese karate don't have a jab. But the jab works in the sportive context of Western boxing limited to use of only the fists. In Chinese boxing and Japanese karate with their non-sportive rationale of anything goes including grappling, the jab would not add much. In fact, if it's done sloppily, the jab offers an arm for you to intercept and control. Xingyi and bagua are premised on striking only after first intercepting or controlling an incoming appendage. The better Shaolin and karate systems also incorporate seizing methods. In fact, *qinna* is completely given over to such techniques.

Mo could also have made the point that the standing fist kept near the head in defense that Western (and Chinese Northern Shaolin and *neijia*) boxers use is also superior to the flat fist held in waist-high chamber stance taught in many Asian combatives. Moreover, whereas most jabbing is done to the head in Western boxing, most Chinese systems favor body blows, believing the gut to be: (1) more accessible than the head (you can't bob-and-weave your middle) and (2) just as lethal as head blows.

Also, Mo says that a boxer will use a body blow instead of a head punch on a groggy opponent, knowing that the head punch might awaken him. This is utter nonsense. I've seen instances where it happened, but they are rare. Usually a boxer will go to the body early, causing his opponent to lower his guard and make his head more accessible. If you hit him in the jaw, staggering him, invariably you then target the head. Brain trauma, not body blows, brings knockouts.

Mo admired Ray Edler, a U.S. Marine who became middleweight kick-boxing champion of Japan by punching instead of kicking. One of Mo's Japanese friends likened this to the use of atomic weapons in 1945. However, several Japanese karate champions in recent years also used their fists more than their feet. I have long been critical of gimmicked kickery, but I still believe that the proper karateka in one of the better systems can blend fist and foot (with priority on the fist) and be as competitive as Edler.

Finally, Mo's analysis is neither nuanced nor comprehensive. He condemns Chinese boxing and karate without having the requisite practical or theoretical background to do it. There are boxing frauds in Asia – I've pointed this out since Mo was a child. There were a few in

Taiwan and many more in Hong Kong and the rest of Southeast Asia. Mo should have tried the better boxing systems and boxers before making such sweeping generalizations.

Ultimate Fighting & Rassling

What about so-called Ultimate Fighting? To me this sorry activity reflects nothing so much as the nihilism of current America. Nihilism is the belief Ivan Turgenev exposed in his novel, *Fathers and Sons,* in the last half of the nineteenth century. It shuns rationality and promotes the violent overthrow of principles and institutions. The one thing it worships – vitality – has now replaced the core altruism one used to find in our society. How great it would be if we could return to those quiet seasons when altruism was as common as hello. There are studies now showing that the benefits of helping others flow back to the helper. Doing good bathes us with endorphins which protect us from the harmful effects of stress. Helping others is good for your heart, your immune system, and your overall vitality. (See "Beyond Self" in *American Health,* March, 1988.)

Ultimate Fighting is ridiculous. It has minimal regulation, making for a brutal, dangerous hash that most competent fighters avoid, although their technical competence is much higher than the rag-tag participants Ultimate pulls, and they would have a fairly easy time of it if they entered.

There is a saying, "A gentleman is a man who can play bagpipes – but won't." The competent fighters see Ultimate as a beastly activity reflecting nothing so much as a terribly neurotic insecurity in participants and fans. The competents are of such a quality that they don't have to engage in it – their status is secure and their egos intact.

Terence Allen recently rebutted the myths that have grown up around this squalid nonsense (my comments are bracketed):

- It mirrors street fights. No. In the street, rules prohibiting such things as biting, eye-gouging, and fishhooking the mouth are absent. [In the street, the ambiance is totally different, too. For example, there is no referee, time limit, or padded canvas floor.]
- It displays real martial art techniques. No. Ultimate is simply a helter-skelter free-for-all. [The "warriors" throw baseballs (haymakers) and behave as they did during elementary school recess fights.]
- Only the world's best compete. No. It's a sorry lot for the most part.

[Some are so inept that they don't appear capable of hurting anyone with a hammer. In fact, the danger lies in mismatching the few worthy veterans against woeful untrained novices.]

Allen's otherwise cogent analysis is marred by his conclusion that while Ultimate is bad in itself, its most pernicious danger is that it will give orthodox martial arts a bad name with the public. I think his assertion reflects a commercial bent, and is dead wrong. Ultimate is simply too violent for a civilized society. That is the problem. Its effect on conventional fully regulated martial arts is small potatoes. But not to worry. Though Albert Camus spoke with unforked tongue when he said that "stupidity has a knack of getting its own way," Ultimate is so far beyond zebra, it should disintegrate fairly soon.

Another reason I'm against these all-in fights is that I don't understand them. Why would anyone want to hurt another person? That's what it comes to. Yes, I know that in ancient Rome, some free men joined the slaves as gladiators. Mark Antony's brother was one, in fact. But that was a long time ago. For money? There are several sports that pay much better in which the violence is regulated. Let these "warriors" participate in them.

But there's the rub. Few of the Ultimates have achieved success in the legitimate sports. These all-in affairs are the corollary of excessive violence in the media, which teaches that emotions can only be expressed in violence. Bertrand Russell said there are people who cannot come into contact with others without colliding; he called this his "billiard ball" thesis. In an ordered society, I would add, they would all be sentenced to six weeks of eight-hour-a-day croquet.

Alas, it is not an ordered society.

Some Ultimate fighters decry sumo as merely grappling. Yet none could stand before a middling sumotori. They should learn that it also includes striking techniques. Sumotori can legally:

- hit, thrust, or slap with the open hand
- kick the opponent's legs
- throttle the throat, and
- butt with the head.

Chad Rowan (466 pounds) was the first American to make *yokozuna* (grand champion). Known now as Akebono, Rowan began sumo when he dropped out of college in 1988. During his first six months in Japan he was miserable. He wanted to quit and cried himself to sleep every night. But in two years he was grand champion. How? He practiced and ate bitterness.

Sumotori are the best in the world at what they do. Here's Clive James, one of the best writers in English:

> Just when I thought these [practicing sumotori] were the strongest men I'd ever seen... a man swayed in who made the rest of them seem emaciated. This was [Toshimitsu] Kinanoumi, the champion. He stopped, looked at the others, snorted, and swayed out. That was his training session.

Nihilism rules in "show" rassling as opposed to legitimate ("shoot") wrestling. This rassling is a non-competitive circus. It pretends a malign intent but lacks even a semblance of honest passion. Which ironically makes it superior to Ultimate Fighting. Though most can't wrestle, they rassle better than the Ultimates fight. For the most part, the rasslers are pretty fair athletes and take falls calculated to keep their careers short and arthritic. But both rassling and Ultimate arouse in audiences a fury too dark for decent people. And though I think Ultimate will wither, I wince at the fact that seven of the top ten cable TV shows are rassling "entertainments."

Rassler Argentine Rocca Takes on Judo

The current headliners in Ultimate Fighting are the Gracie family of Brazil, whose scion was active at the same time that Argentine Antonio Rocca was rassling on the American tour. Big, athletic, and handsome, Rocca's trademark was to use his legs against the opponents' person. Prefiguring karate, this legwork made Rocca a boodle of bucks. Not as much dough as legs made Betty Grable, but still the kind of cash they used to throw off the backs of trains.

Anyhow, Rocca got carried away with being a celebrity and conjured up some fibs to Arthur Daley, the top sports columnist for the *New York Times*. Daley bit. As an officer for the official U.S. judo organization, I wrote the following letter in February, 1958. Although Daley responded politely, he not only didn't apologize, but added insult to injury by publishing the article in a subsequent book, saying he'd gotten some static on it.

I never cared much for Daley after that.

Dear Mr. Daley,

... Your article "Fight to the Death" of January 26, 1958, contains a tale by A. Rocca, sometime rassler, in which he kills a 6-degree judo man, Takeo Okitaro, in a fight to the finish in Brazil in 1949. Although you kept the tale confined within quotation marks, your readers will believe forevermore that what Rocca said is gospel and concurred in by you. Therefore, Mr. Daley, give us a break by being objective and publicly noting these facts.

The Kodokan of Tokyo, the international headquarters for judo – the fastest growing sport in the world – has read your article and informed me that Takeo Okitaro is not registered with them. All of the higher masters were queried but none had ever heard of such a person.

Takeo Okitaro – whoever he was, if he was – was not sent to South America by any Japanese agency, governmental or otherwise, in 1949. About 1952 the champion, Yoshimatsu, and several other top-flight black belts including the 150-lb. Osawa, who tossed a line of 25 South American black belts one after the other (where was Rocca?), were sent by the Kodokan to South America. This was the first and only post-World War II group to travel from Japan to South America.

The President of the Brazilian Judo Federation, Mr. A. Cordeiro, is presently in Tokyo and was shown your article. He states that to his knowledge such an event never took place.

There may have been a person called Takeo Okitaro but he was not an officially recognized black belt, not to mention a 6-degree black belter. I incline to the view that either (a) the event never took place, or (b) it was "staged" for professional reasons. I wonder nights now whether the unknown Okitaro has an unlamented widow who scratchingly subsists on an unlikely pension.

Seriously, if Rocca wants to make professional hay, let him do it at the expense of something other than judo. Masahiko Kimura, who owned the Japanese judo crown through the '30's, came to the U.S. in 1950 willing to fight any style for money. He almost starved to death and would have, had not friendly judomen assisted him. After six months here during which he tried the "show" type of pro wrestling – no one would fight the other way – he sickened with disgust and returned to Japan. (Where was Rocca?)

Rocca's rassling fails to impress me. Judo men frown on mixed matches (although Chicagoans still remember the judoman Masato Tamura beating the great Greco-Roman wrestler Karl Pojello in 1:20 in 1943), but if Rocca really thinks he has a corner on strength, agility, and technique let him try any sumotori (Japanese wrestler), Indian wrestler, or Olympic heavyweight from any country. Let him take his $100,000 plus annually but let him leave judo and the remnants of the noble art of wrestling alone.

The Ali/Inoki Caper

The Gracies and Rocca were not the only South Americans in the combatives realm. Late in his boxing career (June 26, 1976), Muhammad Ali did a Tokyo performance against Antonio Inoki, a Brazilian rassler. I wrote the following paragraphs for the *Washington Star* while the stench from Tokyo was still strong:

The British writer, C. E. Montague, once quoted a boatman who would dive into the Thames for a fee: "I dives, gentlemen, I dives. I don't jump. I don't fall. I don't flop. I don't leap. I don't waller. I dives."

The Ali-Inoki "fight" on June 26 in Tokyo was more farce than dive. Mel Brooks at his zaniest couldn't have conjured up such antic inactivity posing as sport.

But it was a dive, too. Ali dived mightily from the dignity (in one of his towering poems, G.K. Chesterton asks: "Where have they gone that did delight in honor?") that he showed in his tall, lonely stand against the Vietnam lunacy. As a boxer, he is an overweight light-heavy with the punch of a pillow who could not stand with earlier heavyweights.

Inoki, for his part, is hardly a samurai. A Brazilian field-hand whose forte is throwing the discus, he was brought to Japan as a show (non-competitive) wrestler. Against any shooter (competitive wrestler) he would fall easily.

So promoters paired this mediocre boxer and sham rassler, and the media (enriched by the advertising) did a disservice to its readers by hyping it. But even as banditry, it was bad. Ali knew that a wrestler will invariably beat a boxer in a mixed match, but he didn't know that Inoki really couldn't wrestle. So Ali hugged the ropes and threw only five jabs in 15 rounds. Inoki stayed defensively on his back throughout. Thus the putative battle was never joined.

Predictably, this smeller elicited boos and cushions from the audience. One boxing buff was heard to comment: "Bring back the good old-fashioned dive!" And a Japanese wag remarked that if the latter-day samurai, Yukio Mishima, were alive, he'd commit suicide again.

Yes, the gullible public got gulled. But, ironically, anyone who glories in the sight of one human beating the noggin of another for money maybe, just maybe, deserves to be cheated.

The last I heard of Inoki, he had dropped negotiations for a wrestling match with a top legit Pakistani wrestler, Aslam Bholu. Why? Aslam would not agree to lose in advance. Inoki was pointedly told that he would only win if he won! So today Inoki is a promoter instead.

Nothing Could Be Finer: Down to Carolina

Over the years things palled in Washington. Because I stayed healthy and always tried to think of myself as a lad of nineteen, advancing age was never much of a problem. Nevertheless, I felt stale and grew restive. Then one day I saw a sign at National Airport proclaiming, "Welcome to the most powerful city in the world." That did it. "What a marvelous place to be leaving," I told Alice.

The boxing had lost its juice and joy and I was out of the loop on judo. Some old friends had died and others changed in smaller ways. Art Broadbent died in a construction accident in 1968 at age forty-two; Donn Draeger in 1982 at age sixty-one; and Johnny Osako in 1983 at age sixty. Johnny had retained his skill for a long time, though he sometimes resorted to makikomi (sacrifice throws) at the end. Finally, his always troubling heart gave out. I recall his heart was acting up at the San Francisco Nationals in 1954 when I got a doctor to examine him. When he first went to Europe and was paired with a big Dutch kid named Geesink and said kid threw unthrowable John in twenty seconds, John got his back the next day at randori when he threw Geesink all over the dojo. Donn Draeger took photographs on that occasion and in them Geesink is continually airborne. Even the memory of one of our last discussions at the World Judo Championship at Salt Lake City in 1967 where, in his cups, he berated the politics of international judo, fades before the stronger memory of the swirling, slashing wonder of his throws and the quiet dignity of his manners.

My old judo friend Ben "Nighthorse" Campbell changed in a smaller way. Following a distinguished career creating exquisite Indian jewelry, he went into politics, becoming a Democratic senator from Colorado. After a good start, standing tall against assault guns and quitting the NRA, he dashed our hopes by changing parties and becoming a Republican. This was a gymnastic move rivaling the most extreme postures of the Kama Sutra for a part-Indian lad coming up from poverty. I wrote chiding him and got no answer. Recently when I jumped him for not supporting a law cleansing corrupt election financing, his response echoed that of his mentor, the egregious Trent Lott: correcting these laws would infringe freedom of speech!

He's picked his crowd, a choice he'll have to live with. I'll stick with H. L. Mencken, "In this world of sin and sorrow there is always something to be thankful for; as for me, I rejoice that I am not a Republican." Al Capone didn't rejoice. The Chicago thug who once beat two men to death with a baseball bat bragged, "I have always been a Republican, and my young men [sic] are 100 percent Republican!"

Republican readers may be solaced to know that I'm about as disillusioned with the Democrats and chameleon Bill Clinton these days. But I'll always be skewed to the Democrats, despite their scarlet sins. Mainly because of their moral slant and also because I can't forget John Stuart Mills' cogent line of long ago, "Although it is not true that all conservatives are stupid people, it is true that most stupid people are conservatives."

A sunny digression on the sin Mencken spoke of above. I may have spoken of Shanghai's sinfulness before. Prewar Shanghai was a place some said was so evil that it was impossible for normal people to sin there. But there is sin everywhere else. What, really, is sin? Catholicism believed that the worst sin was despair. The Pathan tribesmen in northwest India regarded inhospitality as the only sin. Oscar Wilde and Simone Weill thought it inattention. Bali nominated as sinners only those who bored you. Laoshi and the taiji tradition taught that the worst sin was the conscious waste of energy. My favorite definition of sin is an eighteenth century Hasidic teaching, "Anything you can't do wholeheartedly."

Earlier in this book, I found some fault with judo as currently practiced, but let me now leave by saying something more favorable. Unlike so many other martial systems in America, judo never became popular. This jacketed wrestling never achieved a tenth of the popularity of Chinese boxing or karate. Media interest was minimal, participants few, and spectators fewer: We used to say that judo is the only sport where participants outnumber the audience. Judo was more real than some other systems, but – aye, there's the rub – it had contact and pain and lots of falling. Interestingly, it drew more college graduates and had fewer neurotics.

Although it wasn't perfect – I can remember as the host of a major East Coast tournament once having to warn New Jerseyites who were exhorting their judoka with cries of "Go Zoo!" to curb it or forfeit the match – judo was still a sane sport. If a person claimed high rank in judo, he could be tested quickly on the mat. In contrast, the often silly claims of some "grandmasters" and "masters" of other systems could not be tested because they were afraid of killing you with those educated fingers. Also, judo taught effective joint locks but never pretended to have the capability of paralyzing you by a light touch to a pressure point. Finally, as you get older in judo age begins to make inroads. While you compete less, you teach and referee more. In some other systems, as you get older and fatter you get more rather than less deadly.

That digression aside and coming back to Washington, that place had clearly lost its charm for us. So in 1989, we came down to this bucolic community in the Carolina mountains. Every day Alice and I walk to the top of one of them, passing en route a house clutching the mountainside. Going up one day with my sister and her husband, we met a handsome boyish-looking chap, obviously the homeowner, walking down. He was wearing a Chicago Cubs T-shirt and when we greeted him my brother-in-law said, "You're from Chicago? We're from Peoria," and we introduced ourselves.

The man said he was Cyrus Highlander and that he hailed from Galesburg, not Chicago. Galesburg was my hometown and I had known a chap at Galesburg High School named Highlander who, despite the distancing years, suddenly in my mind's eye looked a lot like this fellow.

I told him that I was from Galesburg and that I knew a Highlander in high school but that his name was Clark. He smiled softly and said that he was Clark but had changed to Cyrus when he went off to college.

I could see he didn't remember me. Nor should he. I had gone to a Peoria high school, dropped out after two years, and then stayed only three months at Galesburg High before leaving. For a short time during that period I'd been a second-string football end. However, Highlander had been the golden boy excelling academically and athletically.

Notwithstanding that and a rewarding career at Upjohn Pharmaceuticals, he has turned out well. Currently the mayor of Flat Rock, he's incorruptible. He blends an easy-going manner and a heady intelligence. What I like best about him, though, is that he never interrupts anyone. It's still true: this old world is a small one.

Another neighbor, Reese Mitchell, is a strapping big West Virginian with a droll wit and jokes just this side of awful. Our community's resident expert on birds and nature, the pair of us have built and maintained a string of bluebird boxes through the neighboring fields of a local surgeon – Buster Shealy's cattle ranch. Every year we help sixty or so new bluebird fledglings get started in life.

Reese and I have also helped foreman Ralph King and his sidekick Enoch Reese herd cattle between pastures and with such chores as calving. Every American kid wants to be a cowboy and we were happy to taste that life a bit.

Ralph King was a wiry veteran of eighty-eight summers when he passed peacefully in 1997. (His employer, surgeon Buster Shealy, told me that Ralph had been claiming that age for the fifteen years he'd known him.) Grizzled old Ralph may not have known as much as God, but he probably knew more than God did when He was Ralph's age.

We had many talks with Ralph. He was born a mile from us but had traveled long and far, cowboying ranges from Wyoming to Florida before returning home. A little guy but tough as an anvil, he was a great talker. Once out West he met a new wrangler just signing on. He liked the lad and asked him where he came from.

"You wouldn't know the place," the guy said.

Ralph replied, "Try me."

"I come from Cumberland Gap, Tennessee. When the sun first comes over the top of the mountain in the morning, it shines right in my back door."

Ralph nodded and mused, "Yep, and when it comes over the next mountain, it shines in my back door in Hendersonville, North Carolina."

Again, a small world.

Ralph confirmed my belief that the badger is about the toughest animal going (he'd never seen a wolverine), citing the time he and a buddy had tried to pickax and shovel a badger out of a hole the animal had built in a corral. "All we got was tired trying to break his skin," Ralph muttered, "and we let him have the damned hole."

Ralph remembered a new guy, a quiet and self-contained cowhand said to know jujutsu. When the ranch bully got drunk and went berserk one day endangering Ralph, who was still a youngster then, and the other hands, Mr. Jujutsu stepped up and showed his stuff. He took the knife from the drunk, broke his arm, and threw him "all in the same motion," according to Ralph.

On another ranch there was Oscar, 250 pounds of peace with a sometime hankering for liquor. Once a month he'd get tight and the two local police who knew him would drive him home until the effects wore off. One weekend, though, two new officers were on duty. When they came upon soused Oscar they decided to take him to the station. Peaceful Oscar laughed and declined the invite. After they extended the invitation with their nightsticks, Oscar put his arms around a tree off which they couldn't pry him. (Quick, police readers, how would you peel Oscar off that tree? Tickling him under the armpits probably would have done the trick.)

Ralph came along just then and told the new fellows who Oscar was and asked them to let him drive him home. "They were wore out by then trying to beat the laughter out of Oscar and they gladly let me have him," Ralph recalled, saying that Oscar regarded the thing as a lark.

Tim Geoghegan: I Find a Warrior in America

Irish poet James Stephens mused that, "No good luck is good until by good luck you see." To do that John Masefield advised us to "always keep a bright eye looking, so that when the thing is there the heart will be glad."

After a lifetime searching for and finding a few real warriors, I came south to these mountains for repose. I had no intention of becoming a *xian* (Daoist mountain sage) nor did I expect to find fighting experts beyond the level of American media portrayals.

But I did find one. And not only the best combat master I ever encountered in America, but one of the prime anywhere in my time. His name was Dr. Charles ("Tim") Geoghegan, a broth of a battler from Ireland but with none of the blarney usually associated with the old sod. Irish poet Joseph Campbell catches his like in his "A Fighting Man."

> A fighting-man he was,
> Guts and soul:
> A copper-skinned six-footer,
> Hewn out of the rock.
> Who would stand up against
> his hammer-lock?...
> Giants showed clean heels
> when his arm was bared.
> I've seen him swing an anvil
> Fifty feet;
> Break a bough in two,
> And tear a twisted sheet...

Dr. Tim Geoghegan

One of my students, Allen Pittman, saw this osteopath give a display of combative wrestling in Atlanta and was so impressed he introduced us. I was equally impressed. No Hollywood nonsense of 95% hype and 5% ability, Tim spoke quietly and listened patiently. Harry Johnston said he reminded him of a priest in the confessional making the sign of the cross and murmuring, "Go and sin no more."

But on the mat, cool and never excited, he showed his other, devastating, side by demolishing anyone who stood in front of him. Those tender skillful hands, which applied his osteopathic magic, created havoc in real combat.

Tim regarded most martial arts he'd seen in America with a mixture of amusement and dudgeon. He was shocked by the low fighting level and high arrogance of the stars. In Atlanta, he invited the king karateka to take a free chop at his throat. Despite the man's wife begging Tim to reconsider – her husband's chop could kill, she cautioned – Tim smiled and said he'd chance it. So hubby took a swipe at Tim's seventy-year-old carotid artery (which can cause a heart reflex and death: readers should never try nor willingly allow this!). Tim just kept smiling but he had to be truthful, "It is not very strong," giving the lad a hug.

Later, in a North Carolina workshop, an expert on Filipino methods of self-defense, a student of Bruce Lee's hiding behind a pseudonym, told Tim he could escape his takedown. Tim nodded to him to have a try, and started the takedown. Instantly the guy tried to turn out and counter but was flattened. I asked Tim what the man did then.

"He was only a little one," Tim answered, "maybe 135 pounds. When he turned he went the wrong way – actually, either way would've been the wrong way, circles being what they are – and I put a headlock-sleeper on him and he was out before he hit the floor. Previously he invited me to give a seminar in California, his home, but after this incident, I never heard from him again."

In a lengthy interview I had with Tim for the second edition of John Gilbey's *The Way of a Warrior* (paper, 1992), I commented on the incident above in which Tim said he never heard from the Californian again, "And never will. California has the same relationship to real martial arts that Dracula had to garlic."

Tim at the ready.

Tim came from a fighting family. His dad, a fine boxer, could jump up and touch both feet on the wall at the level of his forehead. At nineteen, after lifting everything and even endangering trees on the family's Leitrim farm, Tim challenged John Moriarity, Ireland's top strongman, and beat him soundly lifting various weights and became the new champion. This got him a job with the John Duffy Circus doing strongman stints as well as taking on all comers in boxing and wrestling.

Tim could lift anything he had a will to lift, and his was a strong will. A big old kettleweight that once belonged to Arthur Saxon, the famous German "Strongest Man on Earth," had been obtained by the powerful Britisher Maurice Fraher. Saxon and Fraher were the only two persons ever able to get it off the ground. Tim heard about it and went to Fraher, looked at the weight disdainfully, then took it and put it over his head. And this at a bodyweight then under 200 pounds. In his career best, he cleared over 1,200 pounds from the ground. But by then he had bulked up to nearly 230 pounds, which let him:

- Lift a 200-pound man sitting on a chair using only his teeth - and then walk him across the room.
- Withstand two giant Clydesdale horses pulling on him from opposite directions.
- Tear a deck of new playing cards still in the original (non-plastic) box in half and, out of the box, into four quarters.
- Let a truck drive over his neck and stomach, and
- In top form, tear big city phone directories in two – from the closed, glued side.

Tim stayed with Duffy's Circus for three years perfecting his strength skills. It nearly killed him once. In Belfast, he supported a platform up which a man rode a horse. Then, Tim would leg press man and horse several times. One night, however, the rider – who may have had a grudge against Tim over one of the circus girls – rode the horse to the side of the ramp where it jumped off. This abrupt shift in weight profoundly displaced his fifth lumbar vertebra and sacrum. Dublin's best doctors agreed that even after six months in a body cast, he would require crutches for the rest of his life. A friend told Tim of a retired osteopath, Dr. D. Byrne, a wizard at bone manipulation in Wicklow, and the pair of them went to see him. His friend and Dr. Byrne strapped him to a table, stabilized his sacrum, and pulled like hell. (This procedure was done sans anesthesia, which Tim disdained.) Says Tim:

> There was a sound like a millstone turning as the fifth lumbar rotated on the sacrum to its normal position. In about a minute I had been made whole by a man who knew how to correct and maintain the body. As I arose, I asked him what I owed him and he said, "Your life." I took him literally, and soon started formal osteopathic training under his colleague, Dr. F. Taylor, one of the best in England and the man who took what Dr. Byrne had restored and made me into the healer I became.

Though Tim had had over 100 boxing matches and thirty to forty crossroads bareknuckle bouts without a loss, when Jack Solomon, head of British boxing, tried to talk him into turning pro, he turned him down. By then he had fallen in love with wrestling. Combining his circus wrestling with Lancashire and other indigenous British styles, he joined the pro-wrestling circuit while continuing his medical studies. He didn't care for the artificiality of show wrestling but endured it for the sake of his osteopathy. But at heart he was a shooter and when he wrestled another shooter he would shoot for the joy of it, though the final result was prearranged. The greatest wrestlers he faced were Bert Assirati, the perennial British champ, and the Americans Lou Thesz and Ed "Strangler" Lewis. Lewis managed Tim for a couple years while

he worked the Canada-U.S. circuit, which was from 1947 until the 1960's. Despite being built short to the ground, Assirati at 270 lbs. could do it all: a one-leg squat shouldering 200 lbs.; squat continuously for a half-hour with a 235-lb. barbell on his shoulders; and for fun jump up on a chair 100 times while holding heavy dumbbells. He was also a

Tim on the circuit:
on an opponent's back
with an armlock.

gymnastics marvel capable of a one-hand stand; a back flip; a crucifix on the rings; and, one of the two best of all time, three repetitions of the one-arm chin.

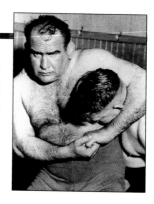

While "Strangler" Lewis was named and known for his chokes, Tim outdid him by doing rapid sleepers: a two-carotid choke learned from Kasutu Higami, a jujutsu adept in his eighties whom he met in London during World War II; and a one-carotid choke he got from Indian wrestling. The latter is

Ed "Strangler" Lewis
– Tim's mentor.

simply the standing clamp of one arm held high against an opponent's head that used to be a fixture in old self-defense books. I tried it as a youngster and found it wanting. I could never find anyone who could make it work, until I met Tim. He made it shine. His unrivaled knowledge of anatomy combined with his enormous power did the trick quick. He littered rings with unconscious rasslers. Though the matches were fixed the sleepers were not. The victims were all challengers from the audience. In Toronto one night, Tim had twenty men asleep at the same time. When Harold "Oddjob" Sakata of James Bond movie fame told Tim he couldn't choke him out, out he went. When Sakata came to, he thought he was back in Montreal a week before and that his opponent there had rendered him unconscious.

But Tim was more than just his sleeper. When he tried to get into the American circuit, the pro rassling tycoon Paul Bowser sent Wilbur Nead (AAU national heavyweight champion in 1940) to test him at the Boston YMCA. Nead tried everything he knew to take Tim off his feet but failed. Every time he leg-dived him, Tim would twist his neck into a dangerous position. Frustrated, Nead said, "You know you're doing something that no one has ever done before." Tim told him maybe not in America, but in Europe that was a standard response to a leg-dive. Nead was a great leg-wrestler and they became close friends.

With his great energy and ready intellect, over the years Tim was able to get degrees and certificates in osteopathy, physiopathy, hypnotherapy, psychology, Hatha and Raja yoga, and jujutsu, with other disciplines. Among his teachers was the esteemed Maurice Nicoll, who did the seminal work on Gurdjieff. Like Zheng Manqing, he had many interests which he turned to good use. He knew as much about arcane skills geared to reconciling oneself with one's body as anyone I ever met.

He taught me much. Before the American medical establishment blessed the egg as edible after decades of bowing to the oleomargarine industry, Tim had already espoused its virtues as the perfect food, "It's got everything in it – the beak, feathers, feet, and meat."

What did he think of current pro-rassling? He regarded it as a degraded thing done by loud, berserk people, most of them pumped up by hormones, almost none of whom can wrestle. He said:

> It is an unseemly business. So bad, it is not even funny enough to be farce. The fact that it commands large audiences says some profound things about the yahoos abroad in this benighted land. Really good shooters, if bucks are more important than their honor, only participate if they are willing to do business.

He knew good shooters and never forgot them. Les Kellett, a buddy in the trade, was regarded as one of the cleverest of the old British wrestlers. A farmer from the north of England, he was tough as nails. Called to the colors in World War II, Les told the army that he could help the country more by raising livestock. The army took him anyway. When he refused to train, they tossed him in an eight-foot deep pit for a month. They fed him, but not much and only meat. Les was a vegetarian and, though he almost starved, they neither bent nor broke him.

After the war, he continued wrestling while working as a bouncer in pubs. He was undersized and very quiet trying to talk trouble out the door. Tim remembered that when a big loudmouth would try to out-talk him, Kellett would mouth clamp him and ease the now-docile drunk out of the place. Tim showed me the devastating lock which instantly immobilized me. (I almost used the clichè "made me say uncle," but that would be wrong: caught in this clamp you can't talk – and don't want to. The technique is too dangerous to detail here.) Tim finished by saying that Les was a good wrestler but would occasionally bite.

Tim and I were friends for nearly a decade. When a back weakened by too many falls or a troubled hiatal hernia caused by too many sit-ups kicked up, I used to go over to his clinic or home and he set me right. He was considered a miracle man in Black Mountain, with patients coming to him from all over the East and South. He didn't charge much and that, coupled with the fact that he cured patients usually on one visit, meant that he was never a millionaire. My son-in-law, considered a top-notch orthopedic surgeon by his peers, has observed Tim up close and says that he was superb, perhaps unique, in his knowledge of the human body.

He was always good copy. A while back, a car spilled off the curve near his house ending upside down on his lawn. Tim went out and rolled the car over, extricating and treating the two women inside. When I asked him about it, he shook it off, saying "It was a small car."

Two bulky gents from Gold's Gym came out to see him five years ago. (He was seventy then.) After a genial chat he invited them to join him on his daily workout on a resistant weight machine. They smirked a bit but, to humor the old fellow, they agreed to go along with him. He moved easily through the routine and at first these guys with magnificent deltoids and pecs and lats maintained the pace. Tim kept breezing along and soon the pace started telling on the youngsters. They heaved, puffed, and finally gasped. And at twenty minutes quit. Amused by such big bodies and so little energy, Tim asked them if they minded if he finished the routine that had another ten minutes to run. And did. They never returned.

I ended my 1992 interview with Tim in a way I can't improve on, so let me repeat it here:

> So there you have it: a real warrior in America. A strong man who scorns steroids and filmic clowns like Arnold and Sylvester – ironically, even their names conjure up pussycats rather than fighters. And laughs at the show rassling and much of the bilge passing for boxing these days. Above all, a quiet man with a voice softer than Dempsey's or Marciano's, a gentle man able to "connect the tender and tough," in Rilke's fine words. In our present manic phase we don't deserve him, but God bless us, let's cherish him.

A Postscript

Poets have called April the cruelest month. It may be so.

On April 29, 1998, Tim Geoghegan, noble athlete, doctor, and man sauntered into the next room. For more than a year, Tim had grappled with cancer only to be pinned by it in the end. Pinned he may have been, but never defeated. Now he plays in some El Dorado among the stars.

Alice and I were with him just hours before he died. The staff at the hospice facility marveled at his big heart that kept beating despite

the voracious inroads of cancer. I felt it as it banged along. Later that day, when he was ready, he took that last long breath. And was still.

Robert Lewis Stevenson's prayer, "Give us courage, gaiety, and the quiet mind," was always Tim's credo. He lived by and in those words.

Tim and author in Hendersonville.

Tim was so well read he also probably knew Cardinal Newman's little sermon. (I've had it in my wallet since 1944 when, as a young Marine in the Pacific, I got the card containing it after Mass one Sunday.) It goes:

> May He protect us all the day long until the shadows lengthen and the evening comes, and the world is hushed, and the fever of life is over and our work is done. Then in His mercy may He give us a safe night and a holy rest and peace at last.

Karate With Doug and Kevin

I've also encountered karate of various kinds down here. Predictably, in Asheville I met a man who is a shihan in a half dozen methods and who came to one of Tim's seminars, not to learn something from a real master but to meet and talk with me. (He sounded like a recording.) Not a wise choice. On the upside, happily I've found Doug Perry (8th-dan) and Kevin Roberts (7th-dan) who teach classic Okinawan Shorin-ryu to many in and around the area. Doug is Kevin's teacher and both are as one on teaching the pure Okinawan form untainted by American additions.

Doug Perry is a legend in these parts. He spent 24 years in the Marine Corps, earning 25 combat decorations including several Purple Hearts before retiring as a major.

D. Perry (l) and K. Roberts
– credits to karate.

Last summer when I visited his local summer camp that brought in over 180 students and teachers from all over the U.S., I felt more comfortable than I ever had at a karate venue. Not only was the real stuff practiced energetically, but the teaching was done in a caring, creative way by top-flight instructors. For me, it was pleasant to see karate played in a happy ambiance of no swagger and no insecurity.

Doug introduced me to his students this way: "I've taught a couple generations of you and you're always telling me that it was my footprints in the sand that you followed. But today we have with us the man who brought the sand...."

Somewhat excessive, but who's to argue with a man who lost out in Marine Corps judo because of an addiction to fouling.

Not that he's a brute. Besides his military and karate honors, Doug is in the shag dancing Hall of Fame. Shag, a style of jitterbug, had its origins in the 1930's and is especially popular in the American southeast. He says that shag, in which he's won two national championships, has helped his kata enormously.

The Music of the Fighting Arts

> ... you are the music
> While the music lasts.
> – T.S. Eliot

Doug Perry, exceptional karateka and dancer, obviously resonates with music. Me too. I was raised on popular music. How lucky that the 1930's were the golden age for the jumpiest tunes and finest lyrics ever. At the Home, we had no radio but the music couldn't be stopped. It came in through the air, I don't know how, and the big girls – my sisters among them – sang and danced the tunes. Everyone harmonized and some did Red McKenzie's thing by taking strips of newspaper, putting them to combs, and blowing up some magic. Others imitated instruments ala the Mills Brothers and could really swing. The sterile cacophony of bop, rock, and punk was junk we would have sneered at. I agree with British poet and jazz critic Philip Larkin who wrote that, after 1945, Charlie Parker wrecked jazz by going from a diatonic scale – the scale you use in a love song, a national anthem, or a lullaby – to the chromatic scale, which is what you use to "give the effect of drinking a quinine martini and having an enema simultaneously."

We denied our penury with rhythm. Music had to stand and move and have a beat. It required no mindless cavorting and snorting, but only thin children to listen to and replicate it.

Without much else to do, I learned the lyrics to these songs and the year they emerged. The film, *The English Patient*, has as hero, a German, who does the same thing with American songs of that period. If you want to see an extended play on this theme, read John Gilbey's, "Pop Songs and Pa-kua" in his, *The Way of a Warrior* (1982). In taverns in later years, this recall skill kept me in beer. There was this piano player who'd bet that he could play a song from the 1930's for which you couldn't give the title, year, or some of the lyrics. If you lost, you paid double price; if you won, the beer was free. In such a place I seldom paid for beer.

Not so strangely, the fighting arts have a beat reeking of the best music. Some of it may be discordant and resolve itself into mere noise, but the finer forms and katas stir and stimulate. Even free fights have a quality of music to them, though the flow can't always be sustained because of the exigent circumstances. The good rhythm in the best fighting arts, however, is never lost. It's a dead life that lacks rhythm. Many activities – making love, walking, even conversing – have a definite rhythm. You can get this from fighting practice. If you don't practice, this rhythm won't come. And though you can't *will* the result – some get it quicker than others – you can *will* the practice.

Language by its power to refer to things is part of the Dao. However, it cannot substitute for music, dance, taiji, or other systems of being. As dancer Isadora Duncan said, "'If I could tell it to you, I wouldn't have to dance."

A little old lady asked Fats Waller once, "What is swing?" Fats came back, "Lady, if you got to ask, you'll never know." What we're talking about here – the rhythm of the fighting arts – is not all that obscure. It's there for you if you can hear and respond to it.

Fats was a great artist ("I wonder what the poor people are doing tonight?"). I never met this organist (sometime in your life try to hear his rendition of "That's All") and pianist ("Blue Turning Gray Over You" will make you denounce the Big Bang Theory on the origin of the universe). I did meet a couple of others, though, who like Fats were tops in their field. They affected me because they kept trying and didn't play to the house. They gave the same superlative performance to an empty house as to a full one.

Billie and Baby

After judo practice one night in 1948, another judoka and I went over to the Blue Note, the best jazz joint in Chicago. It was about seven and there she was, Billie Holiday Herself, standing at the bar near the entry. I braced her, "Billie, I love your singing, let me buy you a drink." Her eyes sparkled. "Sure," she said.

Rye she wanted and a full kitchen glass she got, thanking me. I asked her when she went on. "Fifteen minutes," she said pertly, not bored with the white goofus. I don't recall the rest of the conversation, but when it finished she walked out into the lights and sang "Lover Man" as no one else in the world could do it, to mostly empty chairs.

She continued to sing. Her voice, slightly tart towards the last, was a softly muted trumpet that night. Critic Gunther Schuller commented how great she was in phrasing her "L's". No one ever sang that magic word "love" as she did in "Easy Living" or the "little" and "lovable" as she did so beautifully in "Miss Brown to You." And while she sang, she often looked over at a couple of tired and happy judoka.

Billie inspired others by her singing but she also inspired herself. From being a young prostitute in Harlem for five years, she rose to become America's greatest jazz singer. Like the lotus Zheng Manqing loved, Billie blossomed from the mire. But it never stopped being tough for her. When I saw her, she had just spent a year in the jug on a narcotics charge. Ten years later at Christmas time, she died with seventy cents in her bank account. So seven times down and only six up, somewhat perversely recalling the lines from one of John Donne's haunting sermons:

> Thou knowest this man's fall;
> Thou knowest not this man's wrestling.

Except that we do know Billie's wrestling, her lovely singing that outshone the sin, the rhythms which exculpated her mistakes.

As Billie was our top jazz singer, Baby Laurence (real name Laurence Jackson) was our premier tap dancer. Critic Stanley Dance's poll of leading critics and musicians in the Sixties rated Baby the all-time best. He was too good to be true and too good for America's mass homogenized audiences who crave gimmickry and hoked-up commercial fashion; who resonate to music minus melody and lyrics – a cacophony bereft of beat.

Alice and I caught Baby at a supper club in Rockville, Maryland. Again, here was artistry almost alone. There were less than a dozen people there. We invited Baby to join us for a drink and he obliged. We talked tap and he told us he would give the folks his history of tap, illustrating as he went along. I muttered something about the crowd building once the local newspapers heard that he was here. He smiled and drank his drink, looking at the bottom of the glass as he did so.

It was said of Harry Greb, the old middleweight, that you didn't have to see him box to realize his greatness – all you had to do was watch him climb into the ring. Baby was the same with tap. He labored most of his life in construction to get victuals, but labor couldn't dampen that walk – everything alive and moving to that great rhythm. He could strut standing still. If you let him move, he was a wonder. So when he finished his drink and sashayed out under the lights and began to dance, he was merely magnificent. I've never seen better tap or movement. I have seen Willy Mays cavort an outfield and Dan Gable manipulate a mat, but Baby was even better. As he tapped, he showed and told how the giants before him had done it: the smoothness of Eddie Rector, the perfection of Bill "Bojangles" Robinson, the audacity of Buck and Bubbles, the recklessness of the Nicholas Brothers, even imitating Fred Astaire imitating Bojangles. He did it all. The small audience reveled in it and even the empty chairs seemed to be applauding – inanimate emoting as in the old ballad, "We Just Couldn't Say Goodbye." After 45 minutes of this lyrical lecture on dance, he came back to our table, a bit bushed but as happy as if he had entertained thousands. A year later this genius of dance was dead of cancer at 53.

And the Poetry

Poetry is shot through with rhythm, thus can be said to be a kind of music (surprisingly though, the great Yeats was tone-deaf, unable to recognize any music but "God Save the King"). When I was a boy we memorized and recited poetry in the smallest school every school-day of the year. Literature then was queen of the arts and ploughboys and servant girls were word perfect on such poems as H.W. Longfellow's "Psalm of Life" and J.G. Whittier's "Maud Muller." We recited verse, benefiting our tongues, ears, brains, and heart like Taiwanese children still declaim Sun Yat-sen's "San Min Zhuyi" (Three Principles of the People). I can still recite Edna St. Vincent Millay's "Renascence" and

"Ballad of the Harp Weaver," and other fine poetry, though haltingly in places as befits a veteran of seventy-two summers. The great thing is that even in patches where the words don't come, the old rhythm remains and I can still sound it out even without the words.

In Alfred Bester's excellent short story, "Disappearing Act," America in 2112 A.D. is a giant toolbox of technological experts run by – you guessed it – a general. It has bountiful Brains and Scientists galore but to save itself it needs a poet and can't find one.

Like music, poetry has been as necessary for me as bread. If it had heart and art and style, it had me. The way things pile up, life gets very Confucius. When that happens, such bouquets as this by poet William Stafford set it right:

> The cat by the road is one I used to know. A screen door that opens bangs like ours on Ninth. Somebody whistles a tune that the milkman always tried. Every day of your life shivers around home to get in. You open each morning softly and stand by the door and look out, the way your mother did.

Boxing has a rich heritage of fine verse, wrestling less. In recent decades, I've liked the British boxer-poet Vernon Scannell's, "Mastering the Craft," with its ending likening poets to boxers:

> Who have never learnt the first moves of the game, they can't hope to win. Yet here comes one, no style at all, untrained and fat, who still contrives to knock you flat." And the same writer's excellent "Comeback" with fetching lines like "My body is my biography: The scars, old fractures, ribs and nose, thick ear; That's what I am, a score of ancient wounds."

Craig Raine, another Britisher, wrote the memorable, "A Hungry Fighter," a son's poignant snapshot of an old fighter and dad. There has been little poetry on wrestling except in American college literary journals but none of it has moved me. Of course if you go further back, you can find some in Shakespeare's, "As You Like It," and Sir Walter Scott's, "Wrestling Match"; and better than both, Mathew Arnold's, "Sohrab and Rustum: An Episode" (1853), though the grappling here was tragically unregulated.

For weapons, one can find poetry from Sir Philip Sidney (1554-80) to Ezra Pound. From Sidney's *Astrophel and Stella* we get:

In Martiall sports I had my cunning tride,
And yet to break more staves did me addresse;
While with the people's shouts I must confesse,
Youth, lucke, and praise, even fild my veines with pride.

As for Ezra, he dedicated his first book, A *Lume Spento*, "For E. McC., that was my counter-blade under Leonardo Terrone, Master of Fence," finishing the eulogy:

Struck of the blade that no man parrieth,
Pierced of the point that touches lastly all,
'Gainst that grey fencer, even Death,
Behold the shield! He shall not take thee all.

En route, he quotes the old sword-rune, "If thy heart fail thee trust not in me." Terrone, their master, had no such trouble – he had an abundant heart. After suffering a stroke, he learned and taught pupils from the left side. Later when mobility on his right side returned, he reverted.

All well and good for boxing, wrestling, and fencing, but what about street combat? Save for British poet Henry Reed's, "Lessons of War" (1946), combat hasn't mixed well with poesie. Here is some of "Unarmed Combat," the third part of that poem:

...until that time,
We shall have unarmed combat.
I shall teach you
The various holds and rolls and throws and breakfalls
Which you may sometimes meet...

[These] will always come in useful.
And never be frightened to tackle
From behind; it may not be clean to do so,
But this is global war.

(You may not know it, but you can tie a Jerry
Up without a rope; it is one of the things I shall teach you.)
Nothing will matter if only you are ready for him.
The readiness is all.

You get the idea: it wasn't much of a suchness. And certainly not on a par with the justly famed first part of the trilogy, "The Naming of [Weapon] Parts."

So though it's lacking in the martial arts, I like any poetry that feels, stands, and moves.

The great poet Carl Sandburg and I shared two things: We were both raised in Galesburg, Illinois, and we agree that the most lyric poem in English was this by Bliss Carman:

> Oh once I could not understand
> The sob within the throat of spring,
> The shrilling of the frogs nor why
> The birds so passionately sing.
> But that was before your beauty came.

And here is Lord Byron's shortest, most heartfelt poem:

> Carolyn Lamb,
> Goddam.

Sent me by Paul Nurse from the Canadian chill, and countered by Hunter Armstrong from the wilds of Arizona with this poignant:

> Mary Sue,
> Phew!

Hoplologist Richard Hayes received a letter from longshoreman philosopher Eric Hoffer in 1967 that he recently shared with me. In it, Hoffer quoted George Santayana saying that America is the greatest opportunity and the worst influence. This is square on target. As I read this, I thought of Dr. Seuss' poem on winning and coping, "Oh, the Places You'll Go" (1991). A few lines run:

> Wherever you go, you will top all the rest
> Except when you don't
> Because sometimes you won't.

Solid solace for all, "Keep cool and collect," Mae West, another sort of poet, advised.

Finally, as things wind down, here is a tanka from Richard Hayes:

Under the harvest moon
Amid the hamlets of Musashino
Old people dreaming of the past
Young people dreaming of the future.

Du Fu (born 712 A.D.), the fine Tang Dynasty poet, weary of war and wanting the farmers to start spring planting, also dreamed ("On Washing Weapons"):

... that there might come some great man,
who would bring down the River of Heaven
cleaning all the weapons of blood,
so that they could be stored away forever,
never to be used again.

We Take Stock

Men have always fought. Few animals kill for fun. Natural instincts prevent it. And none do it for ideology. But, despite his wondrous brain, man kills and often enjoys it. He especially enjoys killing when in groups. Other than the harvester ant, no animal except man engages in organized warfare.

To curb these violent impulses, man long ago began to play at fighting with and without weapons. Unarmed systems sprang up as sports everywhere, pride of place going to wrestling. Historically, wrestling probably preceded boxing since mastery in it could be gained without trauma. It is older even than birth: lovers wrestle in their love-play. The hold of a wrestler, divorced of strength, is an embrace. And it embraces something, hence it celebrates community. Boxing does not embrace. It collides and never becomes community. Despite the shock of colliding, boxing is less effective and must bow to wrestling.

Only in some Asian traditions was boxing practiced non-contact, thus lessening the lethality and giving it an ethical context. Here both individuality and community were served as in wrestling. Over time, the Asian fighting arts developed primarily as a means of self-discovery. Initially, the student is worked so that ego is emptied from the vase. This allows the distilled spiritual/technical essence of the teacher to be poured in. Thus, it is a discipline involving individuality (finding out who one is) and community (adding others to one's essence).

Weapons were simply regarded as extensions of one's hands, and no different from unarmed arts. Everything centered on the Exercise, which paradoxically kept the fighting function controlled. Indeed, in the internal boxing tradition stemming from Buddhism and Daoism, excessive desire to fight was believed to inhibit the disciple. To want to fight and injure others was and is regarded as a sickness. Unimpeded by this and its ancillary desires (competition, ego, success) the Exercise is eased and skill invariably emerged.

Once learned, it is axiomatic that the Exercise is never used. The internal and external are alike in this. Both teach us to say "no" to confrontation (I used to tell judo students that "judo teaches you to run with confidence."). We don't learn these arts to fight but rather to become so expert at fighting that we become secure enough to say no to it. And to say it with the confidence that can only come from long and vigorous training under a qualified teacher.

Where We Come Out

Winding down after this blizzard of words, I paraphrase philosopher Schopenhauer to the effect that we spend our lives in search of something and when, after a great struggle, we finally achieve it, we are not satisfied so much as relieved that the damned quest is over. Yes, relief there is and a body meant for rest, but there remains also the responsibility to leave something coherent for the reader to retain.

I'm sensitive to the charge that I've been overly harsh on the infrastructure and some of the exponents of the fighting arts. No matter that I've used less than half the cautionary tales I could have, stories with an awkward tendency to be true.

Thinking back, in all these years I've had a dozen good students who remained a couple of decades or so. During this period, I've also had a dozen or so I've booted for stupidity and misbehavior. So is it a wash? Was Paul Guo right when he told me to avoid teaching at all costs? Was the time I taught a waste? Was I a failure?

Nope. Like the rabbi I told of in the Introduction, these data miss the fact that I was teaching for myself as much as for the crowd. I derived enormous fun from the teaching. More important, even if the bad dozen cancels the good dozen, that leaves a myriad of others, friends who came for varying periods and took part of the teaching away with them. That they went on with their lives out of our sight does not mean that they were not touched by their experiences. I like to think of them doing untold little acts of kindness stimulated by the relaxation, the root, and the erect body we taught.

Enough about me. On balance, have the Asian fighting arts been beneficial to America? Certainly these arts have had great and good teachers who treat their disciplines as Kano did judo, Funakoshi did karate, and Ueshiba did aikido – as educational systems to develop the whole person rather than just his or her fighting ability. These stalwarts have influenced many. But this tradition has had to fight the commercialization spawned by the media.

Much of my criticism of the martial arts is aimed at actions stimulated by the celebrity machine in America. Fortunately, many people who practice these arts aren't overly influenced by this false nonsense. They go on doing their disciplines in a more relaxed and efficient way than the rabid way they're portrayed by the media. This provides them real self-defense and confidence and in the end makes them better people to be around. Critic Michael Medved said that most Americans don't really want the violent fare that movies and TV present. Similarly, I am saying that many exponents of the fighting arts do not reflect the false nonsense huckstered by the media.

I agree wholeheartedly with Donn Draeger's student, Hunter Armstrong, head of Donn's International Hoplology Society, who wrote me in July, 1992:

> I think I can safely say that in the fighting arts (though not limited to them) organization beyond the dojo level – i.e., the personal relationship between the student and teacher – effectively leads to the deterioration of the combative effectiveness of the system and a corresponding growth of political horse manure. Unfortunately, this represents most systems that have migrated out of their original socio-cultural milieu, and even many that have remained. Such is life and the nature of man.

If it's kept small and non-commercial and competitively controlled, then the teacher/student relationships and fighting methods will work and the manure can be avoided. By and large I think it is. I certainly hope so.

Meeting Tim Geoghegan, Doug Perry, and Kevin Roberts down here in the twilight of my life has been serendipitous. It has reinforced my belief that at the grassroots level of America there are still men and women teaching the fighting arts in traditional and effective ways. People who believe without the need to embellish the gospel that green practice is more important than lectures, articles, and books (ouch!) on gray theory.

So where we come out is to get out as gracefully as possible. The final radio message on March 24, 1939, from famed adventurer Richard Halliburton's foundering Chinese junk en route from Hong Kong to San Francisco is a classic last word:

> Captain John Welch of the Sea Dragon to liner president Coolidge Southerly Gales rain squalls lee rail under water wet bunks hardtack bully beef having wonderful time wish you were here instead of me.

More conclusive, if not as courageous, are the fatal last words spoken by the eighteenth century surgeon, Joseph H. Green. While feeling and recording his own pulse, he wrote, "Stopped." And it had.

I may be slowed, but I'm not stopped, and continue to sing the soaring words of mehitabel the cat:

> but wotthehell do i care
> i neither whine nor fret
> what though my spine is out of line
> there's a dance in the old dame yet.

Mom and Pop
hanging on.

SELECTED BIBLIOGRAPHY - BOOKS

CHEN, WEIMING. (1985). *T'ai chi ch'uan ta wen – Questions and answers on t'ai chi ch'uan.* (B. Lo & R. Smith, Trans.) Berkeley, CA: North Atlantic. (Original work published in 1929)

CHENG MAN-CH'ING & SMITH, R. (1994). *T'ai-chi: The "supreme ultimate" exercise for health, sport, and self-defense.* Tokyo: Charles E. Tuttle Co. (Original work published in 1967)

DRAEGER, D., & SMITH, R. (1980). *Comprehensive Asian fighting arts.* Tokyo: Kodansha International. (Original work published in 1969 as *Asian fighting arts*)

GILBEY, J. (PSEUD.) (1989). *Secret fighting arts of the world.* Tokyo: Charles E. Tuttle Co. (Original work published in 1963)

GILBEY, J. (PSEUD.) (1992). *The way of a warrior.* Berkeley, CA: North Atlantic. (Original work published in 1982)

GILBEY, J. (PSEUD.) (1993). *Western boxing and world wrestling – Story and practice.* Berkeley, CA: North Atlantic.

PITTMAN, A., & SMITH, R. (1990). *Hsing-i: Chinese internal boxing.* Tokyo: Charles E. Tuttle Co.

PITTMAN, A., & SMITH, R. (1990). *Ba-kua eight trigram boxing.* Tokyo: Charles E. Tuttle Co.

SMITH, R. (1958). *A complete guide to judo: Its story and practice.* Tokyo: Charles E. Tuttle Co.

SMITH, R. (1959). *A bibliography of judo and other self-defense systems including cognate works and articles.* Tokyo: Charles Tuttle Co.

SMITH, R. (1989). *Secrets of Shaolin Temple boxing.* Tokyo: Charles E. Tuttle Co. (Original work published in 1964)

SMITH, R. (1967). *Pa-kua: Chinese boxing for fitness and self-defense.* Tokyo: Kodansha International.

SMITH, R. (1980). *Chinese boxing: Masters and methods.* Tokyo: Kodansha International. (Original work published in 1974)

SMITH, R. (1974). *Hsing-i: Chinese mind-body boxing.* Tokyo: Kodansha International.

SMITH, R. (1990). *Chinese boxing: Masters and methods.* Berkeley, CA: North Atlantic. (Original work published in 1974 by Charles E. Tuttle Co.)

SELECTED BIBLIOGRAPHY – ARTICLES

GILBEY, J. (PSEUD.) (1981, November 20). Knock knock. *Montgomery Journal*, p. B1.

GUTERMAN, A. & SMITH, R. (1987). Neurological sequalae of boxing. *Sports Medicine*, 4, 194-210.

SMITH, R. (1962, November). Master of the incredible. *Strength and Health*, 24-25, 46-47.

SMITH, R. (1963, November). Let's take a look at Chinese boxing. *Strength and Health*, 30-31, 52-55.

SMITH, R. (1964, December). The fighting arts – The essentials of tai chi. *Strength and Health*, 42, 45, 77.

SMITH, R. (1968, August). Mastery of mind in weightlifting. *Strength and Health*, 36(8), 34, 71.

SMITH, R. (1970). A salute to master Cheng Man-ch'ing. *T'ai-Chi Ch'uan Body and Mind*, Second Issue, pp. 9-11. Published by the T'ai-Chi Association of New York City.

SMITH, R. (1986, December). Some Taiwan notes. *Tai Chi Player*, (4), 1-3.

SMITH, R. (1975). A master passes – A tribute to Cheng Man-ch'ing. *Fighting Arts International*, 2(6), 8-12.

SMITH, R. (1995). Zheng Manqing and taijiquan – A clarification of role. *Journal of Asian Martial Arts*, 4(1), 50-65.

SMITH, R. (1995). Remembering Zheng Manqing – Some sketches from his life. *Journal of Asian Martial Arts*, 4(3), 46-59.

SMITH, R. (1996). Han Qingtang and his seizing art. *Journal of Asian Martial Arts*, 5(1), 30-47.

SMITH, R. (1996). The masters contest of 1926 – An epiphany in judo history. *Journal of Asian Martial Arts*, 5(3), 60-65.

SMITH, R. (1996). Breathing in taiji and other fighting arts. *Journal of Asian Martial Arts*, 5(4), 20-45.

SMITH, R. (1997). Chen Weiming, Zheng Manqing, and the difference between strength and intrinsic energy. *Journal of Asian Martial Arts*, 6(1), 50-61.

SMITH, R. (1997). Da lu and some tigers. *Journal of Asian Martial Arts*, 6(2), 56-69.

SMITH, R. (1998). General Gao Fangxian and the vitality of northern Shaolin boxing. *Journal of Asian Martial Arts*, 7(3), 32-41.

SMITH, R. (1999). Donn Draeger – A lifelong embodiment of the samurai code. *Journal of Asian Martial Arts*, 8(3), 18-33.

ILLUSTRATIONS

The author and publisher have endeavored to get permission to use all the illustrations included in this book. There were some cases where copyrights have expired, the original publishing company is no longer in business, books containing specific illustrations were out-of-print, or the original owners of the illustrations were deceased. We would like to thank all those who contributed with their photographs and illustrations which helped in portraying a visual image of practitioners and particular martial arts styles presented in this book. Credits are presented in alphabetical order to the person or organization, followed by the page number for referencing the illustration.

- John Anderson 212
- Jon Bluming 43a, 104, 106, 107, 112
- Richard Bowen 72, 74
- Jim Bregman 49-50
- London Budokwai 60, 61, 66, 68, 70, 71, 123
- John Carlson 63, 77a
- William C.C. Chen 227
- Donn Draeger Archives 42a, 75, 85, 86, 87
- W.E. Fairbairn Archives 144, 145, 151, 152, 155
- Tim Geoghegan 362, 363, 364
- Tam Gibbs 291
- Rorian Gracie 131, 135
- Fujiko Gardner & Tamura Family 204
- Paul Guo 179a/b
- Pat Harrington and Betty Huxley 87
- Al Holtman 46
- Hong Yixiang 164, 167, 170, 171
- Bart Ingram 247
- International Hoplology Society 98, 100b (photo by P. Lineberger), 100c, 108
- Jodo Federation of Malasyia 89b, 92
- *The Judo Review* 5(4) [Dec. 1955] 73
- Robert Kostka 271
- Michael Lane - dust jacket cover art
- Laureate Press 125
- Rose Li 250, 251, 257, 259, 260
- Liu Xiheng 309
- Pat Lineberger 89a, 96, 97
- Ben Lo 240, 294, 295, 297
- Wolf Lowenthal (photo by Lynn Saville) 232

- Nishitani, Kelly 36
- Hank Ogawa 39a
- Bill Paul Archives 137, 139, 140, 143
- Henri Plée 118
- Doug Perry & Kevin Roberts 262, 368
- Oscar Ratti 95, 206, 211, 212
- Robert W. Smith vi, vii 2 (photo by James Klebau), 4, 15, 20 (illustrations by Janet Bradley), 22, 24, 27-35, 51, 56-59, 64b (illustration by Pat Kenny), 88, 93, 113, 114, 117, 121, 126, 127 (illustration by Pat Kenny), 148-150, 154, 156, 163, 165, 172, 177a, 179c, 187-192, 193a, 194, 197-99, 207 (illustration by Janet Bradley), 218, 219, 220, 223 (photo by James Klebau), 226, 228, 232, 233 (drawing by William Woodward), 242, 245, 249, 268 (illustration by Janet Bradley), 269 (illustration by Pat Kenny), 277, 280, 286-289, 298, 305, 308, 312, 313, 318, 319, 324, 368, 379
- Shimizu Takaji Archives 100a
- Shinji Kozu 37, 208
- Yuan Dao 174, 175, 177b
- Ken Van Sickle 284, 325
- Yamanaka, Toshio "Punchy" 39b
- Wang Shujin 182-185
- Wang Yannian 193b
- Ed Young 227

GLOSSARY
JAPANESE

seoi-nage (shoulder throw) 16, 29, 82-83, 130-131

shiai (contest judo) 40-41, 82, 132, 213

shihan (highest rank, 10th-degree) 29, 37, 44-45, 368

shime-waza (strangling techniques) 120

shinai (bamboo practice sword) 89

shodan (1st-degree) 65, 76, 152

sumo (traditional Japanese wrestling) 98, 353-354

sumotori (sumo wrestler) 99, 117, 307, 329, 340, 353-355

sutemi (sacrifice throw) 63

tai-otoshi (body drop) 49, 107, 131, 140, 162-163, 218

te-waza (hand techniques) 47, 119

tomoe-nage (stomach throw) 27

uki-otoshi (floating drop) 119

yoko-sutemi (side sacrifice throw) 33

yondan (4th-degree) 86

yudansha (black belt degree) 36, 39, 60-61, 82, 86, 119, 205, 212

yudanshakai (black belt association) 121

waza (technique) 81, 214

 GLOSSARY CHINESE

bagua (pa kua; eight diagrams) 144-145, 163-165, 167, 178, 182, 184, 242-249, 252, 254, 256-257, 260-261, 303, 307

beng quan (peng-ch'uan; crushing fist) 179

dianxue (tien hsüeh; "spot blood," striking vital points) 100, 115, 346

ding (ting; character "ding" step) 186, 191

gongfu (kung fu; skill, proficiency, attainment) 258, 310, 328-329

guoshu (kuoshu; national art) 186

jiaodi ("horn butting" wrestling) 307

jin (chin; tenacious energy) 199-200, 215, 285

liangyiquan (liang-i ch'uan; double attributes boxing) 176

neijia (nei chia; internal boxing styles) 88, 170, 257, 330, 351

qi (ch'i; vital energy) 44, 47, 99, 116-117, 177, 182, 214, 229, 260, 282-283, 296, 309, 311, 322, 338-340, 349

qinna (ch'in na; seizing) 169, 177, 351

sanshou (san shou; free-fighting) 200, 280, 319

Shaolin Luohan (Shaolin Lohan) 169

shizhong (shih chung; proper timing) 228, 300

shuaijiao (shuai chiao; wrestling) 181, 186, 214

taiji (see taijiquan)

taijiquan (t'ai chi ch'uan; supreme ultimate boxing) 1, 47, 88, 101-102, 144-145, 154, 157, 159, 163-166, 170-171, 176, 182, 186-187, 193-202, 210, 214-215, 217, 241-244, 248, 249, 251-252, 254-257, 260-261, 271-272, 277-303, 306-308, 310-326, 329-330, 334, 337-341, 346, 348, 358, 370

tuishou (t'ui shou; push-hands/sensing-hands): 99, 101, 139, 164, 193, 195-197, 199-202, 230, 243, 280, 286-287, 289-290, 293, 295-297, 299-301, 307-310, 312, 314-316, 318-320, 331, 340-341

tuijin (leg energy): 258

wing chun (Mandarin, yong quan) 137, 139, 169, 345-346

wushu (martial arts) 253, 278, 302, 328-329, 347-348

xingyi (hsing-i; mind and will boxing) 88, 163-164, 167, 176-179, 182, 196-197, 242-261, 273, 303, 338-340, 346, 351

yong quan (see wing chun)

zijanmen (spontaneous boxing) 196

INDEX

🌲 ORDER FORM

MARTIAL MUSINGS - A PORTRAYAL OF MARTIAL ARTS IN THE 20TH CENTURY
by Robert W. Smith

Robert W. Smith's *Martial Musings* stands out as the sole literary work which offers readers a unique perspective of martial arts as they evolved during the 20th century. Smith personally escorts the reader on a martial arts tour. He starts with his own initial involvement in the arts, then launches outward, across the nation, over to Asia, and eventually home again. Hardbound, 400 pages with over 300 illustrations.

PRICE: $39.95 each, plus shipping and handling: USA: $5 ground

Outside USA: $6 surface mail

JOURNAL OF ASIAN MARTIAL ARTS

Quarterly covering all historical and cultural aspects relating to Asian martial arts. High academic standards presented in an aesthetically pleasing 8-3/8"x10-7/8" format. Indexed, perfect bound, illustrated, with 124 pages or more. Subscriptions are as follows:

Individuals: ❏ $32 one-year, or ❏ $55 two-year

Institutions: ❏ $75 one-year, or ❏ $135 two-year

Shipping & handling: USA – included in subscription

Canada & Mexico – $6 per year surface mail

Other Countries – $8 per year surface mail

Easy Ordering

➤ Toll Free Telephone   1-800-455-9517 (U.S. & Canadian orders only)
➤ Toll Free Fascimile   1-877-526-5262 (U.S. orders only)
➤ Telephone   1-814-455-9517
➤ E-mail   orders@goviamedia.com
➤ Mail to: Via Media Publishing Co. • 821 West 24th St. • Erie, PA 16502 USA

Easy Payment

❏ Visa ❏ MasterCard ❏ Money Order ❏ Check

Name: _____

Address: _____

Tel./E-mail: _____

Card number: _____

Name on card: _____ Exp. date: ____/____

Description of item/s ordered: _____

_____

Payment is required in U.S. dollars drawn on a US bank or by international money order. Make check, money order or charge card information, payable to: Via Media Publishing Company.

W W W . G O V I A M E D I A . C O M